Josh Levin is the national editor at *Slate* and the host of the
Hang Up and Listen. He previously worked a
has written for *Sports Illustrated*, *The Atlantic*
Times Sports Magazine. He was born and
is a graduate of Brown University. He lives in

Praise for *The Queen*:

"In the finest tradition of investigative reporting, Josh Levin exposes how
a story that once shaped the nation's conscience was clouded by racism
and lies. As he stunningly reveals, the deeper truth, the messy truth, tells
us something much larger about who we are. *The Queen* is an invaluable
work of non-fiction" David Grann, author of *Killers of the Flower Moon*

"Anyone who knew welfare knew, I thought, that the welfare queen is a
myth. Turns out she isn't" Jamie Fisher, *TLS*

"Levin's brilliant exploration of the politics of welfare reform teaches an
essential lesson. When myths and stereotypes predominate, facts, logic and
evidence lose out . . . Levin's story calls upon us to think harder. Gripping"
Lisbeth B. Schorr, *Washington Post*

"Another author would have used the 'welfare queen' as a jumping-off
point to explore stereotypes, welfare politics and political rhetoric. Levin
addresses all that, but his real goal is to put a face to Reagan's bogeywoman,
tracking every alias, every scam, every duped husband and every dodged
arrest. He presents Linda Taylor not as a parable for anything grand, but as a
singular American scoundrel who represented nothing but herself . . . Part
of the fun of Levin's book is burrowing inside his obsessive quest" *New
York Times* Book Review

"Levin nimbly explores Taylor's life in a story that becomes more
complex the more it's revealed. The tale encompasses an astonishingly
prolific criminal career as well as issues of race . . . mental illness. amd
self-invention, to say nothing of politics and the essentialism that Regan
commonly practised . . . A top-notch study of an exceedingly odd moment
in history" *Kirku*

"A wild, only-in-America story that helped me understand my country better. It's a fascinating portrait of a con artist and a nation ... and the ways the United States continually relies on oversimplified narratives about race and class to shape public policy, almost always at the expense of brown people and poor people" Attica Locke, author of *Black Water Rising*

"A stunning account ... His powerful work of narrative nonfiction shows how Taylor victimized a slew of vulnerable people, was a victim herself, and was the cause of Black welfare recipients being stereotyped as 'welfare cheats' ... Levin does a terrific job of balancing his portrait of a criminal, of the racism of police ... and of the widespread stereotyping of Blacks that grew out of her crimes and a president's distortions" Connie Fletcher, *Booklist*

"It is impossible to read *The Queen* without pausing every few pages to marvel at either the brilliance of Josh Levin's research or the sheer wildness of the tale. By pouring years of devotion into piecing together Linda Taylor's bizarre criminal odyssey, Levin has created a work of American history like no other - an enthralling portrait of a nation whose splendid promise has too often been distorted by prejudice and political cynicism" Brendan I. Korener, author of *The Skies Belong to Us*

"For decades, Linda Taylor has been demagogued by politicians and the press, reduced to a cruel stereotype: the welfare queen shamelessly leeching from government coffers. Through meticulous reporting, Josh Levin's *The Queen* illuminates in full the story of a life far more complicated, cunning, criminal, tragic and fascinating than the historical stereotype would have ever allowed us to see" Wesley Lowery, author of *They Can't Kill Us All*

THE
QUEEN

Josh Levin

WILDFIRE

First published in 2019 by
WILDFIRE
an imprint of HEADLINE PUBLISHING GROUP

First published in paperback in 2020 by
an imprint of HEADLINE PUBLISHING GROUP

1

Cataloguing in Publication Data is available from the British Library

ISBN 978 1 4722 6608 8

Offset in 10.12/14.14pt DanteMTStd by Jouve (UK), Milton Keynes

Printed and bound in Great Britain by Clays Ltd, Elcograf S.p.A.

HEADLINE PUBLISHING GROUP
An Hachette UK Company
Carmelite House
50 Victoria Embankment
London
EC4Y 0DZ

www.headline.co.uk
www.hachette.co.uk

To Jess, for everything

Contents

Author's Note

"How old was she?" John Parks asked me. We were sitting outside on a spring day in 2013, a little less than thirty-eight years since his ex-wife, Patricia, had died under suspicious circumstances. "Boy, you waited a long time to come," the seventy-seven-year-old Parks said, struggling to remember details, such as Patricia's age, that had once seemed unforgettable. "At first, it was just on the tip of my tongue. And nobody came."

Patricia Parks had been thirty-seven when she was pronounced dead of a barbiturate overdose on the night of June 15, 1975. Patricia, who'd suffered from multiple sclerosis, had been treated at home by a friend who'd promised to make her feel better. Linda Taylor submerged Patricia in ice-cold water and fed her medications stored in unlabeled bottles. Taylor also took possession of the sick woman's house on the South Side of Chicago and became the executor of her estate. John Parks believed then and remained certain decades later that Taylor murdered Patricia. But nobody had seen fit to charge Taylor with his ex-wife's killing, and nobody in any position of authority, John told me, had bothered to ask him what he thought of Patricia's friend. "All they said was, 'That's another black woman dead.'"

When I started digging into Linda Taylor's life, I hadn't imagined that I'd end up investigating a potential homicide. Taylor rose to prominence in the mid-1970s as a very different kind of villain: America's original "welfare queen." One of the first stories I ever read about her, a squib in *Jet* magazine from 1974, said that she'd stolen $154,000 in public aid money in a single year, "owned three apartment buildings, two luxury cars, and a station wagon," and had been "busy preparing to open a medical office, posing as a doctor." Another *Jet* article depicted her as a shape-shifting, fur-wearing con artist who could "change from black to white to Latin with a mere change of a wig." But when Ronald Reagan expounded on Taylor during his 1976 presidential campaign, shocking audiences with the tale of "a woman in Chicago" who used eighty aliases to steal government checks, he didn't treat her as an outlier. Instead, Reagan implied that Taylor was a stand-in for a whole class of people who were getting something they didn't deserve.

The words used to malign Linda Taylor hardened into a stereotype, one that was deployed to chip away at benefits for the poor. The legend of the Cadillac-driving welfare queen ultimately overwhelmed Taylor's own identity. After getting convicted of welfare fraud in 1977, Taylor disappeared from public view and public memory. No one seemed to know whether she'd really lived under eighty aliases, and nobody had any idea whether she was alive or dead.

I spent six years piecing together Taylor's story and trying to comprehend why it got lost in the first place. The more I learned about her, the more the mythologized version of Linda Taylor fell apart, and not in the ways I expected. As a child and an adult, Taylor was victimized by racism and deprived of opportunity. She also victimized those even more vulnerable than she was.

Patricia Parks's death was a blip for the *Chicago Tribune*; Linda Taylor's public aid swindle was a years-long obsession. For journalists and politicians, the welfare queen was a potent figure, a character whose outlandish behavior reliably provoked outrage. Poor black women saw their character assailed by association with Taylor. At the same time, a woman whom Taylor had preyed on elicited no sympathy. Patricia Parks's ex-husband, John, who died in 2016, believed that his family's race was the reason that Patricia's death wasn't seen as a scandal or a tragedy. "I'd have to be somebody," he told me, explaining why some Americans get justice and others don't.

Linda Taylor did horrifying things. Horrifying things were also done in Linda Taylor's name. No one's life lends itself to simple lessons and easy answers, and Taylor's was more complicated than most. I've tried my best to tell the whole truth about what Linda Taylor did, what she came to signify, and who got hurt along the way. That goal may be unattainable, but we do far more damage to the world and to ourselves when we don't care to pursue it.

THE
QUEEN

CHAPTER 1
A New Victim

Jack Sherwin tossed his day's work on the front seat of his unmarked Chevy. He'd fished five or six burglary reports from his pigeonhole after roll call, enough to keep him and his partner occupied all morning and for a good chunk of the afternoon. Sherwin didn't need any more assignments—he had at least a half-dozen more reports jammed inside his briefcase.

The Chicago burglary detective turned on the police scanner and peeled off his sport coat. August 12, 1974, was sunny, hot, and unbearably humid; the sky felt heavy but it wouldn't rain all day. Sherwin headed east from his unit's headquarters on Ninety-First Street and South Cottage Grove, past the Jewel Food Store where a group of armed men had recently made off with a $1,000 haul.

He parked his car in South Chicago, a working-class, mostly black and Latino neighborhood bordered on the west by the Skyway, a toll road that carried suburban commuters above a part of town they'd rather not drive through. A month earlier, a sixty-six-year-old woman had been shot in the neck a short distance away in Calumet Heights, on the street outside St. Ailbe's Catholic church. She'd died in her pastor's arms. A couple of teenagers, both alleged members of the Blackstone Rangers gang, were charged with the killing. That was one of 970 murders in the city in 1974—more than four decades later, still the most homicides in a calendar year in the history of Chicago.

Sherwin wasn't dealing with anything as messy as a murder case. This

1

was a routine burglary, not a big enough deal to justify his partner, Jerry Kush, getting out of the car.

The two-story, six-unit brick building at 8221 South Clyde Avenue looked like a tiny castle, with a crenellated roof, an arch over the entryway, and limestone ornaments near the windows. Sherwin rang the bell and got buzzed inside. As he knocked on the door of a first-floor apartment, he looked down at his clipboard and rehearsed a sequence of well-worn questions: What's missing? Did anyone see what happened? Is there anything you'd like to add to your original report?

When someone called about a smashed front window or a stolen jewelry box, uniformed officers went to the scene and wrote it up, getting a statement from the victim and enumerating the basic facts: the time, the location, what had been stolen. The burglary investigators followed up, often from a seated position. If you treated detective work like a desk job, occasionally exerting yourself by picking up the telephone, you could push a new report off your desk in less than an hour. Nobody ever solved a case by making a single phone call, but it hardly mattered given how rarely burglary detectives recovered people's losses. There were nearly two hundred thousand burglaries, robberies, and thefts in Chicago in 1974, an increase of 18 percent over the previous year. Sherwin's territory—what the department called Area 2, on Chicago's Southeast Side—was the busiest in the city, with thirty-nine burglaries a day.

A big-picture thinker wouldn't have lasted a week in Area 2. Those stats told a depressing story, one filled with the kind of hopeless characters who subsisted on the proceeds from petty crimes. But Sherwin knew it wasn't on him to fix Chicago. He handled what he could see and what he could touch. He preferred to check out crime scenes himself, to imagine who'd been there and what they'd done. He broke down each new assignment into a series of predictable tasks, doing all the things a conscientious burglary detective was supposed to do: He talked to the right people, chased the right leads, and wrote everything up in clear, concise reports.

The door opened at 8221 South Clyde, and Sherwin took stock of the woman standing in front of him. Four days earlier, Linda Taylor had called Area 2 headquarters to say that her home had been burglarized.

Taylor appeared to be in her late thirties. She was just over five feet tall, with olive skin and dark, heavy-lidded eyes. Her face, a long oval tapering to a sharply jutting chin, seemed vaguely elfin. Her eyebrows, plucked into thin arcs, made her look like an old-fashioned glamour girl. She had a pronounced Cupid's bow in her upper lip, and when she talked, that lip curled back to reveal the glint of gold dental work. Taylor looked as though she was expecting company: Her makeup was pristine, her outfit fashionable and snug.

As he stepped into the apartment, Sherwin noticed that Taylor kept a tidy house. Sometimes, if he went out on a case right away, he could see where a burglar had barged in. But there were no signs of forced entry here. The bolt on Taylor's front door appeared undamaged. Nothing was broken or scattered around. Sherwin glanced again at the uniformed officers' original report. Could they go through that list of missing items one more time?

A large green refrigerator, complete with ice maker.

Yes, she told him. That was gone.

A gold stove.

Yes. Stolen.

It was a weird list. Hospital end tables. A grandfather clock. Two large Chinese lamps. Large elephant figurines. A pair of speakers that lit up to the beat of music. Thousands of dollars' worth of household furnishings, every piece of it insured. Most burglars snatched whatever they could fit in their hands: a ring, a necklace, a stereo, a small TV set. Stealing a refrigerator and hospital end tables, bulky objects you couldn't hustle out of an apartment without attracting attention, didn't make much sense.

Sherwin went back to his clipboard and studied the report. He asked Taylor to explain, again, how the thieves had gotten away with her belongings. She pointed to a window in her kitchen, an opening no more than a couple of feet across. Taylor's version of events was preposterous: To fit a double-door refrigerator through that narrow gap, you'd have to cut it in half. The detective didn't press her for more details. He thanked Taylor for her cooperation, and he promised to come around again just as soon as he developed any leads.

THE QUEEN

On his way out, Sherwin rang some more doorbells, but he couldn't find any neighbors who'd seen a mysterious stranger wander off with a large appliance. As he walked back to the car, he thought about the clean apartment, the tiny window, and the woman with the olive skin and the heavy-lidded eyes. There was something so familiar about Linda Taylor. He was sure he'd had this exact case, with this exact woman. He just couldn't remember where or when.

* * *

Sherwin knew Linda Taylor's street. He'd grown up just a few miles away, in an all-white neighborhood close to what was then the southern tip of the city's "Black Belt." Back then, in the 1940s, segregation had been enforced with covenants that forbade the sale of properties to, for instance, "every person having one-eighth part or more of negro blood." The Black Belt's borders expanded in 1948 when the Supreme Court struck down those covenants, but segregation didn't end with the stroke of a pen. New public housing developments kept black people confined to black enclaves, as did violence perpetrated by whites against those brave enough to breach long-standing barriers. When civil rights activist and "Queen of Gospel" Mahalia Jackson moved to the South Side in 1956, her white neighbors shot BB pellets through the windows of her house. Other black newcomers had their homes ransacked and set on fire.

The Sherwins, like many white families, packed up and moved when Chicago's racial boundaries shifted, settling in the area around Midway Airport. Thirty years later, the detective scoped out South Side neighborhoods that bore little resemblance to the one he'd lived in as a child. Some of the areas in his jurisdiction had changed from middle-class white enclaves to middle-class black ones—the city's most beloved athlete, Cubs legend Ernie Banks, lived with his family on a tree-lined street in Chatham. On his daily rounds, Sherwin passed by black-owned banks; the headquarters of the Johnson Products Company, manufacturer of the hair straightener Ultra Sheen; and the office of R. Eugene Pincham, a renowned black defense attorney and advocate for the disenfranchised.

Sherwin also rolled through hollowed-out streets dotted with liquor stores and check-cashing operations. South Chicago, the part of town where Linda Taylor lived, had long been the city's smoke-belching industrial corridor, home to U.S. Steel's mammoth South Works and countless other plants, factories, and forges. But between 1967 and 1977, the number of people working in manufacturing in Chicago proper would plummet by 33 percent. White flight took both jobs and services to the suburbs, cutting off thousands of black Chicagoans from steady employment and weakening the foundations of once-stable communities.

Area 2 burglary detectives didn't spend their days chasing after master criminals. They arrested juveniles and addicts, young men who were more desperate than cunning. Sherwin drove to Grand Crossing and South Shore and Pullman, stopping off at apartment buildings and restaurants to jot down notes about busted back doors and stolen cash.

He spent most days two feet to the left or right of Jerry Kush, with one man driving in the morning and the other in the afternoon. Kush was the best partner Sherwin had ever had, honest and reliable, but they weren't close friends. While Kush wore flashy clothes, Sherwin looked and dressed like a standard-issue detective, with short hair and a daily uniform of a sport coat and tie. Kush never stopped talking—about his kids, his marital woes, and anything else that came to mind. Sherwin didn't want to probe too far below the surface. Sometimes they'd hit the bars after work, but Sherwin didn't like to drink. He hated the sensation of losing control.

Sherwin felt most comfortable when he was by himself. In high school, he didn't go to parties or dances—he was too self-conscious to look at girls, much less talk to them. He'd found his confidence in the Marine Corps. When he came home after basic training, Sherwin wore his dress blues everywhere, and he sat the way a Marine was supposed to sit, his spine not touching the back of his chair.

In 1962, after a stint as a tank commander on Okinawa, he joined up with the Chicago Police Department. As a beat cop assigned to neighborhoods on the West and Southeast Sides, he could go from helping a woman deliver a baby to disarming a man threatening his girlfriend with a butcher knife. Sherwin loved the unpredictability of police work, and he took pride in protecting Chicago and its citizens.

There were times, though, when he thought those citizens' actions were indefensible. Sherwin watched the West Side ignite following Martin Luther King Jr.'s assassination in April 1968, and he was on duty a few months later during the clashes between protesters and cops at the Democratic convention. A study commissioned by Mayor Richard J. Daley found that the MLK riots stemmed from "pent-up aggressions" among black Chicagoans infuriated by poor schools, inadequate housing, and racially discriminatory policing, while a federal report on the Democratic convention documented "unrestrained and indiscriminate police violence" in response to demonstrators' provocations. Sherwin didn't come to the same conclusions. He'd feared for his life during the West Side riots, and he'd seen protesters attack policemen at the convention. He was certain that he and his fellow officers were the good guys. No matter what was happening in Chicago, nobody had the right to tear up the city.

After Sherwin made detective, his life got a lot more sedate. He and Kush still answered the occasional in-progress call, and they still tussled with burglars now and then. One time, they went to make an arrest and found their suspect hiding in a closet. The man charged out, completely naked, and Kush hit him on the head with a portable radio. Sherwin and Kush talked about that one for years. But naked guys didn't jump out of closets on the average Monday afternoon.

Sherwin believed in the work he was doing but he wasn't always stimulated by it. The job could be relentless and dispiriting. Most days, the detectives added a bunch of new reports to a caseload that was already overwhelming.

After work, the thirty-five-year-old police officer would go back to his two-bedroom apartment and do laundry. Some days, he'd head out to a religion class; he was studying to be a Catholic, so he could share a faith with his fiancée. He'd wake up early, before 3 a.m., to go for a run at Northwestern University before work. With the sky pitch-black and nobody else around, he had time to indulge the half-formed ideas bouncing around his head. The morning after his visit to the tidy apartment on South Clyde Avenue, Sherwin's mind kept wandering back to Linda Taylor. He'd gone to her home on August 12 expecting to investigate a burglary. He'd left a half hour later thinking he needed to investigate the burglary victim.

* * *

Lamar Jones couldn't remember the last time something interesting had happened to him at work. The dental clinic at Great Lakes Naval Training Center was an assembly line, a fifty-chair operation that treated a hundred thousand recruits and seven hundred thousand cavities each year. The twenty-one-year-old knew what each day would bring, and he knew what would happen the day after and the following week. But August 12 was different. That afternoon, a few hours after she'd met Jack Sherwin at 8221 South Clyde Avenue, Linda Taylor drove up to the naval base in North Chicago to get her teeth cleaned.

From the moment Jones saw her swagger into the room, he wanted to get close to her. She was self-assured and beautiful, an older woman with the smoothest skin he'd ever seen. The other sailors noticed her, too. They each took a shot, sauntering over all cool and casual, but she turned up her nose at each "Hey, baby." She treated Jones differently. She joked with him and flirted. He left work that day feeling better than he'd felt in his entire life. Out of all the guys in the clinic, he was the one she'd chosen. Her name, she'd told him, was Linda Sholvia.

Jones had grown up on the South Side of Chicago. His mom had struggled to raise six kids on her own, and he'd fought his own battles in the neighborhood. As gangs like the Blackstone Rangers and the Cobra Stones rose to power in the 1960s, DuSable High School—the alma mater of Nat King Cole and Harold Washington, Chicago's first black mayor—became a prime recruiting ground, and occasionally the setting for violent confrontations. But Jones had made it out, joining the navy and setting himself up for a better life. When he started dating Linda Sholvia, that life looked better than he could've possibly imagined.

Although Jones never saw her doing any work, his girlfriend seemed to have an endless supply of cash. She didn't try to hide her wealth, draping herself in furs and driving a fleet of luxury vehicles. Jones considered himself street-smart—he'd had to be, growing up where he did—but this woman and her money made him drop his guard. On Saturday, August 17, less than a week after they met at the Great Lakes clinic, the couple got married at Chicago City Hall.

The new Mrs. Jones spoiled her husband, giving him a couple of new cars and $1,000 right after they got hitched. She was generous, cosmopolitan, and well educated, a thirty-five-year-old Haitian woman with a degree from a Caribbean university. She was poised, too, sometimes even arrogant, commanding respect every time she walked into a car dealership or bank.

The honeymoon phase of their marriage didn't last as long as their brief courtship. After Jones got transferred from the dental clinic to Great Lakes' security unit, an assignment that required him to gear up like a police officer, he and a colleague decided to play a practical joke. They knocked on the door at 8221 South Clyde, hiding in the shadows so Linda wouldn't know who was there. As soon as she opened the door, Jones's friend shoved a badge in her face. She flew into a rage, slamming the door and screaming that she hated cops. If Jones knew what was good for him, she shouted, he'd never pull anything like that again.

Linda said a lot of crazy things. Just after their wedding, she told Jones he was her eighth husband, and that she'd killed the first one, shooting him in the chest. She said another of her husbands had worked for Greyhound and been crushed to death in a bus accident. Maybe she was telling the truth, or maybe she was just trying to scare him. Either way, he wasn't sure what she was capable of.

Everywhere Jones looked, something was a little bit off. That degree from a Haitian university had been awarded to Linda Taylor, not Linda Sholvia. His wife had four different names on her mailbox at 8221 South Clyde, and she'd get letters addressed to all of them. She had a sister named Constance who seemed more like her adult daughter. Jones also suspected that Linda's two small children weren't really hers.

He wasn't even sure she was from Haiti, or that she was thirty-five years old—on their marriage license, she'd given her age as twenty-seven. Jones thought she was black, but he wasn't absolutely sure—her light complexion allowed her to pass as white one day and Asian the next. When she took off her clothes and slipped into bed, he noticed a long scar near her navel—what he thought was an incision from a hysterectomy. One night, he woke up before dawn and saw that his bride's skin wasn't so smooth—she had a thousand wrinkles on her face. After he caught a glimpse of her without makeup, she locked herself in the bathroom for an hour. When she came out, she looked like a whole new person.

* * *

On the morning of August 13, the day after he'd first stopped by Linda Taylor's apartment, Sherwin grabbed six new burglary reports from his pigeonhole. But before he and Kush started on all the new stuff, Sherwin took a detour to 8221 South Clyde Avenue. For the second day in a row, he rang the bell outside, got buzzed into the front hallway, and knocked on the door of a first-floor apartment. When the door swung open, Sherwin saw an older woman staring back at him. It took him a moment to realize that this, too, was Linda Taylor, her face untouched by makeup and her body draped in a housecoat.

Once more, Taylor told him what had been taken from her. She said, again, that an enterprising burglar had stuffed her jumbo-size refrigerator through a narrow kitchen window. She spoke with a confidence that verged on arrogance, as if she couldn't bear to waste her time explaining something so obvious.

Most burglary victims thanked Sherwin for showing an interest in their cases. But Linda Taylor didn't seem grateful to see a police officer making these trips to South Chicago. She didn't defer to Sherwin's expertise, and she didn't bow to his authority. She hadn't asked for his help, and she didn't need it.

Sherwin had been a Chicago police officer for twelve years, a detective for three. He'd been the lead investigator on hundreds of burglary cases.

THE QUEEN

This didn't look like a burglary, and it didn't feel like one either. There was only one reason to think the place had been knocked over: Linda Taylor insisted that they were standing in the middle of a crime scene.

Taylor hadn't told Sherwin anything new, but going back to her apartment hadn't been a waste of time. Seeing her face again had jogged the detective's memory. That afternoon, Sherwin placed a call to the Michigan State Police. He told the sergeant who answered the phone that he might know the whereabouts of Connie Jarvis.

CHAPTER 2
Covert

In March 1972, two and a half years before Linda Taylor would tell him about her missing end tables and elephant figurines, Jack Sherwin went to a house just northwest of Taylor's apartment on South Clyde Avenue. The woman who answered the door at 1651 East Seventy-Eighth Street told the burglary detective that she'd lost more than $8,000 worth of jewelry and furniture. When he pressed her, she refused to say what exactly had been taken. Sherwin suspected that she'd made the whole thing up—that she was running an insurance scam.

Sherwin hadn't let it drop. He'd called the woman's insurance company, reporting the likely fraud. He'd also gone from door to door on her street until he found a witness who'd seen someone loading furniture into the back of a truck. That vehicle, Sherwin discovered, belonged to a man who lived across the state line in Covert, a small town a hundred miles away on the eastern shore of Lake Michigan.

The Chicago detective had then called the Michigan State Police. He'd told the state troopers he had a lead on a woman named Connie Jarvis who'd staged a theft in her own apartment. He'd asked the troopers to go to Covert to check out the man with the truck. But by the time he'd picked up the phone, the man and his truck had left town. When the Michigan State Police told Sherwin they'd struck out, he knew it was time to end his chase. His bosses in Chicago didn't like him to pursue cases outside the city—he had enough burglaries to solve on the South Side.

A couple of years later, Sherwin thought back to that old, futile investigation. Linda Taylor was using a different name, living in a different place, and sporting a different head of hair. But she was the same woman Sherwin had met in 1972. He was sure of it. Thanks to a random assignment, a report that could've gone to any burglary detective in the district, he'd found himself standing in front of Connie Jarvis again.

When Sherwin called Michigan back in 1972, the state troopers had sent him everything they had on Jarvis. He'd put that report aside, probably lost it in one of his massive piles of paper. In August 1974, he got the report for a second time. When he reread that Michigan case file, he learned the full story of her life in Covert—the people she'd met, the lies she'd told, and the chaos she'd left behind when she ran away.

* * *

The first thing Linda Taylor had done when she got to Michigan in October 1971 was go shopping for a new house. Her real estate agent had been easy to find: Ed Hedlund advertised on the front cover of the South Haven, Michigan, city directory, right above a septic tank–cleaning service and Fidelman's Mai-Kai Cocktail Lounge and Dining Room. When she called him on the phone, Taylor introduced herself as Dr. Connie Walker, a heart surgeon from Chicago.

A cherubic man with glasses and a small pompadour, Hedlund had started out in the real estate business in the 1940s. In the early twentieth century, South Haven had been a major destination for Midwestern tourists, attracting boaters and bathers who poured in from Chicago on luxurious steamships. The tourist trade dwindled after the Depression, and at first Hedlund made his living selling foreclosed resorts and farms on the cheap. Now he built and sold homes throughout West Michigan's Van Buren County.

Taylor told Hedlund she'd just arrived in the state and wanted a new place to live. The "new" part was important. The house had to be spotless, never lived in. It also needed to be close to the highway, so she could tend to her patients at a moment's notice. The Chicago heart surgeon came on strong. She bragged that her husband owned a cab company, and she wore hats so large they entered the room before she did. She also showed off her medical bona fides, flashing hospital ID cards and driving a car emblazoned with the physicians' symbol and the name "Afri-med." The vehicle's interior included a two-way radio, in case of surgical emergencies.

The real estate agent, who was white, had grown up on a farm in Covert in the 1930s and still owned land there. Just a few miles outside South Haven, the township prided itself on its history of racial harmony and equality. Despite making up just 10 percent of the population before World War II, blacks had won elected office in Covert as far back as the 1860s. In the decades since Hedlund's childhood, the town's demographics had changed. Between 1940 and 1970, the number of black residents increased eightfold while the white population declined, transforming Covert into a majority-black town.

Hedlund himself now lived in South Haven, which was about 90 percent white. He'd just built a house in Covert, though, at the corner of Seventy-Seventh Street and Twenty-Eighth Avenue. What sounded like a big-city intersection wasn't much more than a wide-open field with a few residences dotting the landscape. Dr. Walker told Hedlund it was perfect. She put down $400 in cash, promising to pay the rest in full in just two months. The Chicago heart surgeon moved in and parked her Cadillac in the driveway.

* * *

Taylor didn't live by herself in Covert. Not long after she got settled in, she called a nineteen-year-old named Charles Bailey. She wanted him to make the trip from Chicago and join her on the opposite shore of Lake Michigan.

Bailey had met Taylor in Chicago a couple of years earlier, through his aunt Francie Baker; she knew Taylor as Dr. Shfolia, reader of the unknown. Taylor placed an ad in the city's leading black newspaper, the *Chicago Defender*, advertising herself as the daughter of a spiritual adviser called the Great Black Herman. She charged $100 per session to commune with the spirits, draping herself in a long black robe and escorting her customers to a room strewn with masks, dead birds, and a lot of paper currency. As candles flickered, she shared the kinds of secrets that anyone would pay to know: the dates when loved ones were going to die, and who was going to kill them.

Taylor had a feeling, she told Aunt Francie, that Francie's nephew Charles wouldn't live much longer. Taylor called the teenager and said he needed to come see her right away. On the phone, she told him that members of his family were plotting his demise. Without having met him, she was able to describe the clothes Bailey was wearing—information, he'd later learn, that she'd pried out of his aunt an hour before.

Impressed, confused, and worried, Bailey got in a taxi and headed across town. When he got to Taylor's house, he found her standing out front in defiance of the Chicago winter, a $100 bill dangling between her fingers. She told Bailey to take the money, and to let the cab driver keep the change. He did as she instructed, then followed Taylor inside. As he stepped through the door, Taylor turned the bolt behind him. "Now you're safe," she said, tucking the key inside her shirt.

Taylor's house in Chicago was nothing special on the outside, a stubby, two-story brick building on the corner of East Seventy-Eighth Street and East End Avenue. Inside, it looked like a palace, loaded with expensive furniture and the softest, thickest carpets Bailey had ever felt beneath his feet. Bailey thought Aunt Francie was a sucker—he didn't believe in voodoo or whispered messages from the spirit world. He had faith in something more tangible: Taylor's money. Just like the women who leaned in close to hear Dr. Shfolia's incantations, Bailey would learn to obey Taylor's commands.

The nineteen-year-old moved into the house at 1651 East Seventy-Eighth Street, helping out with the cooking and looking after Taylor's three young kids. When her husband, Willie Walker, a black cab driver from the South Side, came over on Fridays, Bailey parked the man's 1969 Cadillac Seville and went upstairs to mind the children. And when the three-day-a-week spouse put on his shiny shoes and walked out of the house on Sundays, Bailey took his place in bed with Taylor. They'd watch television together for hours—the news, Johnny Carson, and anything with Bette Davis, though Bailey couldn't understand why Taylor wanted to look at that ugly woman.

Taylor's taste in movies wasn't the only thing he found puzzling. He thought it was strange that his aunt called her Dr. Shfolia while others knew her as Dr. Whoyon. She'd told Bailey he could call her Connie. Bailey, who was black, also couldn't figure out how the dark-skinned Walker was the father of the three kids who lived with Taylor, given that one of them was white. He thought that Taylor, who he believed was some combination of Irish, Italian, and Gypsy, was probably their grandmother rather than their mother. Sometimes a couple of the kids would disappear for a while, or new ones would come to stay. Taylor had brought home the youngest of the three children, a beautiful black baby boy, without any advance warning—she certainly hadn't been pregnant. The infant got added to the brood, with no explanation given.

For Bailey, it was profitable not to ask questions. Taylor, who dressed in fox fur, silk, and satin, took her young assistant on shopping trips, telling him to buy whatever he wanted. As a guest in Taylor's house, Bailey drank expensive liquor and ate breakfast in bed, the food served to him by a maid. Late at night, he snooped inside her closet, which he unlocked using a key she usually kept pinned to her bra. She kept two purses in the closet, each of them loaded with money. He'd grab $100 at a time, knowing she'd never notice that he'd pinched such a small amount.

Taylor stored her mail in that closet, too, including checks inscribed with a bunch of different names. She'd gather up those checks, wrap a rubber band around them, and head over to a nearby currency exchange, or to Gateway National Bank at Seventy-Ninth Street and Stony Island Avenue. She'd walk into the bank with her head held high, and men in suits would trip over themselves to help her. Taylor liked to bring Bailey along when she ran her errands, but she made sure he knew who was in charge. If he asked questions about the people she was meeting, she'd tell him to "leave it alone."

She could be a lot of fun, momentarily. Taylor would laugh so hard she'd make herself cry, and she loved to wrestle, jumping on Bailey's back to catch him by surprise. Out of nowhere, she'd say she wanted to have a party. Twenty minutes later, she'd bottom out, and the party would be over before it started. The key to living with Taylor, Bailey found, was figuring out how to avoid upsetting her. She loved being in control and hated being disrespected. When Bailey asked for money, she'd huff that he had everything he needed, then demand that he leave. Later, she'd apologize, saying, "I wasn't fussing at you."

Taylor heard everything. She had a scanner in the house, to listen to the police frequencies, and she treated Bailey like a human security system, making him check the doors after every boom or crash. She popped Excedrin constantly—extra strength, in the green bottle. When she ran out, Bailey went to the store to buy more. She trusted him more than anyone else. At least that's what Bailey thought. She'd ask him to keep his eyes on the other members of the household, to let her know whether they'd answered the door or made any phone calls.

But that didn't mean Taylor let Bailey play by a different set of rules. One Saturday morning, she shouted at him from upstairs, making what he thought was an insignificant request. He ignored her once, then raised his voice when she started hollering at him again. After that, the shouting stopped. Twenty minutes later, Taylor came downstairs with a pistol in her hand. She placed it against Bailey's neck. "I'll blow your motherfucking brains out if you ever talk to me like that," she said.

Taylor walked away and sat down at the dining room table. She asked Bailey to come over. He assumed she was going to apologize for losing her temper. She did not. "You ain't going nowhere, nigger," Taylor told him. "The only way you're leaving is in a box."

* * *

Around Christmastime in 1971, Taylor called Bailey and asked him to come to Michigan. Two days later, he got on a bus. When Bailey made it to Taylor's house, he found himself surrounded by farm animals: chickens, pigs, and goats that she'd bought to graze on her land.

While Taylor came and went as she pleased, Bailey was stuck out in the country minding her property. There was nothing to do in Covert, and nobody around except a bunch of children and the woman who helped take care of them. The nanny, Virginia Griffin, had lived in Chicago, too. Taylor had told her and Bailey the same thing: If they didn't join her in Michigan, they were going to die.

Bailey thought that Taylor underestimated him—that she believed he was young and dumb and would always fall in line. He knew the risks of a life with Linda Taylor. But when Bailey weighed his options, he decided he'd be better off as Taylor's lackey than he would be doing anything else. Plus, if he stayed by Taylor's side, he thought, maybe she'd be less inclined to hurt him.

* * *

Taylor used her house in Van Buren County as a base of operations. It was a place where she could escape, make plans, and drop off her children. It was also a place where the mail carrier could deliver checks from the State of Michigan.

On November 16, 1971, she drove fifteen miles southeast of Covert to Hartford, Michigan, a tiny township surrounded by farms that produced a bounty of strawberries, cherries, peaches, and asparagus. Past the town's only stoplight, just off Red Arrow Highway and south of the new fairgrounds, stood the Van Buren County Department of Social Services. Taylor parked her car, cradled the small child she'd brought with her, and walked in to apply for benefits.

Inside, the building looked like the set of a horror movie. The basement was lined with cells that had once housed the mentally ill, and on rainy days water poured through the light fixtures. Idealists didn't last long in that basement—the conditions and the caseloads could cauterize any bleeding heart. Some stories, though, were powerful enough to cut through years' worth of cynicism and fatigue.

How could you not empathize with a woman like Connie Green? She walked into the basement carrying an infant, a boy she called her "little black baby." The eligibility examiner, a woman named Jessie Dinkins, thought he was a beautiful child, with ebony skin just like her own. Dinkins also noticed the boy's unusual name, Hosa—Mrs. Green had corrected her when she spelled it *J-o-s-e*. He was one of seven children, she explained. Their father was a white man, and he'd run out on the family because of the child's skin color. The infant, he'd told her, "was a disgrace to the white race."

Dinkins spoke with up to fifteen applicants each day, but Connie Green's story was one of the saddest she'd ever heard. She approved the request for aid, handing over $81 in food stamps with a promise of an additional $236 every two weeks through the Aid to Families with Dependent Children program. An authorization form listed the seven children who stood to benefit from that money: Hosa Womack, age sixteen months; Willie Womack, age three; William and Francis Womack, a set of seven-year-old twins; and Jimmy, Judy, and Johnny Womack, six-year-old triplets.

Another social worker who reviewed Green's case got overwhelmed just looking at those names on a sheet of paper—she couldn't imagine having to care for so many small children. But no one noticed something odd about those kids: The twins and triplets had birthdays just five months apart. That would've been a medical miracle if the children had actually existed.

* * *

It didn't take long for word to spread about the woman who'd just moved to Covert. A single mother with seven young children was the kind of person who drew attention in Van Buren County. So was a doctor from Chicago. So was a woman who wore enormous hats.

After he sold a house to Dr. Connie Walker, Ed Hedlund went out to eat in downtown South Haven. At Marge's Restaurant, he ran into his friend Claude Mann, a fellow real estate agent. Mann advertised on the front of the city directory, too—his slogan was "Serving you is my pleasure." Just like Hedlund, he'd fielded a call from a Chicago heart surgeon. The woman Mann had spoken with, Dr. Howard, wanted to buy sixty-seven acres of land to build a new medical center. But as soon as he'd started talking dollars and cents, the doctor said she had to leave to perform emergency surgery.

Hedlund always tried to think the best of people, but he wasn't a fool. The state police hadn't yet been introduced to the Chicago heart surgeon. But Hedlund realized right then that he'd never see the rest of the money Taylor was supposed to pay him. Covert also wouldn't be getting a new hospital.

The night he found out that Dr. Connie Walker was a fraud, Hedlund met up with his lawyer. There was nothing he could fix, nothing that could make him feel any less embarrassed about his gullibility. What he could do was drink, so he got plastered. The lawyer kept pace, drink after drink, because he'd been tricked, too. Taylor had come to him to draw up adoption papers—documents for kids he now wasn't sure belonged to her.

* * *

Taylor hadn't bothered to introduce herself to her next-door neighbor in Covert. The only thing Douglas Hale knew was that her last name was Walker. He also recognized her car, a blue and white 1969 Cadillac. One day, after Hale had been away for a while, he came home to find his neighbor's Cadillac parked in his garage. When he asked her to move it, she said that wasn't possible—it had engine problems. Not satisfied with that answer, Hale called the police.

The state troopers knocked on Taylor's door at 10 p.m. on February 12, 1972, but no one answered. They had better luck with the Cadillac. Inside the glove box, they found papers bearing the names Steve Walker, Viola Davis, Constance Nelson, Jackie Taylor, and Dr. C. Harbaugh. The Michigan State Police towed the car that night. They also opened an investigation into the woman who owned it.

The next day, a trooper came back to Covert to look for Linda Taylor. Instead, he found Charles Bailey. Taylor's teenage employee didn't tell the officer everything he knew. He didn't say that Taylor had asked him to move the Cadillac into her neighbor's garage, or that he'd found money along with all those papers in the glove compartment. But Bailey said enough to get the police interested. He explained that he'd met Taylor in Chicago, and that she'd pretended to be a spiritual doctor from Africa. He said he knew her as Dr. Shfolia, Dr. Whoyon, Dr. Constance Jarvis, Dr. C. B. Levan, Connie Green, Connie Harbaugh, and Sandra Lewis. He also told the police that she'd hidden the car so she could report it stolen.

It wasn't just Bailey—everyone the state troopers interviewed had a story to tell. The cops learned about the house Taylor had bought and hadn't paid for, the government assistance she received on behalf of seven children, and the car she'd purchased under the name Connie Jarvis. They also found out about the checks her nanny, Virginia Griffin, was getting in the mail. Griffin would later confess that she wasn't yet old enough to receive Social Security. Taylor had instructed her to use a phony birth date so she could collect benefits before she turned sixty-five.

When the Michigan police visited Bailey again five days later, he told them he'd spoken with Taylor, and had confessed to her that he'd "spilled the beans." Taylor didn't like that at all. She said she'd "take care of him" when she got back from Chicago. Her first priority, though, was arranging her escape from Michigan.

On February 19, 1972, the state police found Taylor standing in the snow and ice, loading up a moving van in front of her house in Covert. They arrested her, snapped her mug shot, and transported her to the South Haven city jail. As Connie Green, she was charged with making willful false statements about the number of children living in her home in order to receive $610 in public benefits. That was felony welfare fraud, with a maximum prison sentence of four years. A district court judge set her bond for $10,000, explaining that this high figure had less to do with the scale of her crime than his belief that Taylor was a flight risk.

He was right. After that preliminary examination, the case was bound over to the state's highest-level trial court, where a different judge reduced her bond to less than $1,000. Taylor got out of jail, left Michigan, and never showed up for trial.

Her arrest hadn't made Charles Bailey feel any safer. The day after the police took Taylor away, he'd gotten a phone call from her adult daughter, who'd said "her husband and brother were coming to Covert to get him." That night, Bailey had seen one of Taylor's cars drive past the house, but it hadn't stopped. A few months later, he went to Tennessee with a neighbor's sister. He never saw Taylor again.

Virginia Griffin had cried when Bailey left, begging him not to go. The nanny stayed in Covert to take care of Taylor's kids, if they were in fact Taylor's kids. The seven-year-old twins and the six-year-old triplets she'd put on her application for social services—those were imaginary. Griffin told the police that four of the children in Covert were Taylor's kin, including the "little black baby" Hosa and a white teenager named Robin. Griffin said she'd once overheard Robin talking to Taylor. He'd told her he was "going to Florida to find out what his real name was."

Taylor left behind a mess when she fled Covert. When Ed Hedlund got his property back, he discovered that she'd been using the crawl space as a kind of makeshift barn. Hedlund found all the animals Taylor had acquired—the chickens, pigs, and goats—huddled together underneath the house, unfed and abandoned.

* * *

A year and a half after Taylor ran away from Michigan, the state dropped the case against her—the prosecuting attorney saw no reason to proceed given that Connie Green couldn't be found. But even if she hadn't vanished, *People of the State of Michigan v. Connie Green* had little chance of moving forward. The Van Buren County Department of Social Services told the prosecutor that Green's entire case history had gone missing. He suspected that someone inside the department, embarrassed that the staff had approved a phony application, had made the file disappear.

In November 1973, the Michigan State Police placed Taylor's old felony case on inactive status—nobody would review her file unless someone called with new information. In August 1974, the state police got that call. Jack Sherwin brought the case back to life.

Along with a stack of old police reports, the Michigan state troopers sent Sherwin a fingerprint card. Now he needed to get some fresh prints, to prove he'd found the right woman. The detective made another visit to 8221 South Clyde Avenue and ran through the same set of questions: What's missing? Did anyone see what happened? Is there anything you'd like to add to your original report?

Taylor hadn't been happy to see Jack Sherwin the first time. After the third visit, she'd had enough. She'd told him what was missing. She'd told the uniformed cops, too—she'd given them a whole long list, and they'd written it all down. That should have been all they needed. If Sherwin was such a great detective, she asked, why hadn't he found her missing property already? Why couldn't he just do his job without bothering her? Sherwin told Taylor he wouldn't need much more of her time. Before he left, he had just one small request: Could he trouble her for a glass of water? Taylor did as he asked. When she came back with his drink, Sherwin kept the tumbler as evidence.

The detective had never played a trick like that before, and he was eager to see if he'd pulled it off. Lifting fingerprints off a smooth piece of glass is much easier than grabbing them from a cloth or a wrinkled sheet of paper. But the process isn't foolproof. In 1974, nearly a third of the latent fingerprints evaluated by the Chicago Police Department turned out to be unusable. Even good prints rarely broke open a case. That year, the city's police officers fielded more than twenty thousand requests to match a set of latent prints. They scored a hit less than 10 percent of the time.

* * *

When Sherwin left her apartment, Linda Taylor called Area 2 head-quarters and demanded to talk to whoever was in charge. She told the sergeant on duty that the detective had lost his mind. He kept stopping by to interrogate her about her stolen refrigerator. He was obsessed with her. He'd ruined her life.

The sergeant listened to her grievances, weighing her trustworthiness against the reputation of a cop with a dozen years of exemplary service. He sided with Taylor. The poor woman had filed a burglary report, the sergeant told Sherwin, and he was treating her like a criminal instead of a victim. He was wasting time, screwing around with a case that wasn't even a case. He needed to worry about clearing his other reports.

Sherwin had always respected the chain of command. As a Marine and a police officer, he'd been trained to follow orders, and he'd been rewarded for his compliance. Now he felt as though his superiors had abandoned him. They seemed to prefer those lazy detectives, the ones who shuffled paper around their desks until it was time to clock out.

A short time later, Sherwin heard back from the department's identification unit. He'd gotten lucky: An evidence technician had found a clean print on the glass of water, and it matched the whorls on the fingerprint card from Michigan.

If Taylor had created a new identity to escape her past, that plan hadn't worked. Now that he'd confirmed who she was, Sherwin was able to trace her criminal history. One of her previous arrests had come in February 1967, when she'd been booked under the name Constance Wakefield and charged with endangering the life and health of two children. Officers had brought her into custody again the following month. This time, as Constance Womack, she'd been charged with a felony: kidnapping a child under thirteen years of age.

She had a remarkable knack for dodging punishment. Every one of the Chicago cases listed on her rap sheet had been abandoned or dismissed. A series of police officers had interviewed Taylor and arrested her. Each time, they'd let her go.

Sherwin wasn't going to make the same mistake. He now knew where she'd been and what she'd been accused of doing. His sergeant had been wrong. Linda Taylor was a criminal, not a victim. And Sherwin had what he needed to arrest her.

CHAPTER 3
Page One

On August 25, 1974, Jack Sherwin and three other Chicago police officers drove to Linda Taylor's apartment on South Clyde Avenue. When Taylor answered the door, Sherwin said good morning and asked if he could come inside. Despite the complaint she'd filed with Area 2 headquarters, she waved him in. Sherwin walked into the front room and sat in a chair facing Taylor's couch. The detective told her he hadn't dropped by to chat or ask questions or get a glass of water. He'd come to take her into custody on behalf of the State of Michigan.

After Sherwin read Taylor her rights, she called someone to come pick up the two children she had with her, then asked the officers for a moment to change out of her housecoat. Taylor stepped into the bedroom and put on a new outfit, a short-sleeved brocade dress. She then took a cardboard suitcase from the closet and placed it on her bed. Taylor shuffled from her dresser to the suitcase and back again, grabbing armfuls of clothes and stuffing them inside the cheap piece of luggage. Five minutes after she'd started packing, one of the other detectives shouted at Sherwin—he thought he'd seen Taylor try to stash something away.

When Sherwin entered the room, Taylor slammed the cardboard suitcase shut. The detective asked her what was inside. "Clothes for the children," she said. Sherwin opened the valise. He found a bunch of children's clothing, as well as green Illinois Department of Public Aid identification cards bearing the names Connie Walker and Linda Bennett. One of Sherwin's fellow officers searched Taylor's purse and found another welfare ID card that had her name as Connie Walker, plus a driver's license that said Linda Bennett. Sherwin seized the ID cards, the driver's license, and every other piece of paper he could find in the apartment. There was an apartment lease, a receipt from a hospital stay, and stock certificates from old-time prospecting firms like the West End Extension Mining Company and the Boulder King Gold Mining Company. Sherwin also found eleven books of food stamps and a delayed record of birth for a Constance Beverly Wakefield. It took six police department inventory forms to write it all down.

"I know you by the name of Connie Jarvis. I know you by the name Connie Walker. This card says you're named Linda Bennett," Sherwin said. He asked Taylor to tell him her real name. The woman at 8221 South Clyde Avenue wouldn't give him a straight answer.

On his arrest report, Sherwin took his best guess. He typed the name "Taylor, Linda," then wrote in more names underneath: "Gordon—Green—Connie." He listed Linda/Connie Taylor/Gordon/Green as an unemployed nurse, height five foot one, weight 130 pounds. Her race was N, for Negro, her eyes brown, hair black, and complexion light. He guessed at Taylor's age, listing it as thirty-nine. That afternoon, the Chicago Police Department took Taylor's fingerprints one more time. She posed for two mug shots, one with her hair hanging down in a loose ponytail and the other with her natural locks hidden beneath a black curly wig. In both photographs, Taylor fixed her lips into a frown, and the flash from the camera reflected off her brocade dress.

* * *

Eight days after he'd exchanged vows with Linda Taylor at city hall, Lamar Jones got a phone call. It was his new wife. She was in the Cook County jail.

"Remember what I told you to do if I got in trouble?" she asked. He remembered.

Taylor had prepared him for this day, though he hadn't known it at the time. Shortly after they'd started going together, she'd brought him to meet a banker on Chicago's Northwest Side. If anything ever happens to me, she'd said, you should go see this man right away.

Jones hadn't thought much of the introduction—Taylor seemed to know a lot of men with money. But now, with his wife behind bars, Jones knew what he was supposed to do. He went to the bank, the man gave him a briefcase full of cash, and he used it to bail Taylor out.

* * *

Sherwin didn't think arresting Linda Taylor would accomplish much of anything. Her criminal history report showed that bringing her into custody had never slowed her down. Besides, these welfare fraud charges were from out of state, and Sherwin wasn't willing to cede this case to an outside agency. The cops in Michigan had caught Taylor two years before, but they'd let her wriggle free. If he gave up now, before he figured out who Linda Taylor really was, she would put on another wig, change her name, and slip away again.

The Area 2 burglary detective knew he wasn't supposed to spend his time digging up dirt on a phony burglary victim. But Sherwin couldn't bear to go back to his daily routine—the morning roll call, the half-dozen new burglary reports in his pigeonhole. This was a case he could crack open. He would find out everything Taylor had done, then put it all in a bundle and drop it on his lieutenant's desk. When the higher-ups saw what he'd put together, how he'd gift wrapped a case they could take credit for solving, they were going to be overjoyed. He knew it.

Jerry Kush had never seen his partner so energized. The detectives worked in tandem to check out leads, taking hour-long detours from the cases piling up on the front seat of their Chevy. With Kush's help, Sherwin learned whatever he could about a woman whose real name he still didn't know.

Linda Taylor was at once impossible to follow and easy to track. She changed her identity constantly, kicking up a trail of new paperwork wherever she went. These documents—government intake forms, real estate records, marriage licenses—told an incoherent story, one populated by dozens of characters of Taylor's own creation. When Sherwin found a name he hadn't seen before, he added it to his working list. Eventually, it would grow to fifty-four aliases, a two-column stack that filled the length and width of a typewritten page.

The first arrest on her rap sheet came in the fall of 1944. She'd been booked in Washington State for prostitution, quarantined on suspicion that she had a venereal disease, and then released. The date of that arrest confused Sherwin. When he'd met her in 1974, Taylor appeared to be no older than her late thirties. Sherwin called the authorities in Washington, who sent along her mug shot. He saw enough—the pointed chin, the Cupid's bow in the upper lip—to know he was looking at Linda Taylor. He also now had confirmation that she was closer to fifty years old than to forty.

Three decades after that 1944 prostitution arrest, Sherwin had gone to Taylor's apartment and found welfare ID cards with the names Connie Walker and Linda Bennett. She'd signed those same names on a series of applications warehoused by the Illinois Department of Public Aid.

As Connie Walker, Taylor had told the Public Aid Department she'd been born on Christmas Day 1934. A single mother, she'd claimed she was incapacitated by heart disease and couldn't work. The State of Illinois made sure Walker and her children didn't go hungry. Starting in January 1973, the Illinois treasurer sent her $416.70 each month to provide for herself, her two daughters, and her five sons. By the following January, those monthly payments had increased to $464.

As Linda Bennett, she'd given her birthplace as Homestead, Dade County, misspelling the state "Flordia." Born in 1940, she requested public assistance due to disability, and to meet the needs of her dependent children—this time, she listed four. On October 30, 1973, one week after Taylor signed the application, the state mailed her a check for $306. A day after that, the treasurer sent Linda Bennett $113.33. The money kept coming, every month. Three days after Sherwin arrested Linda Taylor at 8221 South Clyde Avenue, the Illinois treasury earmarked another $340 for Linda Bennett, 8221 South Clyde Avenue, Chicago, Illinois.

In April 1974, Taylor filled out a third request for assistance, giving her name as Sandra Brownlee. Her birthplace was Oakland, California, and her husband was "IN CANADA, DON'T KNOW WHERE." Her stepfather had supported her seven sons and daughters, but now that he was dead the children were "HUNGRY. NO FOOD IN THE HOUSE OR CLOTHEN." When asked to list her recent employers, she put down "NEVER WORK." On the four-page application, she wrote "none" or "no" 154 times. She scrawled the words horizontally, vertically, diagonally, upside down, and backward. She had no income, no insurance, no property—none, none, none. Had she received any kind of public assistance in the previous two years? No. A Cook County caseworker looked over the application and couldn't believe what she was reading. Only a rubber-stamping fool would've bought that Sandra Brownlee had seven children of preschool age or younger. This time, her request for public aid was denied.

Sherwin knew Taylor had committed welfare fraud in Michigan. He now had good evidence that she'd done the same thing in Illinois. He thought pinning those charges on Taylor would be easy. But when Sherwin and Kush shared what they'd found with the Department of Public Aid, the agency wasn't interested—it didn't do in-depth investigations. The Cook County state's attorney's office suggested they talk with the Illinois attorney general. The Illinois attorney general sent them to the U.S. attorney, who said this wasn't something federal prosecutors pursued. Maybe they'd have better luck with the IRS, or the postal inspectors. The locals said the same thing as the people at the state agencies, who parroted the feds. It was a question of resources. It was out of their jurisdiction. It was somebody else's problem.

It felt as though every bureaucrat in the United States was sending Sherwin the same message: Leave Linda Taylor alone.

* * *

Sherwin's frustration with his bosses inspired him to flout departmental rules he'd never pondered breaking. His colleague Wally McWilliams didn't need some crisis of conscience to challenge authority.

THE QUEEN

Sherwin and McWilliams had both started out as beat cops in the early 1960s, then earned promotions to detective. They worked in the same unit, Area 2 burglary, and they occasionally teamed up on investigations. McWilliams saw Sherwin as dependable, thorough, and unassuming. The feeling wasn't mutual. Sherwin didn't think that McWilliams was a bad guy, necessarily, but he did find Wally a little boorish—he always seemed to be scratching his crotch, and he'd scoot up two inches from your nose before launching into a conversation. Sherwin also thought McWilliams cared too much about his own image; he needed to play the conquering hero. He had a habit of butting in where he didn't belong.

McWilliams considered himself a troublemaker. He loved Chicago—he'd been born on the South Side and never left—but he hated the people who ran the city. He couldn't believe how easy it was for politicians to get away with graft, bribery, and outright theft. The whole system was corrupt. Everyone was out for himself.

The Chicago Police Department had its own problems. McWilliams chafed at how detectives got slotted into discrete divisions: burglary, assault, auto theft. If a burglary detective ran across a crime outside his assigned specialty, his superiors expected him to ignore it. McWilliams thought the department's higher-ups were hypocrites. They claimed to value efficiency, but they did everything they could to discourage hardworking cops from working hard.

McWilliams hadn't gone to Linda Taylor's apartment to check out her supposed burglary. He hadn't arrested her, and he didn't do any of the work to untangle her life story. But the more McWilliams heard about the Taylor case, the more he felt that he needed to get involved. Sherwin was a good cop, but he needed help to overcome a broken system. McWilliams could make sure justice was served. He knew the best investigative reporter in Chicago.

* * *

The day after Jack Sherwin arrested Linda Taylor for welfare fraud, the *Chicago Tribune* printed a front-page story alleging that four doctors had fleeced the Illinois Department of Public Aid. Those physicians, the *Tribune*'s George Bliss reported, received close to $100,000 per year for surgeries they didn't perform and newborns they failed to deliver. In one case, a "doctor collected $50 for performing a circumcision on a newborn baby. A check of the records disclosed that the baby was a girl."

Bliss blew out the story in a page one follow-up the next day, writing that doctors had pocketed as much as $750 for surgical procedures performed by unlicensed hospital personnel. He published another front-pager the day after that, with another killer anecdote: "A nurse at Bethany Brethren–Garfield Park Hospital had to deliver a newborn baby because the mother's public aid doctor didn't show up."

Every reporter at the *Tribune* wanted a byline on page one, but Bliss felt worthless if he went a week without a story up front. A single front-page item made for an ordinary morning. Bliss really crowed when he scored three in one day—a "hat trick." From August 24 to September 3, 1974, he placed eleven articles on page one of the newspaper's final edition. No other writer managed more than two.

The *Tribune*, with characteristic immodesty, billed itself as "the world's greatest newspaper." Bliss was the greatest newspaper's greatest reporter. He knew how every part of Mayor Richard J. Daley's Chicago machine fit together—who got paid off, and who was doing the paying. When he caught a politician lying or stealing, he'd say slyly, "You know, I think he wants to be famous."

Bliss made a lot of people famous. A mid-1970s book on investigative journalism estimated that his stories had sent more than one hundred people to prison. At age fifty-six, he'd contributed to several Pulitzer Prize–winning series, guided the *Tribune*'s award-hoarding Task Force investigative team, and been touted as a potential Cook County sheriff.

Stocky and muscular, Bliss maintained the build he'd developed forty years earlier as an amateur boxer. He dressed like a reporter from a bygone era, wearing baggy, off-the-rack suits and perching a fedora on top of his bald head. His typewriter, a Royal manual, sat on a rolling stand beside his desk. He knew how to mash the keys, but he was no great wordsmith. When a big page one piece appeared under his byline, somebody else had typically written it. A copyeditor once said that Bliss "should not have been allowed near a typewriter."

Bliss's skills as a reporter more than compensated for his deficits as a writer. He'd started out as a copyboy in the 1930s, ferrying drafts to editors, fetching coffee, and sweeping the floors at an afternoon newspaper owned by William Randolph Hearst. He'd been with the *Tribune* since 1942, joining the paper just before he shipped off to the Pacific during World War II. As an up-and-comer on the police beat, he'd learned that news gathering was a competition, and that a successful reporter did whatever it took to win.

The key to racking up victories was cultivating relationships with the right people. Bliss didn't just report on the police. He hung out with them at their favorite bars, played in their poker games, and attended their wakes. When the cops got together for the Chicago Patrolmen's Association picnic, Bliss dropped by with his wife and children. For family vacations, he'd rent a house on a lake and share it with his policeman buddies.

In the 1940s and 1950s, police officers and journalists played on the same team. Many shared the bond of military service, and they lived in the same neighborhoods on the South Side. A bulky Irishman, Bliss could pass for a cop himself. He'd flash a badge, identifying himself as a coroner, state's attorney, or police lieutenant when he needed to get places a reporter couldn't. The real police didn't seem to mind this sort of trickery—they understood the rules of the game. Cops spilled details on criminal suspects; reporters shared what they heard on the street. To make sure the information kept on coming, a writer might help a patrolman type up his reports, or look the other way when he saw an officer working security at a Mob-run cardroom.

Occasionally, Bliss used the power of the press to give his friends a little boost. One of the first times his name appeared in the paper—Bliss started at the *Tribune* years before reporters got regular bylines—was on April 22, 1951, atop a story headlined "Desk Sergeant: Busy Man Who Keeps Police Clicking." In that piece, he praised John L. Sullivan of the Grand Crossing District, who "often is called the politest and most efficient policeman in

Chicago." Four days later, the young *Tribune* reporter snared a spot at the front of the procession honoring Douglas MacArthur upon the general's return from Korea. The man who coordinated that procession was John L. Sullivan.

Bliss didn't just churn out puff pieces. In an unbylined series published in 1950, he detailed abuses at Cook County's juvenile home: allegations of a male employee bribing an underage female inmate for sex, of guards slapping and pulling the hair of their young charges, and of children being placed in solitary confinement. Bliss wrote those stories himself, crafting his copy on a portable typewriter he set up in his kitchen. He took pride in never putting in for overtime.

On June 20, 1959, his wife, Helen Jeanne Bliss—the mother of his five children—died giving birth to his sixth. Bliss's colleagues and children thought he never really recovered from that loss. After his wife's death, work became a compulsion. Bliss thought he needed to prove himself every day, so his editors wouldn't fire him and leave his family destitute.

In 1961, after he'd been promoted to labor editor, Bliss discovered that city employees were forging their time sheets so they could get paid without going to work. He would build that one article into a series of more than eighty stories, documenting overwhelming corruption in the agency tasked with safeguarding the region's drinking water. His exposé of the Metropolitan Sanitary District led to the elimination of 188 phony jobs, cuts the *Tribune* estimated would save taxpayers $1 million per year. The series earned Bliss his first Pulitzer, as well as a laudatory write-up in his own newspaper. That story, titled "George Bliss: Profile of a Top Reporter," was accompanied by photos of the prizewinner; his second wife, Therese Bliss; and their ten children: the six from Bliss's first marriage, three from Therese's, and the couple's infant son.

Powerful people knew Bliss's newspaper was an institution they shouldn't cross. In the early 1960s, the *Tribune* had the highest circulation of any non-tabloid newspaper in the United States, with more than eight hundred thousand readers during the week and 1.2 million on Sundays. Reporters like Bliss got their calls returned, and they got more respect than their rivals at the *Daily News* and *Sun-Times*. The *Tribune* earned its stature in Chicago thanks to its comprehensive coverage of local news. "Colonel" Robert McCormick, the former army man who led the paper from the 1910s until his death in 1955, popularized the term "Chicagoland" and tasked his reporters with blanketing the city, its suburbs, and neighboring states. This exhaustive approach to reportage wasn't accompanied by a similarly expansive worldview. A hard-line, traditionalist Republican, McCormick used his paper to editorialize against the New Deal and the United States' entry into World War II. The Colonel, who served as the newspaper's owner, editor, and publisher, called the *Tribune* "the American Paper for Americans." Chicago newspaper columnist Mike Royko later described it as "the voice of Midwestern Conservative Republican Isolationism and Inhumanity to the Downtrodden."

The only politics George Bliss was passionate about were the ones that played out in the newsroom. Bliss wanted to dig up stories his editors wanted to print. He thought he'd found a great one in 1967, when he sussed out some possible corruption in the office of Illinois secretary of state Paul Powell. The paper's leadership didn't think that story needed to be told. McCormick Place, the lakefront convention hall named for the *Tribune*'s late owner, had recently burned to the ground, and the newspaper needed Powell's support to ensure that a bigger, better monument to the Colonel's greatness would rise in its place. In 1968, a year after Bliss was told that Powell was off-limits, the reporter quit his job at the *Tribune*. Upon Powell's death in 1970, the executor of the politician's will found $750,000 in cash in the secretary of state's closet, $150,000 of it packed into a Marshall Field shoebox—wealth accumulated by soliciting bribes from wannabe state contractors. Bliss had been right.

After he walked out on the *Tribune*, Bliss went to work for the Better Government Association, a nonprofit watchdog group that partnered with Chicago newspapers on big reporting projects. As the BGA's chief investigator, Bliss engineered an exposé of private ambulance companies that refused to serve the poor. Bliss himself posed as a heart attack victim; when an ambulance crew arrived to find that he had just $2, the men stole his money and left Bliss propped up on the kitchen table. The resulting series, which ran in the *Tribune*, featured four front-page, hidden-camera photos of the "dying man." Bliss played his part very well—the ambulance stories won the 1971 Pulitzer Prize for local investigative reporting.

Although the *Tribune* got most of the glory from the BGA-conceived ambulance series, the paper's reputation had suffered in Bliss's absence. In December 1969, police officers detailed to the Cook County state's attorney's office shot and killed Black Panthers Fred Hampton and Mark Clark during a raid of Hampton's apartment. Within a few days of the killings, the city's most influential black-owned publication, the *Chicago Defender*, ran an editorial headlined "Was It Murder?" State's attorney Edward Hanrahan, meanwhile, gave the law-and-order-friendly *Tribune* an exclusive account of what he termed a "gun battle"—a confrontation that the Panthers had allegedly instigated by blasting away with a shotgun through the locked apartment door. That story was a lie. What Hanrahan had claimed were bullet holes in the door turned out to be nailheads. The state's attorney was charged with obstruction of justice, though he was ultimately found not guilty. Hanrahan would, however, pay a price at the ballot box, falling to Republican prosecutor Bernard Carey in 1972, thanks in part to the *Defender*'s dictate that "not a single black vote should help Hanrahan's reelection as Cook County's State Attorney."

The damage to the *Tribune* was no less acute. Clayton Kirkpatrick, who'd become the newspaper's editor in 1969, knew his paper had lost black Chicago. Young readers, too, preferred the politics of the *Daily News* and *Sun-Times* to those of the stolidly conservative *Tribune*. Kirkpatrick used the botched Black Panther story as the impetus to modernize the paper's viewpoints and workforce. He urged his reporters to take a more adversarial stance toward Chicago's leading institutions, and he began to diversify the newsroom, bringing in more women and more black journalists. He also extended a job offer to the city's best investigative reporter. In October 1971, after three years away, George Bliss agreed to return to the *Tribune*.

Kirkpatrick's splashy hire paid immediate dividends. Bliss spent all of 1972 directing an investigation of vote fraud in citywide elections, a series that won journalism's top prize the following year. The *Tribune* won three Pulitzer Prizes between 1962 and 1973. George Bliss had a hand in all three.

* * *

Bliss sat in front of the *Tribune*'s wire room, where the teletypes clacked and dinged, clacked and dinged as stories poured in from around the world. The clamor at Bliss's desk was just as incessant. His sources called all day: politicians who wanted help launching a career-boosting investigation, government employees blowing the whistle, cops telling their buddy George what they'd just seen on the job. When Bliss heard something he liked, he'd hang up the receiver, yank his coat off the back of his chair, and head out to find his next page one story.

In a resolutely corrupt city, and coming off an unprecedented run of professional success, Bliss could pick his next target. In 1974, his byline appeared in the *Tribune* 129 times, above pieces on medical swindles, a judge's shady land deal, and a rigged horse race. But he spent most of his time reporting on a single government agency.

In Bliss's telling, the Illinois Department of Public Aid was an unguarded bank vault, and thieves, charlatans, and layabouts were making off with as much as they could carry. He reported on doctors getting rich off Medicaid and drugstores that bilked the state by writing unneeded prescriptions for welfare recipients, in one instance supplying support pantyhose for a six-year-old girl.

Greedy doctors and pharmacists weren't the only ones with their hands in the till. Twenty-five unnamed welfare cheats were awaiting prosecution, Bliss wrote in a June 21 story headlined "High-salary workers collecting public aid," adding that investigators had "found public aid recipients driving expensive cars and owning other luxury items." Bliss subsequently reported that incompetence and sloth in the Public Aid Department cost the state up to $20 million a year. It was open season, he wrote, and "word has spread among aid recipients that they have little to fear in Cook County if they violate the welfare eligibility rules."

In September 1974, Bliss got tipped off about a new welfare scandal. Wally McWilliams, a policeman he knew from the South Side, told him about a public aid case that defied belief.

Cops and reporters didn't get along as they had in the old days. The rules of both professions had become more formalized—in the 1970s, Bliss couldn't get away with flashing a sheriff's badge at crime scenes—and their once-symbiotic relationship had grown strained after the 1968 Democratic convention. Younger journalists steeped in the anti-war movement saw Chicago officers as out-of-control reactionaries, while the police saw the press as a bunch of pointy-headed intellectuals who'd never understand the dangers cops faced on the street. But McWilliams didn't consider Bliss a typical reporter. He was a friend from the neighborhood and a friend of the Chicago Police Department. George Bliss could always see things from an officer's point of view.

McWilliams would meet Bliss at a coffee shop near Evergreen Park. They'd talk about sports and their families, and sometimes the cop would give the reporter a tidbit he could use. McWilliams got a kick out of seeing his tips—his stories—get delivered to homes across the city. He told Bliss about all kinds of investigations, those he'd worked on and those he hadn't.

This time, McWilliams knew he had something really explosive: reports showing that public aid employees had been told about a flagrant welfare cheat—by the police—and done nothing. His pals in Area 2 burglary, Jack Sherwin and Jerry Kush, had been stymied by the Department of Public Aid and the Cook County state's attorneys, and they didn't know what to do. If Bliss made a little noise, the detectives might find a way around those roadblocks—or could maybe smash right through them.

* * *

Linda Taylor drove a Cadillac. That car was impossible to miss, parked in the middle of the first sentence of the first article that ever mentioned her name. Bliss's piece ran on page three on September 29, 1974, flanked by items on Jews for Jesus and Donald Rumsfeld's new gig at the White

House. The story splashed across four columns in the Sunday *Tribune*, but that opening sentence had most of the essential facts.

> Linda Taylor received Illinois welfare checks and food stamps, even tho she was driving three 1974 autos—a Cadillac, a Lincoln, and a Chevrolet station wagon—claimed to own four South Side buildings, and was about to leave for a vacation in Hawaii.*

Taylor, Bliss wrote, had made a false report alleging that jewelry and furs had been stolen from her apartment. A subsequent investigation by a pair of Chicago detectives had uncovered a series of "false identities that seemed calculated to confuse our computerized, credit-oriented society." Bliss dropped in a bulleted list culled from Sherwin's case file, a set of data points that illuminated Taylor's "highly unusual way of life."

- Goes under at least 27 different names.
- Uses 31 different addresses, all but a few in Chicago.
- Has 25 different phone numbers.
- Has three social security cards.
- Owned stocks and bonds under a variety of names.
- Claims to have had several other husbands who died.
- Was married, under one of her aliases, last month to a sailor at Great Lakes Naval Training Center who is 26 years her junior.

But Bliss's article wasn't really about Linda Taylor. Using the information McWilliams had passed along, Bliss assembled a tale of valiant police officers fighting against an indifferent system. "If trailing Miss Taylor was like putting together pieces in a puzzle," he wrote, "trying to interest county, state, and federal authorities in her case was a study in frustration and burocratic buckpassing." Bliss highlighted excerpts from

---

* Why *tho* instead of *though*? Until 1975, the *Tribune* used a "simplified spelling" system favored by former publisher Robert McCormick. Other *Trib*-isms included *burocrat, clew, employe,* and *kidnaped.*

a fourteen-page report Sherwin had written to his bosses, a diary of his interactions with unsympathetic bureaucrats. The Illinois attorney general had told the detective "he would take up the matter with superiors and be in touch." A U.S. attorney had said "it was a matter of several federal agencies that would be involved but not something that they handled."

On and on it went, a "virtual shopping expedition" in which everyone had claimed that Linda Taylor was somebody else's problem. The story's seven-word headline captured Bliss's thesis: "Cops find deceit—but no one cares."

* * *

By the next day, the Linda Taylor problem had gotten a whole lot bigger—and Bliss had another page one story. The state legislature, he wrote, had launched an investigation into whether "Miss Taylor may be involved in a widespread scheme that may include a well-organized group of persons who have been cheating the welfare system." It wasn't unreasonable to suggest that Taylor may have had help on the inside. Three years earlier, the *Tribune* had written that a group of "at least 16 county public aid employes" had contrived to forge hundreds upon hundreds of welfare checks. Now, Bliss wrote, this latest alleged plot could involve "key Public Aid employes, [who,] either by direct assistance or thru negligence, have helped Miss Taylor obtain aid under numerous names."

Bliss's follow-up didn't just call attention to a new probe of the Illinois welfare system. It also added details to Taylor's biography. She "reportedly drives four expensive automobiles," Bliss wrote, up from the three he'd listed the day before. He noted that Sherwin and Kush "have learned that she posed as a nurse and as a doctor," and that Taylor "allegedly has posed as a Filipino, white, and a black to obtain welfare aid."

It took less than a week for the Linda Taylor story to become a national outrage. Shortly after Bliss's first piece ran in the *Tribune*, United Press International distributed its own version of events to more than eleven hundred newspapers across the United States. The UPI's unbylined article mentioned the purported wide-ranging conspiracy to defraud the Illinois government, a "well-organized scheme…involving welfare cheaters and state public aid employees." But that scheme was an afterthought, an aside in the final sentence. In many newspapers, that sentence got cut for space. In the UPI's telling, this wasn't some kind of bureaucratic failure. The scandal here was Taylor's very existence.

"For Linda Taylor, welfare checks are a way of life," the story began, before listing her fleet of vehicles: the Lincoln, the Chevy station wagon, the 1974 Cadillac. The UPI, unlike Bliss and the *Tribune*, directly quoted one of the Chicago detectives. "She is a small person with nondescript features," said Jerry Kush. "Her skin is sallow—like a medium yellow— and she has no features that make her peculiar to any racial background. So she passes as a Filipino. She puts on a black wig and becomes a Negro, and with other makeup and wigs, she passes for white."

The papers that printed the UPI's item wrote their own headlines, coming up with dozens of variations on the same theme. The *Seattle Times*: "She makes business of cheating welfare." The Charleston, South Carolina, *News and Courier*: "She Used Welfare To Pay for 3 Cars." Illinois's *Harrisburg Daily Register*: "She had a pretty good thing going." One newspaper, the *Democrat and Chronicle* of Rochester, New York, gave Taylor a nickname. The headline ran inside the paper, halfway down page two: "Welfare queen arrested."

* * *

Linda Taylor wasn't the first well-clothed welfare cheat in American history. In 1947, the New York papers worked themselves into a froth over a "lady in mink," an unidentified woman—the *New York Times* called her "Madame X"—who cadged relief payments while living rent-free in a city-funded hotel room. In an essay titled "Horsefeathers Swathed in Mink," press critic A. J. Liebling wrote that the "theme of the undeserving poor recurs as often as Groundhog Sees His Shadow." Indeed, in June 1933— one year after the Illinois Emergency Relief Commission was established to aid those suffering during the Great Depression—the *Tribune* railed

Josh Levin

against the "unscrupulous parasites" who'd been working the relief system. By November, a special court had been set up to prosecute cheaters. That same month, a Chicago woman who'd "collected some $50 in cash and grocery orders" was sentenced to thirty days in jail for claiming falsely on her relief application that her husband was unemployed.

From its creation in 1935 as part of Franklin Roosevelt's Social Security Act, the federally mandated and partially state-funded Aid to Dependent Children program was beset by allegations that the poor single mothers who benefitted from its largesse were neither poor nor single. The *Tribune* published a long investigation of "women relief cheaters" in 1951, showcasing ADC recipients who'd stayed on the rolls by hiding their marriages, their husbands' incomes, and their sexual relationships. In the early 1960s, *Reader's Digest* and *Look* did stories on the "shocking truth" and "scandal" of Aid to Dependent Children, pieces that focused on a series of salacious anecdotes: "A mother of seven [who] made a practice of sending her children out begging while she spent the ADC checks to feed steaks to her paramour," another who "hit the $61,500 relief jackpot by producing 14 illegitimate children," and a family that "picked up four cartons of free relief food…and drove off—in a 1958 air-conditioned Cadillac." In 1973, *Reader's Digest* called out a new group of outrageous rip-off artists, including "able-bodied hippies…financing communes with welfare checks" and a "onetime topless dancer…collecting $15,000 a year under five different names."*

These extraordinary individual claims stood for something bigger: widespread bureaucratic waste, moral decay, and the triumph of the indolent over the industrious. Four years before the *Tribune* found Linda Taylor behind the wheel of a luxury car, former undertaker's assistant Guy Drake hit the Billboard charts with a novelty song called "Welfare Cadilac."** "I get a check the first of every month, from this here

---

* Though it was far rarer for men to be branded public aid cheats, in 1946 the *Detroit Free Press* labeled John O'Connor the city's "Welfare King." O'Connor, who allegedly stole nearly $70,000 in relief funds, did get a mention in the *Saturday Evening Post* in 1949, but his exploits and nickname didn't draw much national attention.
** Drake spelled the eponymous Cadillac with just a single *l*.

federal government," the Kentuckian drawled. "Every Wednesday I get commodities, why, sometimes four or five sacks / Pick 'em up down at the welfare office, driving that new Cadilac." President Richard Nixon liked the song so much he asked Johnny Cash to play it at the White House. Cash declined.

In 1974, an estimated 24.3 million people—12 percent of the U.S. population—lived below the poverty line of $5,038 for a family of four. That same year, roughly fourteen million Americans per month received federally funded food stamps, while 10.8 million—7.8 million children and three million adults—got assistance via Aid to Families with Dependent Children. (The Aid to Dependent Children program had been renamed as part of 1962's Public Welfare Amendments to illustrate a "new emphasis on family services.") Drake's song reflected a pervasive anxiety about who was collecting all these benefits, and how they spent them. In a syndicated column headlined "The Welfare Cadillac," Paul Harvey wrote that the "Department of Agriculture is receiving an increasing number of complaints that poor people are using food stamps to buy steak." Those grievances didn't reflect the reality of people on public assistance. In 1973, a Cook County official acknowledged that lower-income women couldn't afford to buy any kind of meat—not even neck bones. Instead, the *Tribune* wrote, "welfare mothers are being urged to use the new soybean additives in the preparation of hamburger dishes."

The hardships faced by struggling American families didn't generate massive public outrage. The astonishing details of Taylor's parasitic life did. "'Welfare Cadillac' Reality for Woman in Chicago; Also Lincoln, Buildings," read a headline on the front page of Texas's *Lubbock Avalanche-Journal*. Cadillacs were chariots for celebrities. Elvis Presley collected them, and Ronald Reagan had driven one back in his movie star days— he'd once described his California ranch as a "hop, skip, and a Cadillac" from Hollywood. Most Americans didn't have luxury cars on their shopping lists. The inflation rate hit 11 percent in 1974, the highest in three decades. Those lucky enough to have jobs saw their paychecks bring home less and less each week. The median household income in the United

States, $11,101, was less when adjusted for inflation than it had been two years prior. The sticker price of a 1974 Cadillac Eldorado convertible was $9,437. When Linda Taylor bought a new Caddy, she was spending the better part of a typical American family's annual earnings.

Taylor was the lady in mink, and the mother who sent her children out to beg while she fed steaks to her lover, and the woman with the fourteen illegitimate kids. But two things set Taylor apart: She had a nicer car, and she had a name. Taylor was a real person, not some anonymous, maybe even fictional character in a newspaper or magazine. She could be found, and she could be punished for what she'd done.

On September 30, 1974, the day Bliss put her on page one of the *Tribune*, Taylor was scheduled to appear in court to face an extradition warrant. The State of Michigan was ready to take her back into custody on those felony welfare fraud charges from 1972—the case in which Taylor had lied about being the mother of twins and triplets. Taylor's name was called three times in Cook County felony court, but she never answered. The most notorious woman in Chicago had vanished again.

* * *

At the end of September, Jack Sherwin took a few days off to clear his head and forget about Linda Taylor for at least a little while. He had no idea what would be waiting for him when he got back to work. Bliss's first two stories were published while Sherwin was out of the office, as was the item written by the UPI. The detective didn't see those articles, and nobody called to warn him that he'd made the papers.

Sherwin got berated by his boss and his boss's boss as soon as he walked into Area 2 headquarters. It was bad enough that he'd continued working on the case after he'd been told to let it go. Now George Bliss was casting Sherwin as some kind of hero, a steadfast detective with "bloodhound instincts." The *Tribune* praised Sherwin and his partner and made police higher-ups, prosecutors, and public aid workers look dumb, incompetent, and crooked. Sherwin had wanted to gift wrap a case and drop it on his lieutenant's desk. Instead, he'd embarrassed everyone who had a hand in whether he'd rise or fall in the department. Bliss's stories, Sherwin thought, were obituaries for his career as a police officer.

He didn't know how George Bliss had gotten his personal files; he didn't suspect that Wally McWilliams had been the one to leak them. Sherwin identified another possible culprit. After Bliss and the *Tribune* got the scoop on Linda Taylor, Sherwin's partner Jerry Kush had talked to the UPI, describing Taylor's sallow skin and penchant for wearing makeup and wigs. Sherwin was certain that Kush had blabbed to Bliss, too. They'd work together for years after that, but Sherwin would never confront Kush, and he'd never learn that he'd been wrong about who'd passed his case file to a reporter. Before the leak, Sherwin believed he still had a few friends in the Chicago Police Department. Afterward, he felt completely alone.

George Bliss's stories made Sherwin an outcast. They also gave him an opportunity he hadn't anticipated. A few days after the *Tribune* published Bliss's first article on Linda Taylor, an Illinois state senator named Don Moore wrote a letter to the Chicago police, praising Sherwin and Kush for their "perseverance and dedication." Moore, the chair of the Legislative Advisory Committee on Public Aid, believed that welfare cheats were systematically depleting the state's coffers. Now, thanks to Sherwin, he had the evidence he needed to confirm that thievery.

Moore followed up a week after he sent that letter to the police, asking that the Area 2 burglary detectives be made his temporary employees. The state senator's request was granted. Jack Sherwin and Jerry Kush were no longer Chicago police officers. They worked for Don Moore now.

CHAPTER 4

Obtained by Deception

Lamar Jones had thought he was going to be with Linda Taylor for the rest of his life. He'd fallen for her the minute she walked into the dental clinic at Great Lakes Naval Training Center. She was sophisticated and smart, flirty and beautiful. Her bizarre, unpredictable behavior—the tales of dead husbands and the frightening temper tantrums—hadn't quite broken that initial spell, and neither had her arrest. Jones had bailed her out, just as he'd been told to. He wanted to make things work.

That got a lot harder after Taylor came back from the Cook County jail. One weekend, Jones threw a party at Great Lakes, then chose to stay near the base overnight rather than drive the sixty miles back to Chicago. Not long after, he checked in with his mother. She was stunned to hear his voice. When Jones hadn't come home, Taylor had called her mother-in-law to report that he'd been killed in a car accident.

After he got off duty, Jones drove straight to his mother's house on the South Side. She was crying, shaken, and confused. He got back in his car, picked up Taylor, and put the two women in a room together. Jones's mother pleaded with Taylor to explain herself. What possible reason could she have had for telling a woman her son was dead? Taylor said it was very simple: She was mad because Jones had stayed out instead of coming home to her. This is what happened when you disrespected her. She hoped he'd learned his lesson.

Jones couldn't believe his wife could be so callous. He told her he'd kill her if she ever treated his mother that way again. That didn't scare

Taylor, or deter her from trying to drive a wedge between her husband and his family. At one point, she put him on the phone with a man in London, England, someone who claimed his name was also Lamar Jones. This other, older Lamar professed to be the young sailor's real father. When Jones started asking this English guy questions—What was his grandmother's name? His grandfather's?—the man didn't have any answers. The whole thing was very strange.

Jones's mother didn't trust Taylor, and his dog didn't either: Whenever she drove up, the Doberman-boxer mix tried to claw through the window of her car. It was past time, he realized, to extricate himself from this relationship. But that wouldn't be his decision to make. In late September 1974, Taylor skipped out on her bond. On her way out of town, she stole Jones's color TV set. Their marriage was over. It had lasted a month.

* * *

To stay safe, Linda Taylor had to get as far away from Illinois as possible. In a new place, in front of a new audience, she could become a new set of people. But this time she'd have more than a single detective on her trail.

Jack Sherwin had tried and failed to get anyone at any level of government to pay attention to an obvious fraudster. When Linda Taylor's name appeared in the *Chicago Tribune*, however, the FBI launched an investigation into whether she'd stolen Social Security benefits and the U.S. Department of Agriculture began to ask questions about her cache of food stamps. And in Illinois, the Legislative Advisory Committee on Public Aid tried to figure out exactly how much Taylor had stolen, and why nobody had stopped her.

Officially, the Legislative Advisory Committee was supposed to counsel the Illinois Department of Public Aid on statutory changes and budget requests. In practice, the twelve-person, bipartisan group attacked the department from all sides. In 1969, a welfare recipient told the committee that she was allotted only 26 cents per person per meal; one sympathetic legislator asserted that Illinois's food allowances were "hardly enough for a grown, healthy pigeon." Other Illinois politicians saw aid recipients as leeches and spendthrifts. In 1964, some committee members claimed that the allegedly needy were gambling away their welfare checks. The year before, a Republican state representative had proposed the total abolition of public aid, writing, "Consider for example the Negro race.... Substantial segments of their group do not understand or appreciate their responsibilities."

By 1960, the poor widows who'd originally made up the bulk of Aid to Dependent Children beneficiaries had mostly been moved into the Social Security system. Those who remained in the ADC program—unwed mothers and the partners of men who'd absented themselves for one reason or another—were largely seen as unsympathetic figures, women whose dissolute behavior needed to be policed.

"Suitable home" and "man in the house" provisions—typically enforced via midnight raids of welfare recipients' homes—allowed states to cut off funding to women who had illegitimate children, lived or had relationships with men who weren't their husbands, or engaged in any manner of conduct that an aid worker might view as immoral. Some states targeted black women on public aid for compulsory sterilization. (The practice didn't end in North Carolina until 1973.) In 1962, Illinois public aid authorities considered warning women on welfare that they could be jailed for having a child out of wedlock. That idea fizzled out when the federal government threatened to withhold matching funds for Aid to Dependent Children.

While these sorts of proposals placed the blame for rising welfare spending on debaucherous aid recipients, an exhaustive examination of ADC in Cook County showed that was a gross mischaracterization. That report, produced in 1960, concluded that the program's biggest problem was public "hostility to this most disadvantaged segment of our population." In contrast to the "false image ... of a mother who is shiftless and lazy, unwilling to work, promiscuous and neglectful of her children," the vast majority of women on welfare "give their children good care, and they deny themselves in order to give the children nourishing food." Self-denial could stretch a minuscule check only so far. "There is a good probability that the [typical Cook County ADC] family is in debt for food and clothing, and that the school age children were kept home from school at some time last winter due to lack of warm clothing and suitable shoes," the report said.

Such deprivations weren't unique to Illinois. As of 1970, the Associated Press reported, thirty-nine states were "illegally denying the poor either due process or deserved relief benefits." By then, the states were supposed to have less freedom to refuse aid to those who needed it. Thanks to changes at the federal level, welfare had shifted from a privilege for the "deserving poor" to an entitlement for all those living below the poverty line. In 1968, the Supreme Court deemed "man in the house" laws unconstitutional; two years later, the justices ruled that welfare benefits couldn't be taken away without an evidentiary hearing. The federal government also began encouraging states to move to a simplified "declaration" system for determining eligibility for the rechristened Aid to Families with Dependent Children, one in which agencies trusted clients to fill out a basic, unverified application. All the while, neighborhood legal aid clinics and leaders of the burgeoning welfare rights movement were fighting to ensure that people who'd historically been excluded from social services—primarily poor black women—received their entitled benefits.

The liberalization of welfare rules coincided with President Lyndon Johnson's War on Poverty, a suite of initiatives that included the Food Stamp Act of 1964; the Economic Opportunity Act of 1964, which funded those neighborhood legal aid clinics; and 1965's Social Security Act Amendments, which birthed Medicaid and Medicare. These programs, along with a booming economy, improved the lots of millions of the nation's poorest citizens. In 1959, 22.4 percent of Americans overall and 55.1 percent of black Americans lived below the poverty line. By 1974, those numbers had dropped to 11.2 percent overall and 30.3 percent for blacks.

It cost money to make people less poor. Medicaid and AFDC, though paid for with the help of federal dollars, placed a significant strain on state budgets. Between 1963 and 1973, the number of Illinois residents on the

AFDC rolls grew from 265,000 to 774,000. During that same period, the state's annual public aid outlays increased more than sevenfold, rising to $1.5 billion. This state-level spending crisis, the *Washington Post* explained in 1971, "is really the reform—namely that poor people are finally getting some money."

In Illinois, state senator Don Moore warned of "fiscal chaos, and perhaps bankruptcy" if the state didn't make drastic cuts. In 1972, he called for a federal takeover of the welfare system, claiming that such a handoff would save Illinois $750 million per year, which the state could then spend on education.

The Republican, a former assistant state's attorney, wore his hair slicked back, and in photos the corners of his mouth drooped down into a glower. He looked like a man who was easy to disappoint. Moore represented Midlothian, a village south of Chicago proper. When whites fled the city, they ended up in places like Midlothian, a tree-lined town with a country club and homes that middle-class families could afford to buy. In 1973, Moore shepherded an antibusing bill through the legislature, explaining that "both black and white people in my district want to maintain their neighborhood schools." In reality, he protected the interests of white suburbanites—by 1970, Moore had 186 black constituents and 15,697 white ones. The people of Midlothian felt particularly aggrieved by welfare fraud. In the early 1970s, the senator got a letter from a man who complained "that some of these people using food stamps are often dressed in fine clothing and purchasing items considered for expensive taste."

Moore, who was eager to bolster his own reputation as a welfare reform crusader, looked west for guidance. In 1971, Ronald Reagan had termed public aid a "cancer eating at our vitals," and as governor of California he'd devoted himself to ridding the state of this so-called disease. Reagan worked with legislators to tighten eligibility rules, reduce the size of grants for those with outside income, and implement work requirements for some able-bodied public aid recipients. The state's welfare rolls shrank in the aftermath of these policy changes, thanks in part to a simultaneous, unrelated reduction in unemployment. Nevertheless, the governor was celebrated as a conservative hero: *National Review* founder William F. Buckley Jr. termed California's welfare reforms the "Reagan Revolution."

In 1973, Moore and seven other members of Illinois's Legislative Advisory Committee flew to California to study what Reagan had done. After his trip, Moore introduced a bill mimicking the Reagan regime's flat grants, eliminating the extra stipends for rent, food, and clothing that had gone to some recipients with special needs. Though welfare rights organizations threatened to sue, Illinois's governor, Democrat Dan Walker, approved the legislation without any public hearings.

* * *

Don Moore knew that plenty of Illinois residents truly needed government assistance, and he believed it was his mission to do right by them. In the fall of 1974, the state senator from Midlothian succeeded in lobbying to override the governor's veto of a cost-of-living increase for all public aid households. "When you start paying 61, 62, 63 cents for a loaf of bread and a buck-15 for a pound of hamburger, you can get an idea of how far money does not go today," Moore said.

At the same time, Moore rarely declined the opportunity to assert that the state's taxpayers were being victimized by fraudsters. On June 21, 1974, George Bliss wrote that investigators had found welfare cheaters who were "earning nearly $30,000 a year in their jobs," as well as people "receiving aid payments for children they never had or members of the family who were dead." In that article, tagged a *Tribune* exclusive, Bliss cited Moore's estimate that "millions of dollars a month can be saved by continuing probes of cheaters in the Chicago area." A day after that, Bliss reported the politician's declaration "that cheating amounts to more than $100 million a year."

Bliss's stories blended provable fact and reckless conjecture. While there was ample evidence that at least some people on public aid shouldn't have been eligible to get checks, Moore's statistics had no clear basis in reality. When it came to documenting the scope of welfare fraud in Illinois, the state senator preferred to work backward, making wild claims in the press and then looking for the proof to back them up.

Moore was convinced that the Illinois Department of Public Aid hadn't done nearly enough to clamp down on welfare fraud. The director of the Illinois Department of Public Aid agreed with him. In August 1974, Joel Edelman stepped down as the leader of that agency, telling the *Tribune* that his staff couldn't handle the "mounting problem of fraud in welfare programs." The next month, Edelman officially signed on as the executive director of the Legislative Advisory Committee on Public Aid. The two men immediately got to work building a miniature police force.

The legislative committee's initial two hires were Neal Caauwe, a white detective from Midlothian, and Fred Pennix, a black policeman from the Cook County suburb of Robbins. On their first day, the cops took an orientation course on fraud detection designed by one of Reagan's top welfare fraud experts.

Less than a week later, on September 29, 1974, the *Tribune* published Bliss's article on Jack Sherwin and Linda Taylor. Moore and Edelman's fraud fighters had the subject of their first big investigation. Within days, they also had two new colleagues, thanks to the Chicago Police Department's willingness to loan out Sherwin and his partner, Jerry Kush. Their mission: Find Linda Taylor.

* * *

Even after she left Chicago, Taylor would call Lamar Jones at Great Lakes Naval Training Center. On the phone, she didn't act as though she was on the lam—she was happy to tell him where she'd settled down. Maybe she was taunting him, or maybe she assumed he wouldn't turn her in. But Jones could take only so much. His wife had abused his trust, and now he would abuse hers. After Taylor called him one day in October, two months after their hasty wedding, Jones went to the police.

Jones told Jack Sherwin he'd been an innocent bystander. He said he'd had nothing to do with Taylor's various schemes—that he hadn't known who his wife really was. Sherwin believed him. How could he not? Taylor had duped him, too. Sherwin was less certain about some of the other things Taylor had told Lamar Jones—that she'd been married eight times, and that she'd shot and killed her first husband. But all of that could wait. He now knew where Taylor was hiding. He needed to tell the Tucson Police Department to be on the lookout for a fugitive from Chicago.

* * *

Taylor's new home had been listed in the *Tucson Daily Citizen* classifieds as "large, tastefully & newly furnished." It was a two-bedroom place in a quiet building, with a small courtyard and a spot where she could park her 1974 Chevrolet Impala station wagon. When she rented the apartment, she told the landlord her name was Dr. Velma Weshmare.

In Arizona, Taylor had everything she needed to make a series of new impressions. She carried Illinois driver's licenses with two different names. Her car title and vehicle sticker had a third and fourth alias, and she addressed envelopes with a fifth and sixth. She set up a doctor's office inside her apartment, filling it with certificates that attested to her educational bona fides. One identified her as Dr. Linda Bennett, MD, ESP, PhD, Doctor of Occult Science. Another said she was Dr. Constance Womack, who belonged to the Sigma chapter of Epsilon Delta Chi, a fraternal organization for members of the clergy. That document included the Latin inscription *Nosce te ipsum:* "Know thyself."

Thanks to Lamar Jones's tip, it took detectives from the Tucson Police Department less than a week to find their woman. Though they had to wait for fingerprint cards to come in the mail from Michigan, the officers identified Linda Taylor—a.k.a. Constance Green, a.k.a. Dr. Velma Weshmare—based on the name tattooed on her upper left arm: Joe Fick. None of the police officers in Illinois or Michigan or Arizona had any idea who Joe Fick was, but that hardly mattered. All they cared about was grabbing Taylor before she got away again.

On October 9, 1974, the Tucson detectives found Taylor driving her Chevy station wagon and placed her under arrest. A photo published in the *Daily Citizen* showed her in a striped tank top, with pursed lips and her hair rolled up in giant curlers. The caption related the story of her capture in the shortest possible form: "Husband 'told.'"

The cops impounded Taylor's driver's licenses and diplomas, as well as ads she'd clipped from newspaper classifieds and the magazine *Fate: True Stories of the Strange and Unknown*. The police discovered that Taylor had planned to purchase a sixty-day supply of E-Longe Lotion, a "newly developed amino extract" that promised longer, thicker hair in a week's time. She'd also wanted to buy a $10 guide to making $2,000 per day; a tip sheet that touted a system for "cashing big" by betting on horse races; and the books *How to Tell Fortunes with Cards* and *Psychic Perception: The Magic of Extrasensory Powers*, the latter of which promised to unlock "avalanches of abundance, and discoveries of hidden treasure." Dr. Joseph Murphy, a minister in the Church of Divine Science, told his followers they could earn immense sums by using "the miraculous mental instrument of the mind." One of Dr. Murphy's testimonials came from a woman who had once been a secretary: "If someone had told me a year ago that I would be driving a Lincoln, wearing a mink coat, expensive diamonds and sapphires, living in my own home and married to a wonderful man, I would have laughed out loud."

Forty-eight hours after Taylor's arrest, Don Moore's welfare fraud cops Neal Caauwe and Fred Pennix flew to Arizona to pick her up. Taylor's daughter, Sandra, came down, too, to get the two children Tucson police had found living in Taylor's apartment. When child protective services handed them over, Sandra complained that the kids didn't have any shoes. Taylor sat beside Caauwe and Pennix on the flight back to Chicago. She didn't say a word the entire trip; she just looked at the police officers and smiled. Taylor had chosen this destination, albeit from a limited set of options. On the advice of her Arizona public defender, she'd refused extradition to Michigan but consented to return to Illinois. Her fate would be decided in Cook County.

When Taylor's plane landed at O'Hare Airport, Jack Sherwin was there to greet her. He placed her under arrest for grand theft and bond forfeiture on behalf of the State of Illinois. Her bail was set at $100,000.

THE QUEEN

★ ★ ★

Though Taylor was now in custody, the basic details of her life remained elusive. On this latest arrest report, Sherwin listed her as fifty years old and unemployed. A month earlier, he'd described her as a thirty-nine-year-old nurse. The *Tucson Daily Citizen* reported one day that she was forty-seven, the next that she was thirty-nine. A short AP article said Taylor was forty.

In his October 12 piece reporting the news of Taylor's Arizona arrest, George Bliss repeated the long list of damning facts he'd first laid out two weeks prior: She drove a Cadillac, a Lincoln, and a Chevrolet, and had at least twenty-seven different names and thirty-one addresses. This time, though, he put a price tag on Taylor's larceny, writing that "her alleged take might have run to $300,000 in welfare funds." Bliss made it clear that his newspaper owned the Linda Taylor story. It had been the *Tribune*, he reported, that "first alerted authorities to her activities here," highlighting the type of blatant graft the Illinois Department of Public Aid had been too incompetent to ferret out on its own. This story, Bliss's third on the case, deployed an identifier that reflected the grandeur of her crime. She was "Linda Taylor, the 47-year-old 'welfare queen.'"

Although the moniker wasn't in wide circulation before October 1974, it did occasionally show up in newsprint. Seven years earlier, a woman named Patty McGowan wrote a letter to the editor of the *Cincinnati Enquirer* complaining about a proposed federal "allowance" for children, writing, "I'm already a drone bee for the Social Security queen, the Medicare queen, and the welfare queen—to name a few." And in 1969, Vermont's *Burlington Free Press* noted that a public aid recipient named "Mary Black"—a pseudonym—"is known as the 'Welfare Queen,' and people in the area claim she runs the streets at night and frequents the beer gardens."

The movie *Claudine*, released in April 1974, pushed back against the welfare queen stereotype even as it was still emerging. "Haven't you heard about us ignorant black bitches? Always got to be laying up with some dude, just grinding out them babies for the taxpayers to take care of," said Diahann Carroll's title character, a black single mother with six kids. "You know, I'm living like a queen on welfare." The *Tribune*, by contrast, used the term uncritically and unrelentingly. Bliss's piece on October 12, 1974, was the first of more than forty articles in the newspaper that referred to Taylor by that epithet. It was the *Tribune* that made the welfare queen a recognizable figure, and that helped spread the term nationwide.

In the absence of confirmed facts, Taylor's nickname was the one thing every publication could agree on. In December 1974, the Gannett News Service published a long story on the "woman who's been dubbed the 'Welfare Queen.'" According to unnamed investigators and agents, Taylor was "either black, white or Latin, a native of the U.S., Haiti, England or South Africa," and had possibly plundered the state treasuries in New York, New Jersey, Ohio, and California. One of those anonymous agents added that the children who'd been with her during her Illinois arrest were "not hers." Another said, "She can look as tacky as she wants and she can look as good as she wants. She is a very well-built woman."

A few days earlier, the UPI had done its own piece on the "welfare queen," a woman who "turns from black to Latin to white with the change of a wig." The wire service quoted Joel Edelman. "When the entire story is told," the executive director of the Legislative Advisory Committee on Public Aid said, "I believe this will prove to be the most massive case of welfare fraud that has ever been perpetrated in the 50 states."

In California, a public relations man named Peter Hannaford filed that clip away. He thought his boss, Governor Ronald Reagan, might want to read it someday.

★ ★ ★

George Bliss's reporting had proved that welfare cheaters existed. The Legislative Advisory Committee's investigation of Linda Taylor promised to uncover how much one woman could steal. It would also reveal whether the Illinois Department of Public Aid had been complicit in Taylor's crimes.

Jack Sherwin took control of the operation, doling out assignments to the other investigators. Though Sherwin worked for the Legislative Advisory Committee on Public Aid, he didn't see this as just a public aid case. He would go wherever the evidence led him and develop a comprehensive list of possible charges.

Sherwin began by scrutinizing Taylor's applications for public assistance. Though the information on those forms was mostly fictional, the names she wrote on the signature lines had some basis in reality. Connie Walker came from her husband Willie Walker, the Chicago cab driver. She got Linda Bennett from another husband, Aaron Bennett. She'd taken the name Sandra Brownlee from her own daughter.

On October 24, 1974, the legislative committee brought the real Sandra Brownlee in to answer some questions. Taylor had told Lamar Jones that the twenty-three-year-old Brownlee was her sister, Constance. The family resemblance was clear—like her mother, Sandra had dark hair, dark eyes, and skin the color of milky coffee. In a series of interviews, she said she'd been born in Paris, France, and that she'd lost the hearing in her right ear due to injuries suffered in a 1958 fire at Chicago's Our Lady of the Angels School. Brownlee admitted she'd cashed welfare checks on her mother's behalf at a Chicago currency exchange. She also told state and federal investigators she knew that her mother had filed Social Security and Veterans Administration claims using the name Sandra Brownlee.

There were some things Brownlee said she just didn't know. An FBI agent wrote, "She is not sure of her origin. She recalled being with her mother, Linda Taylor, at various times during her life, but her mother really confused her at times by telling her she was not who she thought she was." The FBI's memo continued,

> Sandra stated her mother is a member of the black race. She could not explain how her mother presently had two children, one black [Hosa] and one white [Duke], with straight blond hair. She claimed that [Hosa] was her mother's child by Willie

Walker, who is now dead. Sandra displayed photographs of her brothers, [Johnnie] and Robin, who are also white males with sandy brown hair. She further advised that her mother has had several children over the years but she is not sure how she got them.

Sherwin found one of those brothers in Joliet state prison. Johnnie Harbaugh had been arrested at least twelve times in the past decade, for offenses ranging from loitering to disorderly conduct to unlawful use of a weapon, though only a handful of those episodes had resulted in convictions. This time, he'd been locked up for theft. When Sherwin leafed through Harbaugh's arrest reports, he found his own name and badge number. The detective, it turned out, had arrested both Linda Taylor and her son. Sherwin and Kush drove the forty miles to Joliet to talk to Harbaugh. He was twenty-four years old, and dark ink covered the white skin on his arms and hands. His tattoos—including a black panther, a symbol of the Blackstone Rangers—marked him as a South Side gang member.

Sandra Brownlee had said she didn't know where all of her mother's children had come from. Her brother had an explanation: Taylor bought and sold kids on the black market. Sherwin knew Linda Taylor was a liar, and he knew she was a thief. He knew she'd been arrested for endangering the life and health of a child, and he knew she'd been charged with kidnapping. Buying and selling children was different. It was monstrous. Lamar Jones had told Sherwin that Taylor shot and killed her first husband. Now Taylor's son was saying his mother was a child trafficker. Sherwin wasn't sure if either of those claims was true, but he did understand one thing very clearly: The people closest to Linda Taylor believed she was capable of absolutely anything.

* * *

So long as Taylor was behind bars, Sherwin had the time and space to develop all these new leads, and he knew she couldn't make any more trouble in the meantime. It was a comforting feeling. It lasted for two weeks.

On October 24, the day her daughter, Sandra, talked to state and federal agents, Taylor appeared in Cook County Circuit Court for a bond hearing. The legislative committee's investigators hadn't been warned about this court date. As soon as they heard, they rushed over to 2600 South California Avenue to meet with the prosecuting attorney. The Taylor case had been assigned to the special criminal prosecutions division of the Cook County state's attorney's office, the group that handled the county's most challenging and highest-profile fraud and corruption cases. The work could be politically risky: In 1975, the *Tribune* reported that the Chicago police had kept a secret file on Kenneth Gillis, the head of the bureau.

Gillis liked to hire unschooled attorneys, ones he could teach and mold. Bridget Hutchen, the lawyer assigned to the Linda Taylor case, had just graduated from law school. She'd never even appeared in traffic court. Hutchen had been given a folder that enumerated Taylor's Illinois arrests for bond skipping and theft but didn't include her bond forfeiture and welfare fraud warrants from Michigan. She also didn't present any of the new evidence that Sherwin and his team had uncovered. "Two members of the legislative committee were in court prepared to testify that she had collected up to $200,000 in payments, and at one time was collecting welfare under 14 separate aliases, driving late model luxury cars, and claiming ownership of several apartment buildings," the *Tribune* reported two days later. "But the committee members never were asked about any of this by the prosecutor."

While the State of Illinois relied on a novice, Taylor had the best civil rights lawyer in Chicago by her side. R. Eugene Pincham told Judge Wayne Olson his client had never been convicted of a crime and had resided at 8221 South Clyde Avenue for twenty-five years. Olson gave Pincham and Taylor the benefit of the doubt. The judge reduced Taylor's bond from $100,000 to $10,000, explaining that "no evidence of the seriousness of the crime was presented in court." Olson said he'd read about the allegations against Taylor in the newspaper, "but I cannot decide a motion on the basis of a *Chicago Tribune* story."

Sherwin was incensed. So was state senator Don Moore. After the hearing, the head of the special prosecutions bureau told them he'd had more important things to worry about. Earlier in the week, a gang of thieves had busted into a vault owned by Purolator Security. They'd stolen $4.3 million—the largest cash heist in American history. The *Tribune* reported that three hundred local, state, and federal agents were working the Purolator theft. Gillis said his most experienced attorneys had been tied up with the vault break-in, too. That excuse wasn't good enough for Moore. He told the *Tribune* he was demanding a "full-scale investigation" of the state's attorney's office.

By the mid-1970s, the paper's chief investigative reporter had essentially become an adjunct member of the Legislative Advisory Committee on Public Aid. Bliss was copied on the committee's memos, and its chair and executive director fed him tips. The information flowed both ways. Bliss had called the legislative committee as soon as he heard about the Taylor case—he'd been the one to kick off the group's investigation. He'd also passed along a rumor that Taylor might have contracts out on the investigators' lives.

It was a mutually beneficial relationship. Bliss provided Moore with evidence of the state government's lassitude and perfidy, and Moore gave Bliss tangible proof that the *Tribune*'s exclusives had spurred at least one politician into action. On October 26, Bliss and Charles Mount wrote a piece that began, "Accused 'Welfare Queen' Linda Taylor could not have bilked Illinois of an estimated $200,000 in public aid payments without help from welfare workers, a state legislator charged." Moore told the reporters he had "no doubt that there was connivance with public aid employes to cheat the state out of this much money." Now prosecutors had made it possible for these connivances to continue. "With this low bond, she could skip again," Moore said. "We found her only after a nationwide search."

Even George Bliss didn't have the power to get Taylor's bond increased. The newly crowned welfare queen scratched together $1,000—the requisite 10 percent of her bond—and won her release.

* * *

Don Moore's play for publicity didn't fail completely. His fuming about Taylor's October hearing, delivered to Chicagoans' doorsteps under Bliss's byline, essentially forced the hand of Chicago's top prosecutors. In a vacuum, the Cook County state's attorney's office might have deemed Taylor's alleged theft of public aid money too insignificant to pursue. But with Moore and Bliss publicizing Illinois's supposed welfare fraud crisis, the head of the special prosecutions division had no choice but to treat the Taylor case seriously. Kenneth Gillis encouraged the legislative committee to keep up its work, urging its investigators to go across state lines if necessary.

On a trip to Michigan, Sherwin discovered that one of Taylor's dead husbands was actually alive. Taylor had told Lamar Jones that a Greyhound bus had crushed her previous spouse. But Aaron Bennett was decidedly uncrushed, residing in Grand Rapids and employed by an industrial equipment firm. He told Sherwin that Taylor had been into voodoo, and that she'd gotten a bunch of checks in the mail that she hadn't let him look at. She'd left their home in 1973, after they'd been married for a few months. He'd been happy to see her go.

By early November, the state's attorneys believed they had enough to take the case to a Cook County grand jury. Sherwin testified about the public aid cards he'd found in Taylor's apartment, and welfare intake workers described what she'd written on her applications. Lamar Jones and Aaron Bennett shared a car to the courthouse—one of the investigators had introduced the two men, saying they had something in common. Jones told Taylor's other husband he'd just seen a movie in which someone testified against a mobster, then got gunned down on the courthouse steps. They were both afraid to take the stand and were relieved to make it out of the courtroom alive. The welfare fraud investigator Neal Caauwe was scared, too. Caauwe had heard that Taylor might have a contract out on him. He carried a gun everywhere he went, even to take out the garbage.

The grand jury indicted Taylor on November 13, charging her with stealing twenty-one public aid checks between January and September 1974. The indictment said those twenty-one checks—which she received simultaneously under two different names, Connie Walker and Linda Bennett—had been "knowingly obtained by deception." The payments added up to $7,608.02, a figure the *Tribune* said "may be only a fraction of the amount of Illinois welfare money Miss Taylor received illegally." Taylor was also indicted on seven counts of perjury, for telling a series of lies on the application she'd filled out as Sandra Brownlee, and on a single count of bigamy, for marrying Lamar Jones without divorcing Aaron Bennett.

The legislative committee's after-action report, written later in November, laid out how Don Moore's men had brought down Linda Taylor. The twenty-two-page narrative included the following preamble, written under the heading "What brought about the founding of the Commission."

> Everyone in the Nation is well aware of the abuses in the Public Aid Program. Exemplary is the State of Illinois with its swollen welfare roles and the ever ominous cloud of fraud hanging over it.
>
> An all too familiar example of this is the well dressed lady in the grocery line with her multiple food carts filled with choicest meats and top named products, most of which are regarded by the public as luxuries. Then having the frustration of waiting in line and seeing this person paying for those items with food stamps. Insult is added to injury when these items are loaded into a Cadillac.

This was a political document, written for an audience of politicians and designed to lionize the state senator who'd commissioned it. The investigators had been "confronted with a lack of interest and only nominal participation in obtaining the information needed," the report explained. "Only through the stern guiding hand of Senator Don A. Moore did the faucet of information start to trickle."

The Taylor case wasn't finished. The state could still indict her on additional charges, and the feds were just getting started. But Don

Moore wasn't pressing the state's attorneys to look into allegations of kidnapping or baby stealing, or anything aside from welfare fraud.

Jack Sherwin shouldn't have been surprised to discover that the Legislative Advisory Committee was a nakedly political operation. He'd been seduced by the opportunity to lead a real investigation, but he'd never been in control. Senator Moore had an ax to grind. Sherwin had been brought in to wield that ax. Now the detective's monthlong detail was over, and it was time for him to go back to the Chicago Police Department. Sherwin's stint with Moore's committee had left him convinced that Linda Taylor was dangerous. He also believed he'd just lost his best chance to stop her.

CHAPTER 5
Friend

Patricia Parks had needed help. The thirty-six-year-old schoolteacher had three children—nine, seven, and five years old—and she was in the middle of an acrimonious divorce. Parks had multiple sclerosis, plus recurrent bladder and kidney problems, and she alleged in her divorce proceeding that her soon-to-be ex-husband wasn't helping with her medical bills. Just making it through each day felt like a major accomplishment. She'd been desperate to find someone to look after her kids—she'd emigrated from Trinidad, and none of her relatives lived close by. Linda Taylor had been a godsend.

The women had met on the South Side at Our Lady of Peace Catholic Church, though Taylor wasn't strictly Catholic. She and Parks were introduced by a mutual acquaintance, who'd explained that "Linda Mallexo" was an African voodoo priestess. Taylor invited her new friend to a séance, and told her she'd had an alarming vision: Parks would be dead in six months. Taylor promised to change the sick woman's fate. In November 1974, the month after she paid $1,000 to get released from custody, she brought her belongings to Parks's house at 8046 South Phillips Avenue, a small brick bungalow just eight blocks from Taylor's apartment on South Clyde. On the day she moved in, Taylor told Parks's nine-year-old daughter, Bridgetta, "I'm here to take care of you."

Patricia Parks had hired nannies before. Bridgetta hadn't liked all those women, but none of them had made her feel uncomfortable. While Taylor always seemed to have a couple of her own children with her, she showed no interest in being around kids. She wasn't friendly or nurturing; she didn't read Bridgetta and her siblings bedtime stories. On the rare occasions when she spoke, she issued commands. Go stand over there. Go to bed. Go away. The kids could do whatever they pleased, so long as they stayed in the back of the house, away from their mother's room. Taylor had taken over her friend's care, dispensing medication and putting strict limits on visiting hours. It was important, she explained, that Patricia get her rest. "I'm taking care of your mom," she told Bridgetta. "She's going to get better."

Just in case her health didn't improve, Parks wrote her last will and testament. She bequeathed her entire estate to a trustee, who'd be responsible for doling out her assets to her three children. She also named an executor, whom she empowered to "sell, lease, mortgage, deed, and convey any real estate" in her possession. She appointed the same person to fill both roles: "My friend, Linda."

* * *

Near the end of her first month as Patricia Parks's housemate, Linda Taylor went to Cook County Criminal Court and pleaded not guilty to bigamy, perjury, and theft by deception. The executive director of the Legislative Advisory Committee on Public Aid did not presume her innocent. She "is without a doubt the biggest welfare cheat of all time," Joel Edelman told George Bliss. In an AP item that got picked up by the *New York Times*, he described Taylor's criminal behavior as "uncanny, like some science fiction story." The details of this yarn were both unbelievable and incredibly specific. "In about one year, it has been determined that she got $154,000 under 14 aliases," Edelman said. He added that Taylor had used eighty names and made claims on twenty-seven children in as many as eleven states, had been receiving Social Security checks for twenty-eight years, and had bought three federally insured houses.

These were astonishing figures, ones that didn't line up with the charges the State of Illinois had brought against Taylor in criminal court. Edelman, Don Moore, and the Legislative Advisory Committee's welfare fraud investigators believed Taylor had pilfered much more than the $7,600 she'd been charged with stealing. The prosecutor assigned to the case agreed that Taylor was getting off easy, but she didn't see any alternative. According to the UPI, Bridget Hutchen "said most of the investigators' stories about [Taylor] probably are true," but added that "most of them are not indictable. We simply don't have the facts on all of those things."

Though an indictment had already been secured against Taylor, the Legislative Advisory Committee didn't stop trying to prove that she was the biggest welfare cheat of all time. Edelman would later articulate his suspicions in a private letter to the committee's allies at the *Chicago Tribune*. "One of the reasons, in my opinion, that the state's attorney has settled for charges against Linda Taylor amounting only to $8,000 worth of welfare fraud, instead of the $100,000 or more we know of, is the failure of the [Illinois Department of Public Aid] to follow up on this case," he wrote. "Their failure is partly due to ineptness, in my humble opinion, and largely due to embarrassment and a desire to suppress the matter and avoid further publicity."

Jim Trainor, Edelman's successor as the head of the Illinois Department of Public Aid, scoffed at the claim that Taylor had stolen "$100,000 or more," and at the implication that his agency had something to hide. He repeatedly asked Edelman and Moore where they were getting their figures. If he got a reply, it hasn't been preserved in the Illinois State Archives, and it was never recorded in the press. In January 1975, three months after the legislative committee's investigation began, Trainor sent along his best guess at Taylor's total take: $40,000 in public aid, for cases under the names Linda Bennett and Connie Walker. That was a lot more than the $7,600 that Taylor had been formally accused of stealing, and far less than the $154,000 that Edelman had touted to reporters.

The Legislative Advisory Committee kept fighting to close the gap between the official record and what it believed to be the truth. That same month, Moore and Edelman's investigators wrote their bosses a memo indicating that they were "still receiving inquiries on this case from other states, and we ourselves are still following up on leads we are getting." They added, "very soon the Federal government will have their indictments ready." Several agencies had indeed started looking into whether Taylor had dipped into federal coffers. The U.S. Department of Agriculture chased after proof that she'd signed up for food stamps using multiple names, the Veterans Administration wanted to figure out if she'd been stealing survivors' benefits, and the FBI asked Taylor's mail carrier about a Social Security check he'd delivered to her apartment. On January 21, 1975, a special agent from the bureau declared in a memo that an assistant U.S. attorney "will prosecute TAYLOR when fraud confirmed."

To convict Taylor of theft by deception, Cook County state's attorneys would need to prove that the woman Jack Sherwin arrested had signed the names Connie Walker and Linda Bennett on checks issued by the Illinois treasurer. The FBI could help with that. The feds had their own interest in scrutinizing Taylor's writing, and the bureau's laboratory in Washington, DC, was stocked with equipment and experts that states didn't have. On November 12 and 13, 1974, the same days a grand jury heard prosecutors lay out the state charges against her, Taylor visited the FBI's Chicago field office on the orders of a federal judge. On a handwriting assessment form developed by the Chicago police, the alleged welfare cheat wrote "Lake Parker, Washington" in cursive and "THE MONEY IN DOLLARS WHICH DICK ZASS RECEIVED FROM VIRGINIA" in block-letter print.*
With her right hand, she drew the curves and swoops of individual letters—twenty-eight lowercase *g*'s followed by twenty-four *z*'s and twenty-three *w*'s. She also inscribed her various names on a stack of blank white pages, filling each sheet with *Linda Taylors*, *Connie Walkers*, and *Linda Bennetts*.

Her signatures didn't always stay on the same horizontal plane. They'd bend up and down, lengthening and contracting. Sometimes *Linda* was obviously *Linda*. It could also look like *Linde*, *Zinda*, *Zeinda*, or *Lindon*. The FBI's document examiner, David Grimes, eyeballed all these

---

* The document examiner who developed that handwriting form explained in a scholarly article,
   To obtain material for comparison in obscene letters, we combine the last part of Virginia McLong's last name with the first name of Dick Zass. Dropping the last two letters in "Virginia" and the capital letter "Z" in Zass exposes words that show up on obscene letters.

signatures and came to a quick conclusion: Linda Taylor had disguised her true handwriting. The thirty-four pages she'd filled out, under the supervision of a federal agent, were totally useless.

* * *

John Parks couldn't see what was going on inside his ex-wife's house. He'd lost the place to Patricia in their divorce, and he mostly stayed away from 8046 South Phillips Avenue—his lawyer had said that would be for the best. He'd get little snippets of information, sometimes from Patricia, and more often when he saw their children every other weekend. One day, the Parks's youngest child told him their mother's new friend had taken the kids shopping on Seventy-Ninth Street.

"Daddy, Daddy," the five-year-old said, "that woman wants us to steal."

Mr. Parks gave his son a message: "Tell your mommy . . . that she's not supposed to be with Linda Taylor."

John Parks considered himself a people person; Taylor curdled his good nature. He hated the sight of her face, he hated what she was telling his kids, and he hated that Patricia listened to her instead of him. Patricia was kind, open, and trusting. But John didn't see how anyone could be this credulous. He thought Taylor had brainwashed his ex-wife. Whatever she said to do, Patricia did.

Patricia Parks had been a teacher in Trinidad. She went back to school in Chicago, getting her master's in education at Erikson Institute in 1972. She got a job at a preschool on the South Side and socialized with women she knew from work or her graduate program. It was a small, tight circle, and Linda Taylor didn't fit in. Parks's friends were polished and posh. Taylor looked as though she'd been around the block a couple of times and was getting started on her third lap. She was flamboyant, not refined. Everyone noticed when she pulled up in her Cadillac.

Taylor would leave the house if she had some important business to attend to—an arraignment or a court-mandated writing exercise. The Parks's three children didn't know anything about what happened beyond the front door at 8046 South Phillips Avenue. After Taylor entered their lives, Bridgetta and her two younger brothers stopped going to the big department stores downtown. They stopped seeing their friends. They stopped going to church. Sometimes they'd play with the two young boys, Hosa and Duke, whom Taylor had in tow. Taylor's daughter, who was in her twenties, would also come around occasionally—Sandra was a lot nicer than her mother, Bridgetta thought. But the Parks children mostly had no adult supervision. They were left to fend for themselves.

Their mother had always served big, delicious meals: seafood, rice, freshly baked bread. Now Bridgetta went to bed hungry, and her little brothers scrounged for food. Hosa and Duke taught the Parks kids to eat whatever they found lying around. One time, Bridgetta caught the boys hiding in the pantry, shoving dog biscuits into their mouths.

By February 1975, around the time of her thirty-seventh birthday, Patricia Parks had stopped going to work. The previous year, she'd told the judge in her divorce case that her husband was "tired of my sick butt." Her multiple sclerosis was affecting her speech; a doctor had prescribed her tranquilizers. Now she filed another petition with the circuit court, requesting that John Parks be forced to pay child support. She needed the money, she wrote, because she was "physically ill and in a weakened condition."

Taylor had precipitated some of that weakness. Not long after predicting Parks's death during a séance, Taylor had immersed her new friend in freezing cold water. Parks's body temperature had crashed, and she'd pulled herself out of the bathtub and made her way to a nearby hospital as quickly as she could. The bath hadn't made her feel better, and neither had the potions that Bridgetta found scattered around the house. But Parks still believed in nontraditional cures. Her mother would send letters from back home in Trinidad, encouraging her to try various West Indian remedies. Parks had gone to see regular doctors, and they hadn't done much for her. She was willing to try anything.

But no matter what treatments Parks tried, she kept getting sicker. As Parks's health declined, Taylor put her in isolation, moving her into her daughter's bedroom. Bridgetta, who turned ten in 1975, got crammed into a smaller room with her brothers—she slept in one of the two beds and the boys shared the other. Taylor installed herself in the master bedroom.

In May, Parks checked into South Shore Hospital. Five months earlier, she'd made Taylor the trustee of her estate and the executor of her will. Now she updated that will, changing the beneficiary on her life insurance policies from her ex-husband to her three children. Her lawyer, Jeannette Nottingham, handwrote this addendum on a Saturday night, and Parks signed it from her hospital bed. The other witness was Linda C. Jones, address 8046 South Phillips Avenue.

Taylor was no longer a guest in the Parks family's brick bungalow. On April 30, 1975, Patricia had given Linda the title to her house. The Cook County quitclaim deed—an instrument typically used to transfer property between family members—identified the grantor as Patricia Marva Parks and the grantee as Linda C. Wakefield. The deed said the house changed hands "for the consideration of one dollars."

Parks was released from the hospital on June 11. She was found unconscious at her home four days later. Patricia Parks was judged dead on arrival at South Shore Hospital at 7:10 p.m.

The coroner's certificate of death described Parks as a divorced schoolteacher. Her middle name was misspelled—"Marvel" rather than "Marva"—as was her birthplace, "Trinadad." In the middle of the page, below the names of Patricia's father and mother, was the informant's signature. Name: "Linda C. Wakefield." Relationship: "friend."

* * *

Bridgetta never thought her mother was going to die. Everything had been fine until Linda Taylor showed up, and Bridgetta had figured everything would return to normal when Taylor left. They'd shop at the big department stores, they'd see their friends again, and they'd go back to church. But now Bridgetta's mom was gone and Linda Taylor was still there. The ten-year-old was in shock. She wanted to get to her father, but Cook County social workers weren't sure that was the right move. They needed to figure out who should have custody of the three children: Patricia Parks's ex-husband, John, or her friend Linda.

While that got sorted out, the county placed Bridgetta and her two brothers in emergency foster care. John Paul, the seven-year-old, didn't understand what was happening. He didn't know how his mother had died, or why they kept moving from house to house. In the car on the way to their second short-term foster home, Bridgetta told a county social worker that she had to go to her mother's funeral—that she needed to say goodbye. The bureaucrat said that she'd already missed it. The funeral had been that morning.

The second foster home was crawling with roaches, and the kids got peanut butter and jelly sandwiches for dinner and for breakfast the next morning. The three children shared a single bed, but Bridgetta never went to sleep. She stayed up for twenty-four hours straight, trying to will her life back to normal.

A month after Parks's death, a Cook County judge made his decision: The schoolteacher's ex-husband would get custody of the three children. The kids were delivered to their grandparents' house; after the divorce, John Parks had moved back in with his mother and father, who also lived in Chicago. Bridgetta's grandmother and grandfather were shocked when they saw her—she looked emaciated and malnourished. Her grandparents told the children that they could eat until they puked. They'd feed her and her brothers all day long, bringing home their favorite pies from Bakers Square. It took Bridgetta's brother John Paul some time to adjust to a more normal life. He would hide picked-over bones and seeds from discarded fruit underneath his bed, just in case this new bounty got taken away.

Although he was now the children's legal guardian, John Parks wasn't around to do any parenting in those first few days. He'd barricaded himself inside the house at 8046 South Phillips Avenue, and he wasn't letting Linda Taylor or anyone else inside.

* * *

John Parks blamed Taylor for his ex-wife's death, but he also blamed himself. He'd been angry, and he'd let his rage overwhelm him. Patricia had claimed in the divorce case that he'd come to the house two days before

Christmas and removed "lingerie and various personal items belonging to the housekeeper"—Linda Taylor. Patricia's attorney also said that John had made harassing phone calls in November, December, January, February, and March. In April, May, and June he'd gone silent. Now it was too late. He couldn't take back those calls or change what Linda Taylor had done. But he could take back his house.

Parks knew that Taylor would be away from home on Thursday, June 19, 1975, the day of his ex-wife's wake. He skipped the viewing, seizing the opportunity to break into his old house via a side window. When Taylor came back, he refused to let her in. He turned her away on Friday, too. By Saturday, the confrontation had made the local news.

Parks, the *Tribune* wrote, had changed the locks at 8046 South Phillips and was guarding the property with a 12-gauge shotgun and two Doberman pinschers. "They're looting, vandalizing, and destroying her personal possessions while police stand by and watch," Jeannette Nottingham told the newspaper. Nottingham had been Patricia Parks's attorney; she'd handwritten the addendum to Parks's will. Now she was representing Parks's friend Linda Taylor, who she believed was the rightful owner of the Parks family home. Nottingham said she and Taylor would return on Sunday at 10:30 a.m. "We will use what force is necessary to take and secure the property," she explained to the *Tribune*.

The women did return, and this time they brought backup. Taylor, who'd accessorized a sporty striped twinset with a bucket hat that shielded her face from the summer sun, directed a team of armed security guards to bust inside the locked front entrance. Neighbors came out on the street to gawk. Reporters, who'd headed out to South Phillips Avenue after hearing the Taylor camp's promise to "secure the property," staked out the best spots to watch the show. A *Tribune* photographer got an image of one of Taylor's guards kicking the door. It ran on page one, above the caption "Welfare Queen can't get in." The *Chicago Defender* published a story with the headline "House under siege by many-named lady." The Parks children saw the face-off on the TV news. Their father emerged from the family home only briefly, poking his head out to declare that he wasn't going anywhere.

After a half hour, a Chicago police sergeant told everyone to disperse. "Armed guards don't belong here," he said. "Everybody move out or everybody's going to jail." When Taylor heard talk of arrests, the *Tribune* wrote, "she quickly called off her guards, climbed into her car and sped away."

Taylor's belongings were trapped inside that small brick house. But she had much bigger problems than a locked front door. On June 26, four days after the standoff on South Phillips Avenue, the *Tribune* reported that the Cook County state's attorney's office had launched an investigation into the death of Patricia Parks.

* * *

Like the Legislative Advisory Committee on Public Aid, the state's attorneys had their own team of investigators. Those sleuths, the *Tribune* wrote, got suspicious when they "learned that Mrs. Parks reportedly had willed her home to Miss Taylor and had made her...the guardian of her three children." The facts they uncovered about the last days of Patricia Parks's life weren't any more comforting. The funeral director had told someone from the coroner's office that Parks had suffered from cervical cancer. But the doctor who'd treated her most recently was adamant that she'd never had that diagnosis; he'd refused to sign her death certificate. The information about cervical cancer, the funeral director explained, had come from Linda Taylor.

The state's attorneys had tried to take possession of Parks's corpse prior to her funeral, but their investigators didn't get there fast enough. They'd had to settle for moving her body to the morgue after the service was over, before it could be interred. On June 29, the *Tribune* reported that coroners subsequently "found an excessive amount of medical drugs, including barbiturates, in a sample of the dead woman's blood." That didn't prove Parks had been murdered. It did raise plenty of questions about Parks's caretaker, and how she'd insinuated herself into the Trinidadian woman's life.

In a story in the *Defender*, a spokesman for the state's attorney's office described Taylor as Parks's "housekeeper, nurse, and companion."

Though out on bond after an indictment for welfare fraud, Taylor had somehow been "approved by the Illinois Department of Public Aid as a paid housekeeper for Mrs. Parks," the *Tribune* wrote. The state hadn't sent her any checks this time, though, "after she was questioned by investigators from the Legislative Advisory Committee on Public Aid."

Taylor's attorneys said she hadn't been Parks's employee, insisting that the women had been friends for years. A preacher named Frances Fearn countered that she'd introduced them only very recently, in the fall of 1974. Taylor herself said she and Patricia were related by blood. On February 1, 1975, she'd been detained by Chicago police for driving her new Cadillac without a license. According to the *Defender*, Taylor had told the cops that the woman riding with her—Patricia Parks—was her sister.

Though Taylor didn't deign to speak with the welfare queen–publicizing *Tribune*, she was willing to talk to Chicago's black newspaper. The *Defender* wasn't just an institution in black Chicago—it had helped create black Chicago. In the 1910s, the paper had been a major catalyst for the Great Migration, urging men and women who'd been deprived of economic opportunity and terrorized by lynchings to come north for better wages and better treatment. The *Defender*, which published the likes of W. E. B. Du Bois, Gwendolyn Brooks, Langston Hughes, and Martin Luther King Jr., served an audience whose perspectives weren't represented in the city's white-owned media outlets. That need was particularly acute during the civil rights movement, when the *Tribune*, for instance, suggested quelling anti-police unrest on the city's predominantly black West Side in 1966 by ordering rioters "to get out of the city within 30 days and never to come back." The *Defender*'s reply: "The *Tribune*'s prescription for getting rid of a disease seems to be the banishment of the patient."

By the 1970s, the *Defender*'s cultural influence had started to wane, in part because its competitors belatedly recognized the importance of hiring black staffers. The newspaper's daily circulation of twenty-five thousand was a tiny fraction of the *Tribune*'s 751,000. Even so, sitting for an interview with the *Defender* was a great way to make common cause with black Chicagoans, plenty of whom would recognize Taylor's complaint that the police had subjected her to a bogus traffic stop. In the 1974 book *Working*, a black patrolman named Renault Robinson told Chicago author and broadcaster Studs Terkel that cops in the city used trumped-up traffic violations to hassle law-abiding black citizens. "Black folks don't have a voice to complain," Robinson said. "Consequently, they continue to be victims of shadowy, improper, overburdened police service."

In February 1975, Taylor told the *Defender* that she'd turned to the police for help—that she and Parks "had gone to collect a long overdue debt from her ex-mother-in-law and were confronted by the woman's daughter who waved a gun at them." But instead of helping her and "her sister, Patricia," fend off this armed assailant, the cops had given Taylor a series of traffic citations, then held Taylor and Parks for "three hours while they were asked such questions as 'where did you get that fancy ring,' and 'aren't you the welfare cheat?'" The police had hassled a sick woman, Taylor told the newspaper: "Mrs. Parks, who was not feeling well, had planned to go to a doctor after their errands were completed."

The *Tribune* didn't air Taylor's side of this particular story. Five months later, Chicago's most popular newspaper reported that Patricia Parks "evidently was the subject of voodoo sessions before she died."

> When investigators entered the dead woman's bedroom they found five lamps directed toward a hospital bed, a pair of witch doctors' masks hung on walls, candles, a voodoo manual, and a religious statue on a nearby table.
>
> Sources close to the investigation said it appeared that witchcraft spells had been used in an attempt to cure Mrs. Parks of internal hemorrhaging.

Taylor responded to this accusation in another interview with her preferred publication. "I don't believe in that mess!" she told the *Defender*, denying any knowledge of the dark spiritual arts. She claimed that her supposed "voodoo artifacts" were pieces of art she'd bought in Nigeria.

Taylor demurred when asked if she was really related to Parks, saying, "Yes and no—I rather not discuss that." She did take the opportunity to speak out against John Parks. "I wish I did know voodoo," she said. "If

I knew it I would practice it on him because he's in my home and his white lady is eating my food." Taylor, who didn't specify which white lady she was referring to, said she'd been Patricia Parks's savior. She'd "tried to prevent Mrs. Parks from taking non-prescribed medication," she explained. She blamed her friend's death on Frances Fearn—the preacher who said she'd introduced Linda and Patricia. In Taylor's telling, Fearn was "a voodoo worshiper who was defrocked." Fearn had been the one "giving Patsy something to take."

* * *

By June 1975, the Cook County state's attorney's office had assigned a new prosecutor to the Linda Taylor welfare fraud case. In the previous four years, Jim Piper had handled the prosecutions of police officers for murder, battery, and auto theft; the conviction of a firearms dealer; and the breakup of a prostitution ring. Piper was young, smart, and ambitious, but his aggression could sometimes get the best of him. Once, when a bond court judge held him in contempt for sustaining a line of questioning the judge didn't approve of, Piper's boss had to go in and apologize on his behalf. The head of special prosecutions liked to say that the brash assistant state's attorney operated under "Jim Piper rules."

Although Piper was one of the more seasoned attorneys in the special prosecutions division, he'd never shared a courtroom with such an infamous defendant. Piper read the papers—he recognized that he could boost his career by convicting the Chicago welfare queen. Based on what he already knew about Taylor, he believed she was a world-class con artist. Given what he was hearing about Patricia Parks's death, he was starting to think she might be a killer, too. He wanted the FBI to help him prove it.

On July 9, Piper shipped the bureau a packet of evidence: samples of the drugs found inside the house at 8046 South Phillips. He also sent along a memo laying out what he'd learned up to that point, and what he still needed to figure out.

Patricia Parks, negro female, died 6/15/1975 at her home, 8046 South Phillips, Chicago, following hospital treatment which ended 6/11/1975. Linda Taylor was introduced to Parks in 11/74 as a "Voodoo Doctor." Parks, reportedly a native of Trinidad, allowed Taylor to move in her home and treat her for reported bleeding and/or hemorrhaging of Parks' vagina. Welfare caseworker visiting Taylor at Parks' home was witness to Taylor, in possession of approximately 25 drug containers, stating that she had to give Mrs. Parks her medicine. Following Parks' death from an apparently minor medical problem and disclosure of her will which designated Taylor as beneficiary of all assets, an autopsy was performed after Parks was embalmed and disclosed death due to an overdose of Phenobarbital. The death of Parks and Taylor's suspected involvement are the subjects of a special investigation presently being conducted by the Office of the State's Attorney.

The Physics and Chemistry Section of the FBI Laboratory is requested to perform quantitative and qualitative analyses of evidence items...which were obtained from the Parks home after her death. These items contain various drugs which either do not necessarily match the prescribed contents or appear to have been used for mixing drugs as Taylor's "Voodoo Training" may have dictated. These items have not been previously examined by another agency. In view of their special investigation, the state's attorney has requested that this examination be expedited.

Piper's request wasn't an absurd one. The FBI and the Cook County state's attorneys had been collaborating on the Taylor investigation for nine months. Bureau document examiner David Grimes had helped the State of Illinois by analyzing Taylor's signatures. When she'd provided an obviously disguised writing sample, Grimes had advised agents from the FBI's Chicago field office on how to compel Taylor to jot down a more serviceable sheaf of cursive signatures and printed letters.

The Legislative Advisory Committee on Public Aid had also fed information to the FBI. Thanks to a lead from the legislative committee, the bureau had started looking into payments Taylor received as the widow of a navy enlisted man named Paul S. Harbaugh. Between 1968 and 1975, she'd collected around $7,000 in survivors' benefits from the Social Security Administration on behalf of her daughter, Sandra. Taylor had gotten that money even after Sandra turned eighteen in 1969 because she'd been designated a "helpless child." A form that came via the Department of Veterans Affairs indicated, based on information given by Taylor, that Sandra Brownlee "has a mental age of 10 and IQ of 66 percent, is hard of hearing, has heart disease with dyspnea, and is unable to handle funds." Sandra would tell the authorities on multiple occasions that her hearing had been damaged in the 1958 fire at Our Lady of the Angels School. That conflagration had killed ninety-two elementary schoolers and three nuns. George Bliss had been assigned to go to the morgue that day, to watch as mothers and fathers claimed the bodies of their dead children.

Linda Taylor's daughter hadn't been hurt in the fire at Our Lady of the Angels. The FBI learned very quickly that she hadn't even gone to school there. She didn't have a mental age of ten—federal agents and the legislative committee's investigators figured that out when she sat down with them for interviews. She'd also gotten married in 1972 and was thus ineligible for benefits as anyone's dependent. Taylor had exploited her own daughter, and it had worked for years, netting her thousands of dollars in government checks.

The feds marshaled significant resources to chase down Taylor's financial crimes, interviewing her daughter, gathering medical records and birth certificates, consulting with the Veterans Administration, and contacting officials from Our Lady of the Angels. But when Piper sent a request for help with a potential murder case, the bureau wasn't willing to pitch in. The state's attorney received a curt reply to his memo on Parks: "The FBI does drug analyses only in cases under direct investigation by the FBI." The samples Piper had sent along for analysis were never examined. They were returned to Chicago as "unopened evidence."

After getting rejected by the FBI, Piper tried another approach, asking South Shore Hospital for samples of Parks's premortem blood. The hospital, though, told him the woman's blood draws had been misplaced. The prosecutor believed that Linda Taylor had killed her friend. But without those samples, he doubted he had enough evidence to go forward.

On the other hand, Piper had copious documentation that the *Tribune*'s welfare queen had stolen public aid checks. The Taylor welfare fraud case was a huge opportunity for him—his first really big prosecution—and he couldn't afford to screw it up. Piper was wary of being labeled a publicity hound; he didn't want to add a couple more rings to a court case that already looked like a three-ring circus. This time, he saw the virtue in tamping down his aggression. He decided to forget about the homicide and focus on the case he knew he could win.

* * *

When a thirty-seven-year-old black woman died under suspicious circumstances in Chicago in 1975, no journalist bemoaned the failure to prosecute her possible killer. No crusading state senator pushed the state's attorneys to keep their investigation alive. The Chicago Police Department could've done its own intensive investigation of Patricia Parks's death rather than defer to the state's attorneys. It didn't. Police higher-ups could've asked Jack Sherwin to take a few days off from the burglary beat to take a look. They didn't. This was something for the homicide division, if they wanted it. They didn't. John Parks waited for someone to ask him what he knew about his ex-wife's death. No one ever did.

The Cook County coroner and his deputy signed Parks's death certificate on August 18, 1975. The cause of death was listed as combined phenobarbital, methapyrilene, and salicylate intoxication. They declined to rule the death an accident, suicide, or homicide, instead writing the word *undetermined*.

CHAPTER 6
A Woman in Chicago

On January 15, 1975, President Gerald Ford stood before a joint session of Congress and announced that "the state of the union is not good." Ford began his prime-time address by detailing everything he'd failed to fix in the five months since Richard Nixon's resignation. "Millions of Americans are out of work," he said. "Recession and inflation are eroding the money of millions more. Prices are too high, and sales are too slow."

Ronald Reagan claimed to know why prices were high and sales were slow. In a radio commentary taped a week before Ford's State of the Union address, Reagan explained that American businesses were being choked to death by unnecessary regulations. A pharmaceutical manufacturer had to generate seventy-two thousand pages of data to license a new drug. A baker had to choose between filling out paperwork and making his daily bread. A small businessman had been forced to build separate men's and women's bathrooms for his two employees—himself and his wife.

Reagan, who'd just finished his eight-year tenure as the governor of California, declared that he'd now be spending his time "preaching the gospel of free enterprise." In radio spots, a syndicated newspaper column, and corporate speeches, the actor-turned-politician lamented the government-induced decline of a once-mighty nation. Reagan, however, paired his recitation of the country's ills with an optimistic vision of America's future, one in which meddlesome bureaucrats and high taxes no longer troubled business owners and the working class. On November

19, 1975, he called Ford to say he wanted to make this vision a reality: He was going to challenge the sitting president for the 1976 Republican nomination.

Despite the *Bedtime for Bonzo* star's name recognition from his Hollywood days and his reputation as a capable governor, Reagan's White House bid was still seen by many as a fool's errand. "The astonishing thing is that this amusing but frivolous Reagan fantasy is taken so seriously by the news media and particularly by the President," wrote veteran columnist James Reston in the *New York Times*. Reagan needed to prove the doubters wrong, and he needed to do it quickly. His handlers planned an ambitious itinerary leading up to the New Hampshire primary, loading Reagan's schedule with visits to dozens of small towns. It was extraordinarily cold in the Granite State in January 1976, even for New England in winter—at one campaign stop in the White Mountains, the temperature dipped to seventeen below zero. Reagan, who would turn sixty-five on February 6, often braved the wintry weather without a hat or topcoat, conducting a series of outdoor question and answer sessions in which he spoke directly to voters.

Although these "citizens' press conferences" were carefully stage-managed, Reagan couldn't dodge the press entirely. Reporters demanded answers about a speech he'd made in Chicago the previous September, one in which he'd proposed cutting $90 billion from the federal budget by transferring control of education, housing, welfare, food stamps, Medicare, and Medicaid to the states. While nobody had paid much attention to the idea when it had first been floated, the Ford campaign brought this forgotten scheme to the press's attention, declaring that Reagan wanted to "throw old people in the snow."

The insurgent candidate was now on the defensive. "I guess I made a mistake in the speech that I made in Chicago," Reagan said at a campaign event, declining to address what that mistake had been. Later, he insisted he could pay for the $90 billion transfer by repurposing federal taxes on alcohol and cigarettes. He also said that if a specific state didn't fill in the gaps after he eliminated the federal safety net, poor people could "move elsewhere."

Reagan had long been criticized for pushing simplistic proposals. No matter what after-the-fact explanations the ex-governor came up with, this seemed like another plan he hadn't thought through. But Reagan's connection with voters didn't depend on his mastery of policy details. On January 15, he pivoted to a topic that played to his strengths. "No one knows how many people are on welfare," he told a crowd in the mill town of Hinsdale. "They only know how many checks they send out." He said there was a woman in Chicago who exemplified the welfare mess. That woman, Reagan said, used eighty names, thirty addresses, and twelve Social Security cards to collect all kinds of public benefits. The former California governor made it clear that the federal government was preventing the country from reaching its true potential. But this unnamed woman in Chicago—she was the enemy, too.

* * *

Linda Taylor's new address had a heated pool, a cocktail lounge, and a spectacular view of the Lake Michigan shoreline. The 50th on the Lake Motel billed itself as the largest in Chicago, with 301 luxurious rooms that provided guests with "the ultimate in comfort and pleasure." The motel, which sprang up at the intersection of East Fiftieth Street and South Lake Shore Drive in 1958, quickly became a way station for black celebrities. Muhammad Ali moved to the motel in 1965, after a fire coincidentally destroyed his South Side apartment on the same night as Malcolm X's murder. He also bunked there in April 1967, in the days before he formally refused to join the U.S. military, and reporters rushed to East Fiftieth and Lake Shore Drive to interview the boxer on June 28, 1971, the day the Supreme Court overturned his draft-dodging conviction.

Taylor was facing a daunting set of legal issues when she arrived at 50th on the Lake in 1975. In September of that year, a Cook County grand jury issued an updated, fifty-four-count indictment in her welfare fraud case—a substantial increase from the twenty-nine counts she'd been hit with the previous November. Prosecutors brought forward more public aid checks Taylor had cashed as Connie Walker and Linda

Bennett, bumping her alleged take to $8,865.67. In addition to "theft by deception," Taylor now stood accused of having "knowingly exerted unauthorized control" over each of the checks she'd pocketed—that is, having stolen money from its rightful owner, the State of Illinois. The new indictment did include one piece of good news for Taylor: She was no longer being charged with bigamy.

As she continued to await trial, the most pressing item on Taylor's legal calendar was the matter of the estate of Patricia M. Parks. By the late summer, the Cook County state's attorneys had decided Taylor wouldn't be charged with murdering Parks. Now a probate court judge would determine whether she'd get the dead woman's money and house.

In a hearing on September 3, Taylor testified that Parks had been of sound mind and memory when the Trinidadian woman had amended her will less than a month before her death. Taylor told the court that she'd been bereft since Patricia's ex-husband had locked her out of the house on South Phillips Avenue—that her food and clothing were trapped inside the Parks family's brick bungalow. Under cross-examination by John Parks's attorney, Taylor misstated her husband Lamar Jones's name—she called him Lamont—as well as the year of their marriage, saying it had been in 1975 rather than 1974. Though her welfare fraud prosecution was ongoing, she denied being known as Linda Taylor in any other legal cases. She stated, falsely, that "Taylor is the name the detectives gave me after Mr. Parks had broken into my home." And while she'd already told the *Chicago Defender* that Patricia was her sister, Taylor now demurred when asked if they were related by blood: "Your honor, I prefer to not say at this time whether we are or we aren't."

The judge, Robert A. Sweeney, insisted that Taylor answer the question. "Well, I'm going to say this," she responded. "We were allegedly to have the same father." Taylor said that man was named Lawrence Wakefield, and that he was a resident of Wakefield, England. She added that Patricia Parks wasn't her sister's real name—that "Patsy" had been written on her Trinidadian birth certificate.

Sweeney didn't believe anything Taylor said. On October 24, 1975, he appointed John Parks administrator of his ex-wife's estate. Taylor wouldn't get the contents of Patricia Parks's safety-deposit box at Hyde Park Bank and Trust Co., and she wouldn't get the house on South Phillips Avenue. That outcome didn't get written up in the *Chicago Tribune* or in any other paper. Nor had anybody followed up on the status of the investigation into Patricia Parks's death. The allegation that Linda Taylor had killed Parks just disappeared.

That didn't mean reporters had lost interest in Taylor entirely. On October 24, the same day she lost her claim on the Parks's home, the *Tribune*, the AP, and the UPI all ran items on a new Taylor-related intrigue. According to George Bliss, the accused welfare cheat had told the police that "two men came in carrying guns, took her cash and rings, and forced her to remove all her clothing in a bathroom." In an interview with the *Defender* published the next day, Taylor said that one of the robbers had held a gun to her young son Hosa's head and threatened to "blow his brains out"; that the other supposed perpetrator, who went by Chucky, had snatched her friend's two-month-old and flung the baby against the wall; and that the two men had stolen $500 in cash and seven diamond rings worth $17,000. "When I couldn't get [the rings] off fast enough, 'Chucky' grabbed my hand and yanked them off, leaving bruises and scratches on my fingers," she said to the *Defender*, which identified her in a photo caption as "Mrs. Linda (Welfare Queen) Taylor." That photo, which ran on the front page of the newspaper, showed a concerned-looking Taylor with her left arm wrapped around Hosa. Taylor comforted the boy while seated on the hood of a Cadillac, her feet dangling in front of the grille.

While Bliss did note that Taylor had a history of filing fake burglary reports, the *Tribune*, the *Defender*, and the wire services never questioned the veracity of this latest purported theft. This was something of a pattern for the Chicago papers, which published a bunch of lurid, one-off stories about Taylor in 1975 and left all of them unresolved. In February, the *Tribune*'s William Griffin had reported that Taylor had tried and failed to lay claim to the estate of South Side gambling kingpin Lawrence Wakefield—the man she'd told Judge Sweeney was her and Patricia Parks's father. A month after that, Griffin and Bliss had written a pair of articles indicating that Taylor had been a suspect in the 1964 kidnapping of an infant from a Chicago hospital and suggesting she may have purchased children as part of a welfare fraud scheme. In May 1975, the *Chicago Daily News* had noted that Taylor was accusing one of her ex-husbands—Willie Walker, the taxi driver—of faking his own death to get out of paying alimony and child support.

Just as the question of whether Taylor murdered Patricia Parks had come and gone, so, too, did all these other allegations. The only other Taylor-connected development that got national play in the latter part of 1975 was her daughter Sandra Brownlee's indictment. The AP reported that Brownlee had been charged with receiving public aid while her husband "was earning $10,000 a year as an employee of Western Electric Co."

For Bliss, Taylor's theft of welfare checks had served as the defining example of the Public Aid Department's apathy. This had been a crime aided and abetted by an agency that didn't know where its money was going and didn't care to find out. Bliss's subsequent reporting had done nothing to change his view of the department. In January 1975, he'd written that Governor Dan Walker "was accused of covering up a widespread public aid scandal, while state officials were attacked for refusing to cooperate with an investigation of welfare cheaters, who are costing the state $400 million a year." In December, Bliss revealed that the Department of Public Aid had ignored rampant Medicaid abuse by Chicago pharmacists. But none of those white-collar professionals got a catchy nickname or became a political symbol. The welfare queen—not the bill-padding, prescription-forging pharmacist—was the villain the press and the public wanted.

In May 1976, Bliss would win yet another Pulitzer Prize, this one for an investigation he'd done with his colleague Chuck Neubauer on malfeasance in the Federal Housing Administration's mortgage insurance program. Linda Taylor wasn't Pulitzer material. By 1976, Bliss's pieces on the larger public aid scandal no longer mentioned Taylor's name, and his pieces on Taylor didn't address the larger public aid scandal. She'd become a fascinating triviality, less a symbol of systematic fraud than a case study of the outer limits of human behavior.

Though Bliss typically didn't talk about his works in progress, Linda Taylor turned him into a newsroom gossip. "Oh my God, I've got another one," he'd tell his fellow reporter Bill Mullen, boasting about his latest tip and laughing at the brazenness of the public aid cheat with all the names. But nothing Bliss published connected Taylor to a bigger story, and he never answered the basic questions he'd raised in his own reporting: Had anyone on the inside helped Taylor fleece the government? How much money had she really stolen?

Bliss didn't write in shades of gray. He identified villains, and he shamed them. In his initial stories, Taylor stood for an institution that had lost its way. By 1975, she stood alone. In the end, the only person implicated in the Linda Taylor scandal was Taylor herself.

* * *

In New Hampshire, Illinois, North Carolina, and Florida, Ronald Reagan won over conservative voters with an endless stream of stories about the hilarious, alarming ineptitude of the United States government. At a $5-a-plate luncheon in Asheville, North Carolina, on January 27, 1976, he said a judge had ordered a public aid cheat to repay $1,511 "at the rate of fifteen dollars a month, and then ordered the welfare department to increase her grants fifteen dollars a month so she could pay off the debt." He talked about a family that had its welfare checks forwarded to the Soviet Union, and he said there was a housing project in New York City, Taino Towers, where "you can get an apartment with eleven-foot ceilings, with a twenty-foot balcony, a swimming pool and gymnasium, laundry room and playroom" for just $113.20 per month including utilities.

Reagan also told a convoluted but well-received story about a welfare recipient who stole a country ham, sold that ham to a store, and bought it back with food stamps. He said the "executive editor of a metropolitan newspaper in the East" had been urged by a welfare worker to "purchase food stamps even though he informed them he owned a forty thousand dollar home, a three-acre lot, two late-model motor cars, and has had a salary of four hundred dollars a week." He claimed there was a "student in California who was getting food stamps by virtue of being in school." The kicker: "She's studying to be a witch." And though he didn't mention her by name, the Republican presidential candidate also brought up Linda Taylor, again and again. "In Chicago, they found a woman who holds the record," he said at the luncheon in Asheville, cribbing from the 1974 UPI article that his aide Peter Hannaford had clipped and filed away. "She used eighty names, thirty addresses, fifteen telephone numbers to collect food stamps, Social Security, veterans' benefits for four non-existent deceased veteran husbands, as well as welfare."

The former radio announcer had a way of making the hoariest yarn sound like a fresh outrage. Reagan's casual, confiding delivery assured his supporters they were the upstanding "us" fighting to save the country from the corrupt, dishonest "them" of Washington bureaucrats and the undeserving poor. "If someone set out to design a welfare program that wouldn't work, they couldn't do better than food stamps," he said in Asheville. "You've probably had the same idea when you were standing in the checkout line at the market with your package of hamburger, watching the strapping young fellow in line ahead of you buying T-bone steaks with food stamps."

The people in Asheville applauded after Reagan's riff on T-bone steaks, and they laughed when he talked about the food stamp–nabbing witch. But the mood changed when he talked about the woman in Chicago. When he said "her tax-free cash income alone has been running a hundred and fifty thousand dollars a year," the crowd at the luncheon gasped. This wasn't funny.

Reagan had built his political career on stories of profligate government spending. In his star-making 1964 speech, "A Time for Choosing," a televised endorsement of Republican presidential candidate Barry Goldwater, Reagan told the story of a woman who "wanted a divorce to get an eighty-dollar raise"—her husband's salary didn't match what she could get from Aid to Families with Dependent Children. When he first ran for governor in 1966, a pair of advisers—behavioral psychologists Kenneth Holden and Stanley Plog—pushed Reagan to make welfare a major focus of his campaign. Reagan, who'd thought it "might be a dangerous subject," quickly learned that he'd been mistaken. "I am becoming more aware that the man on the street has decided he's supporting too many families not his own, and he wants something done," he wrote in a letter eight months before Election Day. Reagan would defeat Democratic incumbent Pat Brown by nearly one million votes.

While *welfare* was typically understood to be a synonym for cash assistance programs such as AFDC, the term's vagueness made it a versatile political tool. For middle- and upper-class voters, particularly white ones, *welfare* didn't encompass a program like Social Security. Rather, it came to stand for any government benefit they themselves didn't receive.

Although Reagan tended to center his anti-welfare pitch on fiscal sanity, Goldwater and many others framed their objections to public aid in moral terms. "I don't like to see my taxes paid for children born out of wedlock," Goldwater said in 1961. "I'm tired of professional chiselers walking up and down the streets who don't work and have no intention of working." Eleven years later, Russell Long, a Louisiana Democrat who spearheaded a Senate Finance Committee investigation on welfare fraud, said "the welfare system, as we know it today, is being manipulated and abused by malingerers, cheats, and outright frauds."

The loosening of welfare's strictures in the 1960s and 1970s had made it much easier for needy people to get emergency relief. It had also made it simpler for determined thieves to cheat the system. In 1971, the *Washington Post* reported that a group of women in Prince George's County, Maryland, had stolen roughly $40,000 in welfare and food stamps by giving phony addresses and disguising themselves with wigs. When a public aid worker confronted one of the fakers, the woman said she'd been schooled in the art of welfare subterfuge "by a man named Red Willie who drove a brown Cadillac." Red Willie and his brown Cadillac were never found.

Whether or not Red Willie roamed the earth, public aid fraud did exist. In 1978, the federal Department of Health, Education, and Welfare reported that it lost between $5.5 and $6.5 billion of its $150 billion annual budget to fraud, abuse, and waste. However, just 15 percent of that $5.5 to $6.5 billion—less than 1 percent of HEW's yearly spending—

got siphoned away due to "unlawful, willful misrepresentation (fraud) or excessive services and program violations (abuse)." Further, less than $500 million of the agency's losses was attributable to the partially federally funded AFDC program. The vast majority of those debits, around $4 billion, came via Medicaid and other health care initiatives.

While AFDC wasn't, at least relative to Medicaid, a colossal money pit, it also wasn't managed all that efficiently. A 1973 HEW survey revealed that 22.8 percent of families on AFDC were overpaid, 8.1 percent were underpaid, and 10.2 percent were entirely ineligible for payment. Some of those ineligible cases could've been the handiwork of wig-wearing women with fake addresses. In an earlier report, though, HEW had said that most instances of ineligibility stemmed from "honest mistakes" by people on welfare and local administrators, not out-and-out fraud. The next largest group of ineligible recipients, everyone in the field agreed, was those who'd failed to report outside income—the wages from a job or a family member's contributions to the household purse. Families on AFDC needed whatever cash they could scrape together to afford food, clothing, and shelter. In 1974, when the federal poverty line for a family of four was $5,038, the basic grant for a four-person AFDC family in Cook County was $288 per month—$3,456 annually. After the state legislature finally pushed through a 10 percent cost-of-living increase, that figure rose to just more than $3,800.

Most Americans didn't feel sorry for the men, women, and children who received a monthly, taxpayer-funded allowance. A June 1976 survey by the pollster Louis Harris found that 89 percent of respondents believed "the criteria for getting on welfare are not tough enough," while 85 percent thought "too many people on welfare cheat by getting money they are not entitled to." In a poll conducted a month earlier, 66 percent of Americans had fully agreed with the notion that "the American way of life is superior to that of any other country." In the year of the bicentennial, hating welfare cheaters was more American than loving the United States itself.

Americans' views on the poorest of the poor had shifted dramatically in just a few decades. Michael Harrington's 1962 book *The Other America* had awakened politicians and the general public to the deprivations of the white rural poor and had played a key role in inspiring Lyndon Johnson's 1964 War on Poverty. Over the subsequent ten years, the amount of Americans receiving some form of public aid grew from roughly 2 percent to 6 percent. During that same period, the racial composition of the Aid to Families with Dependent Children caseload had stayed roughly the same, with the proportion of black recipients cresting in the early 1970s at just more than 40 percent. But in the aftermath of riots in the Watts neighborhood of Los Angeles, on the West Side of Chicago, and in other inner cities, the image of American poverty had changed. In 1964, just 27 percent of the photographs in newsmagazine stories about poor Americans showed black people. In 1972 and 1973, that number jumped to 70 percent.

Even before the 1970s, black Americans had taken much of the blame for the country's "welfare mess." In 1961, the city manager of Newburgh, New York, lamented that an influx of nonwhite residents had hastened the departure of "more constructive or productive citizens." Newburgh instituted a welfare reform plan that, among other things, required public aid recipients to report to the local police station on a weekly basis. Though the Newburgh plan was deemed illegal by the New York courts, it won broad popular and political acclaim. When Barry Goldwater said he didn't like to see his taxes go to children born out of wedlock, he was speaking out in favor of the Newburgh plan.

In his influential 1965 report *The Negro Family: The Case for National Action*, assistant secretary of labor Daniel Patrick Moynihan framed public aid as an explicitly racial issue. Aid to Dependent Children had been "established in 1935 principally to care for widows and orphans," Moynihan wrote, but "the steady expansion of this welfare program, as of public assistance programs in general, can be taken as a measure of the steady disintegration of the Negro family structure over the past generation in the United States."

Although he never used the phrase "welfare queen" on the campaign trail and he never mentioned Linda Taylor's race, Reagan would've had to have been incredibly naive not to anticipate how the "woman in

Chicago" would be perceived. He prefaced the Taylor story by saying that "no one in Washington…knows how many people in America are drawing welfare. They only know how many checks they're sending out." But the crowd in Asheville wasn't gasping at the government's inability to balance a checkbook. The audience knew what this welfare-swiping villain looked like. She was a lazy, black con artist, unashamed about cadging the money that honest folks worked so hard to earn.

Reagan had opposed the 1964 Civil Rights Act and the 1965 Voting Rights Act, saying the latter was "humiliating to the South." He also failed to condemn Alabama governor George Wallace, Jimmy Carter's rival for the Democratic nomination, who'd risen to prominence thanks to the rallying cry "Segregation now, segregation tomorrow, and segregation forever." And on the trail in New Hampshire in January 1976, Reagan declared, "I would do everything in my power as president to eliminate and make unlawful the forced busing of school children for the purpose of integration." Yet Reagan's campaign aides bridled at the suggestion that he was prejudiced. Reagan, for his part, described himself as racially enlightened. In one of his first speeches after announcing his presidential candidacy, he'd said that in his youth, Americans hadn't understood "that we had a racial problem. It wasn't even recognized. But our generation, and I take great pride in this, were the ones who first of all recognized and then began doing something about it." As a young man, Reagan had invited two black football teammates to stay with him in his home when they'd been refused admission to a hotel. One of those teammates, who maintained a lifelong friendship with Reagan, later said the politician's claim that nobody knew about racism in the 1920s and 1930s was "the dumbest thing a grown person could say."

Reagan's racial consciousness, or lack thereof, became a matter of public concern during the 1976 presidential campaign. On February 5, the *New York Times* reported that he'd altered his typical script at a rally in Fort Lauderdale, Florida, describing a "strapping young buck"—not the usual "strapping young fellow"—buying T-bone steaks with food stamps. "In states like New Hampshire where there is scant black population, he has never used the expression 'young buck,' which, to whites in the South, generally denotes a large black man," the *Times* story said. Reagan's Florida state chair, a Panama City Chevrolet dealer, denied that racism played any role in the governor's campaign. In the same interview, the Chevy seller said that in "Florida we are wasting our time to get black people registered. There's no way we can out-promise the Democrats." He added that black people "would rather be promised a ham and get a loaf of bread than [be] promised two loaves and get it. It's just the way they think."

No matter whether he had zero or several dozen racist bones in his body, Reagan benefited from racism adjacencies. The words he used and the behaviors he didn't denounce gave the most prejudiced members of the American electorate a reason to believe he was on their side. This was a difficult needle to thread. According to the campaign's internal polling, voters in the 1976 primaries saw Reagan and George "Segregation Forever" Wallace as ideological twins. As a consequence of that polling, Reagan's campaign manager, John Sears, told his boss he needed to tone down his rhetoric. Per Sears's instructions, Reagan modified the grocery store line, changing "young buck" back to "young fellow." But there was one story the Republican candidate wasn't yet willing to revise. On February 13, Reagan told a crowd at a Holiday Inn outside Kankakee, Illinois, that it was time to "give back to the people of this country the right to run their own country and determine their own destiny." He told a few jokes, he mocked the Democrats' "wild spending ideas," and he talked about a woman in Chicago, a welfare cheat with an income of $150,000 a year.

* * *

In Ronald Reagan's stump speech, Linda Taylor had eighty names. Taylor's lawyer thought even 10 percent of that total was too many. Not even the most fair-minded juror, R. Eugene Pincham argued, would be capable of giving such an alias-happy defendant a fair trial. The Honorable Mark Jones agreed. On January 23, 1976, the Cook County judge decreed that prosecutors could identify their quarry by just four names: Linda Taylor, Connie Walker, Linda Bennett, and Sandra Brownlee.

Pincham had filed all manner of motions and petitions since signing on as Taylor's attorney in the fall of 1974. That December, he'd managed to get the case transferred to a different courtroom by asserting that five different judges were prejudiced against his client. He'd failed a year later in his bid to dismiss each of the counts against Taylor; Jones hadn't bought Pincham's claim that "the Defendant does not know Jack Sherwin, has never talked to Jack Sherwin, and Jack Sherwin has never talked to the Defendant." His motion to secure Taylor a separate trial for each welfare check she'd been accused of stealing had also been shot down. The state's attorney, Jim Piper, had called that idea "so staggering in its wastefulness and lack of efficiency and impracticality that the concept boggles the mind."

Though his gambits didn't always work, R. Eugene Pincham had a gift for persuasion. When the eminent black lawyer argued a case, young defense attorneys crowded into the gallery to hear his booming baritone, a voice the *Tribune* said "bore the rhythm and intensity of a country preacher delivering a sermon." The fifty-year-old Pincham was a brilliant, incisive cross-examiner, and his summations sometimes inspired onlookers to burst into applause. In his closing arguments, he'd explain to jurors that as a young boy he had a habit of swiping sugar from his mother's supply to sweeten his glass of milk. He never got away with it, though, because she inevitably found the granules he'd spilled on the floor. Those tiny sugar crystals, he'd tell the ladies and gentlemen of the jury, were the perfect analogue for all the reasonable doubts the prosecution had failed to clean up.

Growing up in Limestone County, Alabama, Pincham had picked cotton before and after school and from dawn to dusk each Saturday. In 1931, when he was five years old, nine black teenagers had been accused of raping two white women on a freight train bound for Memphis, Tennessee. The nine "Scottsboro Boys" were pulled off the train in Paint Rock, Alabama, less than forty miles from Pincham's home in Athens, and nearly lynched by a wrathful mob. Two weeks later, eight of the nine defendants had been sentenced to death.

The Scottsboro case didn't end there—the Supreme Court ordered the defendants retried twice, first due to ineffective counsel and later because black men had been systematically excluded from the jury pool.[*] Though there was no evidence to support their conviction, seven of the Scottsboro Boys ultimately spent time behind bars; none were executed. The horrific treatment of those nine young men inspired Pincham to become a lawyer. The Scottsboro trials also filled him with terror. When Pincham was in high school, his mother demanded that he leave Alabama because she feared he might be lynched—a white girl had made eyes at him at the grocery store, and the Pincham family's cook had overheard her father saying he wanted to do something about his daughter's crush. Pincham eventually landed in Tennessee, where he attended the historically black colleges LeMoyne and Tennessee State, then went to Chicago in 1948 to attend law school at Northwestern University. The only black student in his class, he shined shoes and waited tables at the Palmer House hotel to pay his tuition.[**]

Pincham, who moved into private practice in 1951, stepped away from his firm briefly during the Freedom Summer of 1964; he was working as a lawyer in Mississippi when civil rights workers James Chaney, Andrew Goodman, and Michael Schwerner were abducted and murdered. Back in Chicago, the civil and criminal litigator developed a knack for winning unwinnable cases. In 1969, he was part of a team that defended six black men accused of arson during the previous year's West Side riots; an all-white jury acquitted all six. Two years later, he defended seven members of the Black P Stone Nation gang who stood trial for murdering a white Chicago detective in a back-alley ambush. Pincham told the jury that the men had been framed, citing Matthew 25:40 in his closing argument: "If ye have done it unto the least of these my brethren, ye have done it unto me." All seven defendants were found not guilty.

Jesse Jackson, among others, saw Pincham as a leader who could help bring black Chicagoans where they needed to go. In 1971, Jackson

---

[*] Women weren't allowed to serve on juries in Alabama until 1966.

[**] Harold Washington, the future mayor of Chicago, was one year behind Pincham at Northwestern; Washington was also the only black student in his class. Dan Walker, the future governor, was one year ahead of Pincham.

demanded the resignation of Edward Hanrahan—the state's attorney who'd presided over the raid in which police killed Black Panthers Fred Hampton and Mark Clark—and named Pincham as an ideal candidate to replace him. Instead, Hanrahan lost his reelection bid to Republican Bernard Carey. A little more than a year after his victory at the polls, Carey created the special prosecutions division that was pursuing the case against Pincham's client Linda Taylor.

Pincham worked out of an office in Chatham, a middle-class community that had transformed from 1 percent to 98 percent black between 1950 and 1970. His firm rented space on East Eighty-Seventh Street right off the bustling commercial thoroughfare of South Cottage Grove Avenue, in a building filled with other black-owned businesses—a life insurance firm, a dental office, a beauty shop. The waiting room of Evins, Pincham, Fowlkes, and Cooper overflowed with men and women desperate to see a lawyer. They'd crowd into the reception area until 1 a.m. some nights, hoping Mr. Pincham might spare a moment to listen to their pleas. He got referrals from his fraternity, Kappa Alpha Psi; from his fellow congregants at Trinity United Church; and from people he knew in the neighborhood. The other lawyers at Pincham's firm didn't always know where his clients came from. Pincham's junior associate Isaiah "Skip" Gant thought Linda Taylor had some sort of connection to Edward "Flukie" Cain, the proprietor of Flukie's Restaurant and Lounge on Cottage Grove. Gant had no doubt that Taylor was a con artist. But if Pincham had taught him anything, it was that every client deserved the strongest possible defense.

In addition to pulling every conceivable legal lever, Pincham sought to change Taylor's public image. The *Tribune*'s welfare queen was, in her attorney's view, a woman of the people—an inner-city martyr who'd done what she needed to do to keep her head bobbing above the poverty line. "When you cut through everything, she's being accused of taking money not entitled to her," Pincham told the *Tribune* on January 27, 1976. "It would be a pretty sorry situation if the state tried to prosecute and send to jail everybody from the South Side that took welfare money they didn't have coming. There'd just be nowhere to put them."

Although Pincham didn't shy away from taking on high-profile clients, he saw himself as a champion of the underclass. In a 1973 interview with the *National Black Law Journal*, he said that the "people who need me are the victims of unjust accusation, poor folks, and ignorant folks, not the rich nor the famous." Was Linda Taylor a poor, ignorant victim or a rich and famous criminal? It depended on what stories you read, and whose stories you believed.

* * *

Ronald Reagan built his campaign for the presidency anecdote by anecdote. He brought out his favorites more than once each day, regaling each new crowd with wit and wisdom gleaned from friends, staffers, and magazines. For many Americans struggling to find work and pay their bills, Reagan's florid stories of government incompetence felt deeply, viscerally true. They weren't.

On February 4, 1976, the *Washington Star*'s John J. Fialka published a front-page report gleaned from his observations of eighteen of Reagan's citizens' press conferences. The candidate's talking points, he found, rarely stood up to scrutiny. Reagan inflated his own record, claiming he'd cut 400,000 rather than 230,000 welfare recipients from the rolls in California. He said that the U.S. taxed its businesses more aggressively than any other nation; in fact, Canada, France, West Germany, and Ireland all had higher corporate tax rates. He reported that "three-fourths of all the Christmas tree decorations in the U.S. are made in Japan." The president of the National Ornament and Electric Light Christmas Association told Fialka that the correct figure was more like 10 percent, with another 50 percent originating in Taiwan, Hong Kong, and Korea.

Reagan's description of New York's Taino Towers—the public housing complex with a swimming pool and $113.20-per-month apartments with eleven-foot ceilings—had made it sound great to be poor. The swimming pool, it turned out, was open to anyone who lived in East Harlem, and those apartments with eleven-foot ceilings would cost a family between $300 and $450 a month.

And then there was the Chicago welfare cheat with eighty names and an annual tax-free income of $150,000. Reagan "referred to her at nearly every stop" on his New Hampshire road show, Fialka reported, and "people's jaws dropped in Dublin and Jeffrey and Peterborough and Salem and in all the other little towns where he appeared." But just like every other anecdote in Reagan's arsenal, Fialka wrote, this one "doesn't quite check out." The *Washington Star* reporter had learned that Taylor stood accused of "using not 80 aliases but four. The amount the state is charging that she received from her alleged fraud is not $150,000 but $8,000." Though various Illinois officials believed she'd stolen more than that, Cook County prosecutor Jim Piper told Fialka, "You have to go with what you can prove."

Fialka's piece, a professor at the Columbia University Graduate School of Journalism said, was such "an excellent example of reportorial journalism" that it was slated for inclusion in a textbook. Journalists would absorb the story's lessons long before that textbook was printed. At a press conference in Daytona Beach, Florida, on February 7, a reporter accused the candidate of hypocrisy for citing "unverified reports" about a single welfare recipient while refusing to condemn Richard Nixon for his well-substantiated role in Watergate.

> In recent weeks, you've been going up and down the coast telling people about a woman in Chicago who allegedly bilked the welfare agency there out of a hundred and fifty thousand dollars using eighty names and thirty addresses and fifteen phone numbers.
>
> Yet your own briefing material indicates that this woman has never been found guilty of anything, and in fact has been only charged with one count of fraud relating to using four names to defraud them of seven thousand dollars. Do the rules change depending on who you're attacking?

Reagan had come prepared. Upon hearing "never been found guilty of anything," he pursed his lips, shook his head from side to side, unfolded a single sheet of white paper, and pulled a pair of reading glasses from his breast pocket. "Maybe I've been careless at times and not said 'reported,'" Reagan began. A second later, he retracted that mea culpa: "Usually I have said this was reported." (In reality, Reagan almost never used words like *reported* or *alleged*—betraying uncertainty wasn't his style.) "Now, it was widely reported in all the newspapers at the time," he continued, "and you know I believe everything that you fellows print in the newspaper, except when you're writing about me." He then glanced down at his sheet of paper and started to read aloud.

> Late November 1974. Her name is Linda Taylor. The Illinois Legislative Advisory Committee on Public Assistance investigated. Came up with eighty-two charges of welfare fraud, perjury, and bigamy. Among other things they discovered one hundred aliases and fifty false addresses.

Reagan looked up from the podium and raised his eyebrows. "I've only been saying eighty and thirty," he said, complimenting himself on his self-restraint. Back to the sheet of paper.

> The point I was making is summarized in a wire-service story quoting Joel Edelman, executive director of the Illinois committee. He said, "When the entire story is told, I believe this will prove to be the most massive welfare fraud that has ever been perpetrated in the fifty states."

Reagan didn't mention Linda Taylor's name at campaign rallies—her identity had never been important. Now it was. So long as the woman in Chicago was a real person, he seemed to think, he had nothing to apologize for.

The national press corps didn't agree. A week after Reagan's disquisition in Daytona Beach, the *New York Times* reprinted a shorter version of the Fialka article under the headline "'Welfare Queen' Becomes Issue in Reagan Campaign." The *Times*' imprimatur solidified the perception that

Reagan didn't let the facts get in the way of a good story. The *Philadelphia Daily News*'s Chuck Stone called the welfare queen Reagan's "latest con job." John Osborne wrote in the *New Republic* that Reagan's "stories are peopled by misty characters whose identities and adventures tend to go unverified."

But while Fialka had proved that Reagan was a serial exaggerator, the journalist's gloss on the welfare queen story was misleading in its own way. Yes, it was true that just four aliases had been deemed relevant in Taylor's welfare fraud trial. But that didn't constitute any kind of proof that she'd restricted herself to four identities. Likewise, the Cook County prosecutors' decision to charge Taylor with stealing $8,865.67 worth of welfare checks didn't mean that was the extent of what she'd taken. The Illinois Department of Public Aid, which had an interest in suppressing the true extent of Taylor's crimes, had estimated privately that she'd stolen something on the order of $40,000.

Fialka's version of the truth didn't go unchallenged. Reagan's favorite publication, the magazine *Human Events*—he once said it "helped me stop being a liberal Democrat"—reported that the former California governor actually "may have understated the facts concerning Chicago's welfare queen." Joel Edelman, the executive director of Illinois's Legislative Advisory Committee on Public Aid, told *Human Events* that Reagan had been right about everything. Linda Taylor had used eighty names and thirty addresses, Edelman said, and $150,000 was a fair approximation of what she'd stolen. The Illinois official continued at great length, revealing more details of the sordid welfare queen saga.

> You know, there're some interesting sidelights to this. You know it's kind of humorous, but it's tragic. This woman, after the whole exposé and after she was indicted, befriends a woman already on public aid who had gone into the hospital for some medical care and returned home to be confined for a couple of weeks, so our friend, the welfare queen, poses as a homemaker because the Department of Public Aid will pay private individuals to go into the homes of recipients who are recovering from

a serious illness, and who need to have their house cleaned and shopping done for them and that kind of thing.

She went in there—talk about gall, she's under indictment, remember—and used a new alias. We'd never seen this one before, and the Department of Public Aid was issuing a check to her for a couple of weeks running as a homemaker. She gave up her cars—she was driving two Lincoln Continental Mark IVs, but a couple of weeks later she's got another one. She has also taken trips out of the country.

The woman Taylor had befriended, the one "who had gone into the hospital for some medical care," was Patricia Parks. Although the *Tribune* had reported in 1975 that Taylor hadn't succeeded in securing any payments from the state during her stint as Parks's housekeeper, it's possible Edelman was correct that she had been paid "for a couple of weeks." Regardless, Edelman, *Human Events*, the *Washington Star*, and the *New York Times* hadn't seen fit to mention a pair of more salient facts: Patricia Parks was dead, and Linda Taylor had been suspected of killing her.

George Bliss and the *Chicago Tribune* introduced Taylor to the world as the ne plus ultra of welfare fraudsters. In his presentations on the stump, Reagan both cemented Bliss's depiction of the welfare queen and stream-lined what had been a complicated narrative. Taylor changed identities by changing wigs. She could be white, black, or Latina. She lived with children who may or may not have been hers. Later, the *Tribune* had floated the idea that Taylor might be a kidnapper and a murderer. Reagan's version of the Taylor story was mind-boggling but simple. A woman in Chicago had used eighty names to steal $150,000 a year of welfare money. The wigs and the kids and the murder allegation—those were extraneous details. Welfare cheats were bad. Linda Taylor was the worst of them all.

Just as Reagan had defined Linda Taylor, this woman in Chicago came to define him. More than anyone or anything else Reagan talked about during the 1976 campaign, Taylor represented the forces preventing the

United States and its citizens from achieving the greatness that was their birthright. Reagan's supporters understood that. So did his detractors. When Reagan said that Linda Taylor epitomized America's decline, she became a hammer that competing political factions could use to bash the other side. If she'd used four aliases and stolen less than $10,000, that meant Reagan was a liar. If she'd used eighty aliases and stolen $150,000, that meant he was divulging the secrets liberals were too squeamish to reveal.

On February 24, Reagan lost the New Hampshire primary by fewer than sixteen hundred votes. "I feel what's happened tonight is a victory," the runner-up told reporters. "That is a lot of baloney," replied President Ford's state campaign director. As the two Republican candidates made dueling claims on reality, newspapers in Chicago and elsewhere were printing up another series of welfare queen headlines. The day after the New Hampshire results were tallied, Linda Taylor was taken into custody once again. The arresting officer was Jack Sherwin.

CHAPTER 7
Concerned Neighbors

When Linda Taylor walked out of Judge Mark Jones's courtroom, camera operators from all the local stations scrambled to capture her image. The moment she reached the lobby of the Chicago Civic Center, a guy from the city's NBC affiliate jumped in the elevator, grabbed some quick footage of her backside, then sprinted through a set of double doors to shoot her from the front. As Taylor strolled across the plaza outside the rust-colored skyscraper, she was bracketed by lights and lenses.

Taylor had gone downtown on February 25, 1976, for a hearing in her long-delayed welfare fraud case. Her lawyer, R. Eugene Pincham, had filed a motion alleging that Jack Sherwin had confiscated his client's public aid ID cards without a warrant. That search was unreasonable and invalid, Pincham said, a "fishing expedition" that violated the First, Fourth, Fifth, Sixth, and Fourteenth Amendments of the U.S. Constitution. He argued that every piece of evidence seized from Taylor's apartment should be tossed out. Pincham, though, wasn't quite ready to immolate the prosecution's case. He asked Jones for a continuance, and the hearing got pushed back to April 1. Taylor came striding out of the Civic Center just a few minutes after she'd strode in.

The defendant had arrayed herself for criminal court in a full-length black fur coat, a look she accessorized with a black-and-white-striped scarf and a sun-shaped rhinestone brooch. Taylor, whose left arm was tucked beneath the elbow of a male companion, bowed her head to protect herself from the howling wind, then threaded the fingers of her right hand through the bangs of her wavy black wig. She didn't look at the cameras.

"Would you talk to us?" a reporter shouted. "How'd you do, Linda?"

Taylor kept moving forward. A few moments later, she spat back an answer.

"Well, compared to some of you white people, I think I done pretty damn good to be black."

"Thattagirl," the reporter said. It was a great soundbite.

Taylor's daughter, Sandra Brownlee, told her mother to cut it out. "Don't say nothing," she said. "Just smile. Do another pose so they can get a different picture of you. I'm getting sick of that old one."

Taylor giggled, baring her gold teeth.

"Throw your hair back," Sandra said, encouraging her mother to show her face.

"Aw, shit," Taylor replied, again riffling her bangs. After that, she closed her mouth, crossed the street, and unlocked the door of a 1975 Buick Electra. The cameras hadn't noticed Jack Sherwin trailing behind the crowd, watching Taylor climb into her car and drive away.

* * *

Although the hearing on his search of Taylor's apartment had been postponed, Sherwin had another reason to be at the Civic Center on February 25. The day before, he'd met with state's attorney Jim Piper, and the two men had agreed on a course of action. As soon as Taylor exited the building, Sherwin and a couple of his fellow officers would arrest her on a new set of charges. The month before, Sherwin and Piper believed, Taylor had burglarized a house. Among the items she'd allegedly stolen was a fur coat. Burglary was Sherwin's area of expertise. This time, his bosses at the Chicago Police Department couldn't tell him to leave Linda Taylor alone.

Sherwin knew that the Chicago press loved to chronicle Taylor's every sashay, but he still hadn't expected a phalanx of cameras. The chaos outside the Civic Center—the lights, the shouting, Taylor declaring "I done pretty damn good to be black"—forced Sherwin to change his plan.

Rather than arrest the fur-clad Taylor in full view of every major news outfit in the city, he decided to wait for a less conspicuous moment. When Taylor drove off in that 1975 Electra, Sherwin put a tail on the car.

She parked in front of a two-story brick house on South Normal Avenue, four miles from where Sherwin had arrested her in 1974. By midafternoon, Piper, three investigators from the state's attorney's office, and five additional Chicago police officers had assembled at 7450 South Normal. At 3:30 p.m., Sherwin and his nine-man crew entered Taylor's South Side apartment and told her she had the right to remain silent. In the kitchen, the detective spotted a Van Wyck electric can opener. In the bedroom, he found a GE portable color television with a brown wood finish. Both items had been reported stolen.

A year and a half earlier, Sherwin had been struck by the tidiness of Taylor's apartment at 8221 South Clyde Avenue. This place was filthy. Taylor had two children living with her on South Normal, just as she had on South Clyde. The two boys—seven-year-old Duke, who was white, and five-year-old Hosa, who was black—didn't appear to have anywhere to sleep. There was just a single cot in the apartment, and Taylor had been the one using it. The children looked downcast and dirty, and they were dressed in tattered clothes. Sherwin called for an evidence technician and a pair of youth officers to come to the scene, to take pictures of the house and the two boys, and to transport the seven-year-old and the five-year-old to the Illinois Department of Children and Family Services.

Taylor already hated Sherwin. Eighteen months earlier, to the day, he'd found incriminating evidence in her cardboard suitcase. He'd hassled her and arrested her and confiscated a bunch of her belongings. She'd called Sherwin's division to complain, and a sergeant had told her Sherwin would back off. But now he was hassling and arresting her again. On the afternoon of February 25, Taylor waited, handcuffs around her wrists, for two policewomen to come to her apartment and take away the two children. Taylor didn't want to remain silent—there were a few things she needed to say. She didn't yell and scream. She didn't raise her voice. "No matter how much money it takes," she told Sherwin, "I'm going to get your badge." She explained, flatly and calmly, that he wouldn't be able to have children when she was done with him. She said she'd find his wife and tell her about all the "black ass" he'd been fooling around with. She also threatened Sherwin's life. From now on, Taylor said, the detective needed to be more careful. There was a bullet in the streets of Chicago with his name on it.

* * *

The day after George Bliss's first Linda Taylor story appeared in the *Chicago Tribune*, Don Moore declared that he'd be leading an investigation into the alleged infiltration of the Illinois Department of Public Aid by a cadre of welfare cheaters. The state senator never found those supposed villains, and he didn't uncover any evidence that Taylor's thievery had been an inside job. His failures, though, were quickly forgotten. Moore's legislative committee credited itself with corralling Taylor, noting in a self-congratulatory press release that it had "sought to publicize various of its more dramatic activities" as a means to "create an awareness among Illinois residents of the scope of welfare fraud in our state."

For Moore's committee, the welfare queen was good for business. On account of the group's work on the Taylor case, the superintendent of the Chicago police instructed the city's cops to bypass other state agencies and send the names of possible welfare swindlers directly to Moore's investigators, a move that effectively placed the legislative committee in charge of determining who was a cheater and who wasn't. In 1975, the state legislature also increased the committee's annual budget from $100,000 to $188,000, a bump that Moore and Joel Edelman used to hire more welfare detectives. By the following year, Moore was telling reporters that the Legislative Advisory Committee had saved taxpayers more than $1 million. In an interview, the state senator said his group could potentially save the state even more money. He just needed an even bigger budget, and still more investigators.

Moore knew that public aid fraud could take many different forms. In his keynote address at the National Welfare Fraud Association convention in October 1975, he acknowledged that "the greater crimes are being committed by the white-collar cheaters who are hustling the Medicaid program through financial manipulations." But in speeches and interviews, he spent just as much time discussing how the state might prevent individual welfare recipients from gaming the system. At the end of that same keynote address, Moore rhapsodized about a "developing technology"—"an odorless, tasteless, inkless substance" that could grab a fresh fingerprint "each time the recipient cashes his or her check." A "highly sophisticated computer" would then match that print against one in the Department of Public Aid's master file, eliminating the possibility of identity-based fraud.

Don Moore didn't always get what he wanted. Compulsory finger-printing for welfare recipients never came to pass in Illinois. Neither did Moore's proposal to set up an entirely new agency, the Office of Welfare Fraud Investigation, to deal with public aid swindlers. The Legislative Advisory Committee did, however, succeed in lobbying for legislation mandating that welfare cheats pay restitution money directly to the state's attorney's office that convicted them. That kind of financial inducement, Moore hoped, would convince reluctant prosecutors to start treating public aid fraud as a serious criminal act. A few months before, Republican state senator Karl Berning had tried and failed to push through a more expansive piece of legislation, one that would've paid a "finder's fee" of up to $2,500 to anyone who turned in a welfare scammer. "Hopefully," Berning had said, "this bill will eliminate the normal public reluctance toward reporting cases of welfare cheating, and stimulate involvement in the fight against fraud."

Contrary to Berning's claim, much of the general public was eager to throw haymakers in this particular fight. In a survey conducted by a state representative who, like Don Moore, hailed from Chicago's mostly white south suburbs, 96 percent of respondents said that "too many people on welfare are receiving benefits to which they are not entitled." Moore urged those aggrieved citizens to call the committee's office or to drop in personally whenever they spotted untoward welfare-related activity. They did so with great alacrity, no cash payments necessary.

These volunteer guardians of the state treasury also sent a steady supply of angry, anonymous letters to the Illinois Department of Public Aid—notes signed by "Concerned Neighbors," "An Irate Taxpayer," "A U.S. Citizen," and "An Interested Party." These missives listed the names, addresses, and license plate numbers of supposedly suspicious persons. One letter, sent in 1976, carried the header "Re: MEXICAN WELFARE QUEENS" and featured a map of the alleged queens' neighborhood.

In May 1975, the Department of Public Aid made calling out a welfare cheater as easy as picking up a phone, launching a 24-hour, toll-free welfare fraud hotline. Although California and Massachusetts had preceded Illinois in creating inform-by-phone systems, Linda Taylor's home state was the first to grant callers anonymity.

At 9:07 a.m. on August 14, 1975, an unidentified whistle-blower lodged a complaint about a woman named Kathy.

> The reason I think she is cheating [is] because she has a baby that her boyfriend paid for and they are living together and she's getting state aid which she don't need and he's always bragging about going out and buying a bunch of stuff with the money he is making off of it.

Another accusation came in at 9:47 a.m., this one about a woman in Chicago who'd just purchased a blue Chevrolet.

> She is a recipient of the aid and she is running and chasing around with other men and she works for a gas station to help a former boyfriend....I don't care about her personal life but this woman is definitely wrong in receiving aid.

At 9:54 a.m.:

> Now, you said this is confidential. I don't want you to play this tape because you would really mess me up. She is now at Sara Lee's. She works there....I tried to get on aid myself. You refused to let me on, so why should she?

At 11:32 a.m.:

> She came into this apartment with two children and now
> she has four and [she's] driving a big Chrysler. It's a black
> four-door, vinyl top. She has asked public aid for a stove and a
> refrigerator and she tells me that she is working part-time for
> the street department in Saint Louis. I just don't understand
> these big black Cadillacs . . .

The phone rang all day with news of cheaters. In the first twelve months after the agency plugged its fraud phone into the wall, the hotline received more than five thousand tips. Two-thirds of those callers chose to keep their identities to themselves. As of June 1976, just 0.7 percent of those calls—37 out of 5,133—instigated legitimate fraud investigations, with those three dozen or so cases adding up to $325,044.97 in losses for the Department of Public Aid.

The welfare fraud hotline cost $25,135 a year to maintain—$8,549 for labor, $806 for the recorder, and $15,780 for the phone line. By that measure, the toll-free number paid for itself. In May 1976, the head of the Public Aid Department's bureau of special investigations told the *Tribune* that the hotline had in fact "been too successful"—that it "generates more cases [than] prosecutors can handle." The agency's chief investigator added that "most people call because of jealousy. They feel they are taxed beyond belief, and don't want their dollars supporting someone who doesn't need them." In case *Tribune* readers felt jealous themselves, the paper printed the hotline's digits in the last line of its story.

The Department of Public Aid's embrace of toll-free vigilantism didn't win universal acclaim. The *Chicago Sun-Times* wrote that the agency had cast ordinary citizens as "Big Brother's helper," then suggested it change its name to the "Ministry of Fear." After reading that editorial, the Reverend Samuel M. Carter, a minister from the majority-black community of North Lawndale, wrote the department to condemn the hotline as "dangerous and un-American," likening it to something out of Hitler's

Germany or Mussolini's Italy. "It seems to me that this is just another punitive practice against people who are poor," Carter wrote.

> There seems to be a middle-class American attitude to haunt, to curse, and to damn people because they are poor, as if being poor is a disgrace, a crime....
>
> I want you to understand, sir, that I do not condone fraud or cheating on any level of society, but in America we have blessed and glorified the Vanderbilts, the J. P. Morgans, and the Harrimans, who stole and cheated the railroad systems of America blind.... We have had shoebox episodes in Springfield and even more recent misappropriations of state government funds.

George Bliss had wanted to write about Paul Powell, the bribe-soliciting Illinois secretary of state who'd secreted away wads of cash in a shoebox and other receptacles, a haul discovered only upon his death in 1970. Back then, higher-ups at the *Tribune* had told Bliss to leave Powell alone—the newspaper needed to maintain a good relationship with a powerful if ethically compromised state official. There was no such institutional pressure to protect the reputations of welfare cheaters, a group seen as both amoral and politically useless.

* * *

Linda Taylor's latest booking photos looked like the head shots of a fallen Hollywood star. The "CHIGO PD" placard that hung around Taylor's neck obscured the regal, oversized collar of her black full-length fur coat—the same garment she'd worn to her most recent court appearance. She sported a longer wig than she had in 1974, the dark hair covering her ears and curling down to her shoulders. But her cheeks appeared more sunken than they had two years earlier, the look on her face less defiant than downcast.

Taylor had been carrying a handful of documents at the time of her arrest, one of which revealed that she had a new husband. A month before, she'd married Sherman Ray, a twenty-seven-year-old Vietnam veteran. The marriage license, Taylor's third in less than three years, listed her name as Linda C. B. Wakefield and her age as twenty-nine. The janitor at 7450 South Normal Avenue, Arthur Krueger, told Sherwin that the newlyweds had moved in at the beginning of February. Krueger said he'd known Taylor for a long time—she'd been using the building on South Normal as a drop for welfare checks since the early 1970s. When she'd rented an apartment this time, Krueger said, a mail carrier had brought her "some type of questionnaire from the welfare office."

On the night of Taylor's burglary arrest, the victim of her crime came to Sherwin's division to identify her stolen property. Everleana Brame had been Taylor's roommate for several months starting in the fall of 1975, after Taylor had gotten locked out by John Parks and left her room at the 50th on the Lake Motel. Brame told the police that the women had agreed to "split certain expenses," but Taylor had never paid any rent. After what Brame described as "several disagreements," she'd asked her boarder to leave. On move-out day, Taylor showed up at Brame's house with two Chicago police officers—she'd told the cops she "feared that she would have trouble obtaining her possessions if the police were not present." When she left, she pocketed a key to the back door.

A few weeks later, on January 29, 1976, Brame came home and found her can opener and television missing. A set of white china dishes with silver edging was also gone, as was her silverware, a pink radio and record player, a makeup mirror on a flower-adorned pedestal, and a silver wedding band with five small diamonds. Someone had raided her closet, too, swiping a bunch of jackets, a three-piece polka-dot pantsuit, and a black broadtail coat with gray fur trim.

This wasn't a difficult case for Sherwin to crack. Brame's neighbors had seen a woman who matched Taylor's description carry several boxes from the rear entrance of 7719 South Oglesby Avenue, load them into a black Cadillac Eldorado convertible, and drive away. Taylor had done nothing to disguise herself. She'd grabbed Brame's possessions in the middle of the afternoon.

Less than twelve hours after they'd arrested Taylor, at 1:30 a.m. on

February 26, Sherwin and his fellow officers went back to her apartment on South Normal Avenue. This time, they had a search warrant. The detectives found Brame's makeup mirror and dishes, though the china service was missing one cup. They didn't recover the polka-dot pantsuit or the broadtail coat. Taylor, it turned out, had an extensive collection of black furs—the one she'd stolen from Everleana Brame's house wasn't the same coat she'd draped over herself in her most recent set of mug shots. The police gathered, bagged, and labeled the detritus of Taylor's unsettled life: motel keys, lottery tickets, attorneys' business cards, and papers marked with the names Dr. Connie R. Walker, Constance Howard, and Linda Ray. Sherwin also found a Carson Pirie Scott department store credit card that had belonged to Patricia Parks, and he inventoried another document as "deposition of Patricia M. Parks, dated 5/24/1975." That was the day, three weeks before her death, on which Parks had modified her will from her hospital bed.

Most of the stories written about Taylor's arrest focused on a single large object. On February 28, the UPI wire service reported that the Chicago police had impounded Linda Taylor's car. "No carriage for Queen of welfare," read the headline in the *Ottawa Journal*. "'Welfare' Cadillac seized," said Pennsylvania's *New Castle News*. The *New York Times* ran its one-paragraph article with the title "'Welfare Queen' Loses Her Cadillac Limousine," misidentifying Taylor's Eldorado convertible. The *Times* piece noted that the car had been "used to transport a fur coat, television set, diamond ring and kitchen appliances allegedly stolen from an occupant at a residence where Miss Taylor formerly lived." It didn't mention that the police had also seized a pair of children that had been under Taylor's care.

A grand jury indicted Taylor on two counts of felony theft—one each for the GE color television and the fur coat—and one count of burglary. Taylor had been transported to Cook County's Women's Correctional Center after her arrest, and she stayed there after her indictment. The threat she'd made to have Jack Sherwin killed had not gone over well in bond court; a judge set her bail for $50,000, and Taylor wasn't able to post the $5,000 she needed to get released. Seven weeks later, R. Eugene Pincham filed a motion arguing that the five-figure bond was "exorbitant, prohibitive, punitive, unreasonable, and unconstitutional." Taylor, he wrote, wasn't a flight risk—she'd appeared in court for her welfare fraud case "on at least two dozen occasions."

On April 14, a month and a half after she'd shown up for a hearing in a body-length fur coat, Taylor was escorted to criminal court in a correctional center jumpsuit. Pincham sparred with a team of Cook County state's attorneys for nearly four hours, interjecting so often that a frustrated prosecutor pleaded with the defense lawyer "to have some respect for the court even if you don't have any for me." (Pincham's response: "I assure you that I have the utmost respect for the court.") This was less a bond hearing than a referendum on the "welfare queen" label, and the fairness of punishing one particularly flashy woman for the supposed crimes of a whole class of people. It was a debate, in the *Tribune*'s words, over whether "Linda Taylor is a champion of deception and deceit or the innocent victim of a vendetta by overzealous prosecutors."

Judge Russell DeBow sided with Pincham, reducing his client's bail to $7,500. The next morning, Linda Taylor posted $750 in cash and walked out of the Cook County Women's Correctional Center. That same afternoon, she vacated the rear apartment at 7450 South Normal Avenue and left the court no forwarding address. It had taken her less than a day to violate the terms of her release.

* * *

If Ronald Reagan's close defeat in New Hampshire could be spun as a kind of victory, his losses in Massachusetts, Vermont, Florida, and Illinois looked like the death throes of a candidacy that had never really stood a chance. Although his advisers claimed to be pleased with Reagan's string of second-place finishes, they knew that the challenger was running out of time. On March 15, 1976, the campaign's chartered plane almost didn't take off due to a lack of funds. Nancy Reagan urged her husband's press secretary, Lyn Nofziger, to quit chasing the White House while they could all still maintain a bit of dignity.

Reagan's first few months on the trail hadn't been a total fiasco. After the New Hampshire primary, he'd found a crowd-riling foreign policy message to pair with his more well-developed domestic agenda. The ex-governor earned loud ovations by condemning the policy of detente with the Soviet Union as a symbol of the "collapse of the American will." He also adopted an aggressive posture on U.S. sovereignty over the Panama Canal, denouncing President Gerald Ford and Secretary of State Henry Kissinger for their plan to gift an important American asset to a Communist regime.

By March 1976, the Panama Canal had become Reagan's new Linda Taylor. In a campaign advertisement, he parroted a line inaugurated by Senator Strom Thurmond: "We bought it, we paid for it, and [Panama's] General Torrijos should be told we're going to keep it." As he had with Taylor, Reagan got dinged for peddling a misleading, simplistic story— his old Republican ally Barry Goldwater, for one, said his gloss on the canal situation contained "gross factual errors." But Reagan had latched on to a deeper truth. "The Panama Canal issue had nothing to do with the canal," a campaign aide told reporter Jules Witcover. "It said more about the American people's feelings about where the country was, and what it was powerless to do." When Reagan topped the polls in North Carolina on March 23, earning his first win of the primary season, a Ford organizer credited the triumph to "Miss Sally Jones sitting at home, watching Ronald Reagan on television and deciding that she didn't want to give away the Panama Canal."

Reagan knew that his campaign manager, John Sears, wanted him to stop talking about the woman in Chicago. The Republican contender's discovery of a rich new vein of crowd-pleasing material made it easier to heed that advice. But despite putting Linda Taylor aside, Reagan continued to benefit from bigotry. Desperate to resuscitate the flagging campaign, Sears had ceded control of the North Carolina operation to Tom Ellis, a close ally of Senator Jesse Helms. In the run-up to the primary, Ellis's crew had distributed flyers insinuating that Gerald Ford might select a black man, Massachusetts senator Edward Brooke, as his running mate. Reagan reportedly demanded that the flyers be confiscated the moment he learned of their existence. Whether they'd been distributed against his will or not, those leaflets marked him as the candidate of racial grievance.

Earlier in the year, Sears had sought to distance Reagan from George Wallace. Now, in advance of the May 1 Texas primary, staffers produced radio and television ads featuring a Wallace supporter. "As much as I hate to admit it," the man said, "George Wallace can't be nominated. Ronald Reagan can. He's right on the issues." With the help of the state's Wallace-loving ex-Democrats, Reagan won Texas by a landslide. When he took the primaries in Georgia, Alabama, and Indiana three days later, the campaign crowed to reporters that Reagan had swiped the delegate lead from the incumbent president.

The new GOP front-runner barnstormed across the country, championing fiscal prudence at home and strength abroad. At a speech at a Baptist college in Chattanooga, Tennessee, on May 21, the crowd cheered when he said, "Welfare is destroying human beings, not saving them," and again when he suggested that "the answer to saving human beings is to see that able-bodied welfare recipients work at useful community projects in return for their welfare grants." A few weeks later at Oregon State University, a student shouted a question from the balcony: "What do you propose to do to welfare families in Harlem?" Reagan repeated the question, then quickly pivoted to more familiar territory. "There is no one in Washington, DC, who knows how many people in this country are on welfare. Washington only knows how many people they're sending checks to," he said. With his campaign ascendant, Reagan didn't restrain himself. "And in Chicago," he continued, "they're sending checks to a woman who's been on welfare under eighty names, thirty addresses, and fifteen telephone numbers." He made no mention of welfare families in Harlem.

From May 25 through the end of primary season in June, Ford and Reagan each topped the ballot in six different states. With the nomination fight showing no signs of wrapping up before the Republican convention, the candidates' public statements became less important than the words they whispered in private to uncommitted delegates. While the Reagan campaign had built up an impressive grassroots network, Ford bested him by wooing delegates with tantalizing perks: a one-on-one meeting in the Oval Office, a seat alongside Queen Elizabeth II at a state dinner, a perch on an aircraft carrier to watch the bicentennial fireworks in New York Harbor. On August 18, 1976, after three anxious days at Kansas City's Kemper Arena, Ford won the party's presidential nomination with 1,187 delegates to Reagan's 1,070.

The next night, the president invited his worthy opponent onstage to say a few words. In his concession speech, Reagan crowed that "the Republican Party has a platform that is a banner of bold, unmistakable colors with no pale pastel shades." He urged his fellow members of the GOP to "go forth from here united, determined, that what a great general said a few years ago is true: There is no substitute for victory." In the crowd, a Reagan organizer reported hearing a Ford partisan exclaim, "Oh my God, we've nominated the wrong man."

* * *

Having lost the battle for the GOP nomination, the sixty-five-year-old Reagan went home to his California ranch, an American Cincinnatus waiting to be called back into service by the nation he loved. With his political career on hiatus, Reagan relaunched the daily radio commentaries he'd set aside during his run for the presidency. Two weeks after he'd been edged out by Gerald Ford in Kansas City, Reagan dropped by a Hollywood studio to record a dozen new spots. After he'd finished up for the day, he celebrated his return to the airwaves by drinking champagne with his friend Jack Webb, *Dragnet*'s Sergeant Joe Friday.

Radio was Reagan's medium. He'd been a broadcaster for much of his life—his first job out of college had been at WOC-AM in Davenport, Iowa, in 1932—and he knew how to talk so people listened. Reagan composed his radio addresses himself, filling yellow legal pads with the neat cursive he'd learned as a boy in small-town Illinois. He'd steal time on airplanes and car rides crafting as many as three weeks' worth of monologues in one go. Writing for the radio brought Reagan tremendous joy. He grinned widely every time he handed his secretary a new stack of yellow paper.

On October 18, 1976, the Republican runner-up read from a script titled "Welfare." He began, "A news item about welfare foolishness has brought back some campaign memories I'd like to share with you." Those memories centered on a woman in Chicago with eighty different aliases. Though Reagan didn't say Linda Taylor's name, he did refer to her as "the 'welfare queen,' as she's now called"—possibly the first time he'd been recorded saying that phrase.

Reagan's three-minute monologue was a rhetorical double bank shot, one that targeted the American public aid system and his critics in the media. "Even though the story had been widely carried in the press, campaigns being what they are, I would run into cynics who thought I'd padded the story for political purposes," he told his radio audience. "Well, thanks to the chief investigative reporter of the *Chicago Tribune*, I can verify and update my story—and it won't do anything for the image of welfare workers who tried to hush the story up."

Ensconced in that Hollywood recording studio, Reagan told the tale of Linda Taylor in far more detail than he ever had before. He described the Chicago detectives who'd uncovered her fraud, the state's attorney's office that didn't want to prosecute it, the newspaper that publicized Taylor's crimes, and the heroic chair of the Legislative Advisory Committee on Public Aid who'd investigated the whole mess. He then offered this "update" to his original story.

> The trail extends through fourteen states. She has used a hundred and twenty-seven names so far, posed as a mother of fourteen children at one time, seven at another, signed up twice with the same case worker in four days, and once while on welfare posed as an open-heart surgeon, complete with office. She has fifty Social Security numbers and fifty addresses in Chicago alone, plus an untold number of telephones. She claims to be the widow—let's make that plural—of two naval officers who were killed in action. Now the Department of Agriculture is looking into the massive number of food stamps she's been collecting. She has three new cars, a full-length mink coat, and her take is estimated at one million dollars.

Reagan finished up with one last dig at the bureaucrats who'd allowed Taylor to steal all that money. "I wish this had a happy ending," he said, "but the public aid office, according to the news story, refuses to cooperate. She's still collecting welfare checks she can use to build up her defense fund." With that, the almost-nominee signed off: "This is Ronald Reagan. Thanks for listening."[*]

Although Reagan cited the chief investigative reporter of the *Chicago Tribune*, his source material hadn't appeared in the *Tribune* itself. In September 1976, George Bliss had published a twenty-five-hundred-word essay titled "The Unbelievable Case of Chicago's 'Welfare Queen'"—the most expansive article he'd ever written on Linda Taylor. That story ran in Reagan's favorite magazine, *Human Events*.

Bliss's two-page feature wasn't going to win any journalism awards. It was littered with misspelled names and inflated numbers, including the assertion "that the trail of frauds left by Linda amounted to more than a million dollars"—an estimate Bliss had never made in any of his stories for the *Tribune*. As Reagan noted in his commentary, the piece declared that Taylor was building up "her defense fund" with a secret stash of public aid checks, though no prosecutor or public official had alleged such a thing. The story said that Jack Sherwin had arrested Taylor for calling in a fake burglary after finding a "mass of public aid checks" in her apartment, and that Sherwin had then reported that arrest to the *Tribune*. Though none of that was true, nobody at *Human Events* was going to second-guess a three-time Pulitzer Prize winner.

The article that ran under Bliss's name read too smoothly, his *Tribune* colleagues believed, for him to have written it himself. Most likely, Bliss provided a set of facts and his good name, and *Human Events* wrote up the story, printing the text in its September 18 issue alongside a pitch to potential advertisers. ("The new *Human Events* readership study is filled

---

[*]   Reagan would say "welfare queen" at least one more time in a public setting. In 1981, during his first year as president, he'd argue that his cuts to social services had been "aimed at the abuses in the program," as exemplified by "the welfare queen" who was "collecting welfare under a hundred and twenty-three different names" and "also had fifty-five Social Security cards."

with decision-making information for businessmen," the ad boasted, "statistics which reveal, for example, that over 2,000 millionaires read *Human Events* every week.") Reagan left out some of the most salacious details from the *Human Events* piece, such as the claim that Taylor might have been involved in the theft of a newborn baby, a child who was "snatched from his mother's arms in 1964 in…Michael Reese Hospital by a woman dressed in white." Reagan had a specific story to tell, and it didn't have anything to do with kidnapping.

Bliss didn't have any interest in furthering Reagan's career or propping up the conservative movement. He didn't care about national politics, and he didn't subscribe to a particular ideology. Two years earlier, he'd done a piece on police brutality for the *Nation*, a magazine as revered on the Left as *Human Events* was on the Right. For Bliss, freelance writing was less a passion project than a paid gig. He needed to provide for his blended family—seven biological children and three stepchildren, ranging in age from fourteen to thirty-five. If *Human Events* wanted to pay him for an item on Chicago's welfare queen, he was more than willing to cash the check.

At age fifty-eight, Bliss was still in peak physical condition. He'd challenge young writers to a dash up the stairs of the St. Clair Hotel, with the finish line at the Chicago Press Club on the twenty-second floor. He never lost a race. But by 1976, people at the *Tribune* had started to notice a change in his disposition. Bliss was susceptible to depressive moods, and they'd gotten worse since his first wife had died in childbirth in 1959. His second marriage wasn't a happy one, and he was rarely satisfied by his accomplishments at work. Bliss drank heavily; although he'd duck out of the office for Alcoholics Anonymous meetings, he couldn't always stop himself from slamming down martinis at lunch. Some of his friends believed all that drinking was going to wreck his life. Others thought Bliss needed those drinks to dull his anguish.

In the latter part of 1975, Bliss had checked into a Chicago hospital to get psychiatric treatment. During that stint, he called the *Tribune*'s Chuck Neubauer to share a tip about a friend of Mayor Richard J. Daley who'd scored a break on his personal property taxes. They worked on the piece together, and it landed on the front page with both men's bylines. That was George Bliss—obsessed with getting his name in the paper, no matter the obstacles. The George Bliss who Neubauer saw in the newsroom a short while later seemed like an impostor. He was staring at the Saturday *Tribune*, pausing over the ads for what felt like hours. Bliss would sit at his desk and talk on the phone, but he couldn't manage to put out a story. In the first three months of 1976, he had forty-four bylines in the *Tribune*. In the last three months of the year, he had ten. Jim Strong, who'd succeeded Bliss as the *Tribune*'s labor editor, started to get calls from his predecessor at three in the morning. "I need a story for tomorrow," Bliss would whisper into the receiver. "You got anything?"

* * *

Jack Sherwin and Linda Taylor had it down to a routine. He'd arrest her, she'd make bail, and he'd find her and arrest her again for something else. On the morning of July 8, 1976, Sherwin drove to a community just on the Chicago side of the city limits, closer to Don Moore's suburban district in Midlothian than the Civic Center downtown. Three months earlier, Taylor had signed her name to a salmon-colored piece of paper, promising that she'd keep the clerk of the circuit court apprised of her whereabouts or risk having her bond revoked. She'd broken that agreement, and Sherwin had been tasked with bringing her back in.

Taylor hadn't improved her circumstances since she'd moved out of the dirty apartment on South Normal Avenue, the place where Sherwin had arrested her for stealing a fur coat. Her new neighborhood, West Pullman, had been exclusively white until the 1960s, when predatory lenders ushered in black residents just as the South Side's factories started shutting down. In the 1970s, the number of people living below the poverty line in West Pullman grew by 151 percent. Taylor professed to be one of them. Her only income during this period, she claimed, came from her Vietnam veteran husband Sherman Ray's unemployment checks.

In his police report, Sherwin didn't document any confrontations or death threats. He arrested Taylor for bond forfeiture, and some other officers transported her to police headquarters at 1121 South State Street. There was no dramatic bond hearing, no debate over whether Taylor was a victim or a victimizer. A new judge set her bail for $10,000, just a bit more than the amount she'd run out on. Again, Taylor paid up and got out of jail. The only thing that could break this pattern, it seemed, would be the start of Taylor's perpetually postponed welfare fraud trial. By the summer of 1976, that proceeding had been on the verge of getting under way for almost two years.

The docket sheet for *People of the State of Illinois v. Linda Taylor* listed more than thirty court dates as of the fall of 1976, very few of which included anything of substance. Taylor's February 25 evidentiary hearing had been continued to April 1, then to May 6, June 2, August 9, September 7, and October 25. These sorts of holdups weren't unusual in Chicago. The Cook County state's attorney's office was one of the largest in the nation and one of the most overburdened, with more than eight thousand felony indictments on the books in 1975 alone. The county's twenty-two criminal judges had backlogs of their own—one told the *Tribune* in 1976 that he had 350 pending cases—which meant that scheduling a trial could be a challenge even when all parties were ready to move forward. But in the Taylor case, as in most criminal matters, the bulk of the postponements came at the request of the defense attorney. In 1976, Taylor's lawyers were granted seven separate continuances, with most of those delaying the proceedings by at least a month.

A mere thirty defense attorneys handled the bulk of Chicago's criminal cases, and R. Eugene Pincham spread himself thinner than most. Pincham and his partners had so much business they couldn't have gotten it all done even in a fifty-day workweek. They also knew that delay, delay, delay could be a winning strategy. "Right after an incident emotions may run high," Pincham told the *Tribune* in 1971. "Time works in favor of justice." Time didn't always work in Pincham's favor. In November 1976, his associate lawyer Skip Gant was found in contempt of court after he asked to postpone a case that had already been delayed seventy times. The perturbed judge told the *Tribune* that Pincham "can't try every criminal case in Cook County"—that he owed it to his clients and the courts to parcel out some of that work to other lawyers.

By the end of 1976, Pincham had acceded to that suggestion. After twenty-five years as an attorney, the Chicago civil rights icon had been elected to a circuit court judgeship. As a consequence, Pincham needed to off-load his clients. *People of the State of Illinois v. Linda Taylor* got passed along to his younger colleagues, Gant and T. Lee Boyd. A change in counsel meant another continuance, to allow the defendant's new lawyers to get acquainted with her case. When Taylor's legal odyssey began, Illinois governor Dan Walker was announcing that "welfare abuse cannot be ignored" and Mayor Daley was celebrating his twentieth year in office. As of January 1977, Walker had been voted out, Daley was dead of a heart attack, and Taylor was still awaiting trial.

While Taylor's defense team deserved most of the credit or blame for the long interregnum between her arrest and trial, prosecutors hadn't been eager to rush things either. Given Taylor's notoriety, state's attorney Jim Piper felt an obligation to put her in prison for a very long time. The state's public aid code, though, stipulated that the theft of any amount of welfare money—even, hypothetically, $1 million—should be considered a misdemeanor. It would probably be easier, then, to lock up Taylor for stealing Everleana Brame's fur coat than for stealing thousands of dollars from the Illinois treasury. But that didn't seem like a fitting conclusion to the welfare queen story. If Piper couldn't score a heftier sentence, it would look as though Cook County had gone soft on America's least favorite welfare cheat.

Two years into the state's prosecution of Linda Taylor, Piper decided that his best move was to do nothing at all. The FBI, the Veterans Administration, and the Social Security Administration were all still investigating whether she'd committed federal crimes. In November 1976, Piper told U.S. attorneys from the Northern District of Illinois that he didn't want to go ahead with his case—the feds, he thought, would be more likely to deliver the punishment Taylor deserved. After more than a year of digging, representatives from various U.S. agencies suspected that Taylor had indeed filched federal money. The amount she'd allegedly stolen—$3,250 from the Veterans Administration and $3,757.40 via Social Security—was sizable but not staggering, less in total than what she'd been charged with taking from the State of Illinois. An FBI memorandum from July of that year indicated that at least one assistant U.S. attorney wanted Taylor prosecuted for those thefts. Federal lawyers also discussed charging her with mail fraud. Ultimately, though, the Northern District's indictment committee decided to let Illinois clean up its own mess. In the words of one U.S. attorney, "Any federal prosecution would only serve as saving face for the locals." Another FBI memo quoted a prosecutor as saying, "It was the state that blew this matter way out of proportion in the newspapers."

With the U.S. attorneys unwilling to help, it would be up to Jim Piper to finish what Jack Sherwin, George Bliss, and Don Moore had started. Piper got the break he needed in December 1976, when the Illinois Supreme Court ruled that welfare fraud could be prosecuted under the state criminal code rather than the public aid code. So long as you could prove intent, stealing a public aid check worth in excess of $150 would be considered a felony, just like stealing a fur coat. If Taylor was found guilty of numerous counts of theft and perjury, she could go to prison for up to twenty years. That would be long enough to set an example for all the other welfare cheaters, and to win Piper acclaim as the man who brought Linda Taylor to justice.

Given that favorable ruling by the state supreme court, Piper pressed to take the case to trial as soon as possible. Judge Mark Jones sympathized with the prosecutor's new sense of urgency. On February 22, 1977, in a building that had been rechristened the Richard J. Daley Center in honor of the recently deceased mayor, Jones told Taylor's attorneys that "this case has been on the docket too long." He demanded that all parties be ready to go to trial in two days. In a brief interview with the *Chicago Defender*, Taylor accused Piper of breaking into her apartment and stealing her ring, television, and dishes. The charges against her, she said, were "all lies, all lies."

"When this is over," she said in a manner the *Defender* described as "spritely," "I plan on suing all of them."

CHAPTER 8

The Fashionably Dressed Mrs. Taylor

Before he walked inside the Daley Center on February 24, 1977, Skip Gant stopped by a downtown flower shop to pick up a fresh carnation for his boutonniere. A few years earlier, Gant had rescued a blossom that a colleague had deemed unsuitable for his own lapel. It took less than twenty-four hours for that flower to become Gant's calling card. When he wore it to court the next day, a potential client flagged down the young lawyer. The building's shoeshine man had told him that if he needed a good attorney, he should look for the guy with the "beau-kwet."

Gant didn't feel particularly at ease at the Daley Center. Although his law degree came from Chicago's Loyola University, he'd gotten his education at the Cook County Criminal Courts Building, where the old folks in the gallery were happy to tell him if he'd flubbed a cross-examination. The neoclassical courthouse at West Twenty-Sixth Street and South California Avenue hadn't changed much since Al Capone had been convicted of tax evasion there in 1931. The air-conditioning didn't work and the overhead lights didn't illuminate much at all. Rodents and roaches sometimes scurried across the floors. The Daley Center was a whole lot fancier, a sleek modernist tower with a Picasso sculpture standing in the plaza outside. When the skyscraper opened for business in 1965, court personnel had a hard time keeping cases moving—all the lawyers were busy gawking at the spectacular skyline views. The Daley Center's courtrooms, with their private washrooms and glass-and-wood doors, had been built to handle civil cases. But within a couple of years, overcrowding at

Twenty-Sixth and Cal had bumped a bunch of criminal matters into these less grubby municipal quarters. A South Side lawyer with a South Side client, Gant would need to figure out how to win a case in the Loop.

Gant's mentor, R. Eugene Pincham, had told the *National Black Law Journal* in 1973 that "trying a criminal case is basically a situation of selling a product." Linda Taylor was a tough product to sell in any courtroom. Gant found her to be a reasonably cooperative client but not a trustworthy or deferential one. Some days she looked and acted like a schoolmarm, others like a central-casting caricature of a flamboyant Louisiana lady of the night. Everything she said and did felt like an act, and not one that would help Gant build a credible defense.

In her public appearances, Taylor did not dress like someone heeding the advice of counsel. On November 27, 1974, the date of her original indictment, she wore a thigh-length leather coat with shearling trim around the sleeves and collar. When a gust of wind threatened to blow off her black hat, she secured it to her head with her right hand, which was encased in a leather glove. A few months later, Taylor dressed for a hearing in a white blouse with a cleavage-baring cutout, a different leather coat with fur-trimmed cuffs and collar, white satin slacks, and a white tam-o'-shanter. In February 1976, Pincham—wearing a black pin-striped three-piece suit—stood beside a client who'd swaddled her body in black fur. Gant had no more luck getting Taylor to adopt a conservative look. During the trial, the Associated Press took note of her "brightly colored mod outfits with sparkling rings and bracelets." Among those outfits was a blue denim pantsuit, which Taylor had paired with a ginger Afro wig. Her husband, Sherman Ray, sported faux crocodile shoes with little goldfish embedded in the plastic heels—a gift from Taylor. Gant assumed the fish were as fake as the crocodile, but he never got close enough to know for sure.

When Taylor first got indicted, Gant hadn't yet passed the bar exam. As a law student in the early 1970s, he'd hounded Pincham in the hallway of the Criminal Courts building, looking for a chance to slip his résumé into the legendary lawyer's pocket. When that ploy didn't work, he camped out at Pincham's office at Eighty-Seventh and South Cottage

Grove. He'd sit in the waiting room from 3:30 p.m. until after midnight, one of many young black men hoping that the city's best black attorney might give him a minute of his time. Pincham eventually rewarded Gant's persistence, offering him $100 a week to go from courtroom to courtroom, asking for continuances in all the cases Pincham couldn't fit into his schedule. Gant spent his days as a jurisprudential punching bag, getting held in contempt of court and sometimes even sent to jail. As soon as he got out of his cell, he'd head to a different courtroom to ask for another postponement.

After Gant got his law license in 1975, he found his clients in a four-drawer, stand-up cabinet—the final resting place for small-time gambling and drug cases, and ones in which the defendants owed money the firm hadn't been able to collect. When Pincham became a circuit court judge in 1976, the Taylor case got shoved into that cabinet. The welfare queen hadn't been important enough to hand off to one of the other partners at Evins, Pincham, Fowlkes, and Cooper. It would be up to Gant and T. Lee Boyd to win at trial, and to get Taylor to pay her bill.

Gant knew that the evidence against Taylor was overwhelming. There was little doubt that she'd signed up for public aid as both Connie Walker and Linda Bennett, that she'd received checks under both names—under Illinois law, that was considered both "theft by deception" and "exerting unauthorized control" over state money—and that she'd perjured herself on her welfare applications and in front of a Cook County grand jury. Gant's best hope, then, was to make all that evidence go away. One year and ten continuances after Pincham had first sought to invalidate Jack Sherwin's search of Taylor's apartment, Gant called Taylor to the stand. When he asked the defendant to state her name, she didn't identify herself as Linda Taylor, and she didn't use any of the other aliases—Connie Walker, Linda Bennett, Sandra Brownlee—that Judge Mark Jones had deemed admissible. On this day, she said her name was Linda Wakefield. She said it again a few seconds later, speaking loudly enough this time that everyone in the room could hear her. Linda Wakefield was the name she'd signed on Patricia Parks's death certificate.

In this pretrial hearing, she told the story of her arrest in simple declarative sentences. On August 25, 1974, she was living at 8221 South Clyde Avenue. That morning, a group of Chicago police officers entered her home. They conducted a search. They seized her property. They did not show her a warrant. She did not consent to the search. She had not been in violation of any laws. Although Sherwin had written "Linda Taylor" on his arrest report, she denied ever giving the detective that name. Under cross-examination, she said she'd met Sherwin earlier in August 1974, when "he was searching Mrs. Taylor's home across the hall from me." When Sherwin brought her in on August 25, she said, he'd stolen the food she'd packed to feed her two children, just as the prosecutor Jim Piper had stolen her ring, television, and dishes.

Sherwin remembered their encounter differently. He testified that Taylor had invited him inside, and that they'd chatted for twenty minutes before he showed her a Michigan arrest warrant. Although he didn't have a warrant to search her apartment, another detective had waved Sherwin over after spotting possible contraband: Illinois Department of Public Aid ID cards. "None of them had the name that I knew the defendant by at that time," Sherwin said, "nor were any of them issued to that house, nor were any of them issued to the same person or at the same address." Gant countered that the detective had used an out-of-state arrest warrant as a pretense to invade Taylor's privacy: "Judge, the U.S. Constitution as well as the Illinois Constitution guarantees every person, every citizen— that includes Linda Taylor, Linda Bennett, Linda Smith, Linda Jones— the right to be secure in their homes."

Jones didn't buy that Linda Wakefield, Linda Taylor, or whoever it was sitting at the defendant's table had been done a grave injustice. "Obviously, the policeman in the exercise of his duties would be required to take the cards," he said. "No question about it in my mind." The motion to suppress evidence was denied. Gant's first tactic hadn't come close to succeeding, but he had learned an important lesson: No matter how many Bibles she swore on, Linda Taylor wasn't going to tell the truth. She wouldn't take the stand again.

* * *

Pincham had taught his protégé that jurors need someone to latch on to, to tell them what to think and how to feel. When Gant opened the door to Mark Jones's well-appointed, air-conditioned fifteenth-floor court-room, he acted as though he was still in the friendlier, grimier confines of the Criminal Courts building at Twenty-Sixth and California. Taylor's lawyer, a new carnation affixed to his suit, pantomimed friendship and familiarity with the clerk and bailiff, trying his best to make them laugh. If the defense attorney looked comfortable, the people deciding his client's fate would feel comfortable with him.

It took four days to pick a jury, a process that just one of the Chicago papers deemed worthy of scrutiny. The *Chicago Defender* reported that prosecutors Jim Piper and James Sternik had "used eight of their ten peremptory challenges to dismiss the first eight prospective jurors—all of whom were welfare recipients." The city's black newspaper was also the lone media outlet to note the jury's racial makeup. Eight women would sit in judgment of Linda Taylor, five of them white and three of them black. They were joined by four white men.

Given that he'd failed to make those public aid ID cards disappear, Gant needed to convince a mostly white jury to empathize with a South Side welfare cheat. On March 4, 1977, the defense attorney told the jurors that Linda Taylor wasn't who she'd been made out to be. "The term 'welfare queen' gives the image of a cunning, slick woman who could dupe the all-massive, politically job-laden Department of Public Aid," he said in his opening statement. "This welfare queen syndrome was an effort of the State of Illinois and Department of Public Aid to cover up their own frailties. This woman is the fall guy."

Piper countered that Taylor was no scapegoat. Rather, she'd made marks out of the kindhearted social workers who tried to ensure that everyone in Chicago had enough to eat. If well-intentioned bureaucrats had been Taylor's dupes, then Jack Sherwin was the cop she couldn't fool twice. Piper described how the detective had first run across Taylor in 1972, then tracked her to Michigan, grabbed her fingerprints, and arrested her. Sherwin hadn't taken part in any kind of cover-up. He was the only man who'd cared enough to stop an unrepentant thief.

Sherwin led off the prosecution's case, repeating his account of Taylor's 1974 arrest for the benefit of the jury. He said he'd held up one of Taylor's Department of Public Aid ID cards—one of them identified her as Connie Walker, the other as Linda Bennett—and urged the arrestee to take a closer look. "Is this your card?" he'd asked.

"No," Taylor had responded.

"I am looking at this card," Sherwin had said back in 1974, "and I am looking at you, and I am looking at this card, and I am looking at you, and I am looking at this card, and I am looking at you, and you are telling me this is not your card?"

According to Sherwin, Taylor eventually confessed that she'd received public aid as Walker "for a while" and as Bennett at some indeterminate time in the past, "but not anymore." That was the closest she ever came, at least in Sherwin's presence, to an admission of guilt.

The *Defender*'s Nathaniel Clay saw the defendant as the day's clear loser. Taylor, he wrote, appeared "pained and pensive," sitting "in worried silence as her two young black defense attorneys were overruled time and again." That evening, Walter Cronkite narrated a report on the *CBS Evening News*, one that told the familiar story of Taylor's role in the 1976 campaign.

> During last year's race for the Republican presidential nomination, Ronald Reagan talked often about welfare abuses, and he almost always cited the case of an unnamed Chicago woman he says used eighty names to collect more than a hundred and fifty thousand dollars in tax-free income. Well, testimony began in Chicago today in the fraud trial of that woman, forty-eight-year-old Linda Taylor, called by newspapers the "welfare queen." The amount she's charged with receiving is not a hundred and fifty thousand dollars but eight thousand dollars. The prosecutor says he must go with what he can prove.

The nation's most-watched newscast, helmed by the journalist known as the most trusted man in America, beamed Taylor's unsmiling visage and Gant's red carnation into more than ten million homes on March

7, 1977. As Cronkite said the words "welfare queen," the screen showed Taylor walking through the Daley Center, her torso sheathed in a tight-fitting caramel-colored leather jacket. When he mentioned her hypothetical prison sentence, the camera zoomed in on the left side of Taylor's face. At that moment, she brought her hand up to scratch her nose, revealing the huge, dark stone on her right ring finger.

While television cameras crowded the halls of the fifteenth floor, national print coverage of the Taylor trial was sparse. Collectively, the big papers ran a solitary takeout on the welfare queen's legal imbroglio, a *Washington Post* piece that noted how "details of Taylor's escapades have been reported with great relish by Chicago newspapers, providing some tongue-clucking reading for the citizenry." Even the Chicago papers kept their relish to a minimum, playing the trial as one local story among many. The *Chicago Tribune*'s first dispatch, a 230-word news brief by Daley Center beat reporter Charles Mount, ran in a small box on page ten of March 8's final edition.

That same day, the *Tribune* published a front-page piece by George Bliss and Michael Hirsley on the many failings of the Cook County probation system. The *Tribune*'s city editor, Bernard Judge, didn't think he needed Bliss at the Daley Center. Bliss was a reporter, not a wordsmith, and there wasn't much left to uncover about a human-interest story in which the human interest had expired. Between March 4 and March 18, the *Tribune* ran three separate front-page stories about the clubbing of baby seals, but Linda Taylor—the villain Bliss and the *Tribune* had introduced to the world two and a half years earlier—never made it to section one, page one.

During the second week of testimony in Jones's courtroom, the *Tribune* did publish a front-pager on a Cook County court case. A onetime Chicago police officer had been acquitted of trying to kill his son—the boy had survived after his father had allegedly hit him on the head during a fishing trip and tossed him in Lake Michigan. "Ex-cop rejoices," the subhead said. "Youth, 18, stunned." Taylor's days in court weren't nearly so shocking or lurid. What had gained purchase in the press as a story about luxury cars and dead husbands had transformed, in a court of law, into a mostly humdrum tale of canceled checks. But for those who cared to look and listen, the trial served as a weeks-long answer to the question the *Tribune* had asked but never satisfactorily pursued: What had Linda Taylor done, and how had she done it?

* * *

When Taylor applied for government assistance as Linda Bennett, she didn't use a driver's license, Social Security card, or birth certificate to prove she was who she said she was. At 9 a.m. on October 24, 1973, she showed a public aid eligibility worker her wrist, which carried an armband from Cook County Hospital. She'd just been discharged, she said, after getting treated for the lung disease sarcoidosis. Using an armband as a form of identification was unconventional, but Annette Slimkowski allowed it. This woman was sick and desperate, and intake workers weren't in the habit of shooing away sick and desperate people.

On March 9, 1977, three-and-a-half years after she'd sat across from Taylor at the public aid office at East Eightieth and South Cottage Grove, Slimkowski testified that Linda Bennett had told her she'd never received public assistance before. "She did not know the whereabouts of all of her husbands," Slimkowski said, and she had four children under the age of five: William, Duke, Joseph, and Electra. The two oldest boys had a white father and had been born in Arkansas, the applicant said. The father of the two younger children had left the family in 1973. In addition to lung disease, she had a heart condition that would soon require surgery. She hadn't been able to pay rent for three months. She'd sold her last item of jewelry, a ring, to a neighbor that very morning.

Slimkowski quickly put through an approval for emergency aid. She gave Taylor food vouchers that day, and a pair of checks totaling $419.33 arrived at her door the following week. The intake worker had spent less time pondering whether the state should send Taylor money than she had puzzling over her race, which she was obliged to ask about to ensure that the department didn't violate applicants' civil rights.

"You had a hard time telling whether this person was white or was black?" defense attorney T. Lee Boyd asked on cross-examination.

"I would have to ask her," Slimkowski said.

"Have you ever observed a pale black person?" Boyd continued.

"Yes," she replied.

"Would you say that it is nothing to see a pale black person?"

"If the paleness is the only problem, but it was not the only feature."

"Tell us the other problem."

"She had as I recall Caucasian features," Slimkowski said.

Boyd had no further questions.

In subsequent testimony, public aid employees said that Taylor's push to get emergency aid was a ploy to cement her name on the rolls with minimal vetting. Once the department fast-tracked emergency relief, it would also start mailing out monthly Aid to Families with Dependent Children payments. It might take ninety days or longer for anyone in the department to give a new file a second glance, and Taylor did her best to expand that timeframe. Whenever she moved to a new neighborhood, her paperwork would transfer to a caseworker who covered that specific region, restarting the clock on a potential in-home visit to verify her eligibility. While both Sherwin and one of Taylor's landlords testified that they'd seen her with only two children, she goosed her payout by listing four on her application. By claiming that those kids were very young, she also ensured that the Department of Public Aid wouldn't be able to confirm their existence by checking school records. It was a simple system, one that preyed on the sympathies of overworked bureaucrats and exploited rules designed to help the vulnerable and destitute. Most of the time, it worked.

In April 1974, when Taylor was already getting welfare money as Connie Walker and Linda Bennett, she dropped into the public aid office at 1010 North Milwaukee Avenue and launched into her usual routine. She told the intake worker that she was Sandra Brownlee—her daughter's name—and that she'd never been on AFDC before. She was penniless after the death of her stepfather, and she needed emergency aid for a set of triplets and two sets of twins. It was essentially the same story she'd told an eligibility examiner in Michigan in 1971—the case that had clued Jack Sherwin in to Taylor's history of scams. This time, the intake worker got suspicious. Rather than grant Taylor's emergency request,

Etta Tomczyk sent an investigator to Taylor's alleged home address of 439 North Kedzie Avenue. When she couldn't be found, her application for public assistance was denied.

No newspapers or wire services reported on any of this testimony. The *Tribune*'s Mount did write, however, that the prosecution "suffered a setback" when Slimkowski and another public aid official failed to identify Taylor in the courtroom. After three or four years and thousands of client interviews, they explained, they couldn't pick Linda Bennett out of a crowd. The prosecutors, undaunted, told the jury that Taylor's looks weren't all that material. The man they described as their "key witness" was someone who'd never seen Taylor in person.

David Grimes had been eyeballing Linda Taylor's handwriting since the fall of 1974. After Taylor's arrest, the Cook County state's attorney's office had sent the FBI document examiner a package full of Illinois treasury checks. The back of each of those checks carried the all-caps admonition "KNOW YOUR ENDORSER," followed by a longer warning to potential fraudsters: "I understand that the endorsement hereon or deposit to the account of the within named payee is done with the understanding that payment will be from federal and/or state funds and that any false claims, statements, or documents, or concealment of a material fact may be prosecuted under applicable federal or state laws." Taylor didn't always keep her aliases straight when putting her pen to the endorsement line. On one check issued in August 1974, she signed "Connie Walker," crossed it out, and wrote "Linda Bennett" instead.*

The prosecution's case depended on those signatures. Grimes had compared the backs of Taylor's welfare checks to her known handwriting, including nearly a hundred pages' worth of samples the FBI had procured from her under court order in 1974 and 1975. Any writing obtained under duress was suspect, though, especially when it had been acquired from a likely scammer. More valuable was the scribbling Taylor

---

* Three of the canceled treasury checks submitted to the FBI carried an additional signature on the back: Robert Taylor. Although this Robert Taylor seems to be the likeliest source for Linda Taylor's best-known surname, no individual by that name ever materialized in court or in the press.

had done of her own free will. At the FBI laboratory in Washington, DC, Grimes had pored over the all-caps scrawl on Taylor's applications for public assistance, the neat script on her driver's licenses and car titles, and the loops and slashes on the order forms for *How to Tell Fortunes with Cards* and *Psychic Perception: The Magic of Extrasensory Powers*. He'd learned to copy Taylor's penmanship, writing her various names on blank sheets of paper and drawing arrows to point out distinctive characteristics: the downward curl at the top of the capital *C* in *Connie*, the horizontal slash that crossed the double *t* in *Bennett*.

About a month before the trial, Piper had asked Grimes if they could get together to talk about his testimony. "I don't know what we have to talk about," the document examiner told the state's attorney. "I saw what I saw." Grimes had told Piper he didn't need to bring any comparison charts to show the jury. "I've testified dozens of times," he'd said. "I say what my opinion is, and that's good as gold."

Grimes's opinion was that the Connie Walker and Linda Bennett signatures on thirteen of the twenty-three checks at issue matched Taylor's known writing. Eight of the remaining ten endorsements were probably a match, while the other two "may have been the same." Although he didn't feel confident enough to issue a definitive opinion about every signature, Grimes testified that he was absolutely certain about those thirteen checks. If the jurors believed him, they'd have no choice but to find Taylor guilty.

* * *

Skip Gant began his closing argument as R. Eugene Pincham once had: by invoking the Gospel of Matthew. "So the last shall come first and the first shall come last," the defense attorney said, telling the eight women and four men in the jury box that they'd been "called here for a particular purpose." They'd been chosen to serve because of their impartiality, and impartiality was what this case demanded. Gant said that guilt should not be determined by the number of witnesses the state calls, nor "by the number of documents that you see spread before you." Rather, it should be decided based on the quality of the evidence. By that measure, he told the jurors, the prosecution of Linda Taylor had been a colossal failure.

David Grimes had given Gant an opening to ratchet up the jurors' reasonable doubt. The document examiner had come off as arrogant and aloof—he hadn't deigned to walk through his analyses or explain how he'd gone about assessing Taylor's letter forms. "I asked him, 'Mr. Grimes, did you use any microscopes?'" Gant reminded the jury. "What was his answer? 'Well, that depends on what you mean by a microscope.'" Grimes had told everyone in the courtroom that they should just take his word for it. Gant argued that the "almighty handwriting expert from Washington, DC," hadn't done enough to earn their trust.

Taylor's attorney also questioned the integrity of Jack Sherwin. Under cross-examination, Sherwin had said that another detective had looked through Taylor's purse. Piper's notes, however, indicated that Sherwin had searched the purse himself. "Something is either mistaken or someone is lying," Gant said. "If they are mistaken, then they can be mistaken about half the other things in this case. That constitutes proof beyond a reasonable doubt. And if they are lying, they can be lying about other things."

Gant didn't claim that Taylor was a victim, and he didn't say her acquittal would represent a triumph of good over evil. He simply urged the jurors to follow the law, even if it left them nauseous. "You may feel that that little lady sitting over there, she done something," Gant said, gesturing dramatically in Taylor's direction, his voice rising.

You may feel that maybe she signed one of these documents. You may feel that, but you have to be convinced beyond a reasonable doubt that they proved it.

Now, you may say, "Well, Mr. Gant, that seems a little unfair." You may think, *Well, the system is not right*. And I am not here to quibble with you as to what is right and what is wrong....

You may feel the law ought to be changed. But this, ladies and gentlemen, this is not the forum wherein you will accomplish that.

The young carnation-wearing lawyer wrapped up his thirty-minute monologue by saying that the only thing more foolish than trusting Linda Taylor would be trusting the U.S. government. "If there is one thing that the citizenry of this country has learned in the last ten years, especially in the mid and late nineteen seventies as a result of the Watergate incident," Gant said, it's that "it is healthy for we as citizens to scrutinize the conduct and the actions of government officials."

When Gant sat down, a government official got to his feet. Jim Piper told the jurors that Sherwin could've left Taylor's apartment when he saw those welfare ID cards; instead, he chose to stick around to protect the taxpayers' money. David Grimes, too, "was a person...of integrity," a credentialed analyst who deserved the jury's deference. "He is the expert, ladies and gentlemen," the prosecutor said. Linda Taylor, by contrast, was "just a parasite." If she'd been singled out, Piper argued, that wasn't necessarily a bad thing. "When the public learns that this defendant was proven guilty beyond a reasonable doubt of welfare fraud and a jury of her peers convicted her on all counts and counts on perjury...it will have some deterrent," he said. Piper added, "It is not welfare that is on trial....It is the fraud. It is the depriving. You know, there is only so much water in the well."

Taylor, who was wearing glasses and a white pantsuit, "sat stoically through the summations," reported the Associated Press. The *Defender* saw something different. "With her face pinched and drawn, the fashionably dressed Mrs. Taylor twitched nervously at the defense table," the black newspaper wrote. As Taylor either twitched or sat impassively, Jones read the jurors their instructions, then sent them off to deliberate.

A few seconds after the alternate juror collected her coat, Gant and Boyd requested a mistrial, telling the judge that he'd read the jury instructions out of order. "You seriously offer that as grounds for mistrial?" Jones asked. The defense attorneys were serious. So was the judge. The motion was denied. A short while after this failed maneuver, Boyd blew up. "All you have done throughout this case, judge, is turn around and let [the prosecutors] do exactly what they want to do," he said.

Boyd's accusation would've been more credible in almost any other courtroom in Chicago. Although he hadn't given the defense's Hail

Mary motion much consideration, Jones was known as a fair and incorruptible arbiter in a city where such a thing couldn't be taken for granted. Six years after the Taylor trial, the *Tribune* revealed the existence of Operation Greylord, a sting operation in which undercover federal agents planted bugs in Cook County judges' chambers. Among the fifteen judges convicted of bribe collecting and case fixing was Wayne Olson, who in 1974 had reduced Taylor's bond in a court hearing after her extradition from Arizona to Illinois. Although no allegations were ever made about Olson's behavior vis-à-vis Taylor, he was sentenced to twelve years in prison for soliciting and accepting bribes as a narcotics court judge. The evidence used to convict Olson included a recording in which he'd enthused, "I love people that take dough, because you know exactly where you stand."

Attorneys had a tougher time knowing where they stood with Mark Jones. A contemporary of Pincham's, Jones had been the first black lawyer to work in the civil division of the Cook County state's attorney's office before winning election to a judgeship in 1963. His easygoing manner on the bench belied his fierce resolve. In the mid-1970s, Jones had insisted on hearing a case involving the head of the American Nazi Party despite receiving anonymous threats that he'd be killed if he didn't stand down. He wasn't going to be flustered by an angry defense lawyer. "You may feel that way," Jones said in response to Boyd's complaint that he'd given the prosecution preferential treatment, "but there is no facts to support that."

Taylor's attorneys didn't have much time to feel sorry for themselves. It took just six hours for the jury to reach a consensus.

On the evening of March 17, the foreman passed a pile of papers to the clerk. The first sheet was the verdict form for count one, theft by deception of State of Illinois treasury check PB 7454065, a payment of $306 issued to Linda Bennett on October 31, 1973.

"We, the jury, find the defendant, Linda Bennett, also known as Connie Walker, also known as Linda Taylor, guilty of theft of property of value in excess of a hundred and fifty dollars." Linda Taylor was guilty of a felony.

Next was count two, exerting unauthorized control over the same Illinois treasury check.

"We, the jury, find the defendant, Linda Bennett, also known as Connie Walker, also known as Linda Taylor, guilty of theft of property." Another felony.

Count three, theft by deception of a check for $249.33, issued to Linda Bennett on December 14, 1973:

"We, the jury, find the defendant, Linda Bennett, also known as Connie Walker, also known as Linda Taylor, guilty of theft in excess of a hundred and fifty dollars."

Count four, exerting unauthorized control:

"We, the jury, find the defendant, Linda Bennett, also known as Connie Walker, also known as Linda Taylor, guilty of theft of property."

After the clerk read guilty verdicts for three more counts, she got permission to stop reading each sheet of paper in full.

"Count eight, guilty. Count nine, guilty. Count ten, guilty. Count eleven, guilty. Count twelve, guilty. Count thirteen, guilty."

Before the case went to the jury, the prosecutors had dropped three of the perjury counts as well as two theft counts that weren't tied to specific checks. Taylor was found guilty of the remaining three counts of perjury and forty-six counts of theft. After the clerk said "guilty" forty-nine times, Jones asked the twelve jurors to affirm that these were indeed their verdicts. All twelve said yes.

Now that Taylor was a felon forty-nine times over, Jones had to decide whether she could remain free while she awaited sentencing. When asked about her living situation, Taylor told the judge that two of her children had been taken from her. "Mr. Piper had them put in the juvenile home because one of them was a white child and another one was dark," she said.

That accusation made Piper angry. He said the children had been taken away by the juvenile court, and that blood tests were being done to determine their parentage.

"I don't want to get into that," Jones said. "She may remain at large on the same bond she has now."

THE QUEEN

The *Tribune* published a short, dry account of Taylor's conviction on page three of the Friday paper. The *Chicago Sun-Times*, which put Taylor on the front page, added a bit of courtroom color, writing that "Miss Taylor showed no emotion at the reading of each guilty finding by the clerk," an observation echoed by the Associated Press. The *Defender*, again, had an alternative perspective. Taylor appeared "nervous and gloom-stricken," Nathaniel Clay wrote. "Fighting back the tears, Mrs. Taylor, awaiting the jury's verdict, was overheard to murmur, 'Only God can help me now.'"

Skip Gant had set out to change one juror's mind. In Clay's view, he'd never had a chance. "Although it was obvious from the very beginning of her two-week trial that she was 'guilty as hell,'" he wrote, the predominantly white jury, one from which welfare recipients had repeatedly been struck, "had their minds made up before they retired to deliberate the defendant's fate."

Everything Gant had said in his opening statement was true. The Illinois Department of Public Aid was a dysfunctional agency, and Taylor had been the fall guy for a state government whose failings were monumental. But Taylor wasn't just the fall guy for the Public Aid Department. She was the fall guy for everyone who'd lost his job, or had a hefty tax bill, or was angry about his lot in life and the direction of his country. R. Eugene Pincham had made his career by winning over white jurors, but even the great Pincham couldn't have done much with Linda Taylor. She was guilty as hell, and she was someone it felt good to punish.

When Taylor emerged from the courtroom, she didn't look ashamed or chastened. The newly convicted felon grinned broadly as she strode past a swarm of lights and cameras. When she stopped at the elevator, waiting for a ride down from the fifteenth floor, the press pushed in tighter.

"Ms. Taylor, what are your feelings after the verdict?"

She turned her back and stared at the wall, ignoring the handheld microphone bobbing near her mouth.

"Ms. Taylor, you said earlier that the verdict would be in the hands of God. Do you feel that it was a fair verdict tonight?"

She jammed her right hand on the down button, impatient for the elevator to whisk her away.

"What do you intend to do now, Mrs. Taylor?"

She tilted her head upward, haughty and dismissive.

"You're not going to talk to us, are you?"

She shook her head no.

CHAPTER 9
She Couldn't Stop

Linda Taylor's probation officer couldn't find her. The residence she'd listed on South Harvard Avenue was a vacant lot, and nobody on the block had seen her or knew who she was. A few days after she'd been found guilty of forty-nine felonies, Taylor had dropped out of sight.

And then, suddenly, she reappeared. When Taylor showed up at the Daley Center on March 25, 1977, she was carrying an enormous Bible. At her bond revocation hearing, she told Judge Mark Jones that she'd gone into hiding "to avoid police harassment." Jack Sherwin was in attendance, and Taylor faced him as she spoke. "Since you came and searched my house, I've got several places I can stay," she said, with the *Tribune* noting her additional claim that "she attended church meetings at different locations and often spent the night where the meetings were held." She told the judge her primary residence was a different place on South Harvard Avenue, where she lived with her husband, Sherman Ray; four children; and two dogs.

Jones was skeptical. "I'm not sure where she lives," he said. "We couldn't find her, and the state couldn't find her." The judge declared that he was revoking Taylor's bond and sending her to jail.

"Judge, can I say something?" she asked. "They're looking for Linda Taylor, and I'm not Linda Taylor."

Jones's response: "Take her away."

While the Bible was a new accessory, Taylor didn't say or do much in the last week of March 1977 that she hadn't said or done before.

A month earlier, she'd denied that she was Linda Taylor in a pretrial hearing. In July 1976, she'd gone to jail for changing addresses without informing the court. That punishment hadn't deterred her, and neither had anything else. In his closing statement, Jim Piper told the jury that Taylor had cashed welfare checks even after getting arrested in August 1974. She'd also conned the Public Aid Department into paying for her personal housekeeper, taking advantage of a service the state provided for those too ill to take care of their own children. It was a scam on top of a scam. "She was so greedy she couldn't stop," the prosecutor said.

At Taylor's sentencing hearing on May 12, Piper described her "cold, calculated plan to collect welfare checks like clockwork," a scheme that was "an insult to all the hardworking people of the county." The prosecutor asked Jones to give Taylor a sentence that would deter other potential cheats. Piper thought two decades in prison would do the trick.

In arguing for leniency for his client, Skip Gant again brought up Watergate. "If there is anybody in the history of mankind who duped anyone, it was Richard Nixon," he said. "He didn't even get probation." Gant also cited French singer and actor Claudine Longet, who was serving just thirty days behind bars for criminally negligent homicide after killing her Olympic skier boyfriend, and newspaper heir Patty Hearst, who'd been sentenced earlier that week to five years' probation for her role in a 1974 Symbionese Liberation Army crime spree. Taylor should get probation, too, Gant proclaimed—she was "much less a threat" than the machine-gun-toting Hearst. "Black schoolchildren in Chicago will take a more cynical view of the criminal justice system," he said, if Taylor's punishment was disproportionate to her crimes.

In addition to figuring out where to place Taylor on the spectrum of mid-1970s female notoriety, Mark Jones had to sift through a huge stack of mail. The judge told Piper and Gant that he'd been besieged by letter writers—that people around the country had been "telling me what to do." Jones definitely wasn't giving Taylor probation, but twenty years behind bars seemed like an absurd sentence for stealing just less than $9,000. The judge's first move was to reduce the forty-six counts of theft against Taylor to twenty-three, one for each check she'd stolen. That was a consequence of an Illinois rule that prohibited a defendant from being convicted of two offenses that arose from a single act (i.e., the theft of one welfare check). Jones eliminated each count of "theft by deception," leaving in place the jury's twenty-three guilty verdicts for exerting unauthorized control over state property. For each of those counts of theft, he sentenced Taylor to a minimum of two years and a maximum of six years in a state penitentiary, with those terms to be served concurrently. When she'd done that time, she would be imprisoned an additional one year and one day for perjury.

Taylor, who was dressed in a white pantsuit—the same muted ensemble she'd worn for closing arguments—didn't make a scene upon hearing that she'd be locked up for three to seven years. The *Chicago Defender* reported that she'd "quietly replied 'No'" when asked if she had any words to offer in her defense, while the *Sun-Times* added that she had tears in her eyes when Jones read the verdict. "Linda Taylor, the so-called welfare queen, was sentenced in a Chicago courtroom today," Walter Cronkite announced on the *CBS Evening News*. The report lasted just fifteen seconds.

* * *

Before, during, and after her trial, Taylor acted as though she had a compulsion to lie and steal. Prosecutor Jim Piper argued that there wasn't anything complicated about Taylor's behavior: She was greedy, and she took what she wanted with no regard for the consequences. A new member of Taylor's legal team offered an alternate explanation. "I'm concerned about her mental capacities," William Starke said in a hearing in Jones's Daley Center courtroom.

Starke wasn't one of Chicago's most respectable lawyers. His law partners had shut down their firm earlier in the 1970s because money from Starke's clients never seemed to leave his own pocket. A decade after Taylor's trial, he'd be disbarred due to "dishonesty, fraud, deceit, and misrepresentation." But in 1977, with Skip Gant and T. Lee Boyd having failed to stave off a multiyear prison stint, Starke presented Taylor with a new legal strategy. "If she was convicted at a time when she was mentally incompetent, then the trial would have to be declared a nullity," he told the *Sun-Times*.

At a hearing on March 31, Starke persuaded Jones to have Taylor evaluated by a pair of psychiatrists. But when the judge looked over the psychiatrists' report several weeks later, he wasn't swayed by the argument that Taylor had been mentally incompetent to stand trial. Starke disappeared from the scene just as quickly as he'd arrived, and that psych evaluation wasn't written about in the press or included in Taylor's court file. The report's conclusions did surface a year later, as part of a petition in Taylor's other outstanding legal matter—the case in which she'd been accused of stealing Everleana Brame's fur coat, TV set, and electric can opener. In that petition, another of Taylor's lawyers wrote that he'd spoken with Boyd, R. Eugene Pincham, and Jeannette Nottingham—the woman who'd represented Taylor in the fight over Patricia Parks's estate—all of whom said that she "was incapable of knowing whether or not she was telling the truth." Taylor's attorney in the Brame burglary case also said he'd looked over "the reports of two psychiatrists who examined her which referred to her as being psychotic and unable to understand the nature of the proceedings of which she was a defendant."

In an interview with the *Defender* in early May, the pastor of Chicago's St. Paul Church of God in Christ said that Taylor "should be given psychiatric help, not an extensive jail sentence." This was a minority opinion. If Taylor wasn't entirely responsible for her own actions, that would undermine the larger narrative that had been constructed around her, one in which she had come to represent the archetypal welfare fraudster. And so, like every other circumstance that complicated the Linda Taylor story, the psychiatrists' report got cast aside.

On the day of Taylor's sentencing, her lawyers filed a notice of appeal on their client's behalf. Over the prosecutors' objections, Jones set an appeal bond of $50,000. Taylor's daughter, Sandra Brownlee, said that she and her family would get to work raising the $5,000 in cash they'd need to get her mother free.

* * *

Although he hadn't stayed on the Linda Taylor beat, George Bliss still kept in close contact with the Legislative Advisory Committee on Public Aid. On March 20, 1977, he quoted the committee's executive director, Joel Edelman, in a piece about the Public Aid Department's largely failed efforts to track down absentee fathers. According to Edelman, many of those missing dads weren't really missing—they just hid from caseworkers to ensure that their families would continue to qualify for aid. The agency's policy of informing welfare recipients in advance about home visits, Edelman said, was like "a bank telling a bank robber when guards at the bank will be absent."

By the early part of 1977, though, Bliss had mostly moved away from public aid stories. In addition to working on the articles on the Cook County probation system that ran during Taylor's trial, Bliss devoted three months to reporting on child pornography and child sex trafficking. The four-part series he co-bylined with Michael Sneed led to U.S. Senate hearings and the passage of the Protection of Children Against Sexual Exploitation Act, the first federal legislation to make the production and distribution of child porn a criminal act.

That was the last great success of Bliss's professional career. Doctors had diagnosed him as bipolar, and no treatment eased his symptoms. Bliss spent most of the workday sitting at his desk making phone calls. He'd ring up his adult children, telling them the paper's top brass wanted to let him go. "Larry," he'd tell his thirty-four-year-old son, "they're looking at me." One morning, he called his colleague Bill Mullen before work. Bliss was in tears, saying he couldn't remember how to drive to Tribune Tower. He'd really started to panic after he'd turned his car around and realized he didn't know how to make it back home.

Management at the *Chicago Tribune* didn't have any intention of firing George Bliss. In August 1977, after Bliss had checked into Lutheran General Hospital in Chicago's northern suburbs, the newspaper's editor, Clayton Kirkpatrick, sent him a note on *Tribune* letterhead. "We miss you around here," he wrote. "There are all kinds of projects awaiting your return, and I hope that you can be back on the job soon. However, there is no need for you to rush your recovery—we want you completely restored and with your old enthusiasm when you return."

Bliss was given shock treatments at Lutheran General. They didn't help. Shortly after that inpatient stint, the *Tribune* sent him to a psychiatric facility in New Jersey. That didn't work either. When he came back to Chicago after six months on the East Coast, Bliss was prescribed lithium. The medication flattened him out. The last vestiges of his old enthusiasm were gone.

When Bliss walked back into the *Tribune*'s newsroom in May 1978, his colleagues were dismayed. His face was sunken, and his emaciated torso disappeared inside his baggy off-the-rack suits. Bill Recktenwald, who'd worked with Bliss at the Better Government Association before joining the *Tribune*, noticed one day that his friend had blood on his collar. Later, he learned that Bliss had thrown himself down a small staircase. His ten children heard their father's cry for help very clearly. In August, Bliss's son Larry insisted on taking him to see another doctor. At that appointment, Bliss said he couldn't stand to be alive anymore. Larry couldn't believe that the doctor had just let them leave the office.

On September 2, the family convened for Bliss's daughter Carol's wedding. Bliss had told the doctor that he was terrified he'd make a fool of himself. The father of the bride managed to walk his daughter down the aisle, then faded into the background. Unless you were looking for him, you wouldn't have known he was there. A photo taken at the reception showed twelve people looking straight at the camera. Bliss was in the middle of the frame, staring off to the side, unsmiling.

The day after the wedding, Bliss asked three of his sons to play a round of golf. He'd dug up some of his best stories on the course—politicians, he found, talked more freely when they were roaming the fairways. But golf wasn't just an amusement for Bliss. He'd been the *Tribune* champ for years, and was such a great shotmaker that some of his playing partners thought he could've gone pro. That Sunday, he shot a 44 on the front nine and a 36 on the back. An 80 was a relatively poor round for him, but Bliss's children were amazed that he'd played so well considering how bad he looked.

The following weekend, on the night of Sunday, September 10, Bliss and his wife, Therese, went to a birthday party in Western Springs, a Chicago suburb fifteen miles from their home in Oak Lawn, Illinois. They were celebrating the father of Bliss's first wife, Helen. Although thinking about Helen's death in childbirth caused Bliss tremendous pain, he loved his former father-in-law, a man who was crowned "king of the family" each Christmas by his children and grandchildren. On their way home, Bliss and Therese stopped by his son Larry's house to say a quick hello. Therese told Larry the party had been good for her husband. "I think your dad's doing better," she said.

At around five thirty the next morning, Bliss's sixteen-year-old son, Terry, and twenty-two-year-old stepson, Charles, woke up to the sound of gunshots. When they opened the door to their parents' bedroom, they heard their mother moaning, "What happened? What happened?" Charles ran to call the police, while Terry stooped to the floor to give his father mouth-to-mouth resuscitation. When an officer arrived at the house a few minutes later, he found no sign of forced entry, and no evidence that the home had been burglarized. Therese had lost consciousness. She was lying in bed, with gunshot wounds to her right arm and the back of her head. Bliss was on the floor, faceup. He, too, was unconscious, and had a bullet wound on the side of his head, four and a quarter inches above the midpoint of his right ear. On the ground, twelve inches from his right hand, was a .38 caliber Colt revolver. Paramedics transported both of them to the emergency room at Christ Hospital. The fifty-one-year-old Therese Bliss was rushed into surgery. George Bliss was pronounced dead on arrival at 6:42 a.m. on September 11, 1978. He was sixty.

While there wasn't any kind of note at the scene, nobody who'd been in the room had any doubts about what had happened: Bliss had shot his wife, then shot and killed himself. The revolver was a blue steel snub-nosed Detective Special, the kind plainclothes officers concealed in their coat pockets. A check of the weapon's serial number showed that it was registered to Bliss's friend John L. Sullivan, the man he'd praised in the *Tribune* in 1951 as "the politest and most efficient policeman in Chicago." The police officer and the police reporter had grown up together as young men on their respective beats, and they'd stayed close in the decades since. Sullivan told the Oak Lawn police that Bliss had asked to borrow the gun on September 9, saying he needed protection in case a burglar tried to steal the gifts that had piled up after his daughter's wedding. Bliss had never previously kept a gun in the house—he thought it was too dangerous with all the kids around. Thirty-six hours after getting hold of Sullivan's revolver, Bliss fired the weapon twice, leaving four rounds in the cylinder.

Therese Bliss died of her injuries on the night of September 14, 1978. Her death certificate listed her as the victim of a homicide. George Bliss's death was marked down as a suicide by self-inflicted bullet wound. An autopsy found that he had a gastric ulcer and coronary atherosclerosis. A toxicological analysis came back negative for alcohol, barbiturates, opiates, and tranquilizers.

In his remembrance of Bliss, the *Tribune*'s Bob Wiedrich wrote that his longtime colleague had taught him understanding, compassion, and honesty. It had been Bliss who'd mentored him when he was a cub reporter in 1948, and who'd consoled him on the front steps of Our Lady of the Angels School following the 1958 fire that killed ninety-two children. Bliss had given the paper and its readers "his integrity, his expertise, and his heart," Wiedrich wrote. "And the only way any of us can ever repay that is by carrying on his tradition of helping still others become good newspapermen."

Clayton Kirkpatrick, who'd helped revive the *Tribune*'s fortunes by luring Bliss back from the Better Government Association, did his best to encapsulate the great journalist's life and death in one long quote. "George Bliss was, in effect, a victim of his own intense devotion to journalism," the *Tribune*'s editor said in the paper's front-page obituary.

> He was a perfectionist who never was satisfied with his stories. He agonized over details of the brilliant investigative work that resulted in three Pulitzer Prizes.
>
> Some time ago he began to suffer from severe mental depression. Medical treatment, including institutional care, did not

bring relief. The terrible burden of mental illness compounded by an awareness of its presence ultimately proved too severe.

The tragedy that followed ended the career of a man who undoubtedly was the foremost investigative reporter in the nation.

An editorial published in the *Tribune* on September 12 expressed "hope that his death will help spur researchers in the field of mental health to the same tireless dedication that he showed in his career, and that the means will be found to conquer or at least tame the kind of illness that conquered him." A newspaper out of Central Illinois, the *Decatur Herald*, wrote that "people like Bliss need understanding and care, not punishment for a problem that's not their fault." That item, which didn't mention Therese Bliss, ended with a request for empathy: "Bliss, who could afford private psychiatric care and who had many friends even among his professional competitors, met a tragic end nevertheless. Think of the lives of the mentally troubled people with no money, no fame, and no friends. . . . What happened to George Bliss could happen to anyone else."

* * *

Linda Taylor's welfare fraud conviction in Illinois could've been the first of a hat trick for prosecutors. She was still wanted for felony welfare fraud in Michigan, where she'd jumped bail in 1972, and the FBI continued to write regular status updates on a potential federal case in connection to her misappropriation of Social Security and veterans' benefits. After Taylor's sentencing in Chicago, a prosecutor in Michigan's Van Buren County told the local press that her three-to-seven-year sentence was "really not enough." The time and expense required to extradite and prosecute Taylor didn't seem worth it, though, given that she'd been charged with receiving just $600 or so in relief money in Michigan. That was a felony, but not one that would warrant locking her up for a long stretch, even with the extra time she'd likely get for absconding on her bond. The feds, too, eventually decided not to pursue a case against Taylor. In

May 1977, an assistant U.S. attorney from the Northern District of Illinois affirmed the office's earlier decision not to go forward, saying that Taylor had already been convicted in state court "on very similar charges." A federal prosecution would've been redundant. That decision was final.

In Cook County, state's attorneys Jim Piper and James Sternik still had one more Taylor-related welfare fraud case to close out. On June 20, 1977, Taylor's daughter, Sandra Brownlee, pleaded guilty to eighteen counts of theft for receiving public aid checks worth $271.76 each without reporting her husband's earnings. She was sentenced to three years' probation and ordered to pay the state $2,414 in restitution. Upon her conviction, at least one newspaper referred to her as the "welfare princess."

Illinois prosecutors never asked Taylor to pay restitution directly; in 1978, they managed to claw back $7,000 of the $8,865.67 she'd been convicted of stealing by taking possession of various bonds she'd paid to stay out of jail. The state had worse luck getting Taylor's daughter to replenish its coffers. Brownlee told her probation officer that poor health prevented her from working. She said she'd gone partially deaf in the Our Lady of the Angels School fire—a claim the FBI had disproved in 1975. She also reported that she'd had surgery for sarcoidosis in 1973, the same year her mother had told a Public Aid Department employee that she'd been receiving treatment for that lung disease. Taylor's health hadn't improved, her daughter said. An August 24, 1977, entry in Brownlee's probation ledger noted that "her mother is going in surgery in the morning so she will have to be there with her."

In a November interview with the *St. Louis Globe-Democrat*, Piper affirmed that Taylor had been admitted to "a hospital for treatment of an undisclosed ailment." The prosecutor told the *Globe-Democrat* that Taylor had applied for welfare during her hospitalization and that "investigators believe she is financially solvent and may have falsified information on the welfare application."

While that allegation never led to criminal charges, Taylor's behavior had by this point exhausted the patience of every stakeholder in the Cook County legal system. On November 18, 1977, the judge in Taylor's burglary case sent her to jail for missing three consecutive court appearances. She spent the next three months in the county's Women's Correctional Center. In January 1978, Skip Gant and T. Lee Boyd withdrew as counsel in that case. Gant never succeeded in getting Taylor to pay her bill. In February, the attorney Taylor hired to replace Gant and Boyd also withdrew, telling the court he "had absolutely no cooperation whatsoever with the defendant" and that "Linda Taylor should seek other counsel to represent her in this matter." That same month, the appeal in her welfare fraud case was dismissed. In March, Taylor's newest lawyer filed a petition for a behavioral-clinic examination in the burglary case, writing that he "has been unable to substantiate any of the information relayed to him by his client" and that he doubted "whether or not the Defendant is capable of understanding the nature of the proceedings herein." That petition was denied.

After three and a half years of motions and petitions, Linda Taylor was out of options. On March 27, 1978, she pleaded guilty to stealing Everleana Brame's fur coat, television, and can opener. When Judge Robert Sklodowski asked her if that plea was correct, Taylor said "Yes." She said yes again when asked if she understood the theft provision, and once more to affirm that she was waiving her right to a trial by jury. She said yes ten times and no just once, to indicate she hadn't been coerced to plead guilty. The fifty-two-year-old defendant uttered only a single lie, when she told the court she was forty-two.

Sklodowski sentenced Taylor to five and a half years in prison, to be served concurrently with her preexisting three-to-seven-year term for theft and perjury. The burglary case was closed. There were no more outstanding warrants for Taylor's arrest, in Illinois or any other state. She didn't have anything more to run away from, and she didn't have anywhere to run. Linda Taylor had been stopped.

* * *

Jim Piper had spent years toiling as an ordinary assistant state's attorney, one of hundreds of lawyers in the second-largest prosecutor's office in the United States. After his successful shepherding of the Taylor case,

Piper became a star. In the fall of 1977, he was asked to head up a new division: a dedicated unit in Cook County that would ensure that welfare fraudsters paid the price for their actions.

The State of Illinois had at one point considered taking a very different approach to corralling cheaters. In 1975 and 1976, the Department of Public Aid had experimented with offering amnesty to rule breakers who turned themselves in and arranged to make restitution. That program didn't last, though, and the prevailing political mood made it a certainty that amnesty wouldn't be on the table again. "I think the welfare queen Linda Taylor brought about a change in thinking," Piper told the *Tribune* the following spring. "Millions each year are being stolen and we decided to do something about it."

In interviews, Piper emphasized that he had his sights on only the most egregious criminals. "We don't prosecute the mother of 10 on welfare and one afternoon a week she works a couple of hours at the Dairy Queen," he told the *Sun-Times*. The prosecutor estimated that 35 to 40 percent of the people he investigated were government workers, including public aid staffers who cashed welfare checks in addition to dispensing them. The news stories that reported those indictments, though, mostly presented white-collar scofflaws as an undifferentiated mass—a list of names, ages, addresses, and dollar amounts.

Piper understood the unique power of Linda Taylor's story—how a single outlandish case generated more publicity than a long list of indictments. "The thing that made this case draw so much attention was that she fit the welfare abuser stereotype—it was so blatant," he said in an interview with a UPI reporter. "She would drive an Eldorado to the court and wear these flowery hats, diamonds—the whole shtick." Before Taylor, the fur coat–wearing, luxury car–buying public aid chiseler had been something akin to the abominable snowman. The welfare queen had been lurking just out of reach for decades, a mythical being rumored to hang around grocery store checkout lines and Cadillac dealerships. Taylor's mere existence gave credence to a slew of pernicious stereotypes about poor people and black women. If one welfare queen walked the earth, then surely others did, too.

A few months before Taylor went on trial, George Bliss wrote that the Legislative Advisory Committee on Public Aid had found "Chicago's second welfare queen," a twenty-nine-year-old woman named Mildred Hawkins who "was using wigs, different addresses, various Social Security numbers, and other phony identifications" to freeload an alleged $21,600 a year. Although *Tribune* readers never got a follow-up, Hawkins would ultimately get convicted of thieving just $1,013; she'd be sentenced to 1 year and 1 day in prison. In 1978, Piper found a woman whose shtick went well beyond wigs and phony IDs. On April 28, thirty-year-old criminal justice graduate student Arlene Otis went to the Criminal Courts building at Twenty-Sixth and California to interview a judge for a school project. A few minutes after leaving his chambers, Otis was arrested and charged with stealing $118,456 from the Department of Public Aid. "She had to write a report with four other students on how the judicial system compares with reality," explained the judge, Earl Strayhorn. "She's a good student. Now she can write a good report."

Piper's indictment charged Otis with perpetrating the most elaborate, largest-scale recipient fraud scheme in the state's history. Otis's ruse lasted for six years and involved five different public aid cases. She swiped one of her identities from a Chicago actor, Greta Stewart, who'd starred in the national tour of the musical *Hair*. A black woman whose behavior pushed beyond the bounds of reason, Otis offered the strongest confirmation yet that Linda Taylor was a type rather than an outlier. "Atrocious things are going on in the welfare system, and the taxpayer is catching it," Piper told *U.S. News & World Report*. "If this Otis case doesn't prove to the taxpayer that something needs to be done, nothing will."

* * *

Before Linda Taylor came along, the Illinois Department of Public Aid sent caseworkers into the field to spot-check recipients' eligibility. After Taylor made Illinois infamous, the department began a systematic audit of the Aid to Families with Dependent Children, general assistance, and medical assistance rolls, with each caseworker required to conduct eight in-home client interviews per day. In Cook County, the agency also started mailing AFDC checks directly to currency exchanges and banks, requiring recipients to show multiple forms of ID to get their monthly payments.

There were a lot of poor people to monitor in Illinois in the 1970s, particularly in Cook County. In 1970, 483,487 Chicagoans lived below the poverty line. That number would grow to 601,410 by 1980, even as the city's population declined. The Public Aid Department's more aggressive surveillance revealed, if it needed revealing, that a lot of AFDC recipients had been supplementing their welfare checks with cash from off-the-books work. Before the 1970s, such failures to report outside income had typically either been ignored or handled as an administrative matter. As Reagan's welfare policy adviser Robert Carleson once explained with regard to the California public aid system, "The benefits were too low and people really couldn't make it on those benefits, so the whole system was looking the other way." In Illinois in the mid-1970s, the benefits were definitely too low. Between January 1975 and July 1978, when the annual inflation rate in the U.S. ranged between 5 and 9 percent per year, the dollar amounts inscribed on AFDC recipients' checks—$317 per month for a family of four—remained unchanged.

No family could be expected to make it on those benefits, much less get rich off them. Nevertheless, the system had stopped looking the other way when it came to alleged rule bending. When the state's new Republican governor, James Thompson, approved a 5 percent cost-of-living increase for families on public aid in 1978, he tied the appropriation to a parallel jump in spending on fraud investigations. In the late 1970s, there were at least five groups in Illinois tasked with taking on welfare fraud: the Department of Public Aid, the Department of Law Enforcement, the state comptroller's office, Don Moore's Legislative Advisory Committee on Public Aid, and Jim Piper's unit in the Cook County state's attorney's office. Individual recipient fraud was increasingly seen as a matter best handled by the criminal justice system. In the fiscal year that ended June 30, 1970, the State of Illinois terminated 870 public assistance cases due to fraud, with 240 of those—28 percent—referred to law enforcement.

Nine years later, the state terminated 2,638 cases because of fraud and forwarded 1,995 of them—76 percent—to law enforcement. The criminalization of welfare fraud was a nationwide trend. Between 1970 and 1979, the number of AFDC cases referred to law enforcement in the United States rose from seventy-five hundred to just more than fifty-two thousand.

In terms of the bottom line, there was little value in marching cheaters into court. George Lindberg, the former state comptroller whose signature adorned the front of Linda Taylor's welfare checks, said in 1977 that trying to extract cash from fraudsters was pointless: They didn't have any, so the state wasn't getting any. Taylor cost the state money as both a public aid recipient and a criminal defendant. In June 1978, Illinois's Lindsay-Schaub News Service reported that Cook County had spent a minimum of $50,000 to convict Taylor of stealing less than $9,000. Piper didn't think those numbers reflected the real worth of his prosecutions. "For every cheat you get, you also cause others in the community to stop and think about what they're doing," he said.

Linda Taylor and Arlene Otis, though, had as much in common with a typical welfare rule breaker as a bank robber does with someone who swipes a piece of penny candy. The *Tribune*'s embrace of the "welfare queen" nickname and Ronald Reagan's use of Taylor as a metonym for public aid fraud muddled that distinction, ensuring that all welfare recipients would be viewed with suspicion, and that the welfare cheat–hating public would want to see them punished. A survey conducted in Illinois in 1978 found that 84 percent of the state's voters believed that fraud and abuse in welfare and Medicaid were a matter of grave concern, the highest figure for any issue. For certain Illinois politicians, then, chest-thumping about welfare fraud was an essential bit of constituent service.

Don Moore's Legislative Advisory Committee on Public Aid claimed that its fraud investigations saved taxpayers close to $1 million in just the first six months of 1977. That was an exaggeration—the maximum possible total if the Illinois Department of Public Aid had dropped every case the committee sent its way. In reality, the canceled cases amounted to closer to $300,000.

Seventy percent bluster to 30 percent reality was a standard ratio for Moore. In the years after the Linda Taylor case, the legislative committee's investigators spent much of their time digging into big-ticket Medicaid fraud. In 1976, for instance, they'd partnered with George Bliss and another *Tribune* reporter to uncover a scam in which optical firms billed Medicaid for millions of dollars' worth of eye exams they'd never conducted and glasses they'd never dispensed. But the Legislative Advisory Committee on Public Aid never stopped pointing its spotlight at individual, small-dollar welfare cheaters. In the fall of 1977, Moore's group invited members of the media to watch as it filed a batch of twenty welfare fraud cases. These would be the first prosecutions carried out at a special, one-day-a-month welfare fraud court in the south Chicago suburb of Harvey, Illinois—a facility created at the behest of the chief judge of the circuit court of Cook County. Don Moore now had his own committee, his own investigators, and his own hall of justice.

Moore's agenda didn't win universal acclaim in the Illinois legislature. On April 29, 1976, the Republican state senator proposed halving an appropriation to the Department of Public Aid unless the agency could "correct public aid fraud." Democrat Robert W. McCarthy responded to that idea with a long tirade about politically motivated public servants. "I am aware of the fact that there is no more popular political issue that people can understand and complain about than the whole spectrum of welfare payments," he said.

> I know that that's a popular political issue, because my wife informs me of that fact, that what the voters are mad about is food stamp abuses, what they're mad about is overpayment to people who are too lazy to work. Incidentally, I asked my wife where she gets this information. She tells me she gets it at her tennis club, and that she gets it at the beauty shop from other people, and I don't think the people that are playing tennis at the Decatur Racquet Club for eight dollars an hour or getting their hair done are in a position really to know too much about it....

[In] about three weeks, we'll come down and they can play the same old violin about the abuses of public aid, and people understand it, and newsmen know how to write it, and the printers know how to print it, and so, the public will read about it, and my wife will hear about it more vociferously at the tennis club and at the beauty shop, and I'll hear more about it.... We're playing the game of talking about fraud, because they want us to talk about fraud.

A year later, state senator Richard Newhouse declared that it was past time for the Legislative Advisory Committee on Public Aid to shift its focus to protecting recipients' rights. "'Welfare cheaters' has become the new code word for the poor, for minorities in general and those temporarily down on their luck," the black Democrat from Chicago's Hyde Park told the *Defender*.* In 1977 and 1978, Newhouse continually pushed to unseat Moore as the chair of the committee. In a series of votes, the twelve-member bipartisan group repeatedly split six to six on the question of which politician should lead it. Those deadlocks left the incumbent Moore in control. "I think they're trying to give me a message, and I'm hearing it," the state senator said, "but I plan to stay around."

* * *

Nobody from the local or national press took note when America's original welfare queen arrived at Dwight Correctional Center on February 16, 1978. Taylor wouldn't fade slowly into obscurity after heading off to a state prison eighty miles southwest of Chicago. Rather, it would take just a few years for her to get expunged from the historical record. In 1982, the *New Republic* would publish an essay criticizing Ronald Reagan for his frequent mentions of "the celebrated Chicago 'welfare

---

* In 1997, six years after Newhouse's retirement from politics, Barack Obama took over the South Side politician's Thirteenth District state senate seat.

queen' who did not exist." When the press and politicians built her into an archetype, Taylor lost her individual identity. When they anointed a series of successors to her throne, she was forgotten entirely.

She used eighty different names. She stole $150,000 of welfare money a year. She could pass as black, white, Latina, or Filipina. She practiced voodoo. She had a bunch of dead husbands. She stole children. She killed a thirty-seven-year-old mother of three. After three and a half years' worth of newspaper articles, stump speeches, and allegations from outraged public officials, nobody knew or much cared which parts of the Linda Taylor story were true, which were exaggerations, and which were outright lies.

Jack Sherwin had tried to separate fact from fiction, but he'd been marginalized by bureaucrats whose agendas didn't match his own. Sherwin had defied departmental leaders in pursuing the Taylor case in 1974, a move he thought would kill his career. The detective was half right: Although he didn't get pushed out of the force, Sherwin didn't get promoted either. He thought that he'd been held back because he wasn't a suck-up—that he would've made sergeant if he'd played the right political games.

Sherwin would hold on to his notes from the Taylor case for years, hoping someone, somewhere, would have some interest in investigating her for kidnapping and murder. Eventually, he'd throw away those personal files, resigning himself to the reality that no individual or institution would invest the time in figuring out what Taylor had done and why she'd done it.

The key to unlocking her past was in another set of files, a sealed trove of documents from Cook County Probate Court. In Chicago in 1964, Taylor had staked a claim to a massive fortune. On the witness stand, she'd laid out her biography, explaining where she'd come from and how she'd spent her life. Her name, she said, was Constance Wakefield, and her father was one of the richest men in Chicago.

CHAPTER 10

She Knows About the Money

At 4:45 a.m. on February 18, 1964, a pair of Chicago police officers peered down at a dying man. Lawrence Wakefield was lying in a twin bed, fully dressed, and grabbing the left side of his chest. He tried to choke out a message, but all he could do was grunt in pain. The fire department's rescue squad had pulled up to 9312 South Rhodes Avenue at the same time as the cops, but its equipment wouldn't keep the fifty-nine-year-old Wakefield alive for long. He needed to get to a hospital.

Patrolman William Childs stepped out of the front bedroom and glanced around the South Side home. The place looked a bit decrepit, as if all the furniture had been nailed to the floor circa 1945. Given that nothing in the house seemed newer than a decade-old refrigerator, the officer suggested that Wakefield's next of kin call an emergency service that would be willing to transport indigent patients. Rose Kennedy, the seventy-year-old woman who'd summoned the police, said she'd prefer that he travel by private ambulance.

As Kennedy made the call, Childs peered at the old newspapers on the dining room table. It looked as if someone had dropped them there in a hurry. He also noticed four or five men's hats, a stack of unused coin wrappers, and a paper bag filled with what appeared to be $100 or $200 in $1 bills. When Kennedy left the room to check on Wakefield, the policeman lifted the pile of newsprint. Childs found around $50 in silver coins, as well as an adding machine tape with "1,082" scribbled at the end in pencil. The large amount of small bills and coins indicated that someone in the house could be involved in policy, a low-stakes numbers game indigenous to Chicago. Upon Kennedy's return, the officer asked her what Wakefield did for a living. She said he was a freelance real estate broker.

The policemen left before the ambulance came to take Wakefield to Presbyterian–St. Luke's Hospital. When Childs got back to unit headquarters, he called the state bureau of identification to run a record check. Wakefield, he was told, had been arrested multiple times by the Chicago Police Department's vice squad.

After the sun rose, the man in charge of the Kensington police district sent another pair of officers to stake out Wakefield's two-story brick mock Tudor. They sat in their car for a couple of hours on February 18, then again for a short spell on February 19, peeking through the wire mesh that covered the downstairs windows and waiting to see if anybody came out or went in. Nobody did.

At 3 p.m. on that second day, a team of detectives short-circuited the surveillance mission. Although the police didn't have enough evidence for a search warrant, Bernard Kay and George Martis decided they'd try the front entrance. Thirty-six hours after she'd implored the police to hurry over to tend to the stricken Wakefield, Rose Kennedy was dressed in a housecoat and in a disagreeable mood. Later, she'd testify that the detectives had threatened to shoot her dogs if she didn't let them inside. The police denied making any such threats—they said Kennedy opened the door of her own volition and told them they were welcome to nose around.

The officers found what they were looking for down in the basement. In dusty cardboard boxes and a wet and dirty wooden cabinet, they uncovered all the equipment necessary to run a policy operation: the wheels used to select the winning numbers, the printing presses that churned out the daily results, and the thin slips of paper known as onion skins that runners used to jot down customers' bets. As the cops turned their attention to a locked bedroom in the back of the house, Kennedy insisted on speaking to the district commander. On the phone, she told Edward Egan she wouldn't unlock the room for anyone. She owned a collection of valuable coins, she explained, and she wanted to make sure they didn't get swiped. Depending on whose story you believed, Egan either assuaged her concerns or Kay and Martis busted through the door. Either way, that locked room didn't stay locked for long.

When the door swung open, the detectives found a tycoon's treasure vault. There was cash piled on the floor and pouring out of bank bags, stuffed in the closet and jammed between the cushions of a couch. The bills ranged in value from $1 to $500. Some were oversized—a type of banknote that hadn't been in production since the 1920s. None of the officers who showed up to aid in the search had ever seen this amount of money. One of them later claimed he'd almost fainted when he'd spotted the stash.

Although the cops placed Kennedy under arrest for possession of gambling equipment, they treated the back bedroom less as a crime scene than a photo opportunity. Within a couple of hours, the brick house on South Rhodes Avenue was crawling with reporters and photographers. In pictures that ran in the next day's *Chicago Tribune* and *Chicago Sun-Times*, Kay, Martis, and their commander wore stern expressions as they peered at the massive piles of money, their fists full of dollars.

When the men got through with posing, Commander Egan ordered them to confiscate everything in sight—these were obviously the ill-gotten proceeds of a gambling enterprise. The police emptied each of the bank bags, then poured the riches into the biggest vessels they could find. Kennedy watched this bucket brigade while seated in a small chair, with bags of currency below her seat and shoes; the policewomen who'd been brought in to mind the bespectacled septuagenarian caught her dropping stray bills down the front of her dress. Elsewhere in the house, the cops found seven loaded firearms and slips for five safety-deposit boxes. They discovered additional cash reserves beneath the hindquarters of one of Kennedy's dogs.

The money filled thirty-two sacks—the largest of the bank bags, plus some pillowcases and a duffel bag. The police numbered each of those receptacles, loaded the plunder and Rose Kennedy into a squadrol, and drove three miles south to the district police station. At 9 p.m. on February

19, cops from the evidence and recovered property section started counting. They finished the first sack around midnight. It held $120,000.

Kennedy looked on from the corner of the room, doing her own arithmetic with pencil and paper. She kept up a running commentary, shouting that every bill and coin was her personal property. She'd brought $160,000 with her from Canada in the 1920s, she said, intimating to a deputy chief that she'd earned a big chunk of that as a high-priced, World War I–era prostitute. She also admitted that she'd started a gambling business with her first husband; Wakefield had taken over the day-to-day operations after she'd been widowed. Kennedy, who was white, said that her black business manager had doubled as her common-law spouse for more than two decades. He kept his money away from banks, she explained, because "the government would want to know where he got it."

As the count proceeded, an officer called Presbyterian–St. Luke's, then handed the phone to "Mrs. Wakefield." The nurse on the other end told her that Lawrence Wakefield's heart attack had been fatal. He'd died at 8:55 p.m. Kennedy cried when she heard the news. A moment later, she sat back down with her pencil and paper. "I loved him and I am sorry he is dead," she told a policewoman. "Now I want to watch the money."

* * *

Rose Kennedy watched the money all night long and into the morning. The cops worked in shifts, going through the bills by hand and counting the coins with a high-speed sorting machine on loan from a Catholic church. The *Tribune* rolled off the presses with a banner front-page headline: "$500,000 Found in Home." That was just a rough calculation, the paper reported—the police were "up to their necks" in money and wouldn't be done stacking and sorting until noon. At around 9 a.m. on February 20, a phalanx of television crews came through to film the scene. When one of the TV people asked Kennedy where the booty had come from, she said she'd made it selling hot dogs, peanuts, and popcorn on the streets of downtown Chicago.

The *Tribune*'s estimate wasn't nearly high enough. The Chicago Police Department eventually counted $763,223.30* in hard currency, as well as another $30,000 in bank deposits and close to $16,000 in savings bonds. The department couldn't squeeze all those bags of money into its own vault, so a dozen gun-toting officers escorted the hoard to the Continental Illinois National Bank and Trust Company. That money would stay locked away until the probate division of the Cook County Circuit Court determined its rightful owner.

In the days after Wakefield's death, the phone wouldn't stop ringing at Kersey McGowan and Morsell Chapel. "They just wanted to see the man who had so much money—what he looked like," the manager of the funeral home told the *Chicago Daily News*. "Some of them asked me, 'Are you going to bury some of the money with him?'" While most visitors came by to peer into the dead man's casket, a handful presented themselves as Wakefield's long-lost relatives. None of them brought flowers.

More than a thousand people showed up at the South Side's Metropolitan Community Church on February 25 to pay their respects. Kennedy sat in a pew in the front row, flanked by a pair of nurses and dressed in a full-length mink coat. The reverend who delivered Wakefield's eulogy lauded him as "an unostentatious man." "If certain doors had not been closed to him because of his color," the pastor said, "he might have been chairman of the board, the personnel officer of a big corporation. It's not what he was working at that is important. It's what he was living for. It's not what he had in life but what he was in life. He was God's man." When the service was over, the *Tribune* noted, a "long line of Cadillacs" followed Wakefield's hearse south to Lincoln Cemetery.

So far as anyone could tell, Lawrence Wakefield hadn't left a will. The State of Illinois also didn't recognize common-law marriage, which meant Rose Kennedy would have a difficult time reclaiming everything the police had taken from her house. At the end of February, a probate

---

* When the Continental Illinois National Bank and Trust Company did its own tally later in the week, it pegged the fortune at $761,385.66. Bank officials suggested that the difference was due to police officers' "faulty arithmetic."

judge ruled that Wakefield had no known heirs—no living parents, children, siblings, aunts, uncles, or cousins. That meant the money now belonged to the Cook County public administrator. If Kennedy's case got shot down in court and no relatives turned up, the county would keep the cash, minus whatever the Internal Revenue Service took as compensation for unpaid income taxes.

The stash on South Rhodes Avenue didn't just make headlines in Chicago. The *Washington Post* and the *New York Times* both ran stories about Wakefield's cache, and photos of the money appeared on front pages in Indiana, Wisconsin, Michigan, Missouri, Kentucky, Ohio, Nebraska, New Jersey, Delaware, Connecticut, Oregon, and Florida. In the aftermath of that publicity blitz, upwards of a dozen people got in touch with the public administrator to make a bid for the estate. One of them was the woman who'd later be known as the welfare queen. Ten years before the *Tribune* chronicled Linda Taylor's criminal exploits, she declared that she was Lawrence Wakefield's only child, and that his money belonged to her and no one else.

* * *

On April 18, 1964, the *Chicago Defender* published a page one item tagged "Exclusive! Dead Policy King's $763,000 Demanded By His 'Daughter'; Has Papers to Prove Her Claim." The story's first two paragraphs, like the headline, were larded with scare quotes.

> A 29-year-old woman who claims to be the daughter of the late policy king, Lawrence Wakefield, has unfolded a fantastic story of "plots" and intrigues which separated her from her "father."
>
> The claimant, Constance Beverly Wakefield, who lives on Chicago's Northside, showed the *DEFENDER* an array of "documents" which, she claims, prove she is the daughter of Wakefield.

The claimant with the fantastic plots was "of light complexion, with straight black hair," the *Defender*'s M. Wilson Lewis wrote, noting that she was "still attractive and shows signs of having been a beauty in her younger days." Lewis spoke with "Miss Wakefield" at her home after being granted entry by "a man said to be her bodyguard." The house was adorned with "odd figurines," and an "eerie note was provided by a gabby mynah bird, which constantly squawked the name 'Lawrence.'"

In addition to this avian evidence of her parentage, the policy-fortune aspirant presented the *Defender* with a series of official records. Among them was her own Illinois birth certificate, which identified her as the daughter of Lawrence Wakefield and Edith Jarvis. She also produced a family Bible that listed her race as white and that noted she "had a twin brother who died of suffocation at birth."

Constance Wakefield explained that her father was "considerably confused by the race issue." She said her guardians, a couple named Jim and Virginia Collins, had tried to send her to a "colored school" but "daddy had them take me out." The *Defender* related that the policy king's "daughter" had experienced a "strange childhood" in Blytheville, Arkansas, one in which she'd received no formal education and "was never allowed to play ordinary children's games nor lead a normal life, because Wakefield was afraid she might be slained."

The would-be heir saw herself as the central figure in a sprawling drama, one in which a host of enemies were trying desperately to deprive her of her potential inheritance. In the *Defender* interview, she recounted a break-in by "two white men" who were "looking for my father's money," a menacing visit by "a swarthy Italian," and "an attempt to blow her 1964 Cadillac up by switching the electrical current into her gasoline tank." In an accompanying photograph, she exuded solemnity, casting her eyes downward toward her enormous beaded necklace. A day earlier, in a *Sun-Times* story that identified her as Constance W. Stineberg, she said she'd recently had to wave a pistol at a group of five men and six women who'd tried to steal her birth certificate. In the head shot that ran alongside that piece, "Mrs. Stineberg"—who wore cat-eye glasses and a coat with a fluffy white fur collar—looked as though she'd just exited a costume shop.

* * *

By the summer of 1964, Lawrence Wakefield's supposed child had emerged as one of the two leading candidates to win control of his hefty estate. Her main competition was Wakefield's common-law wife.

Before his death, Lawrence Wakefield and Rose Kennedy had owned and operated the Night Owl and Speedway policy wheels,[*] local lotteries that the *Sun-Times* noted were "known to a generation of numbers players." Kennedy said her first husband had invested in the wheels in 1929 and that Wakefield had been running the operation for three decades. They'd found a niche in what had long been a crowded industry. Policy had flourished in Chicago since the late nineteenth century, particularly in the city's black neighborhoods. Two days after Wakefield's death, the *Daily News* reported that underground lotteries amounted to a $50-million-a-year business that lured in five hundred thousand regular bettors. "I wouldn't be surprised if 70 percent of the Negroes on the South Side bet on the numbers," an "informed police officer" told the newspaper.

Those nickel, dime, and quarter wagers provided ample salaried employment for bet collectors and money carriers and funneled a huge quantity of cash to a small handful of numbers barons. Kennedy assured her lawyers that the Night Owl and Speedway weren't rigged in any way. Regardless, the odds in any policy game always favored the house to an absurd degree—per the *Daily News*, they were typically "less than half what they should be to make the bet a fair one." For most players, though, fantasies of a big victory offset the quotidian reality of yet another losing ticket. In his posthumously published autobiography, Malcolm X cited

---

[*]   Although the origins of the term "policy" aren't entirely clear, one etymological explanation—suggested in, among other places, an October 1964 *Ebony* story about Wakefield—is that working-class men and women "risk[ed] their insurance policy money" to place low-probability bets.

Wakefield's $760,000 stash—"all taken from poor Negroes"—as a telling example of "why we stay so poor."

Wakefield had been arrested for gambling-related offenses in 1949, 1952, 1960, and 1961, but the cops had never held him for long. The Chicago police and local politicians saw policy as a fixture of urban life, as well as an opportunity for pocket-lining graft. For a black-market entrepreneur like Wakefield, the Italian mob represented a much graver threat to his life and livelihood. In the 1920s, Chicago Outfit boss Al Capone had brokered a deal to cede control of the policy business to the city's black mafia in exchange for unfettered control of the booze racket. That arrangement had expired in 1946, when the policy tycoon "Big" Ed Jones was kidnapped by Italian mobsters, then fled to Mexico after his brother and his associate Teddy Roe paid a $100,000 ransom. When Roe, the last big holdout among Chicago's black gambling kingpins, was gunned down in August 1952, the Italians had policy locked up.

The fact that Wakefield was alive and running an independent policy venture in 1964 was almost as shocking as the discovery that he and Kennedy had squirreled away close to $800,000. The *Tribune* reported that Wakefield hid "behind an appearance of general shabbiness," wearing worn-out clothes, driving an old Ford, and eschewing "flashy jewels that might attract attention." Kennedy told the press that her partner's faux pauperism had tricked the Chicago Outfit. "Two men from the crime syndicate" had come sniffing around, she said, "but after looking things over they decided he was a marginal operator and they would leave him alone."

Wakefield's frugality was more than just a ruse. The papers all quoted the family's maid, who said she'd been shooed away when she asked for a $20 advance on her salary. She'd been told, "There isn't a penny in the house." The *Daily News* wrote that Wakefield's tightwad ways had caused his business to shrivel—that he'd refused to pay his employees competitive salaries, and the disgruntled workers had taken their best customers elsewhere. While the biggest policy wheel in Chicago brought in an estimated $250,000 per month, the police pegged Wakefield's monthly gross income at closer to $7,500. *Ebony* said that the gambling boss, who'd been known as "The Red Streak," "The Blue Streak," and "The Flash" in his heyday, "apparently hoarded his take" from the 1930s and 1940s, then maintained "an unattractive token operation" until his death.

A month after Wakefield's funeral, Kennedy sobbed on the witness stand in Cook County Municipal Court as she recounted the wickedness of the canine-threatening detectives who'd busted into her home. A judge accepted Kennedy's version of events, ruling that the police had conducted a warrantless and illegal search and dropping all the gambling charges against her. That decision freed her to demand that the county return all the money seized from 9312 South Rhodes Avenue—or at least all the money the cops had bothered to itemize. Kennedy told one of her lawyers that she'd offered the police a bribe to forget what they'd seen. They'd refused, she said, because they wanted to skim some cash for themselves. "The fuckin' cops took half the money," she ranted.

In May, Constance Wakefield filed her own petition with the probate court. Rose Kennedy, Constance's lawyer said, was Lawrence Wakefield's housekeeper, not his common-law wife. In her interview with the *Defender*, Constance went so far as to accuse Kennedy of trying to poison her. "The doctors said I had swallowed enough strychnine to kill a dozen people," she claimed, brandishing hospital receipts that allegedly backed up her story.

Two months later, the purported strychnine survivor sat for the first of a series of depositions. But every time attorneys for Kennedy and Cook County got her in a room to answer questions, Constance Wakefield figured out a way to cut the interrogation short. In August, her lawyer filed a motion to delay the proceedings, writing that his client had been in a car accident and had "suffered recurring illness" that had caused her to shrivel from 135 to 100 pounds. She'd been hospitalized, the motion said, and "it may be necessary to perform surgery upon her." By mid-October, she'd recovered sufficiently to show up for another deposition, this one to be conducted in a judge's chambers. This time, she collapsed during questioning and paramedics hauled her out of the building on a gurney. The *Tribune* reported the next day that "she apparently had fainted from an overdose of barbiturates." Her attorney later said her pulse had fallen to zero and that she'd nearly died. Hospital records, however, showed that Constance Wakefield had been released shortly after admission and given a clean bill of health.

In between these near-death experiences, the wannabe beneficiary did put some responses on the record. The most junior member of Rose Kennedy's legal team came to believe that Wakefield's so-called daughter wasn't a total phony. Norris Bishton thought Constance knew enough details about Lawrence Wakefield's life that she'd likely had some kind of relationship with the policy king. But Kennedy insisted she'd never heard of this Constance woman, much less met her face-to-face.

In September, a probate judge had ordered Constance Wakefield to provide evidence that might affirm her connection to Lawrence. She complied with the judge's request, furnishing the court with letters and insurance policies bearing the names of various Wakefields who lived in Missouri. She included a receipt for $54.90 worth of flowers she'd purchased for Lawrence's funeral, an invoice from a retail outfit called Tile City on which the customers' names were written as "Lawrence Wakefield" and "Constance Wakefield (Daughter)," and a note indicating that Lawrence and Constance "had their Pomeranian bred by Tommie's Tiny Timmie Boy" in Rockford, Illinois, in exchange for a stud fee of $25. She proffered a set of photographs, among them one of a cherubic infant that had been labeled "Constance B. Wakefield, date of birth 12/25/34, Doctor Grant Sill, age 9 month, mother and father Edith Wakefield, Lawrence Wakefield." And she gave the court a brown leather billfold with the inscription "To My Dauther From Dad 1947, Lawrence Wakefield." Wakefield's Social Security number had been scrawled on the wallet's inside flap, so there could be no mistaking who'd bestowed her with this special gift.

In addition, Constance Wakefield produced correspondence from a Professor Jasper Herman of Miami, Florida, who explained that he was "better known as Black Herman from coast to coast." Black Herman averred that he had personal knowledge that Constance was the daughter of "Mr. and Mrs. Wakefield," saying, "They were not white just like Constance is not but they passed for white." Constance also obtained a sworn statement from the couple she claimed had raised her in Arkansas. Jim and Virginia Collins affirmed that she was Wakefield's only daughter, writing that Jim's "grandmother raised Constance Beverly Wakefield until she was 15 years old, but Mr. Wakefield paid for her care." They added, "We are colored, but Mr. Lawrence Wakefield was not colored, he was a foreigner. He originated from England."

The Pomeranian-breeding receipt, the baby photo, and these testimonials didn't add up to much in the way of proof that Constance Wakefield was Lawrence Wakefield's daughter. She professed, though, to have something closer to ironclad evidence that she deserved ownership of his nearly seven-figure estate. In October 1964, she filed a pair of wills with the probate court. Both carried the signatures of Lawrence W. Wakefield.

The first will, dated October 25, 1943, had been jotted in pencil on a sheet of paper labeled "Daily Programme of Recitation and Study." The text spilled across the width of the page in a frantic, erratically capitalized, unpunctuated stream of consciousness. It began,

> We Hope This will is Kept in safe in event of our Death we
> Have almost one million Dollars in propety and in Cash stocks
> and Bonds We only have one child a girl Constance Beverly
> Wakefild was bornd Dec 25, 1934 in Chicago

The will went on to list seven people—among them Jim Collins of Blytheville, Arkansas—who'd each be entitled to receive between $1,000 and $5,000. The rest of the money would go to Constance Beverly Wakefield, who could be identified by a scar on her right leg, another scar on her upper lip, and a dark blue mole on "Her Right arm near the shoulder" that was "Hard like a shot." That list of physical descriptors transitioned into a declaration of love for Lawrence and Edith Wakefield's daughter. "She well know That We Dearley lovl Her," the will explained. "We only live for Her for she is all we Have in the world."

The second will, which had supposedly been written in August 1962, looked more official. It carried the seal of a notary public and attested that its author was "of sound and disposing mind and memory, and not acting under duress, menace, fraud, or the undue influence of any person whomsoever." That formal, typewritten preamble was followed by a handwritten block of jumbled prose.

> Constace Beverly Wakefield . . . This is my Daughter and only liveing Blood Kin and she is my Daughter her mother die in 1945 Edith L. Wakefield I leave Constance Wakefield my home at 9312 S. Rhodes and 2 millions doller that is in thy house in a back room lock I have a Key to door and Constance has a Key She Knows about the money and everything about me

While the 1943 will extolled the virtues of Constance B. Wakefield, this one lingered on her nemesis. "Rosa Kennedy" would get just $1, it stated, as she was "no good and will try to take everything from my baby C. B. Wakefield and my Grandchildren." The will wrapped up with a final burst of character assassination: "In event of my death Constance will know what to do for Rosa Kennedy has said she is going to kill me with some kind of Chemical."

The *Tribune* reported on these documents credulously, topping its October 15 story with the headline "2 Wills Back Daughter of Policy King." It was doubtful, however, that anyone in Tribune Tower had seen the full text of the wills, given that a probate judge had sealed the Wakefield case file months earlier. Additionally, it was more than a bit suspicious that paperwork unearthed by Constance Wakefield supported her case so comprehensively—the older of the two wills said, essentially, "Our daughter, whom we love above all else and who has the following marks and scars, shall rightly profit from our abundant wealth." A few of the words on that piece of paper raised even more questions about its authenticity. The first line—"This is our will to Constance Beverly Wakefild"—and the sign-off—"Daddy Lawrnce W. Wakefield"—both contained unlikely misspellings. To accept that this was Lawrence Wakefield's handiwork, you'd have to believe he wrote up a will without knowing how to write his own name.

Kennedy's attorneys took note of those missing *e*'s, hiring the president of the American Society of Questioned Document Examiners to inspect the wills under a microscope. The lawyers also scrutinized the woman who'd brought the documents to the court's attention. The more they learned about this Constance Wakefield, the more certain they became that she wasn't who she claimed to be.

* * *

On the morning of November 9, 1964, Linda Taylor took the stand in a cramped courtroom on the sixth floor of the Cook County building and promised to tell nothing but the truth. Under questioning from her lawyer Milroy Blowitz, she declared that she was Constance Beverly Wakefield, the only living child of Lawrence Wakefield and Edith Elizabeth Jarvis. She said her parents had exchanged marriage vows in Mexico in 1929. She'd confirmed those facts on a recent trip to Tijuana, during which the American consulate in Mexico had certified the Wakefields' marriage certificate. Her own birth certificate, she said, had somehow gone missing from the county clerk's office, so her mother's obstetrician, Dr. Grant Sill, had been kind enough to fill out a delayed record of birth on her behalf. That certificate, which had been accepted and affirmed by the Illinois Department of Public Health, identified Constance Beverly Wakefield as a white female. She'd been born to Mr. and Mrs. Lawrence Wakefield on Christmas Day 1934.

The petitioner had asked for her proof of heirship hearing to be held before a jury, but Judge Anthony Kogut denied the motion, saying his courtroom couldn't possibly house all that extra humanity. While the Cook County building itself was a block-dominating downtown landmark with a lobby fashioned from Botticino marble, room 643 was tiny and unadorned. Kogut typically presided over matters that drew scant attention—hearings attended by the interested parties, their lawyers, and nobody else. This wasn't a typical probate case. In addition to the judge, his clerk, the bailiff, the witnesses, and a bunch of journalists, the courtroom had to accommodate two attorneys each for Constance Wakefield and Rose Kennedy, as well as lawyers representing Cook County, the City of Chicago, and the public administrator who'd been appointed to oversee the Wakefield estate. It was impossible for anyone to confer with the judge privately, and the courtroom was so packed that some onlookers had to line up against the back wall.

As Wakefield's alleged progeny explained how she'd procured her delayed birth certificate, a small army of opposing attorneys prepared to poke holes in her story. She faced four separate cross-examinations before the clock struck noon on Monday, November 9. The lengthiest of these were conducted by Cook County assistant state's attorney Gerald Mannix and Rose Kennedy's lawyer Norman "Jack" Barry. In the lead-up to the heirship hearing, the state's attorney's office and Kennedy's brain trust at the firm of Rothschild, Hart, Stevens, and Barry had joined forces to defeat a common enemy. If Constance Wakefield convinced the judge that she was a legitimate heir, she'd likely wrest away the entire estate.

The man from the state's attorney's office took the first shift. Mannix asked the witness if she'd ever gone by the names Beverly Steinberg and Beverly Singleton. She said yes. She also volunteered that she'd used the last name Miller and had once been known as Constance Steinberg Yarbough. She then added that she'd married a man named Paul Steinberg Yarbough in Oakland, California, in 1948. They'd had a pair of children—twins, Sandra and John—in Arkansas in 1952. She'd had another child, this one out of wedlock, in 1963. That was the extent of it, she said, a complete accounting of her names, relationships, and offspring.

Mannix kept on going, asking about her paternal grandfather and if her mother's mother had any children and whether she had any aunts. As she pleaded ignorance—"I don't know nothing about my grandfather"—her lawyer Milroy Blowitz complained that this was all a waste of time. "What her great-grandmother's name was or great-grandfather's name was...is absolutely immaterial and irrelevant," Blowitz said.

"I am attempting to establish the family tree of Constance Wakefield," Mannix had explained at the start of his questioning, "which I believe is separate and different from the family tree of Lawrence Wakefield." The judge allowed him to proceed.

"Were you ever known as Martha Louise White?" Mannix asked.

"No," she answered.

Jack Barry then took over, asking if she knew of the town of Arab, Alabama. She said she didn't.

"Were you born in nineteen twenty-five?" Rose Kennedy's attorney continued.

"I was not."

"Was your mother's name Linda Lydia Mooney?"

"She was not."

Barry kept on listing names and places, and Constance Wakefield kept on swatting them away. She'd never been married to a Buddy Elliott. She hadn't given birth to a Clifford Lee Harbaugh. She didn't have a sister named Mary Jane. The witness appeared alternately evasive and annoyed. "I don't know no Lucy Miller, and there is no Lucy," she said, responding to one of a series of queries about people with that last name. At one point, she claimed, bizarrely, that she had a child at home named Robert Heilgeist. That was the name of one of her lawyers.

Blowitz, her lead attorney, was apoplectic. After she admitted to sharing a residence with "a Mr. Miller and his wife," he bellowed, "What difference does it make who she lived with? She lived with a dozen men."

The judge told Blowitz to back away from the stand; he was practically sitting in the witness's lap. The lack of elbow room, it seemed, was making everyone irritable and claustrophobic. With no jurors to placate, the lawyers saw no reason to hide their mutual contempt. Barry accused Blowitz of exchanging notes with his client. Blowitz said he was sick of watching her get pushed around by Rose Kennedy's attorney—someone, he said, who was representing a "cheap and phony wife."

When the men got done casting aspersions on each other, Barry asked Constance Wakefield if she knew a man named Hubert Mooney.

"Yes," she said.

"And who is Hubert Mooney?" Barry replied.

"I don't know."

Blowitz, exasperated, said that none of this could possibly be of any importance. The heir-to-be then blew up when Barry asked if she'd known

Mooney for a long time. "I told you I don't know him," she said. "I don't know anything about him, anything about his work or what he does."

"Get Hubert Mooney, please," Barry said. The lawyer sent his colleague Norris Bishton into the hallway to fetch their witness.

"What is this? What's going on here?" Blowitz fumed.

A few seconds later, a short, slender man with a receding hairline walked through the doorway. Although her lawyer had no idea who this person was or what he was going to say, the woman on the witness stand knew what was about to happen. Hubert Mooney had traveled a long way to get to Chicago. He'd come up north to inform the court that his niece wasn't telling the truth about who she was.

CHAPTER 11
Everything Is Fictitious

Hubert Lee Mooney had lived all around the country and traveled across the world. No matter where the forty-three-year-old refrigeration engineer ended up, he always managed to keep tabs on his family. In the 1950s and 1960s, Mooney spent his time off work taking long road trips with his wife and children, leaving from Amarillo, Texas, and stopping off in Arkansas, Alabama, and Tennessee to visit his mother and six living siblings. They'd reminisce for hours, swapping stories about the relatives who'd stayed close and those who'd strayed from the flock.

"Are you acquainted with the lady that we know as Constance Wakefield Steinberg?" asked the lawyer representing Cook County's public administrator.

"I am acquainted with the girl back there, yes," Mooney told the crowd gathered in room 643.

"Will you identify her for the record?"

"Martha Louise White."

Martha had been born in Summit, Alabama, sometime around 1926, Mooney said. Her mother was his sister Lydia, and her father was a man named Marvin White. Mooney, who was born in 1921, had spent a good amount of time with his not much younger niece. For most of the 1930s, he'd seen Martha, her mother, and her stepfather each fall, when they came to Tennessee to harvest cotton. Mooney said he'd then lost track of her for a spell prior to a serendipitous reunion in Oakland, California, in the mid-1940s.

A week after that surprise rendezvous, Martha had called her Uncle Hubert looking for bail money. As soon as he got her out of jail, she'd disappeared. They'd seen each other just two times since then, he said. The first was in the early 1950s, near the Arkansas-Missouri state line. The second time was in November 1964, in the Cook County courtroom of Judge Anthony Kogut.

At the prodding of Rose Kennedy's lawyer Jack Barry, Mooney answered yes to a sequence of questions his niece had waved away. He was certain that she did know of Arab, Alabama, he said; in fact, she had family there. She had been married to a man named Buddy Elliott. She did have a child named Clifford. She did have a sister named Mary Jane.

For Constance Wakefield's attorneys, this was all extremely perplexing. "If we would feel our client's pedigree supposedly was as stated here today, we wouldn't be in court," said Milroy Blowitz's co-counsel Leon Wexler. Barry, meanwhile, reveled in the success of his gambit. "I can understand counsel being surprised," he said. "I am sure they are."

* * *

Barry's young associate Norris Bishton had spent months laying the groundwork for that courtroom ambush. Early in the morning and after his office shut down at night, the twenty-eight-year-old lawyer had pushed aside his other duties and set his mind to solving the puzzle of Constance Wakefield. Bishton had quickly realized that the aspiring heir didn't know all that much about her alleged genealogy. In her depositions and on the delayed birth certificate she'd obtained from the State of Illinois, she'd claimed her mother was Edith Wakefield. She was a generation off: Edith was Lawrence Wakefield's mother, a fact confirmed by Lawrence's own 1904 birth certificate.

Bishton had gotten enmeshed in the Wakefield case as soon as the Chicago police began hauling bags of cash out of 9312 South Rhodes Avenue. Edward Egan, the commander who oversaw the raid and Rose Kennedy's subsequent arrest, had told Kennedy she might want to speak with his son Donald, a lawyer at a fancy downtown firm. Recognizing the inherent conflict of taking on his father's arrestee as a client, the younger Egan had referred her to his colleague Bishton, who'd helped the seventy-year-old widow get bonded out of jail, and had then driven her to the South Side so she could be reunited with her unfed pets. "Just say her attorney went out to buy dog food," Bishton had told a *Daily News* reporter who'd harangued him outside Kennedy's home. He'd then added, with respect to the Wakefield stockpile, "We are going to try to get it all. We are trying to protect her from thieves."

A couple of the higher-ups at Rothschild, Hart, Stevens, and Barry had wanted Kennedy to take her business elsewhere. Among them was future Supreme Court justice John Paul Stevens, an antitrust specialist who didn't think his corporate clients would care to align themselves with a firm representing a gambling magnate's ex-prostitute common-law spouse. Bishton and Egan, not wanting to lose out on a potential windfall, had enlisted the help of Jack Barry, a personal injury lawyer who was more of a courtroom brawler than his starchy fellow partners. "We're the best law firm in Chicago," Barry had proclaimed during a staff conference call not long after Bishton bought Rose Kennedy dog food. "I believe someone with that amount of money deserves the best law firm in Chicago." Stevens had relented, asking Barry to do what he could to keep the matter out of the newspapers. He hadn't always complied with that request. In April 1964, the *Pittsburgh Courier* asked Barry what Kennedy might do with all the cash. "I hope she has a good time," he said.

While Barry did most of the talking in and out of court, Bishton handled the grunt work. He'd spent weeks staring at Constance's wills, trying to figure out the provenance of the loopy signatures at the bottom of both documents. Although Kennedy said she recognized her deceased partner's penmanship, the names looked strangely tiny. Bishton had found an authentic sample of Wakefield's handwriting on his mother Edith's death certificate, which Lawrence had signed as the informant. The Cook County clerk's office had printed the lawyer a duplicate— a copy, Bishton discovered, that came out much smaller than the original. The firm's document expert had confirmed that the undersized

Wakefield signature on the 1962 will matched the inscription on the undersized copy of Edith Wakefield's death certificate. A further forensic examination had revealed a telling series of pencil marks. The prospective beneficiary, it seemed, had acquired a miniature version of Lawrence Wakefield's autograph from the county clerk, then traced it in graphite before putting pen to paper.

By the fall of 1964, Bishton knew that Constance Wakefield wasn't the policy king's daughter. To dismantle her heirship petition, he'd need to do more than show that she was lying about her bloodline. He'd have to demonstrate that she belonged to someone else's family.

Constance's depositions were a mind-bending thicket of illogic, a collection of assertions that Bishton later termed "the biggest morass of contradiction you would ever want to see." The four hundred pages of transcripts on his desk did serve, though, as a kind of dossier, one larded with scores of names and locations. The young lawyer had a long list of clues. He just needed to figure out which were real and which were bogus.

Bishton had chased down every lead he could find, making calls to hospitals, bureaus of vital statistics, and county recorders' offices. He'd used the same opening line each time he got someone on the phone: "I need your help."

Rose Kennedy's attorney had reached out to a surgeon who'd once practiced in Arkansas, an amateur sleuth in Alabama, and a lawyer in Texas. These far-flung aides-de-camp had put Bishton in touch with neighbors and acquaintances and supposed relatives. Eighty-seven long-distance phone calls later, he had something resembling a biographical sketch of Lawrence Wakefield's ersatz daughter. As Bishton watched Hubert Mooney testify on the morning of November 9, he was confident he'd done enough to make Constance Wakefield pack up her phony documents and go home.

* * *

Judge Anthony Kogut adjourned the heirship hearing after Hubert Mooney left the stand, to give Constance Wakefield's legal team a bit of time to "check some of these names and some of these people." Eighteen hours later, having failed to make much progress with his background research, Blowitz accused Barry of purchasing his star witness's testimony. When the judge refused to grant Wexler another extension to prepare for cross-examination, the lawyer groused that he knew nothing about Mooney—that it would be "strictly a fishing expedition."

With no choice but to proceed, Wexler cast out his line.

"Are you a Negro?" he asked the pale-looking Mooney.

"I hope I am not," the witness said. "I don't look like it."

"Are you white?" Wexler continued.

"I think so."

"With reference to Constance Wakefield, is she a Negro?"

"No, definitely not," Mooney said.

"The person who appears in this court with the petition under the name of Constance Wakefield you are identifying as a white woman?"

"Yes. At least I know her mother is white."

Mooney went on to clarify that his niece's father wasn't a Negro either. He then assured Wexler that there were no Negroes at all in the Mooney family tree. "As a matter of fact," he said, "there has never been a Negro lived in Cullman County."

That wasn't much of an exaggeration. The 1930 census, taken four years after Martha Louise White's supposed birth date, listed a total of eleven black people in the Cullman precinct. In the area around Summit, the town where Mooney said his niece had been born, there were zero people listed as "Negro" in 1930. Thirty years later, that number had not changed.

Mooney, who was born in the town of Cullman, grew up in a place where white separatism was official policy. In 1908, a pair of small Southern newspapers reported that Cullman was "the only strictly white town in North Alabama, if not in the entire state." That rule was publicized, the papers said, via a sign affixed to the railroad water tank: "Nigger, Don't Let the Sun Go Down on You Here." Twenty-eight years later, a black newspaper out of Virginia wrote that black "motorists buy all the gasoline their cars can hold in order not to have to stop at Cullman for any purpose." The publication noted with relief that the upcoming trial of two of the Scottsboro Boys—the group of young black men who'd been falsely accused of raping two white women on a train—wouldn't be held in Cullman County. In 1936, a Scottsboro defendant had been shot near the county line after trying to escape custody. The Cullman sheriff lamented that the convict hadn't been mortally wounded, telling his Morgan County counterpart, "You ought to have killed all the niggers!"

"Constance, would you stand up?" Wexler asked.

Constance Wakefield, or Martha Louise White, claimed that her father was black. As she rose to her feet, Hubert Mooney glanced at his niece's skin. She didn't look like most white people from North Alabama.

Wexler pressed on.

"There has never been a Negro living in Cullman County?"

"No, sir," Mooney said.

"Your vision is adequate, I assume?"

"Twenty-twenty."

"You are looking at Constance Wakefield?"

"Yes."

"You are telling me that she is not a Negro, and she is white?"

"Well, if niggers can be born from white women," Mooney said, "she is probably a nigger."

Wexler told his client she could sit down.

* * *

Norris Bishton had concentrated his investigative efforts in Alabama, Arkansas, and Tennessee, the places the ostensible Constance Wakefield talked about the most in her meandering depositions. His collaborators in the Cook County state's attorney's office had focused on a time and place she hadn't seemed as inclined to discuss. Hubert Mooney had testified that his niece had a rap sheet in Oakland. After Mooney was excused, assistant state's attorney Gerald Mannix called Constance Wakefield back to the stand and confronted her with that list of arrests.

The Cook County prosecutor began by showing her a pair of photographs from August 4, 1945—Oakland Police Department mug shots of a woman named Connie Reed who'd been arrested for malicious mischief. The accompanying police report said she'd been born in Missouri on January 24, 1926. At the top of the form, her race was recorded as Mexican. At the bottom, she was identified as white.

Constance Wakefield said she didn't recognize the pictures, and that she couldn't recall if she'd been in California on that date. Mooney, though, hadn't hesitated when he'd been shown State of Illinois exhibit No. 1. "That is Martha Louise White," he'd said.

Mannix wasn't through enumerating her criminal history. On April 25, 1946, she'd been taken into custody on a prostitution complaint under the name Betty Smith. This time, her date of birth was December 25, 1924, and her home state was Tennessee. Two years later, Connie Fay Harbaugh—not Yarbough, as she'd testified earlier—was arrested for contributing to the delinquency of a minor. This police report said her birth date was December 25, 1927, and that her race was Hawaiian. When she was fingerprinted by the Alameda County Sheriff's Office, she gave her nearest relative as Lydia Mello of Luxora, Arkansas. She listed Lydia as her mother.

On the stand, Constance Wakefield claimed she'd never said she was born in 1927, and she wasn't sure if she'd told the cops that Lydia Mello was her mother. One thing on the report did ring true, however: "I do remember saying that I was Hawaiian."

Whether or not they were wholly accurate, these Oakland arrest reports established a few key facts about Linda Taylor's early life. She'd moved out West as a young woman. By the mid-1940s, she'd been in trouble with the law. She'd also tried on different identities—an overlapping set of names, birth dates, races, and places of origin—and she had a habit of dropping hints about the past she'd left behind.

On the afternoon of November 10, a Chicago police officer testified that he'd examined Connie Harbaugh's Alameda County fingerprint card. That set of prints, the officer said, matched one the Chicago Police Department had on file. In 1963, a woman had been arrested near

Wicker Park for assaulting a twelve-year-old girl. That woman had told officers that she was from Hawaii, and she'd given her name as Beverly Singleton—an alias that Constance Wakefield admitted she'd used in the past.

Mannix told the fingerprint technician he had no further questions. He then moved to have Constance Wakefield held in contempt of court for perjury. Judge Anthony Kogut asked the attorneys to step into his chambers. Out of earshot of the press and public, he made his opinion of Constance Wakefield known. "She has been contradicting herself and lying about everything down the line," he said. "Everything is fictitious. Everything she has submitted so far is fictitious."

Her lead attorney conceded that his client didn't have a spotless record. "We admit this girl was arrested," Milroy Blowitz said. "We admit that this girl may have prostituted herself. We admit that this girl used a number of names. We admit that this girl may have said she was born in Hawaii, she was born in Tennessee, she was born in Arkansas, she was born in Chicago." Despite all that, Blowitz argued, nobody had gotten anywhere close to proving that Constance Wakefield wasn't Constance Wakefield.

Kogut wasn't inclined to see her as an honest broker. The judge went on at length about her pathetic lineup of corroborating witnesses. One of the people who'd testified on her behalf was her own paid employee. Betty Day, who'd been drawing a salary from Constance for five years, swore she'd been present when Lawrence Wakefield's daughter came into the world, and added that the petitioner had a twin brother who'd died shortly after emerging from the womb. Constance Wakefield also had Grant Sill in her corner. But the doctor who'd filled out her delayed birth certificate had his own credibility issues, given that he'd recently been arrested for selling prescription drugs to high schoolers.[*] Sill's story also didn't match up with Day's: While the obstetrician said he'd seen a baby

---

[*] A judge eventually dropped all charges against Sill in connection to his 1963 arrest for selling barbiturates. In 1970, though, Sill was arrested again after selling prescriptions to undercover cops on twenty-seven separate occasions.

girl in the Wakefield home on Christmas Day 1934, he denied tending to a second baby. "The only evidence [Constance Wakefield] offered to establish her date of birth and place of birth was by a colored person who was obviously vague," Kogut said. "You have the very doctor, your own witness, in the court, who testifies contrary to her own testimony."

To have any chance of rescuing their case, Blowitz and Wexler would have to furnish a different kind of testimony. They'd need to find an unimpeachable witness, someone who'd help them demonstrate that Constance Wakefield really was Constance Wakefield. They told Kogut they'd found just such a person. Lydia Mooney Blount was on her way from Arkansas, and she was going to testify on behalf of her alleged daughter.

* * *

Since he'd landed in Chicago, Hubert Mooney had reached out to all the relatives he could find, urging them to come up north and help out with what he termed "a little court deal." Mooney testified that one of his sister Lydia's sons had been too afraid to make the trip—he thought Martha Louise White, "as slick as she is," might figure out a way "to bribe me or frame me." Mooney also recounted a conversation he'd had with Lydia herself.

> I told her the only thing—the people are trying to establish facts in this country, and that is what the world should be made out of, not a bunch of criticism and slanderism. And I said, "The fact is, all you got to do is come up and identify the girl."

Mooney said his fifty-six-year-old sister had been unmoved by his monologue. On the evening of November 9, she'd told him she wouldn't leave her home in Arkansas under any circumstances. And yet three days later, Lydia Blount got on the witness stand in room 643 and explained how she'd come to know Constance Wakefield.

Blount's testimony was hard to hear and at times hard to follow. Blowitz told the court she was a "sick lady"—that she'd had multiple heart attacks and had lost consciousness that very morning. He coaxed Blount along, first asking if she knew the petitioner.

"Yes," she said.

"How long have you known her?"

"Since she was three months old."

"Did you know her by any other name than Constance Wakefield?"

"Well, no, I didn't," she answered. "It was Connie Wakefield on her arm on her tag when they left her at my house."

Blount said a woman—someone she'd never seen before and never saw again—had left the infant at her home. Hubert Mooney's sister had raised this tag-wearing foundling in Luxora, Arkansas, until the child was six years old, at which point "they said they wouldn't allow colored kids in the white school." After Connie was expelled from elementary school, Blount said, a group of "colored people" whose names she didn't know took the girl to Dell, Arkansas. Connie had lived with those nameless strangers until the age of twelve, when "a car came and got her."

"Do you know whose car this was?" Blowitz asked.

"They said it was Wakefield's car," she replied.

Blount professed that she wasn't sure of Constance Wakefield's race. "I don't take blood tests," she said. She was certain, though, that she hadn't given birth to the woman sitting a few feet away from her in room 643. Blowitz finished up with a simple question: "Are you her mother?" Blount said no.

She quickly wilted under cross-examination. After a few queries from Jack Barry about names and dates, Blount started to look so peaked that Kogut halted her testimony and sent her home to rest.

Rather than adjourn the hearing for the day, the judge allowed Hubert Mooney to return to the stand to offer additional insight into his sickly sister's state of mind. Mooney said he'd been surprised, after all his sister's protestations, to lay eyes on her in Illinois. He then went into more detail about their phone conversation on November 9, expounding on the arguments he'd used to persuade his sister to tell the truth.

> I said, "[Martha] is up here and she is claiming she was
> a daughter of some guy that had died, and she was born
> in thirty-four up here, and her people were colored people,
> which there never was any colored blood in the county at that
> time, and you know it."

Mooney said he'd told Blount that he couldn't in good conscience allow such falsehoods to stand: "Now the thing that I am up here for is to defend the rights of my people and not to criticize them and run them down into the ground any lower than this so-called—I don't know what her name is—has run them already."

That line of reasoning hadn't moved Hubert Mooney's older sister. He testified that Lydia Blount had told him she'd never reveal her daughter's lineage. "I don't want people to know she is no relation to me or ever has been," Mooney claimed she'd said, "because she was down here in Arkansas last year with a nigger kid and almost got me in trouble with it."

* * *

When Blount resumed her testimony the next morning, she seemed to be suffering from catastrophic memory loss. She said "I don't know" and "I don't remember" 135 times, professing not to recall when she'd gotten married, when her children had been born, and how old she was when the three-month-old Connie Wakefield had been abandoned at her house.

Faced with this sudden burst of amnesia, Cook County assistant state's attorney Gerald Mannix tried a different strategy.

"Constance, would you come up here, Martha?" he asked.

Blowitz, annoyed by the request, told Mannix to use the petitioner's real name.

"Constance Beverly Singleton Harbaugh Wakefield Smith Reed White," the assistant state's attorney said. "Steinberg Singleton," Bishton interjected, alerting his co-counsel to a surname he'd missed.

"Would you come up here, please, Miss Wakefield?" Mannix said, adopting a softer approach. The many-named woman moved closer to the witness stand.

"Is this your daughter?" Mannix asked Lydia Blount.

"No," Blount said.

"What is her name?"

Blount didn't answer.

"What is her name?" Mannix asked again.

Again, Blount didn't answer.

"What is her name?"

Still nothing.

"What is her name?"

Constance Wakefield's attorney got angrier and angrier with each repetition. "Judge, why do we have to have a demonstration as asinine as this?" Blowitz asked, imploring Kogut to put an end to the interrogation. "How stupid can a man be?"

Lydia Blount was almost close enough to reach out and touch her daughter, but she didn't make a move or say a word. She just sat and waited for the yelling to stop, and for somebody to tell her she was free to go.

* * *

By the afternoon of November 13, it was clear to everyone in the Cook County building that Constance Beverly Steinberg Singleton Harbaugh Wakefield Smith Reed White was no policy heir. Even so, Rose Kennedy's attorneys had gone to the trouble of tracking down one more surprise witness, a woman they believed would bring this interminable probate case to a close.

The previous evening, Norris Bishton and Hubert Mooney had slipped away to catch a flight to Tennessee. The Chicago lawyer and the Amarillo refrigeration engineer had rented a car at the Memphis airport and driven sixty miles on rutted mud roads to a small cabin on a farm not far from the banks of the Mississippi River. Mooney had exited the car first, shouting out a warning to ensure that they wouldn't be met by a shotgun blast. They'd been greeted by a rail-thin woman with long gray hair and toothless gums. Once they'd made it inside, Mooney had sat beside a kerosene lamp and gotten to work convincing his mother to go with them to Chicago. Not long after they'd arrived in rural Lauderdale County, the visitors headed back to the airport, this time with another passenger in tow. Sarah Jane Mooney had been born in the early 1880s. This would be her first time on an airplane.

Less than twenty-four hours later, the octogenarian situated herself in the seat that had just been vacated by her daughter Lydia. She was wearing a long-sleeved black dress that had been cinched at the waist, and she had a shawl draped around her shoulders to ward off the autumn chill. She spoke swiftly and decisively, showing off an easy command of her family's history. She told the court that she didn't see her granddaughter Martha for about a year in the late 1920s—a "smart little while"—because the child and her mother had moved across the river to Arkansas.

Sarah Jane Mooney was a midwife, and she'd assisted with the births of a great many of her grandchildren. When asked by Jack Barry if she'd been present when Martha was born, she said, "Yes, yes, I guess I was." Barry then passed her a photograph taken in 1942. It showed a beautiful young woman with olive skin, brown eyes, and long dark hair. The woman, a teenager, had her left arm wrapped around the shoulders of an older-looking man with a busted nose and a cauliflower ear. Sarah Jane Mooney was nearly blind, but she knew who was in that picture. "That's my oldest son," she said, identifying the man as George Mooney. "And that's Martha."

Barry asked the petitioner to come forward again, this time directing her to remove her sunglasses. It had been twenty-two years since she'd posed for that photo, tilting her head slightly to the left to rest it against her uncle's right temple. Sarah Jane Mooney looked at her granddaughter—the baby girl she'd delivered and cradled in her arms. "Yes, I believe that's Martha," she said. Barry then asked Constance Wakefield if she recognized her grandmother. "I saw that lady in 1939 or 1940," she said. "That's the only time I can remember seeing her."

At the end of the day's proceedings, Blowitz asked to take the weekend to find rebuttal witnesses. When the heirship hearing recommenced on the morning of November 16, he announced his plans to bring in his own octogenarian. Constance's alleged maternal grandfather, Joe Jarvis, had gotten held up in Florida, though, "because of his age, and because of a lack of time." Given the circumstances, Blowitz asked for another delay to allow this Mr. Jarvis to make his way to Illinois. In the meantime, Blowitz said, his client had requested that he withdraw as her attorney. Blowitz then introduced a lawyer named J. H. Silver, who asked for thirty days to familiarize himself with the case.

Silver likely would've had better luck asking for permission to punch Judge Anthony Kogut in the face. No one was going to convince Kogut to deal with this madness for five more minutes, much less another month. He denied the motion for a continuance, then zoomed forward to his ruling on Cook County's effort "to strike and dismiss the petition of Constance Wakefield as being unfounded in fact."

"The petition of Constance Steinberg Wakefield to amend the heirship is denied," Kogut said. "The court further finds she has acted with a willful conscience in a deliberate attempt to defraud the estate of Lawrence Wakefield." As a consequence of that "direct contempt," the judge declared, "I commit her to the county jail for six months."

Constance Wakefield had spent the better part of a year trying to corral a monumental sum of money. Now, those riches would land in the lap of the woman she'd accused of poisoning her with strychnine. Rose Kennedy got a payout of $431,385, with $270,000 kept in reserve for other claimants. The final $60,000 of the Wakefield fortune—cash that had been found intermingled with policy slips—went to Cook County as contraband. Norris Bishton, too, got the windfall he'd been hoping for, earning a $25,000 bonus from his firm. Constance, meanwhile, was ordered to pay roughly $23,000 in court costs and attorneys' fees—the expenses incurred by all the lawyers tasked with proving she wasn't who she said she was. She also had to post a $5,000 appeal bond to buy herself a reprieve from jail.

It took more than two years for a three-judge panel to rule on that appeal. On November 29, 1966, the Appellate Court of Illinois decreed unanimously that Kogut had erred in refusing to grant Constance Wakefield's request for a change of venue—a maneuver the judge had seen as nothing but a stalling tactic. On account of that mistake, the appeals court said, everything that had taken place subsequently would be considered null and void. The petitioner wouldn't have to go to jail, and she wouldn't have to pay those court costs and lawyers' fees. In the eyes of the State of Illinois, that humiliating heirship hearing had never taken place.

The case began again in January 1967, this time under the purview of a different probate judge. But Constance and her attorney would fail to show up for their new day in court. Her bid to pry loose Lawrence Wakefield's money was finished for good.

* * *

Based on his own snooping, Norris Bishton thought Constance Wakefield may have worked for Lawrence in some capacity, or that they could've had a sexual relationship. It's possible that Constance's alleged surrogate parents in Arkansas, Jim and Virginia Collins, brought them together: In the sworn statement they provided in advance of the heirship hearing, the husband and wife said their son had worked for the policy king in the 1950s, before the young man was shot and killed.

All that mattered to the probate court and the local press, though, was that Constance and Lawrence weren't related by blood. On November 17, 1964, the day after Kogut dismissed her petition as "unfounded in fact," the *Chicago Tribune* ran a photo of the "phony heiress" in section two, one column over from a wire story on Russia banning the importation of chewing gum. For the Chicago papers, the comeuppance of a moneygrubbing charlatan was an amusing curiosity. For Constance herself, it was a life-altering catastrophe.

As a child and a young adult, the phony heiress had never really had a steady home. In Chicago in the early 1960s, in a series of houses on the city's North Side, she'd found something close to stability. The last of those places was in Ranch Triangle, a residential district not far from

Lincoln Park. The house at 1715 North Fremont Street stood a half block south of a formerly vacant lot that locals had transformed into an ice-skating rink—one of the more prominent markers of a revitalization project called Operation Pride. While nearby communities drew large numbers of Puerto Rican and Mexican immigrants in the 1960s, the gentrifying area around Lincoln Park became less diverse. When white families moved in and restored old row houses and bungalows, poor black and Puerto Rican residents got priced out and displaced.

Shortly after her failed inheritance gambit, Constance Wakefield told her kids Johnnie and Sandra that it was time for them to go. In 1965, the family moved to South Calumet Avenue, in the heart of the South Side neighborhood of Bronzeville. In a segregated city, this eight-mile journey to the south was a voyage to a different world. Lincoln Park was 95 percent white. The area abutting South Park Way—it would be renamed Martin Luther King Jr. Drive three years later, after King's assassination—was more than 99 percent black.

Bronzeville was the long-standing cultural, economic, and intellectual center of black Chicago, the home of luminaries such as Louis Armstrong and Ida B. Wells. The Wakefield family's new home at Forty-Third and South Calumet was just north of the lavishly appointed, Byzantine-style Regal Theater. By the mid-1960s, though, the Regal's grand staircases and marble floors served as more a reminder of Bronzeville's past than an indicator of its current state. The newly completed Robert Taylor Homes, the nation's largest public housing complex, sprawled a few blocks to the west of South Calumet Avenue. Rather than spread public housing units around the city, Mayor Richard J. Daley's administration concentrated low-income black Chicagoans in places that white people didn't live. The construction of the Dan Ryan Expressway, which separated Daley's own Irish enclave of Bridgeport from the Taylor Homes' twenty-seven-thousand inhabitants, ensured that white Chicagoans wouldn't have to see or think about the all-black ghetto.

It's possible that Constance Wakefield chose to relocate her family because she needed affordable housing. Johnnie thought they'd moved because his mother no longer felt comfortable in a place like Lincoln

Park. In probate court, a white judge had waved away the testimony of her friend and employee Betty Day, dismissing Day's account as the unreliable statement of "a colored person." That same judge and a bunch of white lawyers hadn't said a word when Constance's uncle called her a nigger in open court. White people had done nothing but malign and abuse her. In Bronzeville, she'd have the chance to be something other than a pariah.

For Constance, starting over didn't mean letting go of the Wakefield name. When Jack Sherwin arrested her on August 25, 1974, he found the birth certificate she'd fashioned a decade earlier, the one in which she'd willed Constance Beverly Wakefield into existence. A year after that, she would sign Patricia Parks's death certificate as Linda C. Wakefield. And in 1977, when she stood trial for defrauding the State of Illinois, she didn't identify herself as Taylor or Walker or Bennett or Brownlee. Her name, she said in criminal court, was Linda Wakefield.

The self-professed Wakefield descendant didn't always stick to the story she'd told in probate court. Six years after her petition was denied, she'd place an ad in the *Defender* indicating that she was the daughter of Jasper Herman, the Florida spiritual adviser who'd supported her heirship claim during the Wakefield case. But regardless of what Linda Taylor truly believed about her relationship with Lawrence Wakefield, Johnnie and Sandra both thought something had snapped in their mother in 1964. Later in her life, Taylor would maintain that she'd started hearing voices after Lawrence Wakefield's death. She also said she'd felt the urge to kill someone, and to kill herself.

The people who were supposed to love her unconditionally had cast her aside when she was a child, but they'd cared enough to come all the way to Chicago and destroy her plan to secure a better life. Hubert Mooney had said his niece's father couldn't possibly be a black man like Lawrence Wakefield, because there were no Negroes anywhere in the Mooney family tree. He'd testified that her real father, an Alabaman named Marvin White, was "a Portuguese or something." Sarah Jane Mooney had said her granddaughter Martha was a white woman—or at least "she is supposed to be."

THE QUEEN

Martha Louise White's uncle had been telling the truth when he said her father wasn't Lawrence Wakefield. He'd been lying when he said her father was Marvin White.

Norris Bishton spent a lot of time with Mooney, and the refrigeration man came to trust the attorney. In a quiet moment away from the courtroom, Mooney had confessed that Martha's biological father wasn't "a Portuguese or something." He was a black man. Mooney hadn't traveled to Chicago because he cared about the truth. He'd come to make sure a family secret stayed buried in the past.

Linda Taylor's grandfather Ike Mooney and grandmother Sarah Jane Mooney with one of Taylor's first cousins in 1943. *(Mooney family)*

Ike Mooney and his daughter Lydia Mooney—Taylor's mother—circa 1930. *(Mooney family)*

Taylor, around age sixteen, with her uncle George Mooney in 1942.
(Circuit Court of Cook County)

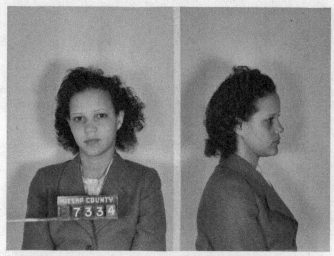

Taylor after being arrested for vagrancy in Washington State in 1944. *(Washington State Archives, Puget Sound – Kitsap County Sheriff's Department, Mug Shots)*

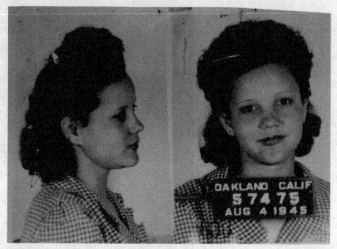

Taylor in 1945, after her arrest for malicious mischief in Oakland. *(Circuit Court of Cook County)*

Lawrence Wakefield, the man Taylor claimed was her father, in 1960, four years before his death. *(Bettmann/Getty Images)*

Detectives Bernard Kay and George Martis and commander Edward Egan of the Chicago Police Department with the money found in Wakefield's South Side home. *(Bettmann/Getty Images)*

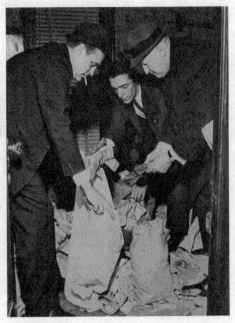

Detective Jack Sherwin of the Chicago Police Department, circa mid-1970s. *(Sherwin family)*

George Bliss (far right) celebrates winning the Pulitzer Prize in 1976 with (from left to right) *Chicago Tribune* colleagues William Gaines, Chuck Neubauer, William Crawford, William Jones, and Bernard Judge. *(Bliss family)*

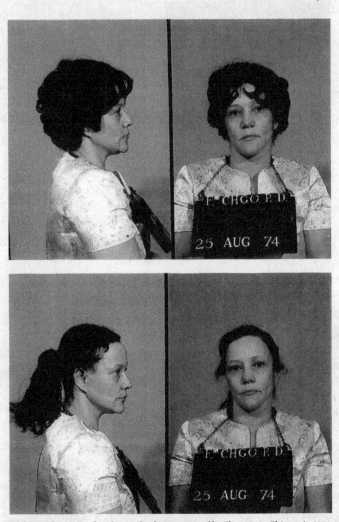
Taylor, with a wig and without, after being arrested by Sherwin in Chicago in 1974.
(*Chicago Police Department*)

Taylor with her husband, Sherman Ray, prior to being sentenced to prison for welfare fraud in May 1977. *(Associated Press)*

Taylor with Ray in a Chicago hospital, date unknown. *(Ray family)*

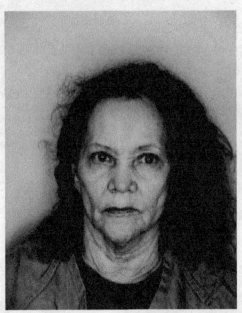

A booking photo taken in Hillsborough County, Florida, in 1995, as federal authorities were evaluating Taylor's mental health. *(Hillsborough County Sheriff's Office)*

Taylor's son Johnnie Harbaugh in 2013. *(Josh Levin)*

CHAPTER 12
Bottom Rats

Lydia Mooney White went into labor during a rainstorm on a frigid winter day. Her family's home, which stood on stilts as protection against the Mississippi River's periodic floods, had no running water, no telephone, and no electricity. It also had no insulation, and the wind off the Mississippi poured through the cypress walls. She tried her best to get comfortable, lying down on a bed next to a small heater. Her mother, Sarah Jane, shooed away Lydia's four-year-old brother, Hubert, confining him to a room on the other side of the small wooden house.

Sarah Jane Mooney had midwifed hundreds of babies, and she knew what to do if a newborn came out feetfirst or looking blue. But there was nothing unusual about this delivery, no reason to call a doctor to tend to the mother or her healthy baby girl.

Even so, this wasn't a wholly joyous occasion for the Mooney family. Lydia's husband, Marvin White, wasn't around, and it wasn't clear if he ever would be. The baby also didn't look like Marvin, and she didn't have Lydia's features or coloring.

Sarah Jane sometimes wrote up birth certificates on behalf of the parents she'd assisted, but this time she didn't bother. There would be no official record to mark Martha Louise White's arrival, nothing signed by a county clerk or state public health director to indicate she'd been born in a particular place at a particular time to a particular mother and father. As far as the Mooneys were concerned, it would be perfectly fine if the outside world had no idea this little girl existed.

THE QUEEN

★ ★ ★

Although Hubert Mooney would later report that his sister had given birth in Alabama, Lydia had actually fled her home state before having her second child. Prior to setting out for Tennessee, she'd spent a week in jail. In the summer of 1925, "Lyda White"—she went by Lyde and Lydie in addition to Lydia—was arrested twice for vagrancy. The State of Alabama stipulated that a vagrant could be "any person who is a common drunkard," "any person who is a prostitute," and "any person leading an idle, immoral, or profligate life." Lydia's transgression was infidelity.

In 1923, her father, Ike Mooney, had sent an Alabama judge a hand-written note to grant his daughter permission to wed. The groom, Marvin White, was twenty-three. Lydia was fourteen, though the county paperwork listed her as three years older. The form specified that the bride and groom were of no blood relation, and the couple's race was penned in with a single *W*—a second dashed line would've been superfluous, as interracial marriage was illegal in Alabama.*

White, a farmer, filed for divorce four years later, alleging that his wife had "[taken] up with one Arthur Head and did commit numerous and various acts of adultery with the said Arthur Head for a long period of time." He later helped send Head to prison, testifying that his romantic rival had defied Prohibition laws by manufacturing whiskey in a still hidden in a thicket of sugarcane. In his divorce petition, Lydia's husband attested that his wife and her paramour had both been arrested for adultery and locked up. White said that Lydia had "voluntarily left my bed and board in the fall of 1925," and that she'd never returned home.

The seventeen-year-old Lydia Mooney White left Alabama with one child in tow—her daughter Mary Jane—and pregnant with another. Lydia's parents and six of her siblings had made the same move a few months earlier, traveling 220 miles northwest to a part of the state known

---

* Although the Supreme Court's ruling in 1967's *Loving v. Virginia* made state-level inter-racial marriage bans unenforceable, Alabama didn't lift its prohibition on miscegenation until 2000.

as the Tennessee bottomlands. Golddust, Tennessee, got its name from a paddle wheel steamer that had carried Mark Twain as a passenger, a stint he documented in his memoir *Life on the Mississippi*. In August 1882, shortly after the town had been christened, the *Gold Dust* exploded due to a faulty boiler, a calamity that killed seventeen people. The town of Golddust, which had a population in the low hundreds, continued on as a small farming community comprising a couple of general stores, a pair of cotton gins, some churches, a post office, and a schoolhouse. The Mooneys worked Golddust's soil with mules, and chopped and picked cotton by hand. Residents of nearby Ripley, a relatively bustling city of just more than two thousand, had a nickname for the laborers who did that brutal work: "bottom rats."

Lydia arrived in Golddust in September 1925, the time of year when the fields bloomed into a bright white blanket. The family matriarch, Sarah Jane, ran the household, took care of expectant mothers, and worked in the fields. She couldn't afford not to earn a wage because her ill-tempered husband had a habit of gambling away whatever money he earned. When she finished baling cotton, she'd harvest pecans and peel bark off trees to make medicine. Sarah Jane covered her thin frame in long-sleeved dresses with a dozen or more buttons down the front, and she laced her long hair into a pair of braids that she wore wrapped around her head. She rarely put on shoes, leaving her bare feet to get dusted with the flour she used to bake tea cakes. Sarah Jane had given birth to ten children, but she liked to say her husband had never seen her knees. If a woman showed off her body, she thought, she deserved whatever trouble came her way.

Sarah Jane Yates had married Ike Mooney in 1898, when she was fifteen years old. Mooney had been born in rural North Alabama to a family that didn't have much money or property. His grandfather Boaz Mooney, who'd owned some land in Blount County, had been lynched in 1861—tied to a tree and shot after being accused of harboring able-bodied men who'd refused to take up the Confederate cause. One of Sarah Jane's great-great-grandfathers, a man named Henry Hill who'd lived in Tennessee, was recorded in the 1830 U.S. census as the owner of eight slaves. Her maternal grandfather had been captured by Ulysses S. Grant's army along with thousands of other Confederate soldiers at the Battle of Fort Donelson. Five months later, in July 1862, he'd died in a fetid, overcrowded Union prisoner-of-war camp. Camp Douglas—a breeding ground for dysentery, smallpox, and tuberculosis that became known as "eighty acres of hell"—was just outside the city limits of Chicago. By the early twentieth century, the Civil War site had been torn down and forgotten, and the neighborhood of Bronzeville had sprung up in its place. When Linda Taylor lived on Chicago's South Side, she was a few miles away from her great-great-grandfather's final resting place, a mass grave in Oak Woods Cemetery known as the Confederate Mound.

Martha Louise White may have gotten her name from Sarah Jane's aunt Martha Louise Rutledge Brown, who died in Cullman County, Alabama, in 1928; her gravestone describes her as "a tender mother and a faithful friend." While Sarah Jane loved her family, she was inclined more toward toughness than tenderness. She'd tell her granddaughters stories about fairies and witches, then remind them to go to sleep with God on their minds, because they might not wake up to see another day. Sarah Jane also warned the girls to stay away from men they wouldn't want to be with for the rest of their lives. Her own husband made her miserable, but she was too devout to consider a divorce.

Lydia had already had one child out of wedlock by the time she got to Tennessee. She'd given birth to Mary Jane at age fourteen, eight months before Lydia's father had signed the letter allowing her to marry Marvin White. When Sarah Jane would take the stand in the Wakefield case, she'd say that Lydia had been impregnated by her first cousin, a man in his early twenties.

Given the absence of a county or state record, Martha Louise White's birth date is also uncertain—it's possible that Martha herself didn't even know it. One of Lydia's younger sisters remembered the birth falling on a cold and stormy school day, and Sarah Jane would testify in 1964 that Lydia had been in Tennessee for roughly three months before Martha was born. Between December 1925 and February 1926, there was just one rainy weekday—January 21, 1926—when the daytime high temperature dropped below fifty degrees in the vicinity of Golddust, Tennessee.

A little less than two decades later, when "Connie Reed" was arrested in Oakland for malicious mischief, she told the police she'd been born on January 24, 1926. It was perhaps the only time she gave a cop, a lawyer, or a bureaucrat a plausible date of birth.

Thirty-eight years later in Chicago, the then eighty-something Sarah Jane Mooney would say that Martha's father was "Marv White." When asked how she could be certain, she'd explain, "Well, they was living together. That's all I know now."

* * *

Sarah Jane knew more than she was letting on. Like her son Hubert, she'd confess to the lawyer Norris Bishton that she'd deceived the court. Marvin White and the bootlegger Arthur Head were white men. In their conversations with the attorney, Hubert and Sarah Jane Mooney would both divulge that Martha's father was black.

Lydia and her relatives had good reason to obscure the truth. In Alabama, where Martha had been conceived, the state code criminalized sexual relations between "any white person and any negro," with violations of the statute punishable with a prison stint of between two and seven years. That law had been upheld by the U.S. Supreme Court, which ruled in 1883 that Alabama had been within its rights to convict a black man and a white woman who'd been living "in a state of adultery and fornication." This precedent would stand until the high court's ruling in *McLaughlin v. Florida*, which decreed that prohibitions on interracial cohabitation were unconstitutional. The Supreme Court would make that decision in December 1964, one month after Lydia, her brother, and her mother lied about Martha Louise White's parentage in Cook County Probate Court.

Even within the Mooney family, the circumstances of Martha's birth were discussed only in whispers. It was a mystery how, in a part of Alabama where black people were de facto prohibited from settling, Lydia had made the acquaintance of Martha's biological father. In private conversations, Hubert and Sarah Jane would say Lydia had professed that her second daughter was conceived in rape.

THE QUEEN

That sort of allegation could be incredibly dangerous. In May 1926 in Osceola, Arkansas—a town just across the Mississippi River from Golddust—a twenty-two-year-old black man named Albert Blades would be mutilated, hanged, and burned by a mob of twelve hundred after an eleven-year-old white girl said he'd sexually assaulted her in a park. Doctors would later examine the girl, according to the *St. Louis Argus*, and find that "she had not been attacked."

Lydia's accusation of sexual assault never became public; if any acts of violence were perpetrated against Martha's father, they weren't reported in the local newspapers or inscribed in Mooney family lore. But neither Sarah Jane nor Hubert believed Lydia had been a victim. While Hubert was too young to have firsthand knowledge of his sister's assignation, he'd later say he'd heard that she would sneak off to a barn with an unnamed black man, and that their sexual relationship had been consensual.

From the 1920s on, the identity of Martha's father shifted depending on the audience. In 1964, Lydia would erase herself from her daughter's origin story entirely, testifying that the girl had been left on her doorstep as a three-month-old infant. That lie embodied a larger truth: No one wanted to lay claim to Martha Louise White. It was a fact she understood from the time she was a very small child.

* * *

Martha got a stepfather before her first birthday. In October 1926, a year before Marvin White filed for divorce in Alabama, Lydia Mooney White married a thirty-eight-year-old widower named Joseph Jackson Miller.[*] "Old Man Joe Miller," as Sarah Jane took to calling him, had left his job at a Missouri slaughterhouse to find agricultural work in the Mississippi River's alluvial plain. Soon after Martha started walking, Lydia and her new husband packed their possessions into a Ford truck that Old Man Miller had bought from his father-in-law, Ike. As of the 1930 U.S. census,

---

[*] Lydia would eventually marry again, taking the last name of her husband Hubert Blount.

Joe, Lydia, and their children—Miller's teenage son, Sam, from his first marriage; a girl named "Murry" (probably Mary Jane); and four-year-old Martha—were living on the Arkansas side of the Mississippi, on property owned by a wealthy planter named Edgar A. Stacy.

Until the turn of the century, the area around Dell, Arkansas, had been a swampy, malarial timberland patrolled by wolves, bobcats, and bears. In the first few decades of the 1900s, loggers cleared thousands of acres of elm, ash, oak, and cypress; dredge boats dug out hundreds of miles of drainage ditches; and state and federal functionaries shored up levees to protect the region from devastating floods. In short order, Mississippi County, Arkansas, had been transformed, in the words of the local chamber of commerce, into the "greatest cotton producing county in the world," home to "super-soil" that nurtured an agricultural bounty.

At its height, the Stacy plantation had twenty-two thousand acres of land under cultivation. Farmhands like Joe Miller planted cotton in April and May, thinned out the crop with hoes when the plants broke through the dirt, and plowed the fields with the aid of mules in June and July. Picking season started at the end of August, whereupon women and children took to the fields to separate fluffy cotton locks from their thick, protective burrs, depositing the white fibers in nine-foot-long canvas sacks worn strapped around their shoulders. Most of the men on the plantation were sharecroppers rather than wage laborers—they were furnished with seed and beasts of burden and gave up half the proceeds from their harvests in return. The greatest cotton-producing county in the world didn't produce anything close to a living wage for the Miller family. Stacy's tenants were essentially indentured servants. At the end of the year, they might be told they'd run up a debt, and they'd have no recourse to contest the boss's accounting.

The front of the Stacy family's residence, a stately two-story home with four towering white columns, looked a bit like the facade of Tara, the fictional plantation house from *Gone with the Wind*. The Millers lived in a shanty fashioned from cypress boards that had been fastened together vertically, with sheets of newsprint stuffed between the cracks. The laborers' shacks had kerosene lights, outdoor pitcher pumps for water, and coal or kerosene stoves for heat. Joe, Lydia, and their children may have had a small garden plot and a pig or calf to raise and slaughter. They bought everything else they needed—cornmeal, flour, lard, dried beans—at the plantation commissary. When Stacy's hands got paid, they received half their remuneration in groceries. If working men had too much money in their pockets, the plantation owner believed, they'd waste it all on moonshine.

The late 1920s and the 1930s were trying years for cotton farmers in Arkansas and Tennessee. The Great Mississippi Flood of 1927—what Secretary of Commerce Herbert Hoover called America's "greatest peacetime disaster"—overwhelmed levees in Louisiana, Mississippi, Arkansas, and elsewhere along the river. The cataclysmic flood, which left the Stacy plantation underwater, necessitated a large-scale, nationalized relief effort. That outlay of federal money primed the nation to support Franklin Roosevelt's New Deal, a package of programs that included Aid to Dependent Children. The disaster of 1927 also accelerated the Great Migration, impelling tens of thousands of black Americans to leave behind the deprivations of rural life and set out for metropolises such as Chicago and Detroit.

In 1930, in the midst of the Great Depression, a ceaseless drought caused as many as 50 percent of the crops in Arkansas to wither and die. The Stacy plantation suffered catastrophic economic losses, ultimately forcing the family to give up all but two thousand of its twenty-two-thousand acres. With farmers unable to purchase staples and Hoover, who was elected president in 1928, slow to offer federal largesse, the Red Cross stepped in to provide food and clothing for hundreds of thousands of Arkansans. The planters and bankers who controlled the distribution of this aid fretted about the risks of excessive generosity, recalling "how hard it was to get labor after the '27 [flood], when people were allowed to loaf and eat."

Seven years after the height of the drought, another great flood washed over more than a million acres of agricultural land in Arkansas and destroyed most every dwelling in Golddust. Lydia's brother Sam, who lived on the Tennessee side of the river, woke up to water sloshing through the floor of his house. A barge eventually plucked him and his family off their tin roof and ferried them to a Red Cross tent city, where they found temporary shelter until the Millers took them in.

Although Lydia and Joe moved from place to place frequently, they never strayed too far from her parents and siblings. Sometimes the Millers and Mooneys even ended up on the same plantation. Hubert would remember playing with Martha several times a week when they were young kids, "eating watermelons and crap like that on the farm." A photograph taken in Arkansas around 1930 showed Lydia and her father, Ike, side by side, their arms touching at the elbow, the expressions on their faces totally blank. She's wearing a dark-colored cloche hat and a rumpled, drop-waist, floral-print feed-sack dress, one that had probably been sewn by her mother. The mustachioed, dour-looking farmer and his heavyset, unsmiling daughter stood in front of an elevated, rough-hewn wooden structure with a busted window—either Lydia's parents' home or her own.

* * *

By 1940, the Millers were living on the Florenden Plantation, a thirty-five-hundred-acre farm on the outskirts of Luxora, Arkansas, owned by Frank O. Lowden, a former governor of Illinois who'd been touted in the 1920s as a potential Republican presidential candidate.* Lowden, who aspired to build Florenden into "the star plantation of the South," wrote to the farm's manager in 1939 that he was "not only delighted but astonished at the yield of cotton . . . which the tenants have produced." According to the 1940 census, the Millers paid $5 per month in rent to live at Florenden. While the census didn't enumerate Joe Miller's income, his adult sons earned $150 and $240, respectively, as wage laborers. That was well below the median annual income for American men, which stood at $298 for agricultural workers and $1,001 for those not employed on farms.

---

* While the ex-governor always managed the property, his wife, Florence Lowden—the daughter of sleeping-car magnate George Pullman—had been the one to buy the land in 1911. She willed the plantation to her husband upon her death in 1937.

The men and women listed above J. J. and Lyde Miller on the 1940 census included a pair of schoolteachers, five farm laborers, a grocer, and the manager of the Florenden Plantation. Eleven people on the Millers' census page were classified as "Negroes." In 1920, the U.S. Census Bureau had distinguished between "blacks" and "mulattoes," with the former group encompassing "all Negroes of full blood" and the latter "all Negroes having some proportion of white blood."* That distinction had been erased in 1930, when the agency adopted the principle that became known as the "one-drop rule," mandating that any "person of mixed white and Negro blood should be returned as a Negro, no matter how small the percentage of Negro blood." The Census Bureau's chief statistician, Joseph Hill, explained that it had been necessary to enact such a provision because the "very nature of things makes it impossible in a census to distinguish accurately between black and mulatto." Until 1960, individual census enumerators were tasked with categorizing the race of every American. Hill reported that the "enumerator must either judge by appearances—which are often deceitful, and he does not by any means meet or see all the persons whom he enumerates—or he must accept the answer he gets to the question if he takes the trouble to ask it."

It's not possible to know if the census takers who visited the Miller family in Mississippi County, Arkansas, scrutinized Martha's pigmentation to determine if she had some "percentage of Negro blood." What we do know is that Martha was marked as white in the 1930 and 1940 censuses, just like the rest of her family. This government-adjudged determination of racial purity affirmed that the Millers were law-abiding citizens. In 1911, the Arkansas legislature had prohibited the act of "concubinage"—that is, "the unlawful cohabitation of persons of the

---

* The 1890 census had included more discrete racial categories. "Be particularly careful to distinguish between blacks, mulattoes, quadroons, and octoroons," the Census Bureau's Instructions to Enumerators explained. "The word 'black' should be used to describe those persons who have three-fourths or more black blood; 'mulatto,' those persons who have from three-eighths to five-eighths black blood; 'quadroon,' those persons who have one-fourth black blood; and 'octoroon,' those persons who have one-eighth or any trace of black blood." The octoroon and quadroon categories did not appear in the 1900 census or any year thereafter.

Caucasian race and of the negro race, whether open or secret." Per that statute, "Any woman who shall have been delivered of a mulatto child, the same shall be prima facie evidence of guilt without further proof and shall justify a conviction of the woman." If Martha had been declared a "Negro," her mother, Lydia, would've been guilty of a felony.

Hubert Mooney would testify in 1964 that he and his niece had played with black children in Golddust. "There are lots of them there, lots of them," he'd say, remarking on the contrast between Tennessee's Lauderdale County and lily-white Cullman, Alabama. The Millers had lived alongside black people on the Stacy plantation as well. All farm-hands faced economic deprivation, but black sharecroppers and wage laborers also had to live with the constant fear of racial violence. Drivers traveling east and west on state highway 18, which bisected the sprawling farm, made a game of throwing rocks at dark-skinned workers they spotted walking down the road. Black men and women rarely left the Stacy property. They worshipped there, in a modest wooden church with a gable roof that itinerant preachers were always promising to fix up. They were also buried on the plantation, in a bamboo-covered cemetery laden with unmarked graves.

Black children rarely had the chance to explore the world beyond the cotton fields. While white boys and girls went to a local public school, the sons and daughters of black laborers went to class on the plantation, if they went at all. Although the 1940 census indicates that the teenage Martha completed the second grade, her aunt Thelma Helms—who lived near the Miller family—didn't remember her niece making it even that far. "She didn't go to no school I went to," Helms would say during the Wakefield heirship hearing, noting that Martha's older sister, Mary Jane, had been given an education. Lydia would testify that Martha had been expelled from an all-white school at about age six. Despite refusing to acknowledge in court that her daughter was biracial, Martha's mother would say that "they wouldn't allow colored kids in the white school." She'd explain that her daughter had gone with "colored people—colored women who took her to Dell and sent her to school."

In her 1964 interview with the *Chicago Defender*, Constance Wakefield said that Jim and Virginia Collins—a black couple who lived near Dell—had been her surrogate parents. The U.S. census, however, always listed her as living in a household headed by her stepfather, Joe Miller. Thelma Helms would say in court that she'd never heard of Martha moving in with a black family, though she did acknowledge that her niece had been a nomad from an early age. "She had been leaving and coming ever since she was about twelve years old, drifting in and out," Helms would explain. "She would come back and stay awhile, and get into a fuss with her stepdad and take off again....It was in and out so much I couldn't keep track of a person like that."

* * *

A light complexion could, in certain circumstances, allow a biracial person in the Deep South to travel between two very different worlds. In the fall of 1919, NAACP assistant secretary Walter White went undercover as a white man to investigate a massacre near Elaine, Arkansas, a town 115 miles down the Mississippi River from Dell. On the night of September 30, a group of roughly a hundred black farmworkers had gathered at a church to discuss forming a union; by banding together, they thought, they might be able to convince white plantation owners to share more of the proceeds from their cotton crop. Although it's unclear who shot first, a conflict outside the meeting ended in the death of a white railroad policeman.

The next morning, hundreds of armed white men descended on Elaine, and they were soon joined by five hundred U.S. Army troops who'd been brought in to quell a supposed black insurrection. ("Vicious Blacks Were Planning Great Uprising," said an October 4 *Arkansas Gazette* headline.) Walter White would later estimate that more than two hundred black people were slaughtered, gunned down by "mobs [that] swept over the countryside hunting down and killing every Negro they could find." He'd gathered that information in interviews with white citizens and public officials who'd believed that the NAACP assistant secretary was one of them.

White—whose mother was purportedly the granddaughter of an

enslaved woman named Dilsia and her master, future U.S. president William Henry Harrison—risked enraging those who'd been deceived by his racial passing. In a 1929 article for the magazine *American Mercury*, he reported that he'd fled Elaine after word began to spread about his identity. On his way out of town, he wrote, a white train conductor told him, "Why, Mister, you're leaving just when the fun is going to start! There's a damned yaller nigger down here passing for white and the boys are going to have some fun with him." When White asked about "the nature of the fun," the conductor explained that "when they get through with him, he won't pass for white no more."

Martha Louise White's family members were happy for her to pass on official forms, but they didn't let her forget who she really was. Her uncle Sam Mooney, who'd found refuge with the Millers after the 1937 flood, didn't allow his niece inside his home in Golddust. Sam's daughter Sarah, who was more than a decade younger than Martha, thought her first cousin was incredibly beautiful, with shiny black hair and full lips. Sarah knew that Lydia's daughter was different, and she knew she wasn't supposed to talk about what made her that way. She mostly admired her cousin from afar. Martha spent one big family get-together sitting in a car, alone. None of the Mooneys spoke to her, and she didn't speak to any of them.

Martha, like her mother before her, would give birth to her first child when she was still a child herself. In 1964, Rose Kennedy's attorneys would introduce into evidence a delayed birth certificate for a white male named Clifford Lee Harbaugh. That record, which had been filled out by an Arkansas physician in 1957, reported that Clifford had been born on July 27, 1940, in Dell, Arkansas. His mother's "color" was listed as white, her name as Connie M. White, her home state as Louisiana, and her age upon Clifford's birth as fifteen. The first of those data points was open to interpretation. The last three were incorrect. As of July 1940, Martha Louise White of Golddust, Tennessee, would've been just fourteen years old.

Lydia would tell the probate court that she'd helped raise her grandson in his infancy. That arrangement would end without any warning. One day, when Lydia was away from home, Martha and Clifford disappeared. Lydia wouldn't see her daughter and grandson again for years.

In Mississippi County, Arkansas, Martha Louise White's life had been circumscribed by events that preceded her birth. Everyone seemed to think they knew who and what she was, and who and what she had any right to be. In a different state, in a different part of the country, her history wouldn't have to be her destiny. She could rewrite her past to tell whatever story she wanted.

CHAPTER 13
The Two Mrs. Harbaughs

The top sanitation official in Oakland, California, said the six buildings owned by William Viera were "the vilest the health department has ever seen." The families that lived in Viera's apartments told of clogged toilet fixtures, broken flooring, and wooden beams that had been gnawed by rats. The squalor at 778 Tenth Street, where tenants reported that "small flies gather around the rotted wood," earned a front-page spread in the *Oakland Tribune* in 1942. Four years later, an Oakland jury found the landlord guilty of a host of violations owing to the "filth and rubbish" that continued to blanket his properties.

The building on Tenth Street made the paper again in 1948, in an article about a pair of women who'd been arrested for abandoning their children. On February 4, the Oakland police got tipped off that a two-year-old and a three-year-old had been neglected by their mothers. The woman who called the authorities also lived at 778 Tenth Street; she explained that she'd agreed to watch her neighbors' kids but had left the youngsters on their own because she had to go to town herself. The two mothers were taken to the city jail. Their babysitter, who called herself Connie Harbaugh, faced no charges for ditching her assignment. The cops would come back for her the following month.

On a Thursday night in March, two officers showed up at Connie Harbaugh's door; their ensuing report noted that they'd "received information" that she'd been seen consorting with "several different men." What they saw inside her West Oakland apartment confirmed the tip. "When arrested the above had a Mexican, Gilbert Ortiz, in her room," the report began. "On questioning, Ortiz admitted several acts of intercourse with above and stated that he has slept all night with above on three different occasions while [her seven-year-old] son, Clifford Harbaugh, slept on a couch in the same room."

The Oakland police detained Connie Fay Harbaugh for contributing to the delinquency of a minor, a misdemeanor that could stem from abetting a child's exposure to "any house of prostitution or assignation" or placing him "in danger of leading an idle, dissolute, lewd, or immoral life." The case history stated that "Gilbert Ortiz admitted that he had a venereal disease which he contracted only last Sunday." The woman at 778 Tenth Street, apartment number two, was deemed the probable culprit.

* * *

Nearly everyone in Martha Louise White's family—her mother, stepfather, and grandmother and most of her aunts, uncles, and cousins—chose to stay in the South forever. Even so, her decision to start over someplace new was far from uncommon. As many as 21 percent of Arkansans abandoned the state in the 1940s, the largest proportion in the nation, with California their most popular destination. The teenager from Mississippi County was somewhat unusual in that those who left Arkansas tended to be more well-to-do and better educated than those who stayed behind. But like most people who relocated, Martha Louise White was young and from a rural area. Race also played a major role in one's willingness to pick up stakes. Between 14 and 18 percent of white Arkansans moved beyond the state's borders in the 1940s. Estimates of the departure rate for black residents ranged from 24 to 33 percent.

Black migrants saw the Pacific Coast as both a gateway to economic prosperity and an escape from the degradations of the Jim Crow South. Among those who made the journey to California was a teenage Maya Angelou, who fled to Oakland from Stamps, Arkansas, shortly after a white man forced her older brother to carry the body of a "rotten dead Negro"—possibly the victim of an unreported lynching.

Oakland, San Francisco, and most everywhere else in the Bay Area flourished during World War II, buoyed by billions of dollars in government shipbuilding contracts. An essay published in the NAACP magazine the *Crisis* depicted California as a Shangri-la for black Americans, a place where black "children go to the same schools as other children" and black men "can walk down the street without having to move toward the curb when a white man passes." Oakland also offered a bounty of opportunities for working women, thanks to massive growth in national defense spending and the dearth of men in the labor market. The around-the-clock nature of wartime shift work fostered a kind of leisure free-for-all in which restaurants, dance halls, and movie theaters stayed open twenty-four hours a day, seven days a week. In the Golden State, it seemed, the rules governing all types of social behavior were subject to change, and the past didn't necessarily have to be prologue.

In 1944, *Fortune* magazine sent Dorothea Lange—whose photograph *Migrant Mother* came to embody the hardships suffered by those who'd gone west in the 1930s—to document the wartime boom in Richmond, twelve miles north of Oakland along San Francisco Bay. One of the images from that series featured a young black woman standing in front of a café, her smiling face drawing attention away from a poster advertising a "free war show" at Berkeley Memorial Stadium. She had a small handbag tucked beneath her left arm, a long beaded necklace wrapped around her neck, and a mid-length fur jacket draped over her shoulders. The caption: "It Was Never Like This Back Home."

The reality of life in California, however, often didn't live up to that dreamy vision. Shipyards mostly passed over black women when hiring for high-paying, skilled jobs, instead offering them less remunerative positions as custodians and cafeteria workers. Connie Harbaugh's rat-infested West Oakland apartment building was abysmal but not atypical. Between 1940 and 1947, Oakland grew by a hundred thousand people and developed fewer than fourteen thousand new housing units. War workers and their families slept on park benches, in chicken shacks and sheds, and in the passageways of Oakland's city hall. Some rooming houses offered beds by the hour. Others rented out chairs for laborers to sleep in.

THE QUEEN

The housing shortage was most acute in West Oakland, a 6.5-square-mile neighborhood that city policy makers quickly transformed from an integrated working-class enclave into a black ghetto. In 1940, there were 8,462 black people in all of Oakland. By 1950, that figure had risen to 47,562. This rapid influx of black migrants inspired local officials to impose the type of segregation that these newcomers had moved to California to escape. The construction of black-only housing projects in West Oakland, as well as the enforcement of restrictive real estate covenants in nearby communities, meant that, in the words of one Oaklander, there was "such a small part of the city that black folk could live in that they were sleeping on top of each other." As of 1950, 85 percent of the city's black residents had been partitioned off in West Oakland, many of them bunking in cramped single-occupancy hotel rooms and Victorian houses jam-packed with boarders. Angelou lived with her brother, mother, grandmother, and two uncles in an overstuffed apartment with a bathtub in the kitchen. The place shook all day long, rocking back and forth whenever a Southern Pacific train rolled past.

That railroad-adjacent apartment was on the western edge of West Oakland, not far from one of the nation's most prominent black boulevards. On Seventh Street, Angelou wrote in her autobiography, "dusty bars and smoke shops sat in the laps of storefront churches." The strip also housed Harold "Slim" Jenkins's nightclub—an elegant establishment that Angelou called "pretentious"—which attracted mixed-race crowds for performances by the Ink Spots, Duke Ellington, and Sarah Vaughan. A few miles to the east, the five-thousand-plus-seat Oakland Auditorium held separate "colored dances" on Monday nights, a policy enacted in 1944 following a skirmish outside a sold-out Cab Calloway concert. Although the city's police chief declared that it "was not a race riot," the conservative *Oakland Observer* blamed the arena fracas on "the influx of what might be called socially-liberated or uninhibited Negroes who are not bound by the old and peaceful understanding between the Negro and the white in Oakland." These new arrivals, the newspaper explained, do "not concede that the white man has the right to be alone with his kind."

In the 1940s, Oakland business owners responded to this influx by posting signs reading "White Trade Only" and "We Refuse Service to Negroes." These public displays were most prevalent in the stretch of downtown abutting the eastern border of West Oakland. This was the area, almost exactly halfway between Slim Jenkins's nightclub and the Oakland Auditorium, where the city's white ruling class came in closest contact with the thousands of black men, women, and children who'd put down roots in California in the 1940s. The apartment where the Oakland police arrested Connie Harbaugh in 1948 was situated in this contested space. So was the sidewalk where she bumped into her Uncle Hubert in the summer of 1945.

* * *

Hubert Mooney hadn't planned to end up in California. The Alabama native had enlisted in the navy in July 1942 and been assigned to the cruiser USS *Portland*. Two months after he'd come aboard, the Pacific-based ship was struck by a torpedo during the Naval Battle of Guadalcanal. The *Portland* had then been towed to Sydney, Australia, where it stayed in dry dock while undergoing repairs. Mooney went AWOL for more than nine days during this extended shore leave, got court-martialed, then vanished for another three days. When the ship made it to San Francisco in March 1943, he was booted out of the navy with a bad conduct discharge—a fact that wouldn't get mentioned when he'd assail his niece's character in court two decades later.

After his unscheduled exit from the armed forces, Mooney drove a Yellow cab in Oakland and lived around the corner from Swan's 10th Street Market, a massive downtown shopping emporium that employed clerks who'd answered ads for white-only positions. He would testify in Chicago that he'd "never thought about running into" his sister's daughter in the Bay Area: "I will guarantee you, not there." But on an afternoon in late July 1945, the ex-sailor heard a familiar voice shouting his name. Mooney had turned twenty-four a few months earlier. His niece was now nineteen. The two of them would spend the rest of the day cavorting and reminiscing, a couple of young adults exulting in the coincidence of finding each other eighteen hundred miles away from the plantations where they'd played as children.

The night's revelry began at the Army and Navy Cafe on Franklin Street, where they posted up in a booth with a pair of friends—one of his and one of hers—had a few beers, and talked about the relatives they hadn't seen in ages. The quartet then drove off to Big Bear Tavern, a roadhouse across from a horse stable in the Oakland hills. "We wound up in Redwood Canyon that night," Mooney would report in 1964, "drinking whiskey and anything in the book." They stayed out for six to eight hours, finally parting ways at two o'clock in the morning. Mooney left his niece at her friend's place in West Oakland, then headed back to his apartment downtown, on the other side of a border that was at once invisible and impossible not to see.

A week after their night out together, Mooney got a phone message at the Army and Navy Cafe. It was his niece. She needed him to bail her out of jail.

On the afternoon of Saturday, August 4, two days before the U.S. dropped an atomic bomb on Hiroshima, Japan, the police had responded to a call about a derelict tenant in West Oakland. The landlord of the eight-unit building at 1131 Market Street told the cops that a woman named Connie Reed owed him rent, and that he "intended to hold all of her clothing until she paid." The police had tried to broker a compromise, asking the complainant to hang on to only part of the woman's wardrobe. She'd ended those negotiations when, in view of the officers, she grabbed a pancake turner and started scraping the paint off her bedposts.

The woman who'd wielded that spatula would tell a very different version of this story during the Wakefield heirship hearing. "The landlord came into my apartment, to my building, and was going to get into bed with me," she'd explain. "I took a butcher knife and hit him, and when I did I cut the bed."

The booking report from August 4, 1945, didn't say anything about a butcher knife or an attempted sexual assault. The police arrested Connie

Reed for malicious mischief, and they confiscated her purse and its contents. The sepia-toned booking photos the Oakland police snapped that night showed a young woman in a girlish checked blouse with a notched collar. Her eyebrows were pencil thin, and her dark, curly hair was piled into a pompadour that crested several inches above her forehead. In the picture taken from straight on, her lips were clasped into the thinnest of smiles. In the one showing her face in profile, the corners of the teenager's mouth tilted a few degrees downward, and her eyes wandered to a place well outside the frame.

As soon as he got his niece's call, Mooney made the half-mile trip to the city jail, located in the upper reaches of Oakland's towering granite and terra-cotta city hall. While he'd never known Martha to use the name Connie, he'd later profess that he hadn't been surprised to hear she'd been arrested. He didn't ask her to pay back the bail money, he'd say, "because that's useless." He also didn't get her address, because he "didn't want it."

On that whiskey-soaked evening in Redwood Canyon, Mooney had allowed himself to lose his bearings. Now he remembered who Martha Louise White was supposed to be. He wouldn't forget again.

* * *

Hubert Mooney's niece had a criminal record before she made it to Oakland. In January 1943, when she was sixteen or seventeen years old, the Seattle police had booked her for disorderly conduct under the name Martha Davis. A year and a half later, the sheriff's office in Port Orchard, Washington—a small town thirteen miles due west of Seattle, across Puget Sound—had arrested her for vagrancy, identifying her as Martha Gordon. Less than a month after that, in November 1944, the Seattle police again brought her in for disorderly conduct.

The circumstances of those three arrests reveal the trap she fell into upon arriving in the Pacific Northwest. In every instance, she violated an expansive statute used to detain those suspected of lewd or undesirable behavior. In 1943 and 1944, the U.S. Army tallied more than 250,000 cases of gonorrhea and 165,000 cases of syphilis among its stateside personnel. Journalists and government propagandists blamed "loose women" for the VD scourge, casting male soldiers as their innocent victims. "She may look clean—but," read the top of a poster depicting a wholesome-looking lass. The message at the bottom: "Pick-ups, 'good time' girls, prostitutes spread syphilis and gonorrhea. You can't beat the Axis if you get VD."

Local and federal authorities sought to control VD by controlling women. In April 1943, Agnes E. Meyer published a two-part series in the *Washington Post* on the exhaustive efforts to rid the state of Washington— home of the Fort Lewis army base, outside Tacoma, as well as the Puget Sound Navy Yard, near Port Orchard—of both "out-and-out prostitutes" and "girls with a curiously perverted sense of patriotism...[who] scorn to accept money."* The Seattle Department of Health and Sanitation noted that summer that the "chief source of infection at present is the promiscuous woman who hangs around taverns and loiters on the streets, 'picking up' with strangers, frequently referred to as an 'amateur' though she is rapidly losing that standing."

In the first few weeks of 1943, the City of Seattle branded Martha Davis a promiscuous woman. After her disorderly conduct arrest, she was denied bail and referred to the health department for a compulsory blood test. That test was administered at the city jail, an unsanitary, overcrowded facility in which women suspected of being infected with venereal diseases were locked up alongside those who'd been convicted of crimes.

The municipal court docket doesn't indicate the result of Martha Davis's VD screening. It does show that she was forced to undergo another blood test the following year, after her second disorderly conduct arrest. By that time, the city had opened a venereal disease treatment center in what had formerly been a home for "unfortunate unmarried mothers." A judge told the *Seattle Times* that the arrestees quarantined at the facility

---

* In addition to writing for the *Washington Post*, Agnes E. Meyer served as the newspaper's vice president. Her husband, Eugene Meyer, had purchased the *Post* in 1933, and her daughter Katharine Graham would later run the enterprise.

were first-time offenders, and that there was "nothing to remind the girls of jail or even a hospital. It's run more like a girls' club."

Martha Davis was likely confined in this "girls' club" regardless of whether she had gonorrhea or syphilis. A social worker at the Seattle treatment center determined that just 17 percent of the more than two thousand women housed there during one eight-month period had any kind of venereal disease. That didn't matter to the Seattle police, who believed they were containing a moral crisis as much as a public health one. A "large proportion" of the women in the facility, the head of the department's vice squad would explain, consisted of "prostitutes, alcoholics, feeble-minded, and extremely unstable persons."

In the 1940s, Seattle, like Oakland, swelled with war workers, men and women who traveled great distances to secure jobs in shipyards and factories and often found themselves with no place to live. In between her various involuntary confinements, the teenager from Arkansas lived in Orchard Heights, a temporary housing project built to accommodate those who worked shifts at the Puget Sound Navy Yard. That's where she was arrested for vagrancy on October 24, 1944. Her name was written in cursive on the front of her booking card: "Gordon—Martha—Ms. (Spanish)." The accompanying photo, which was taken after midnight, showed a young woman with curly hair, thin eyebrows, and puffy eyes. Martha Gordon looked exhausted.

* * *

The back of that booking card from Port Orchard said that Martha Gordon had been found guilty, and that she'd been given a thirty-day suspended sentence on the condition that she leave Kitsap County for good. While she did decamp from Washington not long after that vagrancy arrest, she didn't pick up a new line of work. At 4 a.m. on April 25, 1946, nine months after Hubert Mooney had bailed his niece out of jail, the Oakland police arrested her as Betty Smith, taking her "into custody after complaints from several sailors that she was soliciting in the Station Hotel."

The panic over dissolute, disease-riddled tramps hadn't abated after World War II. The police report laying out the evidence against Betty Smith noted that she might be infected with a venereal disease; on account of that presumption, she was held for four days before being released. Two years later, when she was arrested as Connie Harbaugh after being found with a man in her West Oakland apartment, she was again locked up until she received a clean bill of health. There's no indication that her sexual partner Gilbert Ortiz, who'd admitted to having VD, was either jailed or forced to see a doctor.

The Oakland police arrested 753 people for prostitution in 1946, more than double the figure from 1942. The department's sudden emphasis on vice investigations drove illicit sexual activity indoors, to places like the Station Hotel in downtown Oakland. The three officers who arrested Betty Smith reported that "she had occupied 4 different rooms [at the hotel] since her arrival in Oakland." She'd lied about how long she'd been in the city, saying she'd just turned up the previous week. The police also said she'd "told conflicting stories regarding her whereabouts and her activities."

Betty Smith—also known as Martha Lee Davis, Martha Gordon, Connie Reed, and Connie Fay Harbaugh—used a different name on the occasion of each of her five known arrests in the 1940s. She also assigned herself a unique birth date—December 25, 1924; January 24, 1926; and December 25, 1927—and place of birth—Tennessee, Missouri, and Hawaii—every time she got booked by the Oakland Police Department. Four of her five arrests in Washington and California, though, did have a common thread: allegations of prostitution.

The facts laid out in that 1946 arrest report—the description of "complaints from several sailors"—suggested that Martha/Connie had gotten into a dispute (or a series of disputes) with her clientele. The paper trail she generated in Oakland also indicated that she was making some effort to pick up on-the-books employment. In 1945, the police marked her occupation as "laundry." The next year, she was reportedly an usherette, a position that entailed taking moviegoers' tickets, escorting them to their seats, and padding down the aisles with refreshments. In 1948, the cops had her down as an apartment manager. And many years after she'd left the Bay Area, she'd claim to have worked at the H. J. Heinz Co. factory in Berkeley as a temperature taker.

It's possible that she held all those jobs. Considering the lies she told the police about every other facet of her biography, it's also possible she was never an usherette, an apartment manager, or a factory worker. Either way, she didn't derive much benefit from the Bay Area's wartime economic boom—she was not, in reality or in her imagination, a welder or a riveter or a carpenter. Her lack of formal schooling in Tennessee and Arkansas certainly would've placed some limits on her work prospects. Anti-black animus, too, could've been a factor in limiting the young mother's options.

It's telling, though, that no official records issued in California labeled her a "Negro." The 1945 arrest report for Connie Reed identified her as both white and Mexican. A year later, the Oakland police said Betty Smith was white with a dark complexion. Connie Harbaugh's 1948 booking report had her down as white and Hawaiian. Abbreviations on government forms—*W, N, Mex, Haw*—didn't necessarily reflect public perception. Growing up in Arkansas, she'd been classified as white on the 1930 and 1940 censuses, but the white people she'd crossed paths with hadn't seen her as one of them. Still, it's plausible that no one in California aside from Hubert Mooney knew about her racial background.

During Martha Louise White's childhood in the 1920s and 1930s, the "tragic mulatta"—a woman, typically wracked with self-loathing, whose surreptitious forays into white society lead to personal catastrophe—became a stock character in literature and film, with popular sensations such as *Show Boat* and *Imitation of Life* dramatizing the perils of passing. Magazines also printed the confessionals of women faced with the temptation to live as white. "If I accepted this offer I could go anywhere I wanted. I could do anything I wanted, without question. No saleswoman would ever again refuse to sell me a dress. No hotel clerk would refuse me a room. No head waiter would deny me a table," wrote light-skinned actor Janice Kingslow in "I Refuse to Pass," an essay published in *Negro Digest* in 1950. "What good was fame or money if I lost myself?" she asked. "[Passing] meant stripping my life clear of everything that I was.... Conscience wrestled with dreams of fame and money, and conscience won."

On the one hand, these fictional and nonfictional narratives constituted an admission that a person's racial identity can shift depending on factors that have nothing to do with biology. On the other, they affirmed the near-consensus view that the "one-drop rule" was a fundamental law of nature. It was in no way misleading or inaccurate for the former Martha Louise White to call herself a white woman. She was, after all, just as much white as she was black. But in the first half of the twentieth century, men and women with some "percentage of Negro blood" were presented with a false choice: Either live an honest life as a Negro or perpetrate a deceit by passing as white.

Connie Harbaugh didn't accept that premise. While Janice Kingslow feared that passing might cause her to lose herself, that wasn't a concern for a woman who'd been taught from birth that her nonwhite heritage was a secret shame. In view of the hatred she'd experienced during her youth in Arkansas, the possibility of "stripping [her] life clear of everything that [she] was" likely would've seemed more alluring than terrifying. Besides, given that she'd gone by at least eight different names in her first twenty-two years, what true self did she have to lose?

When Connie Harbaugh was arrested for contributing to the delinquency of a minor on March 18, 1948, the police described her as a Hawaiian female with foreign-born parents. At the top of the form, her race and age were written in shorthand as "W-21." Two weeks after that arrest, Alameda County issued a marriage certificate listing her as Connie Martha Louise White, a twenty-one-year-old born in Tennessee. Her mother was recorded as Lydia Miller from Alabama, while her father was purported to be Marvin White, the man Lydia had married and divorced in the 1920s. He was designated, implausibly, a native of Pearl Harbor, Hawaii, while the bride and groom were both marked as white in the field reserved for "color or race."

In this context, her assumption of a white identity was less a choice than a necessity. Interracial marriage was illegal in California, with the civil code decreeing that "no license may be issued authorizing the marriage of a white person with a Negro, mulatto, Mongolian, or member of the Malay race." The state considered Mexican men and women to be white for the purposes of the marriage, while "the Malay race" may or may not have included Hawaiians, depending on which anthropologist or lawyer you consulted.[*]

The Supreme Court of California would declare the state's miscegenation ban unconstitutional six months after Connie Martha Louise White's wedding. But as of March 1948, Alameda County wouldn't have sanctioned a marriage between a white man and a Negro woman. Concocting a phony Hawaiian lineage allowed the bride-to-be to account for the color of her skin while still conforming to the state's parameters for whiteness.

California bureaucrats might not have been the only audience for this fabricated backstory. She may have wanted her new husband to think she was Hawaiian, too.

* * *

Paul Harbaugh, like his wife, had never had the chance to form a bond with his father. When Paul was five years old, Joseph Harbaugh Sr. had been killed in one of the worst mining accidents in American history, an explosion in Mather, Pennsylvania, that took the lives of 195 men. As a teenager, Paul had worked at the mine company's general store, selling furniture, garden tools, and household goods. But rather than stay in Mather and pursue a career underground, Paul had seized an opportunity to get out of Western Pennsylvania, enlisting in the U.S. Navy in September 1942.

The blond-haired, blue-eyed nineteen-year-old arrived at Illinois's Great Lakes Naval Training Center—the base where Linda Taylor would

---

[*] The language about Malay people had been added by the California legislature in 1933 with the intent of barring marriages between whites and Filipinos.

meet another of her husbands, Lamar Jones, in 1974—at around the same time as the navy's first black seamen, a group that took its classes in a segregated facility. Harbaugh spent six weeks in a white-only camp training to become an aviation support equipment technician, then served stateside for two years before shipping out to the Pacific island of Saipan for the duration of World War II. He reenlisted after the war, eventually getting assigned to the USS *General A. E. Anderson* as a boatswain's mate. The troop transport, which ferried personnel and supplies from the West Coast to bases in Hawaii and the Pacific Theater, typically came and went from San Francisco Bay. He likely met Connie Martha Louise White during one of the ship's frequent West Coast stopovers. Their March 1948 wedding came two days before he sailed to Guam, Japan, China, and the Philippines.

Harbaugh looked as though he'd been born to wear a uniform. The strongly built, square-jawed sailor stood five foot seven and weighed 175 pounds, and he wore his hair in a crew cut. Although he could plaster on a mean mug for a posed portrait, he smiled easily and broadly. At twenty-five years old, he was excited to become a parent. In November 1948, he told a California judge he wanted to adopt his wife's son. His petition said that Connie Harbaugh had been unmarried at the time of Clifford's birth, "that the father of said minor has never supported him or had custody of him," and that he was "well able and anxious to care for, maintain, and educate" the eight-year-old boy. The petition also indicated that Connie would soon have another child. She'd give birth in December 1948. The Harbaughs would name their son Paul Phillip.

Connie Harbaugh's life seemed to settle down in the months following her wedding. The Oakland Police Department didn't find cause to arrest her, and she found socially respectable employment—the city phone directory listed her as Mrs. Paul Harbaugh, dressmaker. But Paul and Connie wouldn't build a life together in California. At around the time their next child was born, in January 1950, the navy reassigned Paul to the country's largest inland base, a facility outside Memphis where he'd teach airplane maintenance and repair to enlisted sailors. The Harbaughs lived east of the Mississippi River in Raleigh, Tennessee, a short drive from Golddust and the cotton plantations of northeast Arkansas. Connie Harbaugh's third son, Johnnie, would be born just a few miles from the farms where his mother had grown up.

* * *

It didn't take long for the Harbaughs' marriage to unravel. In the late fall of 1950, Connie took their two youngest children and drove off in her family's newly purchased Pontiac, explaining that she was going to see her parents in Arkansas. She called her husband from the road, demanding a couple of hundred dollars. She said that Paul "would be sorry" if he didn't do what she wanted.

In the divorce complaint he'd file in 1951, Paul Harbaugh wouldn't reveal whether he'd acceded to Connie's wishes. He would say that she'd lied about every element of her trip: Her father "was not living," her mother was in Missouri rather than Arkansas, and she'd actually set out for "St. Louis and other places." When she came back after a month on the road, their one-year-old and two-year-old sons "were filthy, dirty, and their clothes were torn, and they appeared to have been uncared for for many days." It was during this family reunion that Connie told Paul she wanted a divorce. She also said she was pregnant.

Paul didn't believe this unborn child was his, and he didn't agree to sign the papers his wife pushed in front of him. Annoyed by his noncompliance, Connie again took the children and disappeared. She reemerged two weeks later, confronting him at the naval base with those same divorce papers. Paul once more refused to sign the documents, citing advice from a navy legal officer and a chaplain. She replied with "vile and obscene language," he'd say in the complaint, unleashing a stream of profanities "in the presence of their two small children, and in the presence of others standing nearby." She then grabbed the kids and dropped out of sight for another three and a half months.

Paul Harbaugh's divorce complaint described Connie as a cruel and often absent mother and a willfully malicious partner. She had a penchant for "writing to his superior officers in the Navy and to the American Red

Cross, claiming that he was not sending her any money"—a practice that "caused him a great deal of trouble, embarrassment, and humiliation." She'd also tried blackmail. On May 8, 1951, a few months after cursing him out at the naval base, she insisted that he send her money, or else she would "disclose certain facts to the Navy which might cause him considerable embarrassment and difficulty."

The complaint alleged that Connie was an inveterate liar, and that she'd obscured key elements of her pre-California life. Although she'd "led him to believe that she had never previously been married and that she was a respectable and virtuous girl," Paul had learned after their wedding day that she'd "had an illegitimate child by another man." That child was Connie's son Clifford. In 1948, Paul had told a judge in California that he was "well able and anxious to care for, maintain, and educate" the then eight-year-old. In 1951, he reframed that adoption proceeding as another component of his wife's deception.

In his bill for divorce, Paul Harbaugh said that Connie was "not a fit and proper person to have the custody and care of their children." He asked the circuit court of Shelby County, Tennessee, to either award him custody of Paul Phillip and Johnnie or give him permission "to place said children in a reputable home." He made no mention of Clifford, nor did he file any paperwork relating to Connie's daughter, Sandra, after she was born in August 1951. (Sandra's birth certificate recorded her father as Paul Harbaugh and her mother as Connie M. Miller, a white woman born in San Francisco.) In January 1952, a Shelby County judge granted Paul the divorce he'd requested, finding Connie Martha Louise White Harbaugh "guilty of such cruel and inhuman treatment or conduct towards the complainant as renders cohabitation unsafe and improper." The judge made no ruling on who'd get the children, who were living with Connie in Arkansas and thus outside the court's jurisdiction.

Paul would wait just five months before getting remarried. The navy man would tell his new wife, Jean, that he'd figured out very quickly that his first marriage had been a horrible mistake. Even though Connie had initially been the one to push for a separation, Paul told Jean that he'd finagled a transfer to the South to evade California's strict divorce laws, which required that one spouse prove the other had committed a wrongful act or was incurably insane.* He said that Connie had turned his own mother against him—that she'd somehow convinced Gertrude Harbaugh that Paul was to blame for the dissolution of their marriage, and that Gertrude had gone so far as to send Connie money. He never mentioned anything about his ex-wife's race, but Jean, a white twenty-two-year-old from West Memphis, Arkansas, believed Connie must not have been honest with him about her parentage. She didn't think Paul would've married Connie if he'd been aware of all the branches in her family tree.

Jean Harbaugh crossed paths with her husband's first wife only twice. One of those encounters came when she tagged along on a trip to Connie's house in Arkansas. Paul and Jean didn't make it inside. Connie wouldn't stop cursing at her ex-husband, calling him a no-good son of a bitch and shouting "Fuck you!" Jean was terrified—she'd never heard a woman lose control like that. Later, the two Mrs. Harbaughs sat across from each other at a court hearing relating to Paul and Connie's divorce decree. In that setting, Connie looked and sounded prim and polite, a transformation that Jean found even more unsettling.

Connie was inscrutable and relentless, and she seemed willing to say or do anything to get what she wanted. Once, Jean had a nightmare that culminated with Connie hissing, "Your name will never be Jean Harbaugh." When Jean and Paul bought a house on the outskirts of Memphis, they placed the property under the names of Jean's parents. That small subterfuge, they hoped, would make it harder for Connie to get at their money, and to find them.

Jean, who had a young daughter of her own from a previous marriage, hadn't spent any time with her husband's children. She did know that his son Paul Phillip had darker skin than the other kids. It was difficult for her to imagine raising a mixed-race family in such a deeply segregated

---

* In her 1948 divorce filing, the actor Jane Wyman had been forced to argue that her husband, Ronald Reagan, had subjected her to "extreme mental cruelty." This experience likely contributed to Reagan's decision to sign the nation's first no-fault divorce law in 1969, two years after being sworn in as California's governor.

city. A year after Paul and Jean got married, in the spring and summer of 1953, a white mob threatened to kill the handful of black residents who'd bought houses on East Olive Street in South Memphis. While some black homeowners heeded the warning and cleared out of the neighborhood, a forty-five-year-old utility worker and his fifty-three-year-old sister refused to move. At one thirty on a Monday morning in late June, a stick of dynamite exploded on the front porch of their two-story house, shattering windows and blasting a hole a foot away from a brick support column. The brother and sister were unharmed, as were the three children who'd been inside the home, the youngest of whom was six years old. "I guess they meant to hurt us," the utility worker said, "but we're staying."

A white family raising a dark-skinned child, Jean Harbaugh believed, would invite their neighbors' wrath. It just wasn't tenable. In May 1953, Jean and Paul had a son of their own, naming him Paul Harbaugh Jr. A few weeks before the newborn's arrival, the Shelby County Circuit Court had modified its original divorce decree, deeming Connie Harbaugh a "suitable and proper person" to care for Paul Phillip, Johnnie, and Sandra—the children she claimed were born of her brief and tempestuous marriage—and ordering her ex-husband to pay her $50 each month in child support. Paul Harbaugh was given the right "to visit his said children at reasonable and seasonable times." He never did.

CHAPTER 14
I'll Sue the Hell out of Them

As a small child in the 1950s, Johnnie Harbaugh saw Louisiana from inside a white Oldsmobile and Texas from the back seat of a little green Nash. Johnnie and his siblings never knew where they might be going, or how long they'd stay once they got there. When it was time to move on to the next place, they'd pack up their belongings, climb inside a station wagon or sedan, and hope their mother would steer them away from trouble.

Johnnie got used to being a passenger, the feeling of being carried through the world by forces beyond one's control. Although he couldn't keep track of all the people he'd met and places he'd been, he never forgot his mother's first new ride. Not long after she got it, he watched that 1957 Ford burn up. Back then, he thought racists had set it ablaze. Later, he wondered if the police had questioned his mother because she'd stolen that new car.

Connie Harbaugh had moved back to the South in the late 1940s, but she never really settled there. In his 1951 divorce complaint, Paul Harbaugh wrote that she'd whisked their children away without warning, then brought them back in a diminished state before running off with them again. In her husband's view, this was an obvious case of parental abuse, albeit one he'd done nothing to stop. Her children didn't know what to think of their calamitous lives. At times, they saw themselves and their mother as victims of an unjust world. At others, they felt as though they were getting lashed around by an unstable woman's cruel whims.

THE QUEEN

* * *

In California, far away from where she'd been expelled from an all-white elementary school, Connie Harbaugh had been seen as more than just a biological mistake. But back home in Arkansas, where old acquaintances still thought of her as Martha Louise White, her racial background demanded she be exiled. As an adult in the 1950s, she was subjected to the same slights she'd borne as a young girl. This time, her children would suffer those insults, too.

Hubert Mooney didn't see his niece for seven years after bailing her out of jail in Oakland. They reconnected near the Arkansas-Missouri border in 1952, close to where Hubert's brother-in-law Troy "Buddy" Elliott lived and worked. The Elliotts and Mooneys had known each other for more than a decade, having picked and hauled cotton side by side. As of the early 1950s, Buddy Elliott had recently gotten married to Hubert's wife's sister. Rumor had it that Buddy's older brother was the father of Martha Louise White's oldest son, Clifford.

After her divorce, and possibly before it had been finalized, Martha started seeing Buddy on the sly. The tall, handsome twenty-two-year-old, who, like her first husband, had blond hair and blue eyes, was known as something of a scoundrel. Hubert would testify in Chicago that Buddy was a no-good drifter, adding, "I think that has been verified everywhere in the world."

Buddy's wife, Bonnie Elliott, would leave him when she learned he was having an affair. Before she broke things off, she asked some relatives to drive her to the lovers' hideout. When they reached their destination, Bonnie's husband and his dark-complexioned paramour refused to show their faces. Bonnie's young niece, who'd come along for the ride, wasn't sure why her aunt was crying, or what had compelled her to toss rocks at her husband's car. She was old enough, however, to understand the meaning of Bonnie's slurs. "Come out, you black nigger!" her aunt screamed. She thought Bonnie was going to kill this other woman.

Buddy and Martha escaped that run-in without suffering any physical injury, and in August 1952—seven months after a Tennessee judge granted Paul Harbaugh an absolute divorce—the couple was issued a marriage license in Mississippi County, Arkansas. That document listed the new Mrs. Elliott's maiden name as Martha Louise White. It also included a phony birth date, one indicating that she was twenty-two years old rather than twenty-six. When she had her fifth child in 1956, a son named Robin, the birth certificate labeled the boy's parents as Troy and Connie Elliott. Her "color or race" was recorded as white.

Connie/Martha's second marriage wasn't any happier or more stable than her first. As an adult, Johnnie would recall having seen Buddy Elliott beat his mother and pull her hair. But no matter how terribly her new husband allegedly treated her, she didn't receive much sympathy from Buddy's family. The Elliotts worked with black people in the fields, and they ate lunch beside them while perched on tractor tires. But a marriage between the races wasn't something they could tolerate.

Regardless of what words were typed on those state and county records, the Elliotts knew about Martha Louise White's bloodline. By the time Johnnie was ten years old, Buddy's relatives had told him his mother was really black. The Elliotts didn't seem to hold that against Johnnie, who himself looked white. But his older brother Paul Phillip, who was darker than his mother, wasn't welcome to spend time in the Elliotts' homes.

Martha's side of the family wasn't any more accepting. In court in 1964, Lydia Mooney Blount would deny, unconvincingly, that she'd described one of the children her daughter had brought around as a "nigger kid." She would acknowledge she'd helped raise her grandson Clifford, explaining that he was white and—unlike her daughter Martha—had been allowed to attend an all-white school. Lydia would profess ignorance regarding her other grandkids, saying she didn't remember most of their names. When asked if they were "white children or Negro children," she'd reply, "What am I to judge what kids are?"

* * *

Johnnie didn't know who he was or where he'd come from. He'd heard that his father was a man named Paul Harbaugh, and that he was off somewhere working for the navy. Some of the Elliotts told him that wasn't true—that his stepfather, Buddy, who Johnnie couldn't stand, was his real biological father. His mother wasn't interested in helping him solve this mystery, and she'd beat him up if he asked too many questions. She also avoided the subject of her own lineage, telling him she was "a little bit of everything," and introducing different people as her own mother depending on where she was and who was asking.

The way Johnnie saw it, his family was either absent or might as well have been. His mother alternated between ignoring him and knocking him around; he barely knew his brother Clifford, who left home for good when Johnnie was less than five years old; and his younger siblings, Sandra and Robin, weren't old enough to serve as co-conspirators. Growing up, he felt that Paul Phillip was the only person he could count on. The brothers, who were born just a year apart, clung to each other as best they could, but the day-to-day reality of life in the Jim Crow South meant their relationship was constantly under threat. At a restaurant in Louisiana, Paul Phillip had to go to the back door to pick up his food, then eat his meal outside. When Johnnie joined his brother underneath a tree, the proprietors forced the children to split up. If they were ever seen there again, the two boys were told, they'd get themselves into a world of trouble.

Johnnie called his brother Paul, although some white people in Arkansas referred to him as Tojo—an allusion to Japanese prime minister Hideki Tojo, who'd ordered the attack on Pearl Harbor. During World War II, Tojo's name had gained currency as an anti-Japanese slur. In this case, the nickname may have been inspired by black Americans' purported kinship with the United States' "colored" foe. This had been a matter of some concern in Arkansas: In the 1930s, a Filipino union organizer had been arrested in Mississippi County after allegedly preaching to black sharecroppers that "the world belongs to the colored races. Join us and hell will soon pop around the corner for the white man."

Paul called his brother Rusty, on account of Johnnie's reddish hair. It was Paul's hair, though, that attracted interest from white passersby, who wanted to know how a kid with dark, kinky locks had found a place in such a pale-faced crowd. Paul's appearance marked him as an outsider, and different from the person he felt closest to. When he asked why he and his brother looked nothing alike, his mother was no more forthcoming than she'd been with Johnnie. No matter how much he pleaded, she wouldn't give him an answer.

Martha Louise White had been able, in certain places and at certain times, to conceal her origins from those who might be inclined to use them against her. Three of her children—Clifford, Johnnie, and Robin—had light enough skin not to invite a second glance from suspicious white folks, while Sandra had the same olive coloring as her mother. But there was no hiding the way Paul looked.

Paul's blackness was a problem, and her solution was to fob him off on other people, just as her own mother had done with her. In the mid-1950s, she left him with a family in Missouri, a black couple who sent him to school under his middle name, Phillip. She'd later reclaim him, then give her son away again. Johnnie found these repeated separations confusing and crushing. He missed his brother desperately, and he didn't understand why their mother was unwilling to keep her family together.

Johnnie, too, felt the sting of her abandonment. His mother's marriage to Buddy Elliott had only made her connections with her children more tenuous. The eventual dissolution of that relationship later in the 1950s didn't do anything to strengthen those bonds. She'd leave Johnnie with Buddy's parents and sister for a couple of weeks or months, and she'd bring him to a chicken farm in Albany, Louisiana, where he was fed and cared for by a woman he called Grandma Goldie. Although Johnnie thought Goldie was his biological relative, the truth was that his mother had briefly dated the Louisiana woman's son—a fling during which Martha Louise White had passed herself off as a Filipina. The two women may have seen each other as kindred spirits. Golda Forrest Stevens was married at least eight times. In 1950, she was convicted of manslaughter after shooting and killing one of her husbands during a domestic dispute.

By the time Johnnie met Goldie, she'd done her hitch in prison. In Albany, he chased chickens and stomped on snakes, and he got lavished with the sort of affection he rarely received from his own flesh and blood. But inevitably his mother would retrieve him, and they'd set out for some new place. Johnnie had no idea how she decided where to point that white Oldsmobile or green Nash—to him, it seemed as though she moved around at random. She brought the family to El Paso, Texas, where she got together with a man who supposedly worked in the oil business. They also alighted on the southeast coast of Florida, where she met a dentist who had a big house, a big boat, and a son with two gold teeth. That liaison stalled out when she started bringing people to the dentist's house for voodoo sessions.

That voodoo stuff was just one more thing Johnnie didn't understand. What he was certain of was that none of his mother's entanglements ever lasted. She hadn't succeeded in starting a new life in California, and both of her marriages had been busts. But in the latter part of the 1950s, she'd hatch a new escape plan, one that would allow her to leave her childhood home for good.

* * *

Connie Elliott drove up to Avalon and Annie Mae Moore's plank-walled house sometime in 1956 or 1957, approaching the front door with an offer of transportation and friendship. The Moores' five daughters and two sons didn't know who Connie was—they didn't recognize her from their worship services, and the ones who were old enough to work had never seen her in the cotton fields. Connie sounded more worldly than anyone else the black family had ever run across on their Arkansas plantation, and she had at least a little bit of money, seeing as she drove around in a big Oldsmobile station wagon. The Moore kids didn't think Connie looked black, but they were pretty sure she wasn't white either. After talking it over among themselves, they decided she was probably Mexican.

Annie Mae found Connie easy to get along with and fun to be around. The women would drive into Blytheville to go shopping, and Connie would stop by just to visit, strolling in and helping herself to a glass of water from the bucket in the Moores' kitchen. Connie also brought around her children, no two of which looked the same. Sandra was the Moore girls' favorite—they'd faithfully brush her long hair as if she were their personal doll. Johnnie and Paul mostly kept to themselves. Connie wasn't all that strict with her offspring, but she didn't need to be—they seemed wary of straying too far from their mother, or even opening their mouths.

Connie had an ease around all these children, but she didn't appear attached to any of them. In addition to her own kids, she'd occasionally come around with a child or two the Moores hadn't seen before, then never bring those youngsters around again.

The Moores' oldest daughter, MaLoyce, who was born in 1945, sensed something was off with her mother's new friend. She found it odd that this strange woman had just come out of nowhere, and that she referred to herself by different last names. Connie also hung around with an older boy named Joe, a gangly white teenager who tried to touch MaLoyce's sisters while they were sleeping. All the girls were afraid of him; MaLoyce came to believe he was Connie's henchman.

Although Annie Mae admonished her children to stay away from Joe, she didn't banish the woman who'd brought him into their home. MaLoyce thought Connie was a bad influence on her good Christian mother. The mystery woman was always concocting one scheme or another, and blurting out swear-laden exclamations like "I don't give a damn!" and "Hell no!" She also brought Annie Mae into the grubby company of fortune-tellers. One time, a clairvoyant in Memphis told MaLoyce's mother that someone important in her life would turn on her, but not before doing some wonderful things. The psychic said there was nothing for her to do but wait for it to happen.

* * *

Avalon Moore had come to Arkansas in the fall of 1953 to make a few dollars harvesting cotton. He'd planned to stick around for just a couple of months but scrapped his plans to go back home to Mississippi when a plantation overseer asked him to stay on to sharecrop. Avalon, Annie

Mae, and their children moved into a small wooden house on the out-skirts of Blytheville. They had two bedrooms to split between two adults and six children—they'd have a seventh after arriving in Arkansas—and a woodstove for a heater. The cotton fields were just a few paces away.

Given their duties on the farm, the Moore children didn't make it to school often enough to be in a specific grade. The four oldest kids picked and chopped cotton with their father while their mother tended to the household chores, and they all huddled together in the evening to listen to the radio and laugh at Annie Mae and Avalon's made-up stories. When he couldn't hitch a ride in the back of the boss man's truck, Avalon would walk four or five miles to the plantation store to pick up flour, sugar, baking powder, and lard that he'd buy on credit.

Sharecropping sustained the Moores—barely. It also trapped them in a never-ending cycle of debt. By the late 1950s, they'd managed to move to a slightly bigger house, one with five rooms and a small garden in the back. They'd also replaced their woodstove with a gas-burning one and bought an electric Kelvinator refrigerator. But no matter how hard they worked, and no matter the price of cotton, they never came out ahead. Avalon and Annie Mae taught their children the importance of self-respect—that they should never kowtow to anyone. At the same time, the kids watched their father scrape and bow before the overseer, saying "Yessir" when the boss told him to "get your kids to put a handle on my name."

This was the plight of a poor black sharecropper in Arkansas: Work yourself nearly to death, yessir-ing all the while, just to earn the right to do it again the following year. That's the deal Avalon Moore had made, and that's the deal he'd be held to. At least that's what the Moores had believed before the spring day in 1959 that they thought might mark the end of Avalon's life.

* * *

Annie Mae was picking beans in her garden one Saturday afternoon when her daughter Bobbie ran to the back door, almost hyperventilating.

A white man had marched up to the porch, the eleven-year-old shouted, and he'd pointed a gun at her father's forehead. From the garden, Annie Mae could see Avalon getting into the back of a pickup truck. She watched the vehicle speed away down the field road, kicking up dust until it zoomed out of sight.

The matriarch of the Moore family tried to keep her children from panicking, but they could tell she was worried. Annie Mae told them to climb down into a roadside irrigation ditch, and to keep their voices down and their footfalls quiet. She led them to a bridge, then across a river to a friendly white family's house, where she dropped off her youngest children. Annie Mae and MaLoyce then walked a couple of miles farther down the road to Connie's place. Annie Mae's friend had a car that could get them to the sheriff's department.

When they made it to the station, it was already starting to get dark. Annie Mae told the man on duty that her husband had gone missing, and that he'd had a gun pointed in his face. When she finished telling her story, the man said it didn't strike him as a matter for law enforcement. "If he ain't dead," he said, "there ain't nothing we can do for you."

MaLoyce started crying, and she couldn't make herself stop. The thirteen-year-old didn't know where her father was, and it didn't seem as though anyone cared enough to help. Connie got the teenager even more agitated, taking it upon herself to run through a series of worst-case scenarios. By the time they'd retraced their steps and regathered the younger kids, Annie Mae, MaLoyce, and Connie had all begun to suspect that Avalon might be dead. Instead, they found him sitting on the Moores' front porch, waiting for his family to get back home.

Avalon's daughter Bobbie hadn't seen what she thought she'd seen. One of the plantation bosses had stuck his finger, not a gun, in the middle of her father's forehead. The boss man had reeked of alcohol, and he'd started yelling about all the money Avalon owed him. Avalon had no choice but to endure the abuse—he couldn't risk upsetting a white man, particularly a drunk and angry one. He'd sucked it up and done as he was told, hoisting himself into the back of the boss's truck and going for a ride. They'd ended up outside a backwoods shack on a plot of untended, mosquito-infested land: This is where the Moores would have to live, the overseer had said, if Avalon didn't repay his debt.

Avalon explained all this to Annie Mae, telling her he hadn't been in mortal danger, and that they wouldn't have to move to that mosquito-infested land. But his wife had had enough.

"Avalon," she said, getting out of Connie's station wagon to face her husband. "We're leaving."

Avalon told his wife they should stay a little while longer—that they could break even if they worked for just one more season.

Annie Mae knew the overseer would never let that happen. She also knew her husband could've been seriously hurt, or even killed. Her family didn't deserve to be treated this way, and they wouldn't be treated any differently so long as they stayed in Arkansas. Her children weren't getting out of the car. It was time to go.

"Avalon, come on," Connie shouted from the driver's seat. "Don't be such a scared jackass."

Avalon Moore stepped inside his house, grabbed his favorite cap off a nail on the wall, and squeezed into the station wagon with his wife and children.

The Moores would never see their home again. They'd leave behind that new Kelvinator refrigerator, all the clothes that weren't on their backs, and drawers full of family photos. As she drove them away, Connie assured Avalon and Annie Mae that she'd take care of them. The Moores didn't have any better options. They were going to put their lives in Connie's hands.

* * *

That night, Connie took the Moores across the state line to Missouri, dropping them off in a town none of them had seen before. The older children stayed in a furnished house, one they thought may have belonged to Connie's relatives. Avalon, Annie Mae, and the younger kids slept in a shabbier structure, one in which the most prominent piece of furniture was a large wooden box that looked as though it had once held a casket.

The Moore children typically found comfort in the smell of their mother's cooking—the chicken, greens, and brown gravy she'd have simmering on the stove when they got home from the fields or school. Now they had to make do with bread, mayonnaise, and rag bologna. Annie Mae fixed as many sandwiches as she could, serving them to her family around that casket box. When Connie came by to check on the Moores, she brought over eggs to supplement their meager provisions. She also took them to a very nice house one evening, where a white family treated them to a big spaghetti dinner. MaLoyce didn't know anything about who their hosts were or how Connie knew them—she was just grateful not to be eating bologna.

For MaLoyce and Bobbie and their brothers and sisters, this period in Missouri was a terrifying blur. They'd crawl under their beds whenever a car drove by at night, hiding from the bad people who might be trying to hunt them down. The overseer did find them, just three or four days after they'd gone on the lam. This time, he went after both Avalon and Annie Mae, telling them they needed to make him whole. But the Moores weren't in this fight alone. Connie stood right beside them, and she wasn't afraid to tell the boss man what she thought about his threats. "I'm not going to let you do nothing," she told him.

Annie Mae's daughters had never seen anyone speak to a white person that way. Their mother would later tell them she suspected that Connie had somehow blackmailed the plantation owner—that she wouldn't have been confident enough to tell him off otherwise. Bobbie thought Connie could talk the way she talked because she looked the way she looked. The Moores didn't have light skin, and they didn't have silky hair. Connie didn't seem white to everyone, but on this day, during this face-off, she was white enough to be safe.

Connie succeeded in chasing the plantation boss away, but it felt like a temporary reprieve. The overseer knew where to find them, and there was no guarantee he wouldn't come back. The Moores weren't sure where Connie had been and what she'd seen, but they believed her when she said their lives could be better somewhere else. She'd tell Avalon and Annie Mae they didn't have to live under this tyranny.

After their latest confrontation, the Moores couldn't muster any kind of counterargument.

A good portion of Annie Mae's family had left the South already, moving from Mississippi to Peoria, Illinois. Avalon traveled ahead of his family, leaving just as soon as his in-laws wired bus fare, while Annie Mae and their children climbed into Connie's white station wagon one more time. They drove along the Mississippi River, skirting the eastern border of Missouri until they reached Saint Louis, and then veered into southern Illinois. When they reached their destination, four hundred miles north of Blytheville, Connie didn't turn her car around and head back home. She hadn't just liberated the Moore family. She'd also finally extricated herself from a place she'd never quite been able to leave behind.

* * *

The Moore siblings had never seen white people and black people shopping in the same grocery store. They'd also never lived on a mixed street or gone to an integrated school. And thanks to their erratic educations in Arkansas, they were older than all their new classmates—kids who didn't hesitate to mock their thick country accents.

It would take a long while for the Moores to feel as though they fit in, and to think of Peoria as their home. There was one aspect of their life up north, though, that felt very familiar. Connie's ragtag family lived just two blocks away, and Paul, Johnnie, and Sandra went to the same school as MaLoyce and Bobbie. Annie Mae's friend never asked for permission to stop by, and she didn't defer to anyone else's rules. Soon after they all made it to Illinois, Connie rubbed the Moore girls' earlobes with ice and jabbed needles through their numbed flesh. They were all thrilled with their new piercings, especially eight-year-old Justine. The little girl was crestfallen when her mother said she couldn't keep the holes in her ears. Connie's beauty assembly line, it seemed, had been a rogue operation.

By the end of the 1950s, Peoria had earned a reputation as a clean-living, technocrat-scrubbed dreamscape, one of the National Municipal League's "All-America Cities." In 1955, the feminist writer Betty Friedan proclaimed in *Redbook* that she was no longer ashamed of her once-filthy hometown, writing that the "houses of vice are padlocked. The streets are sparkling clean." Comedian Richard Pryor, who was born in Peoria in 1940 and grew up in a brothel owned and operated by his grandmother, countered in his memoir that the city's sterile self-image obscured a more sinister truth. "They called Peoria the model city," he wrote. "That meant it had the niggers under control."

Although the city of just more than a hundred thousand was a lot less segregated than Mississippi County, Arkansas, the leader of the local NAACP said that, as of the late 1950s and early 1960s, "Peoria wasn't any better than the South." In 1962, six members of the civil rights group filed suit against the owner of a café located six blocks from the Moore family's house; the proprietor, in a bid to shoo away black customers, had charged them $5 each for hot dogs that had a listed price of 15 cents, then had them arrested for disorderly conduct when they'd asked for receipts. Peoria also wasn't brimming with job prospects for men like Avalon Moore. Neither the municipal bus company nor Peoria Water Works had any blacks on the payroll prior to 1963, and the Central Illinois Light Company—which employed six hundred people in the city—had a mere two full-time black workers.

The Moores' move to the Midwest didn't immediately lift them out of poverty. Their two-room rental on Peoria's South Side wasn't much more spacious than the shanty they'd lived in outside Blytheville. Avalon's first job off the farm was on the back of a city garbage truck, and he'd bring home crates of unsold fruit and vegetables that grocery stores had left outside to rot—food that was good enough to eat, and that helped fill his children's plates.

He soon landed a better-paying, fouler-smelling gig at the stockyards, driving pigs to slaughter. Pryor, who briefly worked as a meat-packer in Peoria before launching his comedy career, described it as "nasty work," explaining that "all the shit that got on me during the day, the rock salt, water and whatnot, froze in the cold. By quitting time, my pants were as stiff as a board." But Avalon wasn't one to complain about the condition of his pants. He also didn't grouse about the paltriness of his wages, or how Peoria wasn't much of an "All-America" city so far as black people were concerned.

Connie did launch into tirades about these sorts of inequities, pretty much all the time. She told Avalon and Annie Mae they should be getting checks from the government to pay for their children's needs, and she wouldn't let it go even after the Moores told her they weren't interested in public largesse. She was always talking about money, mostly that it was unfair she didn't have more of it. While Connie wasn't the type to wait for opportunities to come to her, she had the good fortune to stumble into a potential windfall in the last few days of 1959. If everything played out as she thought it should, she was going to be set for life.

* * *

Bobbie Moore was getting a geography lesson when the floor beneath her desk began to shake. At 11:30 a.m. on December 21, 1959, the fluorescent light fixtures affixed to the ceiling of her teacher John Wallace's classroom came crashing down and flames shot up through a hatch in the floor. A photograph in the next day's *Peoria Journal Star* showed a pair of children standing in the snow outside Webster School, looking up at a row of shattered windows.

The fire chief explained that gas from a broken main had built up in a tunnel beneath the school, and this invisible cloud had combusted the instant a plumbing inspector lit a match. The inspector and his colleague had suffered first- and second-degree burns on their faces and hands, and Bobbie and her twenty-six classmates had been knocked to the ground instantly. The twelve-year-old had gotten plenty of practice doing duck-and-cover drills, but she hadn't thought even a nuclear attack could be this loud.

Considering the force of the explosion, it was a miracle none of the students was seriously hurt. According to the *Journal Star*, three kids from Mr. Wallace's geography class "suffered shock and were taken home." The newspaper identified just one other possible victim. Ten-year-old Paul Harbaugh had been "in the classroom next to Wallace's and...was the only student [in that room] knocked to the floor." The paper reported that the child's "mother said he had blood on his shirt."

* * *

The adults at Webster School remained remarkably coolheaded after the explosion. Paul's teacher hurried into John Wallace's classroom to extinguish a flaming bookcase, while Wallace himself hustled students out of the building and across the street. The children's parents mostly stayed calm, too, collecting their frightened sons and daughters from a playground near the school. And then Paul Harbaugh's mother came roaring through, shouting that her children needed to get to a hospital.

Bobbie thought Connie sounded almost gleeful as she huddled with both Paul and her eight-year-old daughter, Sandra, telling them what to say about their supposed injuries. Neither of Connie's kids had been badly hurt, and they didn't seem excited about being asked to lie. Bobbie heard Paul say, "Mom, I don't want to do it." But Connie was determined to milk the accident for all it was worth.

On August 9, 1960, a Chicago attorney named Nathan M. Gomberg filed a complaint against the Peoria Board of Education and the Central Illinois Light Company on behalf of Paul and Sandra Harbaugh. The suit alleged that the defendants should've known about the gas leak, and that as a result of their negligence Connie Harbaugh's children had been "injured and became ill and disordered for a long period of time, and their parents were compelled to and did expend large sums of money, endeavoring to cure them." The plaintiffs asked for a judgment of $250,000 per child from both the board of education and the light company. If Connie Harbaugh won her case, she'd be entitled to $1 million.

Annie Mae Moore was disgusted by her friend's lawsuit, but it didn't catch her by surprise. Connie didn't need much provocation to say "I'll sue the hell out of them"—to turn real or imaginary misfortune into an opportunity for personal enrichment. Annie Mae would tell her children that she wished they could all go back to the barter system. If cash was illegal, she said, then maybe Connie wouldn't be so consumed by greed.

A few months after Connie filed that $1 million lawsuit, Annie Mae closed a door in her house and unburdened herself to her husband. She told Avalon that she found Connie exhausting. Her fixation on money was "unnatural," and Annie Mae wasn't sure how much more she could take.

Unbeknownst to Annie Mae, Connie had been lying on a couch in their living room, and she'd picked up their conversation through the wall. "I heard you talking to Avalon about me and money," Connie told her the next day.

Connie clearly felt betrayed. Her mother had never loved her, and her other relatives' feelings were conditional at best. The Moores had shown her what a real family looked and felt like. Now they'd rejected her, too, after all she'd done for them. Worse, they'd been insincere, acting cheery to her face and running her down behind her back. "You could've just told me," she said.

That was the last conversation Connie and Annie Mae would ever have. She didn't come by for another visit after she left the Moores' house that day, and she didn't call or write. For decades after Connie left, Annie Mae would wonder where she'd gone and what she'd made of herself. She never would figure out why that strange woman had stopped at their door in Arkansas, and why she'd made it her mission to deliver the Moores to Illinois. But Annie Mae would always be grateful to Connie. As the psychic had predicted, her friend had turned on her, but not before doing some wonderful things.

CHAPTER 15
A Helpless Child

Seven months after the gas leak at Webster School, Connie Harbaugh's daughter, Sandra, was admitted to a military hospital. A physician at Illinois's Chanute Air Force Base wrote that the patient—the daughter of a veteran—had partial bilateral deafness, "possibly due to school explosion." By early 1961, her malady had worsened. The director of medical services at another air force base, this one in Arizona, noted that Sandra had "nearly total loss of hearing due to the effects of an explosion." That memo also alluded to a September 1960 audiology appointment at Walter Reed Army Medical Center in Washington, DC. Sandra's doctor's visit had been canceled, the document said, "because the mother was involved in a serious automobile accident and was hospitalized for resulting injuries."

Four years later, Sandra's mother would again use a car accident as an excuse, this time to avoid sitting for a deposition during the Wakefield heirship case. At this point, in 1964, her lawsuit in Peoria was still ongoing. Every piece of paper her lawyers submitted in the school explosion case referred to her as Connie Harbaugh. Meanwhile, 130 miles away in Chicago, a separate team of lawyers told a probate court judge in Cook County that she was really Constance Wakefield.

As in the Wakefield proceeding, the complaints she filed in the Webster School suit included a handful of demonstrable truths. Sandra had been a student at Webster, and she'd indeed been diagnosed with damaged hearing. It was clear, though, that Connie Harbaugh's daughter hadn't been anywhere close to the blast site. None of the initial news reports had mentioned Sandra's name, and all three children who'd reportedly gone into shock due to the explosion had been in a sixth-grade geography class. In 1959, Sandra had been an eight-year-old second grader.

Connie Harbaugh was undeterred by the enormous hole in the middle of her lawsuit. She said that Sandra had suffered "permanent impairment of eyesight, particularly of the right eye"; that the girl had received a supportive letter from President John F. Kennedy; and that her son Johnnie and her friend Annie Mae's daughter Bobbie Moore had been injured in the fiery episode, too. In addition, she supplied a list of eight medical professionals who'd treated Sandra's infirmities. One of those doctors was Grant Sill, the shady Chicago physician who'd later fill out a delayed birth certificate indicating that the supposed Constance Wakefield was Lawrence Wakefield's daughter. But Sill didn't testify in the Peoria explosion case, nor did he provide an affidavit about Sandra's injuries. In the end, Connie Harbaugh didn't give the court any of her daughter's medical records. She also failed to hand over that letter from President Kennedy or anything else that might back up her claims.

In Chicago, a state appeals court would rule in November 1966 that Constance Wakefield wouldn't have to do any jail time for trying to defraud her alleged father's estate. Four months later, a Peoria judge would dismiss Connie Harbaugh's explosion suit after the defendants complained repeatedly that she'd refused to answer their questions. Sandra had been a small child when the ground shook at her elementary school. She was fifteen when her mother lost out on a chance to profit from the accidental detonation.

The potential payout from the Peoria case had shrunk years earlier. Contemporaneous reports on the incident at Webster School had said that ten-year-old Paul Harbaugh, not his younger sister, Sandra, had been knocked to the ground and bloodied. But in 1964, Paul was dropped from his mother's suit without explanation. Two years after that, when opposing counsel asked Connie Harbaugh to reveal Paul's location, she professed to have no idea where he might have gone. She was likely telling the truth.

* * *

In the spring of 1961, Connie Harbaugh wrote to the Veterans Administration to say that Paul had been taken from her. Her letter, handwritten in cursive, said she'd paid someone to "keep him and send him to school" while she was out of town. This caregiver, she explained, had told the local authorities a malicious lie, falsely reporting that the twelve-year-old had been abandoned.

Paul's mother informed the VA that her lawyer had located him at a home for needy children in Peoria. "I had a call from Paul last week," she wrote, "and he ask me to send him some...underclothing and other things that he needed because they did not get him anything and that he needed his glasses fixed because he had broken them." Paul was a "nice boy," she said, and she was worried about him. He needed to be "home with me," not confined in some institution.

Connie Harbaugh hadn't sent this note unprompted. The Veterans Administration had gotten word from a juvenile probation officer that Paul was no longer in his mother's custody. Given that, the VA had notified Mrs. Harbaugh that she wouldn't be receiving any more checks in her son's name. Those benefits had come courtesy of the federal government's Dependency and Indemnity Compensation program, which provides for the children of veterans who've succumbed to service-connected injuries or illnesses.

In 1953, a year after his divorce from Connie, the elder Paul Harbaugh had been discharged from the navy due to rheumatic heart disease. Five years later, he was admitted to the hospital with a blood pressure of 220 over zero. He died during heart surgery on September 24, 1958. He was thirty-five years old.

Connie M. Harbaugh—maiden name Connie Martha White; place of birth Baton Rouge, Louisiana—applied for compensation a month after her former husband's death. She abstained from using commas and periods when filling out the VA form, and she adopted a confiding, conversational tone. She'd separated from Paul Harbaugh because he "refuse to support minor children...he did it so many time I can't tell you." She expanded on that story in a space labeled "remarks."

I writin you a letter askin for help with my minor children for Paul and his wife refused to help me and would not let him see the children and they didn't know thir father had past away until I got a letter from the court telling me

The Veterans Administration approved Connie Harbaugh's claim, mailing her $42.30 per month—$14.10 for each of her three eligible children. Despite her best efforts, she couldn't convince the VA to send money for her son Clifford, who was no longer a minor. She would, though, figure out a way to misappropriate federal funds. Per an FBI memo, Paul Harbaugh's second wife, Jean, reported that "shortly after her husband's death, probably in early 1959, Connie Harbaugh sent a change of address to the Veterans Administration…and had the VA widow's benefit check, which was rightfully hers, Jean Harbaugh's, sent to Connie Harbaugh."

Connie was a master of the change-of-address form. The VA sent her first check to 2020 North Cleveland Avenue in Chicago. A little more than a month later, she'd ask for her money to be delivered to Route 1, Manila, Arkansas. Seven months after that, she'd say she'd moved to 306 Kane Street in Peoria. Overall, the Veterans Administration would process twenty-five address changes on her account, with those adjustments made at the behest of Connie M. Harbaugh, Connie M. Wakefield, Connie Womack, Constance Howard, and Dr. Constance Howard. The last of these modifications, on March 24, 1975, would come after she'd been indicted in Chicago for stealing public aid checks. That final change of address would redirect her monthly VA stipend to 8046 South Phillips Avenue—the Parks family's house on the South Side of Chicago. Patricia Parks would die of a barbiturate overdose less than three months after that request went through.

Back in 1961, the VA slashed her monthly check because of reports she "had deserted [her son Paul] and moved to Chandler, Arizona." Indeed, the letter she'd written about paying someone to "keep" Paul had been scribbled on a blank lab report from the Arizona air force hospital she'd visited with Sandra. In that missive, she'd pointed out that she'd been getting just $14.10 each month from the government for her son's needs, while she'd just bought Paul "$60 of clothes." She'd decided not to ship him that clothing, she wrote, "for my attorney said he would be home in about 2 more weeks."

It wouldn't have shocked Paul to learn that his mother had said one thing and done another—after all, she'd told her son she'd come get him when she returned from Arizona and she hadn't fulfilled that promise. Upon reviewing the available evidence, the Illinois Department of Public Welfare decided it would be in Paul's best interest to get away from Connie Harbaugh. By April 1961, he'd been placed under the custodianship of the superintendent of a state-run school for dependent children.

Four years went by before Connie asked the VA about her son again. In 1965, a year after Lawrence Wakefield's death, she wrote that she'd been praying "to the Good Lord" that the agency might pass along Paul's address. The last she'd heard, he'd been living in Peoria. She said that Paul had been "taken when I [had] to take Sandra Kay Harbaugh to a hospital and now my father is dead." She signed her name Connie Wakefield.

The VA responded brusquely: "We are sorry, but we are not able to furnish [Paul's address] under existing regulations." The government had seized her son, and it wasn't going to give him back.

* * *

The Illinois Soldiers' and Sailors' Children's School opened its doors in 1869 as a home for Civil War orphans. Nearly a century later, the fifty-five-acre campus in the city of Normal housed close to three hundred children of military veterans. That population, according to a 1958 article in Central Illinois's *Pantagraph* newspaper, consisted mainly of teenagers who were "emotionally disturbed as a result of indifferent or difficult home backgrounds."

Most of the boys and girls at ISSCS had been neglected and mistreated. Some of their parents were dead, and others were abusers or just not around. For students like Paul, the school was an oasis. They bunked in two-story brick cottages with houseparents they called "Mom" and "Pop," swam in a thirty-by-seventy-foot pool, and watched a movie in the auditorium every Friday night. For breakfast, they'd get scrambled eggs, and sometimes pancakes and waffles. Dinner would be roast beef, chicken, or ham.

Paul would live at ISSCS for five years. He felt secure at the state-run school, which imposed some structure on his chaotic life and allowed him to experience success. He spent much of his time in the machine shop, mastering the lathe and die cutter. He was also a fantastic athlete—at an invitational track meet in 1964, he finished first in the 220-yard dash, the 440-yard relay, the broad jump, and the shot put.

But Connie Harbaugh's son was never totally comfortable in Normal. Paul was one of just a handful of dark-skinned students at ISSCS. Although sports helped many of the school's black children bond with their white classmates, he always hung back from the crowd. Paul didn't know how or why he'd landed at a school for misfits, and he felt just as estranged from his surroundings as he had in the Deep South. He hadn't fit in down in Arkansas. Now he felt like an outcast among outcasts.

While other students' relatives would come to campus during holidays, he never had a single visitor. He also didn't have the slightest grip on his own identity. Paul's mother hadn't told him much about his father, and what she had said hadn't made any sense. Three years into his stint at the Illinois Soldiers' and Sailors' Children's School, when Paul was fifteen years old, a state social worker tried to get him the answers he needed.

In September 1964, a supervisor with the state's Department of Children and Family Services mailed a letter to the Veterans Administration. "Gentlemen," it began, "we should appreciate learning the race and nationality of the above-mentioned man." That man was Paul's purported biological father, the navy veteran who'd died without his son getting the chance to know him. The letter continued,

> Paul's natural mother seemed to prefer to keep Paul's [siblings] with her but wished to "farm" Paul out....
>
> Paul is very sensitive about his coloring and although his birth certificate lists both his parents as being in the white race, Paul has rather definite Negroid features and coloring.

Our agency has received reports also that his mother was a native of Hawaii and his father a native of Puerto Rico. Paul seems more concerned with obtaining information regarding his father than his mother, as he remembers very little about him.

The note concluded, "We would be grateful for any information or pictures you might be able to give to us to enable us to work with Paul."

The bureaucrats at the VA sent back a three-line response, saying only that the man who was supposed to be Paul's father, "as indicated by our records, was of the Caucasian race." The agency didn't send along any photographs, or any leads on possible blood relatives.

* * *

Nobody had paid attention when Connie Harbaugh filed her $1 million lawsuit against the Peoria Board of Education in 1960. She became a public figure four years later when she transformed into Constance Wakefield. It wasn't just the Chicago newspapers that took notice of the flamboyant, fast-talking woman with the manufactured wills. The FBI also started scrutinizing the so-called policy heir. She got the bureau's attention by reporting a kidnapping.

On April 17, 1964, the *Chicago Sun-Times* published a piece saying that "Constance Wakefield Stineberg" had told the authorities her eleven-year-old son, Johnnie, had been taken on his way to the grocery store. Johnnie's captor, she'd said, had phoned her to demand a $20,000 ransom for the boy's safe return. She'd insinuated that the crime was connected to her bid for Lawrence Wakefield's estate, explaining that she'd taken to carrying a "pistol because of threatening phone calls demanding that she abandon attempts to get [Wakefield's] money."

This story was a sham. A pair of FBI agents had found Johnnie wandering the streets not far from the family's home. The teenager—contrary to his mother's report, Johnnie was fourteen rather than eleven—told them he hadn't been kidnapped by anyone. He'd run away from home after getting into a fight with his sister, Sandra.

Although the *Sun-Times* article didn't indicate as much, the bureau had pushed for Constance Wakefield to be charged with making a false report. The U.S. attorney's office hadn't signed on to that plan. A document produced by the FBI's General Investigative Division said a government lawyer had "declined prosecution as there was no way of proving that Wakefield did not receive the ransom call."

Constance Wakefield talked about kidnappings all the time. The day after the *Sun-Times* ran its piece, the *Chicago Defender* published her assertion that she'd been "kidnapped by two white men on her 13th birthday and held for $40,000." She said the incident had ended happily, at least for her: She'd been released after four days "and the kidnappers were murdered."

She also described additional plots centering on her children. On August 19, 1965—after her heirship claim had fallen apart and she'd moved her family to the South Side—she told the FBI that her daughter had disappeared. The concerned mother said she'd received a threatening phone call: If she ever wanted to see Sandra again, the kidnapper had allegedly growled, she needed to drive south on Route 66 and pull off at the "first unoccupied service station, then turn right into a grove."

The FBI didn't say whether Constance Wakefield had followed the abductor's directive. A separate report issued a month later, however, revealed that Sandra had returned home; her mother said the girl had been "staying with relatives" the whole time.

By 1965, a Cook County judge had decided Constance Wakefield wasn't really Constance Wakefield, and the FBI had concluded she wasn't a reliable source. "In view of background of Wakefield," an agent had written about her latest fantastical yarn, "no active investigation being conducted by Chicago office in this matter."

And yet on February 23, 1966, the bureau dutifully generated a communiqué regarding her latest missing person report.

She reported subject, her daughter, missing to Chicago PD and claims has not received satisfactory action. States at time of subject's disappearance, heard subject scream; subsequently bloody clothes were found but Chicago PD refused to process.

Wakefield claims she received "ransom notes" which were turned over to PD, and received third note instant, which was found lodged in Wakefield's door, and written on paper bag in crayon, "If you want to see Sandra alive again, bring the price of the house in cash one seven one six Halsted......bring no flatfeet...."

The teletyped dispatch went on to say that the complainant had skipped a planned meeting with the Chicago police, that she had "not turned over any ransom notes," and that she "complained about Chicago PD and FBI and claimed to have sent telegram to President Johnson."

While Lyndon Johnson didn't acknowledge receiving this message, news of Sandra's latest kidnapping did make it to the *Defender*. "Sandra Stienberg...has been missing from home for 18 days," the paper reported on March 3. "Her mother, Mrs. Constance Wakefield, says she believes her daughter has been abducted." The photo that ran above that squib showed the fourteen-year-old Sandra with her eyes closed. She had sideswept bangs, and she was wearing a patterned sleeveless top. In that moment, she looked unguarded and happy.

Sandra didn't know what it felt like to settle in a particular place with a particular group of people. She'd spent her whole life getting uprooted from one spot to another, and she'd seen her siblings get dropped off and picked up again and again. Just after her ninth birthday, she'd been made a pawn in a bogus lawsuit, and been dragged to various military hospitals to get poked and prodded. Given what her mother had already put her through, Sandra would've had no reason to believe her teenage years would be any less erratic. That may have been why, in February 1966, she set out on her own.

There had been no scream, no bloody clothes, and no crayoned ransom note. Sandra had run off to a ritzy suburb on Chicago's North Shore and found work as a domestic. Her stint away from home wouldn't last long.

THE QUEEN

She was arrested in Glencoe, Illinois, in April 1966, two months after her mother declared her a missing person. According to the FBI, she was "charged with being a runaway" and was held temporarily in Chicago's Audy Juvenile Home. Constance Wakefield, in turn, was investigated for contributing to Sandra's delinquency, although she wouldn't ultimately be prosecuted for that misdeed.

Sandra's mother likely harangued the FBI and the Chicago police about her daughter for the same reason she'd written the VA about Paul: She wanted someone to tell her where her child had gone. It was in keeping with her proclivities for melodrama and fabulism that her cries for help sounded like plot points from hard-boiled detective stories. But not all her kidnapping tales were entirely fictional.

* * *

Johnnie Harbaugh had a job to do on the morning of Monday, February 6, 1967. Before dawn, he bundled up and trudged through the drift-covered streets to an L station on the city's West Side. A week and a half earlier, the biggest blizzard in the history of Chicago had dumped twenty-three inches of snow on the city in twenty-nine hours, leaving twenty-six people dead and fifty thousand cars marooned in the streets. Railroad firms had shipped some of the estimated seventy-five million tons of frozen precipitation out of state in freight cars bound for Mississippi, Tennessee, and Texas. But that hadn't been the end of it. On Sunday, February 5, another massive storm had covered the ground in eight and a half more inches of white powder. This latest blizzard, the *Chicago Tribune* had reported, "caused snow-fighting crews to moan in despair." Mayor Daley urged Chicagoans to stay off the roads if possible, and to take mass transit to work.

Johnnie got off the train at 43rd Street station, just a few hundred feet from his mother's place on the 4300 block of South Calumet Avenue. The seventeen-year-old walked up the building's back steps, opened a window, and shimmied into her apartment, taking care not to trip the burglar alarm. Once inside, he snatched a baby girl from her crib and reversed course, climbing out the window and going back down the steps. With the wind gusting to twenty miles per hour, he made a beeline back to the L station and got on a northbound train. The whole thing took a couple of minutes. His mother hadn't even woken up.

A few hours later, the Chicago Police Department got a call from a woman on South Calumet Avenue. The complainant, who said her name was Constance Womack, told the police her infant daughter was missing or kidnapped. She said the girl's name was Lena.

Local and federal authorities had determined that Constance's previous kidnapping claims were entirely fabricated. This time, they concluded that she was lying about a real kidnapping. She was not, it turned out, the mother of the girl who'd been taken from her apartment. Also, the child's name wasn't Lena. It was Ana Maria.

Ana Maria Garcia was the daughter of a friend of Johnnie's, Lorraine Termini. When Lorraine had needed someone to watch her child, Johnnie's mother had agreed to look after the girl for a few weeks. At some point during this babysitting gig, Constance had decided she was going to keep Ana Maria and give her a new name. Lorraine pleaded with Johnnie. If he didn't help her, she said, she was going to lose her daughter for good.

Johnnie hadn't gone to school regularly since the fourth grade. Around 1964, the year his mother reported he was being held for $20,000 ransom, he'd started hanging out with Latino gang members on Chicago's North Side. After Constance Wakefield lost her heirship bid in November of that year, he'd moved with her to an almost entirely black neighborhood. Her apartment on South Calumet Avenue was just north of Bronzeville's Liberty Baptist Church, Martin Luther King Jr.'s headquarters during his mid-1960s push to desegregate the city's housing. Johnnie, for his part, had helped integrate the South Side's Blackstone Rangers gang, getting a tattoo of a panther to cement his affiliation.

The Chicago police had arrested Johnnie for the first time in 1965, bringing him in on suspicion of auto theft. Although he ultimately wouldn't be charged with that offense, the police did take a trio of mug shots. Their photographs showed a skinny fifteen-year-old kid with wavy hair and a baby face, a long-sleeved, zipped-up, Nehru-style jacket hiding the tattoo on his left hand. He was standing ramrod straight, his stiff posture conveying the nervousness of a child who knew he'd gotten into trouble. In June 1967, four months after he snatched Ana Maria, Johnnie would get arrested for burglary; that would later get reduced to "criminal damage to property," and he'd be sentenced to probation. In this set of booking photos, he'd look the part of a juvenile delinquent, with a shaved head, slumped shoulders, and a dark shirt buttoned up to the collar.

As soon as Constance Womack reported that a young girl had gone missing, the police went looking for her son. When they tracked down Johnnie on the West Side, he told the officers he'd taken the baby, and that he'd returned Ana Maria to her real mother. Despite the teenager's reputation as a budding criminal, the cops believed he was telling the truth, and they didn't arrest him for his act of vigilantism. His mother wouldn't be so lucky.

On February 7, the day after she'd called the police, Constance Womack was charged with endangering the life and health of a child. The arresting officer's narrative didn't mention a kidnapped girl. Instead, the children she stood accused of endangering were a pair of boys—a white eight-year-old and a black four-month-old—the police had found alone and neglected in her apartment. She was arrested again two weeks later and charged with contributing to the dependency of a minor, though in this case the report didn't indicate which minor she'd neglected. During that encounter, the cops found a six-and-a-half-inch kitchen knife in her purse, a discovery that would lead to a weapons charge. On March 6, she was arrested for a third time in a one-month span and charged with the felony kidnapping of a minor under the age of thirteen. The informant, the report said, was Ana Maria's mother, Lorraine Termini.

Constance had brought all this on herself, alerting the police to a kidnapping she'd committed. The FBI's memorandum on the incident, which called her "a habitual missing persons-kidnapping complainant," was at least the seventh such document the bureau had generated in an eighteen-month span. It was the first of these reports, though, to declare her an out-and-out fraudster—to say she'd lied in court about being Lawrence Wakefield's daughter and was almost certainly lying again.

The FBI's previous memos had all referred to her as Constance Wakefield and nothing else. This one spelled out all the aliases that had come to light during the Wakefield case: She was Martha Louise White, a.k.a. Martha Lee Davis, Martha Lee Gordon, Constance Harbaugh, Connie Johnson, Connie Maxey, Connie Reed, Constance Singleton, Constance Steinberg, Constance Stienberg, Constance Beverly Stineberg, Constance B. Wakefield, Constance Womack, and Mrs. Willie Womack.

The FBI knew who she'd been and what she'd done. But she wouldn't pay any price for bringing the cops to her door. All the charges leveled against her in 1967—endangering the life and health of a child, contributing to the dependency of a minor, unauthorized use of a weapon, kidnapping a minor under the age of thirteen—would go away. It's unclear why she was never prosecuted for any of these alleged acts. Her Chicago Police Department rap sheet doesn't offer any clues, and the relevant court files haven't been preserved.

There was no pressure on the Cook County state's attorney's office to go after Constance Womack. The *Tribune*, which had chronicled Constance Wakefield's moneygrubbing exploits and would publicize Linda Taylor's welfare thievery, didn't print any contemporaneous stories about Ana Maria's kidnapping. But as Taylor was awaiting trial for welfare fraud in March 1975, George Bliss and his colleague William Griffin would talk to the police official who'd interviewed Constance Womack eight years earlier regarding "the disappearance of her [infant]." That investigator would tell the *Tribune* that he'd compiled evidence that she'd been involved in "baby buying…but that it never was used for criminal prosecution." Bliss and Griffin would also report that Taylor had been a suspect in another kidnapping—one of the most infamous child abductions in the history of Chicago.

* * *

On the afternoon of April 27, 1964, a woman dressed in a white uniform came into Dora Fronczak's room in the maternity ward at Michael Reese Hospital. The woman in white stood behind the new mother, watching over her shoulder as she fed her newborn son, Paul Joseph. "Okay, that's all," the woman said. "I have to take the baby down to see the doctor."

Fronczak did as she was told, handing over her day-old infant. When a caregiver came to check on Paul Joseph a few minutes later, the boy's mother explained that she'd "just given the baby to another nurse."

At around that time, a hospital staffer saw a woman in a white uniform walking down a corridor. The woman, who was carrying a baby wrapped in a blanket, passed through a doorway leading to a rear stairwell. As soon as that door closed, the woman in white vanished. So did Paul Joseph Fronczak.

The Fronczak kidnapping scandalized Chicago and the nation. On April 28, the day after the abduction, scores of newspapers published page one stories on the woman dressed as a nurse who'd taken a baby boy from his mother's arms. As many as two hundred police officers and FBI agents were tasked with solving the case. That massive law enforcement contingent interviewed an estimated thirty-eight thousand Chicagoans, a group whose collective knowledge of the caper added up to not much at all. Each new lead turned out to be a false alarm, and every person of interest was quickly cleared of wrongdoing.

After a couple of weeks, the police began to turn their attention elsewhere. The papers moved on, too, checking in with Dora Fronczak only to mark the passage of a series of grim anniversaries. "Our whole life, our plans for the future, still are on the baby," she said in July 1964, three months after the kidnapping. "It's something they say time heals, but so far it hasn't," she said in October, six months after she'd last seen her child. "I believe that God will return Paul some day," she said on her son's first birthday, in April 1965.

That July, a blond-haired, blue-eyed toddler was found abandoned in a stroller outside a New Jersey department store. Given 1960s-era scientific know-how, it was impossible to determine the child's parentage with certainty. Nevertheless, Dora Fronczak and her husband, Chester, decided he must be their missing son. The couple adopted the boy in December 1966, giving him the name Paul Joseph Fronczak.

The woman in white, meanwhile, remained at large. But eleven years after the kidnapping, the *Tribune*'s Bliss and Griffin reported that the Fronczak case had been reopened. The leading suspect, they said, was Linda Taylor.

* * *

The evidence against Taylor, Bliss and Griffin wrote on March 21, 1975, included an allegation from one of her ex-husbands, who'd "told [FBI] agents that Miss Taylor appeared one day in the mid-1960s with a new-born baby, altho she had not been pregnant." Taylor's explanation for this surprise new addition, according to the paper: that "she hadn't realized she was pregnant until she gave birth that morning." The *Tribune* also said that a woman calling herself Connie Reed—a name Taylor had used in the 1940s—had been at the hospital at the time of Paul Joseph's abduction. Finally, Bliss and Griffin noted that the Chicago police had received a tip in May 1964, a week after the Fronczak heist, that a person who could've been the kidnapper had tried to rent an apartment under the name Constance Wakefield.

Two months after the *Tribune* posited that the notorious welfare queen might be connected to the notorious Fronczak kidnapping, Taylor told the *Chicago Daily News* that she'd figured out where this allegation was coming from. She believed her ex-husband Willie Walker—the South Side taxi driver she accused of faking his own death to avoid paying her alimony—had been the one to tell the FBI she'd shown up in the mid-1960s with a newborn baby. Taylor got this wrong: Walker wouldn't talk to the FBI until 1976, a year after Bliss and Griffin wrote their piece. In his statement to federal agents, he'd say that his ex-wife had actually brought home two children he'd never seen before, one white and one black, and he "never knew where the two babies came from."

Other than that *Daily News* article and a short item in the *Defender*, the *Tribune*'s Taylor-Fronczak scoop got strangely little follow-up. It wasn't just the *Tribune*'s competitors that ignored the report: The paper itself published just one more piece on the convergence of the two scandals before dropping the story for two years. The *Tribune* finally picked it back up the day after Taylor was sentenced to three to seven years in state prison for welfare fraud and perjury.

On May 13, 1977, court reporter Charles Mount wrote that a man named Samuel Harper was "certain" that Taylor had stolen the Fronczak baby. Harper told law enforcement officials, among them Jack Sherwin, that he'd lived with her in the 1960s, and that "several children and infants, all white, were staying with the woman." The *Tribune* reported that "Harper said he is sure Taylor was the kidnaper because she left that day dressed in a white uniform, and the description of the kidnaper...matched Taylor." The newspaper added that, according to Harper, Linda Taylor had even "filed a police report after the kidnaping, saying she had seen the kidnaper with the baby."

Mount reported that Sherwin had "no reason to doubt" that Harper was telling the truth. The FBI, however, was less convinced that Linda Taylor had taken the Fronczak baby. Ron Cooper, an agent who worked on the case in the 1970s, would acknowledge decades later that the bureau had looked at Taylor as a suspect, but he'd claim that investigative avenue had turned out to be a cul-de-sac. The FBI "had no cooperation from people around her," Cooper would say, adding that everyone in her orbit "would tell you a story and it would just sort of be a flimflam thing, and it wouldn't make any sense."

No one has ever been charged with carrying out the Fronczak kidnapping. It's unclear if the FBI eventually exonerated Taylor or if the agency just moved on. The bureau has declined to make its case file available for public viewing—releasing those records, the FBI has said, would interfere with its purportedly still-active investigation into the 1964 abduction.

Some of the evidence in the *Tribune*'s Taylor-Fronczak stories can't be easily dismissed. There's no doubt Samuel Harper, who died in 1990, had a relationship with Taylor at around the time of the kidnapping. Taylor's son Johnnie confirmed that Harper lived with his mother for a time, and Harper was identified as a potential witness in the Wakefield heirship hearing, though he was never called to testify. With regards to the white uniform, a witness in Taylor's 1976 burglary case provided a written statement indicating that he'd known Taylor to dress as a nurse in the

1960s. Both Johnnie and Lorraine Termini's sister—the aunt of the girl Johnnie retrieved from his mother's apartment in 1967—said that Taylor would tell people that she was a nurse and would dress in a nurse's outfit. Taylor's daughter, Sandra, would go further, saying her mother worked "at the county hospital as a registered nurse for at least three years." And when Sherwin filled out his police report after arresting Taylor in August 1974, the detective described her as an unemployed nurse.

There are also good reasons to doubt that Taylor absconded with Paul Joseph Fronczak. In the spring of 1964, she was preoccupied with her quest to take control of Lawrence Wakefield's estate, a task that required manufacturing documents, coaching witnesses, and establishing herself in the public eye as Constance Wakefield, the rightful inheritor of the policy king's substantial fortune. The *Chicago Defender* ran a front-page interview with the self-proclaimed Mrs. Wakefield nine days before the kidnapping, and both the *Defender* and the *Sun-Times* published photographs of the ersatz heir. The woman seen in those photos didn't bear much of a resemblance to sketches of the kidnapper. And although she could've theoretically disguised her face, Taylor, whom police typically listed as five foot one, wasn't a match for the suspect height-wise. After initially saying the kidnapper was five foot six or five foot seven, the police eventually revised that estimate to five foot four.

Samuel Harper's 1977 accusation didn't reignite media interest in the Fronczak case. After the *Tribune* aired his claim that Taylor had stolen the infant, the local and national press essentially forgot about the kidnapping for thirty-five years.

The story reemerged in 2012, when the toddler the Fronczaks had brought home from New Jersey in 1966 began to investigate his pedigree. The adopted Paul Joseph Fronczak, who by then was approaching fifty years old, bought three genetic test kits from a pharmacy, filling one with a vial of his saliva and the other two with DNA samples from his adoptive parents. Two weeks after mailing them in, he got the results: "There is no remote possibility that you are the son of Dora and Chester Fronczak."

A half century after the kidnapping at Michael Reese Hospital, the whereabouts of the Fronczaks' biological child remain a mystery. In a series of interviews in 2013 and 2014, Johnnie Harbaugh said he believed his mother had stolen the day-old Paul Joseph from Michael Reese Hospital. He said she'd obtained a new baby at around the time of the kidnapping, a white infant she called Tiger. While she insisted the boy was her own, Johnnie knew she hadn't been pregnant. He said his mother "was capable of anything," and he apologized to the Fronczak family for not telling the police what he knew back in the 1960s.

Johnnie may be right that Linda Taylor kidnapped Dora and Chester Fronczak's son. But Tiger wasn't Paul Joseph Fronczak. He was a different child, one Taylor almost certainly abducted.

* * *

On the first day of Constance Wakefield's heirship hearing in November 1964, the petitioner said she'd recently had a baby, "a little boy." That child, she told the court, had been born on March 3, 1963. Although she was thirty-seven in 1963, the newborn's certificate of live birth—signed by her go-to disreputable physician, Dr. Grant Sill—identified her as a twenty-six-year-old named Beverly Stineberg. The boy's father, the birth record said, was a man named J. C.

There's no record indicating that J. C. and Beverly Stineberg were ever married. Even so, he may have been the "ex-husband" the *Tribune* wrote about in 1975—the man who told the FBI she'd brought home a baby in the mid-1960s despite not having been pregnant. That child, according to the woman J. C. later married, was known as Tiger.

J. C. was sterile, and thus knew he couldn't be the boy's father. Tiger also couldn't be the Fronczaks' son, given that his birth certificate had been filed with the State of Illinois a year before Paul Joseph was born. J. C., who died in the early 2000s, had no idea who the baby's parents really were. He just knew Tiger didn't belong where he was.

Johnnie was used to seeing kids come and go, including a young black girl who'd stayed with the family for just a few months. He watched his mother and J. C., who lived together in the first half of the 1960s, take care of Tiger for as long as a year. And then, just as suddenly as he'd arrived, Johnnie's baby brother was gone, and so was J. C. When Johnnie asked his mother what had become of them, all she'd say was that her live-in boyfriend "went home."

Johnnie thought J. C. and his mother had teamed up to sell Tiger. Years later, J. C.'s wife heard a different story.

Although her husband didn't like to talk about the past, she knew he'd helped raise Tiger. She also believed he'd severed his relationship with Beverly Stineberg before he took the boy. Her in-laws told her that J. C. and another man had retrieved Tiger from his ex-girlfriend's apartment. When they'd opened the door, they'd found a bunch of children—she didn't know how many—living in filth. There had been a pot of chicken on the stove with maggots crawling all over it. The oldest boy had stolen candy bars so the kids would have something to eat.

J. C. had grabbed Tiger, just as Johnnie would take Ana Maria. Rather than keep the child himself, he'd given Tiger to his brother and sister-in-law. J. C.'s relatives had eventually adopted Tiger and given him a new name. So far as J. C.'s wife knew, no money had changed hands. She believed her husband had rescued Tiger, and that it had been an act of love. She never heard what happened to the other children in that apartment, the ones J. C. had left behind.

* * *

Why did Linda Taylor take other people's children? It's possible she sold these boys and girls for cash—there was a known black market for child adoption in Chicago, and Johnnie speculated to Jack Sherwin that she'd been part of it. She may have used these children's names to pad her welfare applications. It's also plausible, maybe even likely, that her child snatching wasn't part of any grand scheme—that it was pathological behavior that served no larger purpose.

What's clear is that Taylor abused babies, young children, and adolescents in different states across multiple decades. Several of her young victims were glimpsed only in passing, seen by those who recognized their plight but didn't know who they were, and couldn't or didn't help them escape. Others, like the white eight-year-old and black four-month-old the Chicago police found unattended in Taylor's apartment in 1967, were identified at the time but have since had their names redacted from public records. Some of the kids she harmed were her own biological children.

Martha Louise White grew up knowing she'd never be the daughter her mother wanted her to be. When she became a mother herself, she did to her five children what had been done to her, making them feel uncared for and abandoning them. The oldest, Clifford, was mostly raised by the Elliott family in Missouri; he left his mother for good when he was about fourteen. Taylor neglected Paul and Johnnie when they were infants and deserted them as they approached adolescence. Paul was twelve when he became a ward of the state. Johnnie, like Clifford, was fourteen when he left home. Sandra, too, was fourteen when she ran away to Glencoe, and she went to Arkansas to live with Clifford two years after that. Taylor's youngest child, Robin, was sixteen when, shortly before his mother's arrest in Michigan in 1972, he said he was setting out for Florida to determine his real name.

All of Taylor's children felt compelled to get away from her. Not all of them stayed away. When Sandra returned from Arkansas in the late 1960s, she and her mother fell back into old patterns. Four months after Sandra's eighteenth birthday, and a decade after the explosion at Webster School in Peoria, Taylor told a team of Veterans Administration doctors that the teenager was deaf in both ears, had a burn across her abdomen, was hampered by a heart condition that made it impossible for her to exercise, and had been diagnosed with mental impairments. "The mother states that she wouldn't trust her daughter with making a purchase over $5.00 because she doesn't always come back with the right change and some people take advantage of her," a neuropsychiatrist noted on December 10, 1969. "Mother states that the doctors at Walter Reed Hospital told her that the patient was mentally retarded and that it was the result of the fire and explosion she was involved in."

Sandra seemed less certain about what she was suffering from, or whether she was suffering at all. "I have no complaints," she told the doctor, then added, "I do have trouble hearing especially when I go to a party and the music is playing loud." Later, she admitted to being depressed and crying frequently. "I don't know what my troubles are," she said, "but I am not crazy." The neuropsychiatrist concluded that Sandra had a "mental age of 10 years." A VA physician cut his examination short after Sandra became "agitated" but nevertheless reported that she had compensated congestive heart failure.

An honest person never would've tried to profit from the explosion at Webster School. A typical con artist would've quit trying to do so after her lawsuit got tossed out of court. But Taylor wasn't the type to let things go. In this case, she was rewarded for her doggedness. Owing to her supposed mental and cardiac impairments, Sandra K. Harbaugh was declared a "helpless child" by the VA. Although she was no longer a minor, she was entitled to government support. Sandra's mother, Constance Howard, was named her custodian and granted a stipend to subsidize her care—an outlay that would reach $125 per month. After trying for ten years, she'd finally made money off the Peoria school explosion. She couldn't have done it without her daughter's help.

While Sandra appeared at least somewhat reluctant to lie to the VA's doctors in 1969, she didn't tell the agency she had a child of her own. Sandra and her mother also failed to inform the VA when, in 1970, she had a second baby, as well as when she married Roosevelt Brownlee in the summer of 1972. Later that year, a VA field examiner noted that the twenty-one-year-old Sandra was "partially deaf...has a serious congenital heart ailment which renders her helpless at times, is severely disturbed emotionally, takes medication, and is rather dull and unresponsive." The examiner reported that "the minor appeared to be receiving good care"; the checks would keep on coming. The spigot wouldn't get turned off until 1975, when the FBI would learn that Sandra had been married for three years. The VA would send Taylor a letter demanding $3,520—everything she'd received since Sandra had ceased to be her dependent. The federal government would never get its money back.

In the 1970s, Sandra would stand up for her mother both in private and in public. Charles Bailey would tell the Michigan State Police in 1972 that Sandra had threatened him, saying her male relatives would make him pay for revealing her mother's welfare fraud schemes. In 1976, news crews captured Sandra walking alongside Taylor after a court appearance. The two women looked like confidantes, laughing together as Sandra joked that the welfare queen should smile for the cameras. And upon Taylor's sentencing in Cook County Criminal Court in May 1977, Sandra told the press she'd help raise the money to bail her mother out of jail.

Taylor had used the alias Sandra Brownlee—her daughter's name—to steal public aid money. A month after Judge Mark Jones gave the older woman three to seven years, Sandra herself would plead guilty to receiving illegal welfare payments from the State of Illinois. The *Pittsburgh Courier*, in reporting Sandra's sentence of three years' probation, noted that "the acorn seldom falls far from the oak."

In December 1974, the FBI interrogated Sandra to suss out whether she was in cahoots with her mother. Specifically, the bureau wanted to know how a self-sufficient adult had been classified as a helpless child. Investigators reported that Taylor's daughter said she'd done nothing wrong—that she hadn't schemed to trick the VA, and that she'd "never learned the basis of [her mother's] claim." Sandra admitted she didn't have any heart problems and hadn't contracted any illnesses that had left her disabled. She did say, however, that she'd lost the hearing in her right ear in Chicago's Our Lady of the Angels School fire, the 1958 disaster that killed ninety-two elementary schoolers. This wasn't anything close to the truth. Sandra hadn't gone to Our Lady of the Angels. Even if she had, the FBI quickly learned that there had been no reports of children suffering deafness as a result of the fire.

Ron Cooper didn't think Sandra was being totally honest. Nonetheless, the FBI agent suspected that she was an innocent victim—or at least that she was a lot more innocent than her mother was. Cooper believed Taylor had orchestrated Sandra's agitation during that 1969 VA medical exam and had fed false information to the agency's doctors. Jim Piper, the Cook County state's attorney who'd prosecute both Taylor and her daughter, knew that Sandra didn't have a mental age of ten. He told the VA she was "very 'sharp' and appears to have greater than average intelligence" and that she had "an extraordinary memory for past events (dating back as far as 20 years)." He also reported that she had "no noticeable hearing disability."

In her interview with the bureau, Sandra never quite said her mother was a criminal, and she didn't give the FBI any new leads. At the same time, she depicted Taylor as a cruel, unfeeling parent, telling the FBI that her mother had purposely misled her about her origins. As a child, Sandra had believed that Paul Harbaugh was her real father. Later, she said, Taylor had showed her baby pictures to prove it was a different man. Sandra told the FBI her mother was black, and claimed that she wasn't sure how Taylor came to have kids of different races. She explained that Taylor had several children of unknown provenance, among them a white boy known as Duke and a black boy named Hosa.

Sandra, again, wasn't telling the whole truth. Those two boys weren't Taylor's biological kids, and Sandra knew where they'd come from. Duke and Hosa were her own children—the sons she'd given birth to in 1968 and 1970, respectively.

In this case, Sandra may have misled the FBI to protect her mother. Just as Taylor used Sandra as a moneymaking tool, she also deployed her grandchildren for financial gain. In Michigan in 1971, she won the sympathy of a welfare eligibility examiner by saying that Hosa—who she called her "little black baby"—had been rejected by his father, who'd declared him "a disgrace to the white race." She also listed both Duke and Hosa as her children on the fraudulent applications she submitted to the Illinois Department of Public Aid.

Taylor didn't just claim those two children as her own on government forms—she fed the same story to at least two of her husbands. First, she tried to convince Willie Walker that Duke and Hosa were her kids, and that he was the boys' biological father; they were the two children, one white and one black, that Walker told the FBI had shown up out of the blue. Later, she told Lamar Jones that Duke and Hosa belonged to her, and that Sandra—whom she called Constance—was her younger sister.

Jones didn't buy that Duke and Hosa were his wife's kids. It did appear, though, that Taylor was responsible for the boys' care, and that as a result they got hardly any care at all. When Taylor went on the lam in Arizona in the fall of 1974, she brought the five-year-old Duke and four-year-old Hosa with her. After the Tucson police arrested her, Sandra came to Tucson to pick up the children and found that they didn't have any shoes. The following year, the two boys came with Taylor when she moved into Patricia Parks's house on the South Side of Chicago. Parks's children got the sense that Duke and Hosa had learned to survive without adult supervision. When there wasn't any food available, the two boys told Parks's young sons they could eat dog biscuits.

The Parks children were left motherless in June 1975. Taylor's grandchildren were shuttled to the next place. When Jack Sherwin and a crew of his fellow officers arrested Taylor for burglary in 1976, they were appalled by what they saw in her apartment. The police described the seven-year-old Duke and five-year-old Hosa as "dirty, hungry-looking, and 'depressed.'" A police investigator told the *Tribune* that "there were no bedding facilities. And the boys hadn't been bathed in a long time. Their clothes were rags falling from their bodies." Taylor was charged with two counts of child neglect, and Duke and Hosa were taken away by the Illinois Department of Children and Family Services.

Sandra may have relied on her mother for child care because she was in dire economic circumstances. It's also possible that she was too unsettled to parent two young kids, or that Taylor simply persuaded her daughter to do her bidding, just as she'd persuaded so many others to abandon their best judgment. Regardless of the rationale, this arrangement perpetuated a cycle of neglect and abandonment. The lack of food, the tattered clothes, the arrival of child services—all of this was familiar. Sandra and Johnnie and Paul and Duke and Hosa were all damaged by Linda Taylor. No matter the circumstances, the results were always the same. The children suffered the consequences. She did not.

CHAPTER 16
Clever, Conniving, Callous

New inmates came to Dwight Correctional Center in handcuffs, their possessions stuffed inside a pillowcase. The warden of Illinois's only women's prison would watch them line up at the iron gate that separated the facility from the outside world, their eyes focused on Dwight's solid stone walls. When the entrance buzzer blared and the gate swung open, they'd march into the warden's office and tell their stories. It didn't matter what they'd done or what kind of life they'd lived. In those first moments, every woman looked at least a little scared.

When she heard that buzzer on February 16, 1978, Linda Taylor was fifty-two years old. In a photograph snapped two months later, prisoner A-87028 looked more defeated than frightened. An intake form listed her age as thirty-nine and her race as black. Taylor had a "short-stocky" build, brown eyes, and "black/dyed blonde" hair. Her occupation was "minister," and her daughter Sandra was marked down as a correspondent.

Taylor had been sent to Dwight for three to seven years after getting convicted of welfare fraud and perjury; shortly after she arrived, she'd plead guilty to stealing clothes and appliances from her former housemate, a crime that carried a five-and-a-half-year concurrent term. In April 1978, the Illinois Prisoner Review Board—the group that would eventually decide whether to grant Taylor parole—received an official statement of facts from a Cook County state's attorney.* Taylor was "a nationally known welfare cheat" and "a career criminal," the prosecutor said. He advised that she be locked up for the full seven years, "the maximum period allowable by law."

Despite arrests dating back to the 1940s, Taylor had never served a long stint in prison. At Dwight, she wouldn't be required to wear a uniform—in that prison photograph, she had on a collared shirt with a paisley print—and she wouldn't spend her nights behind bars. The state penitentiary, located roughly halfway between Chicago and Peoria on a property laden with oaks and spruces, looked like a country club or a college campus. Dwight, like the Illinois Soldiers' and Sailors' Children's School, which had housed Taylor's son Paul in the 1960s, boarded its occupants in cottages, although one journalist argued that calling the brick-and-stone structures "cottages is like calling Aristotle Onassis' yacht a dinghy." The mock-medieval buildings, most of which had been built in the 1920s, looked fancy on the outside, with slate roofs and brass front doors. On the inside, the dormitories were outfitted with shared kitchens and common areas, while the prisoners' rooms were individually decorated and furnished.

As far as Dwight's residents were concerned, the state-run institution wasn't so idyllic. The cottages had balky plumbing and inadequate heat, and up to five women got crammed into each small bedroom. For a time, the guards banned their charges from touching each other, and women suspected of lesbianism were isolated in a high-security unit. "Tell all the people out there that this isn't fun; it's not exciting or interesting," a prisoner told the *Chicago Tribune Magazine* in 1979. Another said, "All this place does is teach you how to really hate."

★ ★ ★

---

* In 1978, the State of Illinois would effectively abolish parole for all future inmates, moving to a system that eliminated subjectivity from the sentencing process. Despite this change, Taylor—whose initial sentence was handed down in 1977—remained eligible for an early release.

Taylor was an outlier at Dwight. More than half of the prison's three-hundred-plus convicts had been sent away for violent offenses. Among them was Patricia Columbo, who'd helped plan and carry out the murders of her parents and thirteen-year-old brother, the latter of whom was stabbed ninety-seven times. In August 1977, Taylor's former attorney R. Eugene Pincham, who by then had ascended to a circuit court judgeship, gave Columbo a two-to-three-hundred-year term; he'd later say he would've sent the twenty-one-year-old to the electric chair if that option had been available to him. While the *Tribune* had noted Taylor's sentencing on page two, Columbo—a white woman whom one of the paper's columnists characterized as a "suburban sylph" with "Frederick's of Hollywood hair"—got front-page billing, with news of her multicentury hitch superseding Ernie Banks's induction into the Baseball Hall of Fame.

Columbo continued to draw attention after she got shipped off to Dwight. In September 1979, the young killer would face accusations that she'd recruited other felons to have sex with correctional officers.[*] Taylor, by contrast, essentially disappeared once she passed through the prison's front gate. In March 1979, the *Chicago Sun-Times* ran a short item reporting that she had a "minor violation on her prison record—she allegedly used state-owned materials to make cushions and sell them." No other major outlet—not the *Tribune*, and not the national wire services—would write a single story about what had become of Chicago's original welfare queen.

Inside Dwight Correctional Center, Taylor was deemed a minimal security risk, a designation that enabled her to roam the grounds without being escorted by a guard. The prison's doctors also declared her unfit for heavy manual labor, prescribing her a medication, Nitrospan, that was typically used to manage chest pain. On account of her condition, Taylor was detailed to clean the inmates' cottages, a job her fellow residents—many of whom earned $5 a day as seamstresses in an on-site

---

[*] Columbo denied the allegations of jailhouse pimping, and the claims were never proved.

factory that produced drapes, pajamas, and dresses—considered a plum assignment.

Taylor's file with the parole board contained just one disciplinary report, a document detailing an incident that took place nineteen months into her sentence. On the afternoon of September 9, 1979, a guard conducting a "routine shakedown following a visit" found a plastic package inside Taylor's bra. That pouch contained twenty pink pills—a more potent heart medication that wasn't stocked by the prison pharmacy. Taylor said she hadn't known the contraband was in her bra and suggested that she may have been "set up by correctional guards." She also requested that a man named Willtrue Loyd be allowed to speak at her disciplinary hearing, falsely claiming that he was her father.

Prison officials didn't speculate about what Taylor intended to do with those pink pills. The most likely explanation is that she wanted a stronger, quicker-acting drug to manage her chest pain, which by all indications was a real affliction. The Prisoner Review Board, though, didn't care why she'd smuggled in the pills, nor did it agree to listen to Loyd's testimony. The board had no doubt that Taylor had broken prison rules, and that she was refusing to admit as much in the face of overwhelming evidence. In November 1979, state authorities would revoke a handful of Taylor's good conduct credits, delaying her eventual release by fifteen days.

The following month, as Taylor neared her first possible parole date, the Cook County state's attorney's office reiterated its view that she should remain in prison for seven years. Taylor, the chief of the felony trial division wrote, "will no doubt resume criminal activity immediately upon her release." The state's attorneys, who in the aftermath of Taylor's successful prosecution had launched a dedicated unit to go after welfare cheaters, also made the perverse argument that she should be punished for giving public aid recipients a bad reputation.

> This "Welfare Queen," as appropriately titled by the media
> has preyed on society and government since 1944. Her actions
> and others of her ilk, deprive decent citizens who may need
> welfare as a temporary measure, of the sympathy of taxpayers

who contribute to that support, and who have become disen-
chanted with the ever increasing tax burden required to meet
those needs. Her actions have tainted the legitimate recipients
to the point where taxpayers believe all recipients are out to
"get all they can."

The parole board didn't listen to the prosecutors' advice. An early
release checklist included in her prison paperwork indicated that Taylor
had no serious juvenile record and no history of crimes related to alcohol
or drug abuse. Her offense also didn't involve a weapon or threats of
force. Taylor, whom the state could've kept under lock and key until
1985, was released from prison on April 11, 1980—two years, one month,
and twenty-six days after she'd entered Dwight Correctional Center.

A year later, Taylor's parole officer reported that she was married and
living on the North Side of Chicago. Although Taylor had planned to "be
self-employed with sewing and crocheting for customers," a "variety of
illnesses and ailments" had left her unemployed. Consequently, she was
receiving $186 per month in public aid.

As of April 1981, the parole officer wrote, Linda Taylor was older and
wiser. "At age 50," the parole officer said of the fifty-five-year-old Taylor,
she "displays no inclinations to return to the criminal acts that caused her
incarceration." A few weeks later, on May 26, the Illinois Prisoner Review
Board granted Taylor her final discharge, expressing its confidence that
"she will remain at liberty without violating the law." Taylor's release,
the board said, "is compatible with the welfare of society."

* * *

The *Chicago Tribune* may have lost interest in Linda Taylor when she
went to prison, but the newspaper didn't forget about the prosecutor
who sent the welfare queen away. On February 16, 1978, the same day
Taylor entered Dwight Correctional Center, the *Tribune* reported that
Jim Piper's welfare fraud unit had won seventy-seven indictments since its
inception the previous fall. Three days later, the assistant state's attorney

was quoted in a story chiding the Cook County courts for being "soft" on welfare cheaters. "These people are crying in front of the judge but laughing all the way to the bank," he said.

Piper's cause was arguably a righteous one: He was going after men and women who stole taxpayer money, with a specific focus on civil servants who collected both government salaries and government benefits. Among the people his division indicted in April 1979, the *Tribune* wrote, were "11 employed by the State of Illinois, 8 by the Chicago Board of Education, 7 by Cook County Hospital, and one by the City of Chicago."

While Piper was happy to push this anti-corruption storyline, the nation's best-known welfare fraud prosecutor also recognized the importance of going after big, media-luring targets—the kind that would keep the public excited about locking up chiselers. Arlene Otis, the thirty-year-old black criminal justice graduate student who'd purportedly stolen in excess of $100,000 in public aid money, was just the type to stoke those feelings of righteous indignation.

Although Piper had won the Linda Taylor case, he knew that it hadn't been a perfect prosecution. In pursuing Taylor's successor—a woman touted as "the new welfare queen" by both the state's attorney's office and the *Tribune*—he looked to fix the mistakes he'd made the first time out. Illinois officials had believed Taylor had a tax-free cash income of $150,000 a year, but she'd been convicted of thieving a tiny fraction of that amount; the charges against Otis, by contrast, reflected the full scope of her alleged actions. For Piper, it had also been vexing to watch Taylor keep getting released on bail; this go-round, he made sure Otis stayed locked up on a $200,000 bond. And while it took more than three years for Taylor to go from arrest to incarceration, Otis traveled the same path in just eight months. In January 1979, Piper reached a plea deal with Otis's lawyer, and the new welfare queen was sentenced to four years in state prison. Like her forebear, she'd serve that time at Dwight Correctional Center.

Otis, too, had a successor, a purveyor of frozen treats the *Tribune* called the "Ice Cream Welfare Queen." That woman, Joyce Williams, reportedly collected almost $11,500 in public aid even as she lived in a luxury apartment building on South Lake Shore Drive and "drove a $23,000 imported automobile." She was held on $100,000 bond in August 1978 after supposedly fleeing to Mississippi and opening another ice cream parlor. Piper also prosecuted Chicago's next "new welfare queen," Hope Beaty, who was denied bail in 1980 after being charged "with illegally collecting $150,682 in checks, $49,858 in food stamps, and $8,844 in medical payments."

The bail rulings in these high-profile fraud cases—the six-figure bonds given to Otis and Williams, and Beaty getting held without any bond at all—signaled that the Cook County courts were in the grip of a kind of anti–welfare queen hysteria. The *Tribune*, stenographer of the state's attorneys' press releases, didn't criticize this or any other practice undertaken by Piper's welfare fraud unit. It would be unfair, though, to say the newspaper lacked compassion for Chicago's poor. In its annual drives for the city's Neediest Families Christmas Fund, the *Tribune* urged its readers to give money to the city's most pitiable welfare recipients: Gloria Diaz, a diabetic mother with three small daughters; John Larkin, an elderly man with an artificial leg and paralyzed arm; and Margueritte Gillian, who took care of foster children until being felled by illness, "has not received her last two [public aid] checks in the mail," and "has no family to help her through these hard times."

In the enormous chasm between Linda Taylor and Margueritte Gillian were untold numbers of people who neglected to report outside income that might render them ineligible for government assistance. All of them were cheaters by the letter of the law, and the *Tribune* rarely if ever defended them. In 1980, the magazine *Chicago Lawyer* published an in-depth feature about one of these supposedly hardened criminals, a black woman named Dorothy Holder who collected $4,730.95 in public aid while working for the Illinois Department of Children and Family Services.

Holder, who'd dropped out of high school to help support her family, had to stop working temporarily at age thirty-six due to a prolonged hospitalization. She'd then earned a bachelor's degree, began to pursue a master's, and got a job with the state, failing to get off the public aid rolls immediately upon finding full-time work. Holder learned that she'd been indicted when a friend told her that her name was in the newspaper—she was the eleventh of twenty-seven Chicagoans on a list of those accused of "bilking the welfare system." For the state's attorney's office and the *Tribune*, these directories of alleged wrongdoers—each person charged was identified by name, age, address, and place of employment—served the dual purpose of publicly shaming supposed welfare thieves and alerting the cheater-hating masses that the city was overrun by leeches.

Holder admitted she'd made a mistake—"I don't want to sound like 'Miss Goody Two-Shoes,' because that's not the case," she told *Chicago Lawyer*—but pleaded to be seen as someone who was trying to do the right thing. "I wanted to work it out so that once I got off public aid I would never have to go that route again," she said. "They kept saying in court that I was a well-educated woman, but they failed to realize how I had to fight to be well educated. I was trying to survive. I was not doing it to buy cars and fancy clothes."

Judge Thomas J. Maloney didn't listen to anything Holder said. He rejected her request that she be allowed to repay the money she'd taken, and he ignored testimony from her boss and co-workers that she was a woman of high character. On December 7, 1979, Maloney ordered Holder to prison for one to five years for what he termed a "clever, conniving, callous rip-off of the taxpayers' money," arguing that if she was "retained on the state payroll, Holder could, and probably would, steal again." Years later, the judge who lectured Dorothy Holder on morality would spend twelve years behind bars after being convicted of fixing multiple murder trials in exchange for cash.

Holder's prosecution in some ways marked the end of a feverish era in Illinois, one that started when the *Tribune* branded Linda Taylor the welfare queen in October 1974. In the final days of 1978, Democratic state senator Richard Newhouse succeeded in ousting Republican Don Moore as the chair of the Legislative Advisory Committee on Public Aid. The following year, the body that had led the charge to prosecute Taylor disbanded its internal police force, effectively ending its run as a publicity-seeking pursuer of individual offenders. At around the same time, Piper began to get fewer referrals from the Illinois Department of Public Aid and the Illinois Department of Law Enforcement, a consequence of arcane changes in those agencies' internal review processes. Finally, in November 1980, Cook County's Republican state's attorney Bernard Carey would lose his reelection bid to Democratic mayoral scion (and future twenty-two-year mayor of Chicago) Richard M. Daley. Although Daley would occasionally ballyhoo his office's welfare fraud prosecutions, he'd dismantle the unit Piper built.

Piper, who'd moved to the state's attorney's financial crimes section just before Carey's ouster, believed he'd done important and valuable work. Between 1977 and 1980, his division would indict 631 people accused of stealing a collective $7.3 million in public aid. In his first meeting with Daley, though, the prosecutor was criticized by the new boss for bringing welfare fraud charges against Chicago Police Department crossing guards. Piper thought those were good cases—if the guards had stolen government funds, he didn't understand why they should get special treatment. But Daley had other priorities.

The relative slowdown of Illinois's hyperactive fraud-fighting regime didn't reflect a shift in the mood of the state's concerned citizens. Call volume to the Department of Public Aid's twenty-four-hour welfare fraud hotline stayed steady throughout the late 1970s, hovering at just above ten thousand reports per year. The nation as a whole likewise remained suspicious of those receiving public benefits. Between 1976 and 1980, a consistent 57 to 60 percent of survey respondents said the nation spent too much on welfare—the highest figures on record until the mid-1990s.

* * *

On June 14, 1978, six weeks after the *Tribune* dubbed Arlene Otis the new welfare queen, the *Los Angeles Times* reported that a thirty-three-year-old woman from Ladera Heights, California, had been "accused of pulling off the biggest welfare fraud in the nation's history." Barbara Williams, who was charged with scamming the state out of $239,857 in welfare checks, allegedly padded her public aid applications with thirty-four, forty-seven, or "more than seventy" phony children, depending on which media item you believed. The judge who sentenced the black, Cadillac-driving, over-sized sunglasses–wearing mother of four to eight years in prison said she was "on a par with somebody who steals from the poor box of a church." The *Times'* enormous page one, above-the-fold headlines told Williams's story in a shorthand that was easy for any reader to understand. "Welfare Queen Surrenders." "Welfare Queen Sent to Prison."

Two years later, another Californian would get touted as the perpe-trator of a "possible record swindle." When police swarmed Dorothy Woods's Pasadena mansion in December 1980, they found a Cadillac with a license plate frame reading "My other car is a Rolls." Her Rolls-Royce was indeed parked nearby. Woods, who was black, would get an eight-year prison sentence for stealing $377,000 in welfare payments using thirteen names and claiming forty-nine dependent children. Before get-ting convicted in California, she'd gone to prison in Illinois for credit card fraud. The state's attorney who'd prosecuted her was Jim Piper. Woods had been released from Dwight Correctional Center in June 1973, a bit less than five years before Linda Taylor showed up at the front gate.

Newspapers touted Woods's ascent to the top of the all-time welfare fraud tote board as if she'd just won a literal crown. "No other known 'welfare queen' has done so well," the *Tribune* wrote, while other news-papers speculated that she'd "unseat" or "dethrone" Barbara Williams. In a 1980 interview with the black newspaper the *Los Angeles Sentinel*, Maxine Waters—then a member of the California State Assembly—argued that these shocking tales of greed emboldened the enemies of social welfare. "I think every year or so we get a spectacular case of fraud and far too often those who would like to deny any welfare systems to the poor point to these cases in an effort to indict all welfare recipients—black, in particular," Waters said.

It wasn't a coincidence that these spectacular cases were concentrated in California and Illinois. Under Governor Ronald Reagan, the Golden State had invested heavily in fraud detection and prosecution; when Illi-nois got serious about fighting fraud upon the discovery of Linda Taylor

Josh Levin

in 1974, state senator Don Moore imported a Reagan official to show his public aid cops the ropes. The knowledge transfer went both ways. California launched its own anonymous welfare fraud hotlines after Illinois pioneered the practice, and both Williams and Woods got found out thanks to unidentified phone tipsters. "She does have a Rolls-Royce," said a caller to the Los Angeles Department of Public Social Services, describing one of Woods's vehicles. "She has a Fleetwood. She has a Mercedes. Uh…she owns a house worth approximately $250,000."

For those Americans inclined to believe that high-living good-for-nothings lurked in every grocery store and car dealership, the welfare queens of past and present were less spectacular outliers than representative case studies. "When I read in the newspapers or hear on television about sensational welfare cheaters such as Dorothy Woods, the 'welfare queen,' I wonder how many small cheaters there are still undiscovered," a *Tribune* reader named M. Freeman wondered in a March 1981 letter to the editor, going on to suggest "that many of the jobless could be trained and gainfully employed in checking on welfare recipients." The woman who proposed building this spy force lived in the village of Grayslake, a northern suburb of Chicago that, per the 1980 Census, had a population of 5,196 white people and one black person.

M. Freeman wasn't a lonely crank. Her views were shared by the letter writer in Minnesota who called that state "the promised land for welfare chiselers, cheats, and the parasites who live off the working people"; the editorialist in Arizona who predicted a "revolt" if the government didn't start "tracking welfare recipients with the same tenacity as it does taxpayers"; and the Kentucky official who said the poor were using food stamps to buy "everything from guns to drugs to Cadillacs." This not-so-silent majority had a very powerful ally in Washington, DC. "No one in the United States knows how many people are on welfare. They only know how many checks they're sending out," President Ronald Reagan said at a breakfast for newspaper and television news editors on February 19, 1981. "And then we turn up a woman in Chicago that's getting checks under a hundred and twenty-seven different names. And just recently in Pasadena, California, living in a lovely big home there, a woman was brought in and charged with collecting three hundred thousand dollars in a welfare scheme."

★ ★ ★

Coming up short in his bid for the presidency in 1976 didn't change Ronald Reagan. In his twice-weekly syndicated newspaper columns, daily radio commentaries, and scores of paid corporate talks, the ex-governor maintained that the world was a very simple place. Individual freedom and limited government were good; socialism and high taxes were bad.

Sometimes Reagan would cite new facts that supported his preexisting views, as when he quoted a prosecutor's explanation for how liars, cheaters, and con artists get on the welfare rolls: "It's easy. They just lie." More often, he rehashed his favorite material. In 1977, a writer staking out a Republican get-together at Disney World reported "stumbling through the palm trees in pitch darkness...in search of a conference luau." Suddenly, he heard Reagan's "soft, resonant, familiar voice." The presidential also-ran was "making the same old tired speech," one in which he marveled at the existence of "a woman on welfare in Chicago who had 127 different identification cards."

For Reagan, these sorts of gigs were a warm-up for his return to the electoral stage. He talked about the woman in Chicago and her 127 names in New Hampshire in February 1980, and he mentioned her in Springfield, Pennsylvania, in April. "There's a woman in Chicago [who] received welfare benefit[s] under 127 different names," Reagan said in advance of May's Texas primary when asked how he'd trim the federal budget. "I think we can eliminate that kind of thing."

As they'd done in 1976, journalists pounced on the candidate's misstatements. Reagan said "there was virtually no growth at all" in California's budget when he was governor; the *Los Angeles Times* said the state's budget had grown 122 percent. Reagan said John F. Kennedy had cut taxes by 30 percent; *Time* said it was 19 percent. Reagan said it "costs [the Department of Health, Education, and Welfare] $3 in overhead to deliver $1 to a needy person in this country"; the *New York Times* said the department "insists that it costs only 12 cents."

This gotcha game didn't hurt Reagan in the Republican primary against George H. W. Bush, and it didn't hurt him in the general election against Jimmy Carter. For Reagan and his supporters, it was less important that the statistics he rattled off were true than that they felt true, and that he projected certainty in an uncertain time. In November 1979, with the country shaken by runaway inflation and a gasoline shortage and a perilous hostage situation in Iran, Carter spoke of a "crisis of confidence...that strikes at the very heart and soul and spirit of our national will." In a televised address a year later, on the eve of the 1980 election, his Republican opponent declared that he'd seen something altogether different. "I find no national malaise," Reagan said. "I find nothing wrong with the American people." Reagan told tens of millions of voters what they wanted to hear. The nation's problems, he assured the people in attendance at his rallies and those tuning in at home, were someone else's fault.

The main obstacles to American prosperity, Reagan made clear, were Jimmy Carter's feckless presidency and the enormous bureaucracy that did Carter's bidding. That bureaucracy, Reagan had explained to an audience of fifteen thousand at Mississippi's Neshoba County Fair in August 1980, had consigned the poor to a life of dependency. Welfare recipients were "so economically trapped that there's no way they can get away," he said. "And they're trapped because that bureaucracy needs them as a clientele to preserve the jobs of the bureaucrats themselves." Thirty seconds later, after stopping twice for applause, Reagan told the nearly all-white crowd, "I believe in states' rights," adding that he would "restore to the states and local communities those functions that properly belong there."

Reagan, as was his custom, presented an argument he'd made count-less times before, one about how Americans should do "as much as they can for themselves at the community level and at the private level." When he expressed support for "states' rights," though, he used a phrase he wasn't in the habit of deploying on the campaign trail, and he did so just a few miles from where activists James Chaney, Andrew Goodman, and

Michael Schwerner had been murdered during 1964's Freedom Summer. Both before and after the killing of those three men, who'd been investigating the burning of a black church, political authorities in the state had invoked states' rights as a kind of threat—a warning that integrationists and the federal government give the state leave to handle its own affairs or face potentially deadly consequences. Carter, in a speech at Atlanta's Ebenezer Baptist Church, where Martin Luther King Jr. had served as co-pastor until his assassination in 1968, lamented "the rebirth of code words like 'states' rights' in a speech in Mississippi," saying that "hatred has no place in this country."

In a then-anonymous 1981 interview with a political scientist, Reagan campaign operative Lee Atwater acknowledged that "states' rights" and "forced busing" (a Reagan hobbyhorse in 1976) were coded phrases, "abstract" appeals that obviated the use of nasty slurs. As Atwater explained, abstracting racism allowed Reagan and other candidates to appeal to racists—blue-collar "George Wallace–style voters," i.e., the "guy who is most threatened by the black"—without being explicitly racist themselves. (Atwater referred to this as "doing away with the racial problem.") Voters got the message. In 1976, 40 percent of respondents to the American National Election Studies survey thought the Republican Party would "not make any special effort to help minorities because they should help themselves." Four years later, with Reagan as the GOP's presidential nominee, that number had shot up to 66 percent.

Reagan did make some efforts to court black voters. Two days after the Neshoba County Fair, he told the convention of the National Urban League that "to too many people, 'conservative' has come to mean 'anti-poor, anti-black, and anti-disadvantaged,'" urging the crowd "to look beyond labels." A month later, when Carter went after Reagan for using "code words," the Republican called it a "shameful" political ploy. Carter then backpedaled, saying he didn't think Reagan was "a racist in any degree."

Orienting the dispute around Reagan's personal beliefs was a dodge, a way to avoid talking about the choices politicians make (or allow others to make on their behalf) to try to win elections. In Atwater's telling, "country club people"—white voters angry that their wealth was getting redistributed to the poor via welfare programs—were essentially a Republican lock. To build a winning coalition in the South, the GOP candidate needed to woo the Wallace types, too. The Neshoba County Fair, the *New York Times* reported, was an event where white politicians had traditionally gone off on "bitter racist diatribes." A week before Election Day, Reagan also appeared alongside former Mississippi governor John Bell Williams, an avowed segregationist. And two days before voters cast their ballots, South Carolina senator Strom Thurmond—Atwater's mentor and the 1948 presidential nominee of the States' Rights Democratic Party— declared at a Reagan rally, "We want that federal government to keep their filthy hands off the rights of the states."* This was less a dog whistle than a full-throated rebel yell, and Reagan did nothing to disavow it.

On November 4, 1980, Reagan cruised to a ten-point win in the popular vote and a 489–49 electoral college landslide. In 1976, Carter had carried every Southern and border state except for Virginia. Four years later, Reagan would win them all save West Virginia and Carter's home state of Georgia.

* * *

In the opening two minutes of his first inaugural address, Reagan said the nation had been "confronted with an economic affliction of great proportions." A month later, the fortieth president of the United States told Congress he could cure that affliction by slashing the federal budget. These cuts wouldn't hurt "those with true need," Reagan explained, as the programs he planned to scythe were unnecessary, duplicative, wasteful, and racked by fraud. Spending on food stamps would be reduced "by removing from eligibility those who are not in real need or who are abusing the program." He also promised to "tighten welfare and

---

* Immediately after Thurmond left the stage, Trent Lott—then a member of the House of Representatives—proclaimed, "You know, if we had elected this man thirty years ago, we wouldn't be in the mess we are today." Twenty-two years later, Lott would resign as Senate majority leader after making a very similar comment at Thurmond's hundredth birthday party.

give more attention to outside sources of income when determining the amount of welfare that an individual is allowed."

Carter, like Reagan, had stormed into office promising to clean up the welfare system. The Democrat's Program for Better Jobs and Income—which called for implementing work requirements for able-bodied welfare recipients and giving a standardized cash payment to those who couldn't work—had been an ambitious proposition, one Congress had no interest in enacting once it became clear it would cost billions of dollars. Carter's pitch to fix welfare had been premised in part on the notion that the system was "subject to almost inevitable fraud." He emphasized, though, that this fraud was rare, and he didn't tell cherry-picked stories about extraordinary thieves.

His successor took a different approach. A few days before Reagan told Congress he'd "tighten welfare," syndicated columnist David Broder wrote that Democratic congressional leaders had asked the president to get into the nitty-gritty of his cost-saving plan. Reagan had then proceeded to tell "his well-worn campaign anecdotes about the 'welfare queen' of Chicago who was on the rolls with 100 different names." Two weeks later, the UPI's Helen Thomas reported that Reagan had brought up "his famous 'welfare queen'" during a meeting with the Congressional Black Caucus.

According to Thomas, most of the black lawmakers in that meeting "left the White House 'steaming.'" Other members of Congress walked away from policy discussions with Reagan feeling totally perplexed. "[Senate Budget Committee chair] Pete Domenici says we've got a $120 billion deficit coming," Republican senator Bob Packwood told the AP in March 1982, "and the president says, 'You know, a person yesterday, a young man went into a grocery store with an orange in one hand and a bottle of vodka in the other, and he paid for the orange with food stamps and he took the change and paid for the vodka. That's what's wrong.' And we just shake our heads."

At a subsequent congressional hearing, an official from Reagan's Department of Agriculture said it was "unfortunate if the president was misinformed." By law, the amount of change dispensed in a food stamp transaction was capped at 99 cents, the official said, and "it's not possible to buy a bottle of vodka with 99 cents." The fact that this orange-and-vodka maneuver would've been illegal didn't prove definitively that the anecdote was a work of fiction. The White House's inability to dredge up a source for the incident, though, suggested pretty strongly that it had never happened. "If there is a major fraud for us to focus upon, it is the fraud upon the public of repeating untrue stories," said House Nutrition Subcommittee chair Fred Richmond, a Democrat. "We don't need to change the program to counter these myths. We need to silence the storytellers."*

Reagan's shallow command of policy matters may have made the likes of Packwood and Richmond shake their heads, but it didn't stop the president from winning on Capitol Hill. Reagan did lose some battles: A national registry for welfare recipients got scuttled due to privacy concerns; a proposed mandatory work requirement for those on public aid became an optional, state-level pilot program. But Congress ultimately approved $35 billion in cuts for fiscal year 1982, $25 billion of which came from initiatives that affected the poor. An estimated 408,000 of the country's 3.9 million Aid to Families with Dependent Children households lost their benefits entirely, while roughly one million people lost access to food stamps. Millions more saw their AFDC and food stamp outlays reduced.

At the end of December, the *Los Angeles Times* published a long front-page story on the human toll of Reagan's first year in office. "I won't be able to survive," said a woman whose $594 monthly take-home pay had made her ineligible for welfare. "I can't find a cheaper apartment unless I move to a ghetto. We have to eat." There was also an unemployed steelworker in Indiana who'd lost two-thirds of his jobless benefits— "We're not having any Christmas this year," he said—and a destitute couple in Tennessee who no longer received Medicaid benefits for their three young kids. "Under new federal regulations, Tennessee has exercised its option not to provide free health care for needy children," the

---

* Richmond would resign from the House five months later after pleading guilty to charges of tax evasion and marijuana possession. Packwood would resign from the Senate in 1995 after nineteen women accused him of sexual misconduct.

Times explained. (One column over on page one, the newspaper ran a parallel article on the big winners of 1981: lumber dealer Robert Spence and petroleum executive Armand Hammer, both of whom profited from the administration's rewrite of the American tax code.)

Stories of hardship were easy to find given that the United States had fallen into a severe economic downturn. At the tail end of the recession, which lasted from July 1981 to November 1982, the national unemployment rate spiked to a post-1948 high of 10.8 percent, while the poverty rate reached 15 percent. As the economy tanked, Reagan proposed additional massive cuts to AFDC, Medicaid, and the food stamp program, and Congress would give him about 60 percent of what he asked for. In May 1982, the *Boston Globe* reported on the proliferation of food banks across the United States, and how "people who are embarrassed to be seen in a soup kitchen" had started lining up for emergency rations.

More often than not, the hungry, jobless people showcased in these sorts of features were white. In the early 1970s, as welfare cheats took the blame for rising public aid costs, 70 percent of the photos in newsmagazine items on poverty had featured black people. As benefit levels crashed in the early 1980s, the percentage of nonblack faces in stories about poverty rose to 67 percent. This dramatic shift couldn't be explained by actual demographic changes: White Americans made up 66 percent of the nation's poor in 1972 and 1973 and 68 percent in 1982 and 1983. Rather, this type of editorial decision-making reflected the belief that the U.S. government was now harming the "deserving poor." A *Newsweek* piece on "The Hard-Luck Christmas of '82" asserted that the Reagan-era recession had produced "a much better class of poor person, better educated, accustomed to working, with strong family ties." Just seventeen of the ninety people pictured in that article were black.

When the president's approval rating plummeted in 1982, he blamed the drop on negative press coverage. Reagan was particularly aggravated by the media's fixation on individual hard-luck cases—what he described as "horror stories about the people that are going to be thrown out in the snow to hunger and die of cold and so forth." All those dire warnings about starvation, the president thought, didn't account for the generosity of the American people, who would compensate for potential shortfalls in government funding via "simple acts of neighbor caring for neighbor." He was also tired of watching himself get criticized on television. "Is it news that some fella out in South Succotash someplace has just been laid off, that he should be interviewed nationwide?" Reagan groused.

The White House wasn't just mad that tales of woe were crowding out pro-Reagan news. Administration officials also protested that these accounts were misleading and inaccurate. One of Reagan's press aides, Larry Speakes, said in February 1982 that the administration had discovered that "a lot of stories of people being deprived...don't hold up." Another aide, David Gergen, said it was unacceptable for the news media to use one-sided anecdotes but perfectly okay for the president to do the same thing. "He has several responsibilities," Gergen said of Reagan. "One is to describe reality, and one is to lead."

* * *

Ronald Reagan never knew the truth about Linda Taylor, and he never cared to know it. The only thing that mattered to him was that she was a specific type of criminal, one whose criminality was politically useful. The State of Illinois, too, had made an example of Taylor for political reasons. In 1967, she was charged with kidnapping and wasn't prosecuted for it. In 1975, she was suspected of murder and wasn't questioned about it. In 1977, she was sentenced to three to seven years in prison for stealing public aid money and lying about it to a grand jury.

By the early 1980s, politics no longer governed Taylor's fate. When Reagan talked about the woman in Chicago with the 127 different names, he was describing a still image. The real Linda Taylor had moved on, and her movements weren't of interest to journalists, elected officials, or anyone else.

The Illinois Prisoner Review Board faced no scrutiny when it convened to decide Taylor's fate. In discharging her prison sentence, the state body relied on the facts of her individual case. The members of the parole board decreed that she no longer posed a threat to society, and they said that she'd remain at liberty without violating the law. They were wrong on both counts.

CHAPTER 17
Beneficiary

Michael Booker was so terrified he could barely speak. It was late on a summer night in Chicago in August 1983 when Booker woke up Raymond Ray to tell him what he'd seen. Booker was like family to the Rays. He lived a few blocks from them near Grand Crossing Park on the South Side, and he was a frequent visitor to their house on South Langley Avenue. This time, he would've preferred to be anywhere else. Booker came through the door, sat down, and said his best friend, Raymond Ray's son Sherman, was dead. He'd watched the whole thing happen.

Booker explained that Sherman Ray had been defenseless—that he'd been backing away from a confrontation with a much older man. The thirty-four-year-old victim, who hadn't been holding a weapon, was standing in front of a tree when he'd gotten blasted in the chest with a shotgun at close range. The person who'd shot him—a relative of Sherman's wife, Linda—claimed it had been a horrible accident. Booker was certain the old man had pulled the trigger on purpose. He was also convinced that Linda had been an accessory to the crime.

Ray's father told Booker he needed to go to the police. Booker wasn't so sure. He thought he'd just witnessed a murder, and he didn't want to be the next to die. Booker told Raymond Ray they were dealing with some evil people. "You don't know them," he said.

* * *

Sherman Ray's parents and siblings had no idea how he'd met Linda Taylor. The first time anyone had seen the two of them together was in 1976, when they'd made a joint appearance at a barbecue. When Ray introduced Taylor as his wife, his relatives were bewildered. Ray had never mentioned her, and he definitely hadn't said anything about a wedding.

While Ray's family was a bit suspicious of his new bride, they were happy he'd found someone to share his life with. Ray had seemed haunted ever since coming back from the Vietnam War. He'd joined the Marine Corps in 1968, when he was nineteen. In June of the following year, twenty-nine of the men in his infantry battalion were killed in action in northwest Quang Tri Province while an additional 114 were wounded. That same month, Ray was hospitalized with what he termed "nervousness." After stretches in military hospitals in Vietnam, Japan, and New York, he'd been honorably discharged on September 11, 1969, three days after his twenty-first birthday.

When he returned to Chicago, Ray told his brothers how scared he'd been in Southeast Asia. Before he'd gone to Vietnam, he'd been easy to get along with and quick to smile. After the war, he was friendly but guarded. He started drinking heavily, downing six-packs of Schlitz most days of the week. His older sister Patricia noticed that he no longer liked to be touched, and that he'd recoil if anyone surprised him.

As far as Ray's sister knew, he'd never been in a serious relationship before he'd started seeing Linda Taylor. Whoever she was and wherever she'd come from, he seemed to love and trust Linda. The biographical information on their marriage license, though, suggested that his wife hadn't been totally honest with him. The document, dated January 20, 1976, granted twenty-seven-year-old Sherman F. Ray permission to wed twenty-nine-year-old Linda C. B. Wakefield; in reality, she was forty-nine or fifty. Sherman and Linda got married the next day at 5546 South State Street, the address of a storefront church called the House of Silent Prayer.

In August 1974, Taylor had gotten arrested for stealing public aid checks eight days after marrying Lamar Jones. That legal predicament had killed their budding romance: Taylor had fled to Arizona, taking Jones's TV set with her, and he'd subsequently helped the police track her down. In January 1976, Taylor burglarized her ex-roommate's house eight days after marrying Sherman Ray, pilfering, among other things, a fur coat, a wedding band, and a pink radio and record player. A month later, she'd get arrested yet again. But this time, Taylor didn't run away. Neither did her husband.

Ray stuck with Taylor when she got charged with that burglary, and he stood by her during her welfare fraud trial in March 1977. On the first day of trial testimony, the *CBS Evening News* showed footage of Ray strolling through the Daley Center alongside Taylor. He was short, stocky, and handsome, with dark brown skin and a thin mustache. While his Afro was a lot trimmer than his wife's billowing orange hairdo, he didn't fade into the background. Ray, whom Taylor's lawyer had once seen sporting crocodile shoes with goldfish in the heels, wore a white Western shirt with a butterfly collar and contrasting gold fabric on the pocket flaps, yoke, and cuffs; a royal blue vest; and a white belt. A few months later, the AP snapped a picture of the duo on the way to Taylor's sentencing hearing. Taylor, her left hand clutching a handbag and pressed against her husband's right hip, appeared untroubled by her looming prison hitch. Ray, who wore a herringbone sport coat over a cable-knit turtleneck sweater, seemed just as relaxed. They looked like a great team.

Taylor, too, supported Ray when he was at his lowest. He was admitted to the VA hospital in North Chicago, Illinois, multiple times in the mid-1970s, with forms indicating a recurrence of a "mental condition." A photo taken during one hospital stay included a small Christmas tree—a marker of a trying holiday season. Taylor, though, appeared to be full of good cheer, sitting by her husband's bedside with a look of pure devotion on her face.

Although Linda and Sherman seemed like a happy couple, Ray's parents had concluded very quickly that their daughter-in-law was a dubious character. But it took more than a burglary arrest for Raymond and Maude Ray to cut off contact with their son's wife. Their breaking point came in the late spring, when Taylor took their granddaughter.

THE QUEEN

* * *

Sherman Ray's brother John was just twenty-five years old when he drowned on June 12, 1976, slipping and hitting his head on a boat propeller. Shortly after the accident, Sherman and his wife went to the morgue to identify John's body, informing the staff that his corpse should be released to the Lena Bryant Funeral Home. It wasn't the first time Linda Taylor had given the South Side funeral parlor her business. She'd done the same thing a year earlier when her friend Patricia Parks died of a barbiturate overdose.

Raymond Ray was irate when he learned that Taylor had started planning his son's funeral. By way of explanation, Taylor said that Bryant—a prominent Chicago entrepreneur who also owned a beauty school and served as the scholarship chair of the Miss Black USA pageant—was her mother. It's not clear if the Rays realized she was lying. Regardless, it was too late to make alternative arrangements, and the burial proceeded the way Taylor wanted it to. Her father-in-law spent the day of the funeral in a rage. He was about to get even angrier.

Diana Ray had adored her new aunt from the start. The eight-year-old, the daughter of Sherman's younger brother Edmond, lived with her grandparents in the family home on South Langley Avenue. Diana had stayed with her Aunt Linda and Uncle Sherman the night of John Ray's drowning, and she was excited when Taylor asked if she wanted to sleep over again after the repast. While everyone was downstairs drinking, Diana went up to her room and dumped some clothes in a Jewel grocery bag. A short time later, she was in Taylor's car, heading to a big, beautiful white house with a stairwell just inside the front entrance.

The next day, Taylor threw out the clothes Diana had packed and took her to a department store to get a whole new wardrobe. She also bought the elementary schooler a bunch of toys, including a life-size doll. Diana found that doll extraordinarily creepy, but otherwise she was having a fantastic time with her aunt. Taylor cooked her breakfast, gave her hugs, and said she loved her. Diana was thrilled to find she had her own bedroom, and she didn't mind that Taylor told her she wasn't allowed to go outside by herself. She played with a little boy who was close to her age; he, too, had his own bedroom, and he got just as many toys as she did. Taylor told Diana he was her Uncle Sherman's son.

Diana was close to her uncle. Before he'd married Taylor, Sherman Ray had been his niece's go-to babysitter—he'd make her peanut butter and jelly sandwiches and they'd watch *All My Children*, *One Life to Live*, and *General Hospital* together. But Diana saw him just a handful of times during this post-funeral excursion; mostly, Taylor was the only adult around.

The little girl never quite grasped that she'd become a missing person. Diana's grandfather had gone to where he thought Sherman and Linda were living and found the place empty. He didn't know anything about the big white house with the stairwell by the front entrance. Diana, in the meantime, had lost track of time. After more than three days, and maybe as much as a week, her grandfather came to the big white house late at night. Diana woke up when she heard Raymond Ray shouting at her to come downstairs. He wasn't alone. After Diana roused herself and walked to the ground floor, a police officer draped his jacket over her pajamas. Her grandfather then carried her to a waiting car, as she wasn't wearing any shoes.

Diana would later find out that it had been her Uncle Sherman who'd told her family and the police where Taylor had taken her. The eight-year-old had a hard time believing she'd been kidnapped, and she didn't understand when her grandparents called Aunt Linda the devil and a witch. Diana thought she had a special bond with her aunt. Her grandfather told her she'd been conned, that Aunt Linda had thought she could pry Diana away because the girl's parents weren't in the picture. He also said the boy in the big white house wasn't really her Uncle Sherman's child. Diana would never see that boy again, and she'd eventually forget his name.

Raymond Ray was horrified that his son had stood by as his wife abducted Diana. He did his best to ensure Taylor could never get close to his granddaughter again, asking his neighbors to be on guard for another abduction. If Aunt Linda called their house, Raymond Ray told Diana, she needed to hang up the phone immediately.

Taylor, already facing prosecution for welfare fraud and burglary, wouldn't be charged with kidnapping Diana. But on July 8, 1976, three weeks after John Ray's funeral, she was arrested on a fugitive warrant after failing to give the Cook County circuit clerk her current address. She'd be jailed in November of the following year for missing court dates, and she'd land in Dwight Correctional Center on February 16, 1978. Taylor wrote Diana when she was in prison, but the girl's grandfather intercepted those missives. Diana did manage to see one of her aunt's letters, a note in which Taylor said the charges against her were "a bunch of hogwash." She also told Diana that she missed her, and that she'd come by for a visit as soon as she got free.

Raymond Ray would succeed in keeping his granddaughter away from his daughter-in-law. Raymond's son, though, stayed with Linda Taylor despite his family's disapproval. After she was released from Dwight in 1980, Linda and Sherman moved further away from his relatives, taking up residence at a pair of addresses on Chicago's Northwest Side in 1981 and 1982. While Ray would still swing by South Langley Avenue on occasion, Diana would see her Aunt Linda just once after she got out of prison. That meeting would come in August 1983, at her Uncle Sherman's funeral in Kankakee County, Illinois.

* * *

For Linda Taylor, Pembroke, Illinois, was just the right distance from home. Like Covert, Michigan, the rural township on the shore of Lake Michigan where she'd run a series of cons in the early 1970s, it was close to Chicago yet seemed very far away—a spot where her infamy didn't precede her. Just sixty miles south of the city and twenty miles east of the county seat of Kankakee, the sand dune–laden, sparsely populated, mostly ungoverned patch of land hugging the Indiana state line had, according to a 1981 *Tribune* feature, "no industry, no policeman, no dentist, no drugstore, no public transportation system, no gas pipeline, no central water supply, and no bank." What the predominantly black enclave did have in abundance was "the flotsam of poverty": busted-looking shacks, piles of worn-out tires, and "stripped, stolen cars [that]…serve as a monument to past crimes."

What looked like a trash-strewn hellscape to visiting reporters represented something very different to black Chicagoans. For much of the twentieth century, racially restrictive housing covenants and violent mobs ensured that large swaths of Chicago and its surrounds remained white-only zones. Brochures handed out to aspiring home buyers on the South Side touted Pembroke as a place free of these impediments—a kind of unspoiled, egalitarian paradise. The wide-open spaces of rural Kankakee County, where black families had settled as far back as the 1860s, offered an opportunity to "own part of 'America' forever" for the price of a $20 down payment. Given Pembroke's lack of jobs, infrastructure, and arable land—a geographer once said the area, with its sandy soil, was "preprogrammed for poverty"—that $20 was often an investment in false hope. Still, it could feel liberating to escape the confines of the city, and to set out for a place where what you'd done in the past had little bearing on the present.

Sherman Ray, ever the loyal husband, tagged along with Taylor when she went to Pembroke in late 1982 or early 1983. The couple was joined by an old man, Willtrue Loyd, who Taylor insisted was her father. Ray's sister Patricia found the arrangement very mysterious. Loyd, who stayed in a trailer not far from where Taylor and Ray lived, acted more like Taylor's crony than her relative.

Loyd was born in December 1919, making him about six years older than his alleged daughter. A veteran of World War II, he worked as a nurse's aide at the VA hospital in North Chicago, the infirmary where Ray spent significant time in the 1970s. Whether or not the trio originally linked up at the hospital, they'd become financially intertwined by the time Taylor and Ray got married in January 1976. One week after their wedding, the newlyweds put down a deposit on a rental apartment using a check issued to Loyd. And that December, the three of them went in together on a two-story stucco house on South Harvard Avenue, a property they purchased with no money down with the help of a loan backed by the Veterans Administration. A foreclosure action would be brought against them less than a year later.

Like his fake daughter, Loyd was a well-practiced scammer. In July 1977, he forged two people's signatures on a check in order to steal $18,000. In January 1978, a month before Taylor went off to Dwight Correctional Center, the Chicago Police Department arrested Loyd for "deceptive practice," accusing him of filching a $2,414.88 check, erasing the payee's name, and writing in his own. His booking photo showed a tall, thin black man with a balding pate and a heavily lined face. Loyd was fifty-eight. He looked seventy.

Ray was arrested himself in 1980, nabbed by the Chicago police for shoplifting. In his mug shot, the man who'd looked so dapper at his wife's welfare fraud trial appeared bloated, unkempt, and possibly inebriated. Ray was hospitalized after car accidents in both 1981 and 1982 and found to have abnormal EKGs, abnormal liver function, and chronic hepatitis. At the tail end of 1982, the VA brushed off the Vietnam veteran's fourth attempt to get compensation for what he claimed were service-connected mental health issues; years earlier, the agency had concluded that Ray had a "history of alcoholism" but "no mental condition."

The two men in Linda Taylor's life didn't get along. On the afternoon of August 25, 1983, their conflict escalated. Ray and his best friend, Michael Booker, who was visiting Pembroke Township from Chicago, were drinking together in the vicinity of Loyd's trailer. Loyd, who by this time was sixty-three years old, would tell a detective with the Kankakee County Sheriff's Police that he'd been having some difficulty with a seven-foot snake—that he "would go down to pick corn for my animals and the snake would always come in between me and the corn." Loyd said he was out hunting for that gigantic snake with his 12-gauge shotgun when his "stepdaughter's husband" came up behind him. "Sherman told me to give him the gun and I said no," Loyd told the police. He said Ray then grabbed at the gun two separate times. The second time Ray reached for the weapon, Loyd said, "is when the gun went off. And Sherman stood up and then fell to the ground."

When the police arrived at the scene, Ray was lying faceup in a yard strewn with garbage. Metal pellets from Loyd's shotgun had perforated his liver, esophagus, and heart. He'd been killed within seconds. Loyd was handcuffed, placed in a squad car, and brought to the Kankakee County Detention Center. He'd be released the next morning without being charged with a crime.

Although the officers who checked out the killing weren't sure Loyd was telling the whole truth, there were a couple pieces of evidence that backed up his version of events. A postmortem toxicology report, which determined that the victim's blood alcohol content was an extraordinarily high 0.333 percent—a level "usually associated with stupor and marked incoordination," the coroner's physician wrote—gave credence to Loyd's claim that Ray had been acting irrationally. And although he didn't make a note of it in his case report, the responding officer would say decades later that Loyd hadn't been imagining that giant snake—that he'd seen the reptile when he'd been out on patrol.

The foremost reason that Loyd was allowed to go free, in the words of the lead detective, was that "everybody that was there stated they didn't see anything." That included Michael Booker, who told the Kankakee police that he "did not see the incident."

Booker came to Raymond Ray's front door with a different story. He told his friend's father that Willtrue Loyd had been the aggressor and that Sherman Ray had been shot in cold blood. He also said Sherman's wife had been at the scene. The case report, by contrast, hadn't mentioned her at all.

It's possible Booker was covering for Sherman Ray, concocting an account that absolved his best friend. But Diana Ray was in the room when Booker explained what he'd seen, and she was certain he wasn't lying. Booker was genuinely scared: He believed that Loyd and Taylor were responsible for Sherman Ray's death, and he believed they were capable of killing him, too.

In Diana's recollection, her grandfather convinced Booker to tell the authorities what he knew. But when the time came for Booker to make his statement, he didn't show. He also didn't pay his respects at his best friend's funeral. The Rays would never see Michael Booker again.

In 1974, Taylor had told her then-husband Lamar Jones that she'd shot and killed the first man she'd married. That claim would never be verified by Jones or anyone else. Taylor's role in Sherman Ray's demise would remain similarly mysterious. Without Booker's eyewitness testimony, no one—not Taylor, and not Willtrue Loyd—would be held accountable for Ray's killing. Ray's death, like that of Patricia Parks in 1975, was of no political consequence. Taylor's husband had been shot in an all-black rural ghetto that was practically off the map. By moving to Pembroke, Taylor had situated herself in a place where nobody knew her names or her modus operandi. It didn't raise much suspicion, then, that Sherman Ray had purchased two life insurance plans before his untimely death, and that his wife was the sole beneficiary of both policies. The Kankakee police never figured out that Linda Ray was Linda Taylor, and no one in the press would connect the shooting to the Chicago welfare queen. By 1983, Taylor had been out of the newspapers and off the TV news for five years. Her husband's killing wouldn't bring her back into the spotlight.

In the days after Sherman Ray's death, Taylor busied herself with funeral preparations. On August 28, she sent the VA a request for an American flag for burial purposes, signing the form "Rev. Linda Ray." The interment took place three days later, at a cemetery just outside Pembroke Township. When Raymond Ray lifted the veil covering his son's face and leaned down to give him a kiss, Taylor screamed, "Don't touch him!" Ray's widow was kinder to her niece Diana, asking the fifteen-year-old to sit with her in the front row. It was the first time they'd been in each other's company since Taylor abducted the then eight-year-old in 1976. It would also be the last time they'd speak to each other.

Taylor's stay in Pembroke Township would be a short one. A month after her husband's funeral, she'd buy a house in Florida, signing the mortgage deed "Rev. Linda Ray." Taylor wouldn't go to the Sunshine State alone. Her husband's killer would move there with her.

* * *

In 1982, one of Linda Taylor's new neighbors, a sixty-three-year-old army veteran and tomato seller, told a reporter he was "friendly to strangers unless they might be bureaucrats, welfare cheats, 'fancy-britches lawyers' or judges who grant convicted killers stays of execution." The residents of Bonifay, Florida, a poor, agrarian, deeply conservative, and over-whelmingly white Panhandle city of twenty-five hundred, didn't know that the world's most famous welfare cheat now lived among them. In Florida, Taylor mostly stole from individuals rather than government agencies. She lied, scammed, and manipulated to get what she wanted, and she never stopped wanting more.

Taylor told the sellers of the house she bought in Bonifay that she "was coming into money." That money never came, and the Reverend Linda Ray got evicted. On her way out, she stole the homeowners' furniture and some cement sculptures of chickens. She told a man named Kenneth Lynch, a partner on a land deal, that she'd make him whole as soon as a sure-thing injury settlement came through. She never paid him what she owed and she swiped his last name, rechristening herself Linda Lynch. After defaulting on a contract to buy yet another house, she was arrested for allegedly stealing the owner's refrigerator. That charge was ultimately dismissed. So was a charge of grand theft, which she picked up after commandeering four bulls that had wandered off someone else's property. Linda Ray Linch—it's unclear whether she misspelled her own borrowed last name or the typo was the fault of the clerk of court—managed to convince a prosecutor that she owned similar-looking bulls, and that it was all just a misunderstanding.

Taylor undertook these scams in Bonifay and elsewhere around the state. Between 1983 and 1989, she'd leave a paper trail in at least six different counties, and courts in those counties would enter at least six civil judgments against her. Some of the swindles she executed were otherworldly. She'd tell people in Florida, as she'd told Patricia Parks, that she could see into the future. At Linda Lynch's instruction, Reta Hunter would collect four new $20 bills from the bank, then watch her psychic friend singe the edges of the currency. This money-burning spell, she promised, would soon bring Hunter prosperity. In the meantime, Linda would keep those $20 bills for herself.

Hunter's husband, Leroy, also got himself entangled with Linda Lynch, building her a set of feed troughs she never paid for. She told Leroy, who was white and in his early fifties, that she had magical powers. He replied that he'd see her "black ass in court." Leroy Hunter would be awarded a $738 civil judgment, thanks in part to an older black man who confirmed that Linda Lynch had promised to buy those feed troughs. Reta Hunter would overhear Linda snapping at that man, presumably Willtrue Loyd, "I told you not to say anything."

* * *

Reta Hunter didn't perceive Loyd as a rabble-rouser. She thought the man who'd spoken up in court was Linda Lynch's lackey, and she felt sorry for him; he looked beaten down and afraid. Sandy Paderewski, a lawyer based out of Sarasota, didn't register Loyd as much of a presence at all. The woman who came into his office, he believed, was the brains of her own operation.

Paderewski was looking for a payday, and he thought his new client could get him one—maybe more than one if he got lucky. Linda Ray Lynch didn't strike the young attorney as all that trustworthy, but she was a great storyteller, and the stories she told were, from the perspective of a personal injury lawyer, extremely alluring. Her husband had been shot and killed in Illinois, she told Paderewski, and her six-figure insurance claim had been denied for no good reason. Also, since moving to Florida, she'd been mutilated by an unlicensed plastic surgeon. That looked like a strong case, too, one that might get decided very quickly if Paderewski alerted the press to her horrific injuries.

In October 1985, the *Miami Herald* reported that thirty-nine-year-old Linda Ray Lynch—she was actually fifty-nine—had gone to a rejuvenation clinic housed in a South Florida motel. Lynch, a police detective said, had been kept a "virtual prisoner" in that motel after being charged $5,900 for a chemical treatment. The detective reported that her "face was red like a tomato." Paderewski gave his diagnosis a bit more oomph. "Her entire face was eaten off," he told the Miami newspaper.

Josh Levin

The front man of the motel clinic, Bernard Gross, had lost his medical license more than a year earlier, after pleading guilty to selling six thousand homemade quaaludes out of the trunk of his Chrysler. Gross was charged with three felonies in connection to his alleged treatment of Linda Ray Lynch, though prosecutors would ultimately choose not to pursue a criminal case against him. His aggrieved patient, however, would move forward with a civil case against the erstwhile doctor and six other defendants, including the physician Gross said had performed the procedure. Paderewski felt good about this motel-chemical-scar-treatment litigation. While his client's face didn't appear disfigured in the present day, she did have some grisly-looking photographs. A civil court judge was less impressed—he'd dismiss the case in 1986, citing a Florida statute mandating that the claimant's attorney do a "reasonable investigation" into accusations of medical negligence.

Despite that courtroom failure, Taylor still had a chance to make a big score. By the time she met Paderewski, Sherman Ray's widow had already collected on one of her husband's two life insurance policies. Although the value of that first policy hasn't been preserved in any public records, Ray's second insurance contract stipulated a payout of $100,000. The firm that had underwritten that policy, Veterans Life, had no intention of paying up. The company's reluctance to cut Taylor a check had nothing to do with the manner in which Ray had been killed or the fact that his wife's so-called father had done the killing. Rather, the pertinent issue was that Ray hadn't reported his heart and liver problems when he'd signed up for coverage eleven months before his death. Paderewski's complaint, filed in September 1985, argued that was irrelevant: The Rays had paid their monthly premiums, and Sherman had died of a gunshot wound, not heart disease or liver failure.

Veterans Life and Linda Ray would fight it out in both state and federal court, filing motions and memorandums and supplemental answers for more than two years. The parties finally reached a settlement in January 1988, with the specific financial terms of that agreement remaining confidential. Taylor didn't get the full $100,000 she wanted, but she did get some more compensation for her husband's death.

Paderewski would represent Linda Ray Lynch in one more matter: a separate insurance case that was still in process when he worked out a settlement with Veterans Life. Given the time and money he was putting into these various legal excursions, Paderewski wasn't satisfied with the return on his investment. He liked having Linda Ray Lynch around—she was far more entertaining than the people who usually sought out his services. But Paderewski worked on contingency, and he was losing patience with his client's long-running, labor-intensive disputes.

Taylor wouldn't give up so easily. In Florida, she preyed on strangers, acquaintances, and friends. Almost everyone she met became a mark. The people who thought they were close to her lost the most.

* * *

Linda Lynch was sitting by herself at the airport in Dothan, Alabama, in 1985 when she struck up a conversation with a twelve-year-old girl. Lynch, who was waiting for her grandsons' plane to touch down, was extremely friendly and a very fast talker—she seemed excited to have some company. She chatted up Karen Snell for just a few minutes before coming over to meet the girl's mother, Queen. Not long after that, she invited the whole Snell family to her property in Esto, Florida, a tiny town north of Bonifay in rural Holmes County.

The thirty-six-year-old Queen Snell and her three daughters, who lived one county over in Graceville, had never had any occasion to visit Esto. The Snells were black, and people who looked the way they did weren't typically welcome in that corner of the state. Holmes County, which was more than 96 percent white, gave 86.4 percent of its votes to George Wallace in the 1972 Florida Democratic presidential primary. Two decades later, members of the Dupree family—reportedly Esto's only black residents—would scuttle plans to bury their 104-year-old matriarch in the all-white town cemetery after getting an anonymous threat that men with shotguns would turn up at her funeral.

Queen Snell's oldest daughter, Jane, who was fifteen, thought her mother's friend looked out of place in Holmes County.[*] Jane suspected she'd come from an island, or some other exotic, faraway place. Linda Taylor, who'd represented herself as black since Lawrence Wakefield's death in 1964, may have tried to blend into her surroundings in Esto. When Taylor was charged with stealing four bulls in 1985, a Holmes County deputy sheriff noted on the criminal complaint that she was white. She didn't, however, tell her neighbors anything about her background. In a place where everyone knew everyone, nobody knew anything about her at all.

Although he wasn't sure, the farmer whose land abutted hers believed that Linda Lynch was a light-skinned black woman. She certainly didn't hide the fact that she had black relatives. The first time Queen Snell and her girls came over to visit, they met a pair of teenagers named Duke and Hosa, the latter of whom had dark skin. Those were the kids—her daughter Sandra's sons—Linda had picked up at the Dothan airport. The Snells would also meet her son Paul, who was in his late thirties. A quarter century after he'd been sent to a state-run home, he seemed to be on good terms with the woman who'd abandoned him.

The Snells were impressed with Linda Lynch's spread. She lived in a big brick house on a ninety-nine-acre plot with a lake full of bass and bream. The property, which she'd settled on after convincing Kenneth Lynch to pay the mortgage, was a working dairy farm, with automatic milkers, a cow lift, and an eight-hundred-gallon milk-cooling tank.

While Duke and Hosa were just visiting and Paul lived elsewhere on the Panhandle, the farm did have two other permanent residents. Willtrue Loyd was pleasant enough but wasn't the type to stop and chat; whenever the Snells saw him, the sixty-five-year-old was busy doing odd jobs. Mildred Markham, who was in her mid-seventies, was mostly

---

[*] There was a history of mixed-race people living in the area. The 1950 census identified sixty Holmes County residents as "Dominickers," a group of "reputed Indian-White-Negro racial isolates" concentrated near the Choctawhatchee River. By the 1980s, the group—whose pejorative descriptor referenced the black-and-white coloring of Dominicker chickens—had dispersed or assimilated, and there was no longer any record of an organized settlement in the county.

noncommunicative. Linda described the elderly black woman as her grandmother—she'd tell other people Markham was her mother—and said her aged family member wasn't allowed to stay inside because she practiced voodoo. Jane thought that was ridiculous—the old lady didn't strike her as evil or dangerous. Even so, it felt rude to stick her nose into another family's business. At dinnertime, the Snells watched in silence as Markham collected her plate, walked out of the main house, and headed into a barn to eat on her own. She and Loyd slept in that barn, too. The entire situation felt bizarre and sad.

Linda Lynch liked to talk about money—how she was related to a family in Graceville that had bushels of it, and how she was working on a bunch of "cases" that would bring in still more riches. She brought Queen Snell in on one scheme, in which they'd procure day-old baked goods from a bread outlet and resell them out of the back of Linda's red pickup truck. But the two women weren't business partners for long. One afternoon in the spring of 1986, Snell's daughters came back from school to find Linda alone in their house in Graceville. Their mother was gone, she explained. She'd be taking care of them now.

Jane, Karen, and their eleven-year-old sister, Sheila, couldn't believe what they'd just heard. Snell's daughters understood that their mother was in a bad relationship, and they knew their uncles had urged her to leave the man she was seeing and come live with them in New York. Still, it wasn't like her to leave without any warning, and it made no sense that she'd appoint a virtual stranger to watch over them. But Linda was telling the truth: Queen Snell was already on her way out of town.

Snell did eventually talk to her daughters on the phone, saying that she was en route to New York and would send for them when school was out for the summer. Sheila, the youngest of the three girls, refused to sign on to this plan, raising such a ruckus that her mother relented and brought her up North right away. The oldest daughter, Jane, didn't trust Linda at all. She insisted on going to her grandmother's house in the nearby town of Noma; when Linda tried to retrieve her, Jane locked the doors and wouldn't come out. Karen was the only one of the girls to accede to her mother's wishes. She agreed to stay in the family's house in Graceville, where she'd share a room with her new caregiver.

This house-sitting opportunity came at a convenient time for Linda Taylor. Nobody had been making the payments on her property in Esto, which was foreclosed on in October 1985, just six months after the purchase had gone through. In early 1986, she'd make herself at home in the Snells' three-bedroom residence, and she'd bring along Willtrue Loyd and Mildred Markham.

Karen, who would turn thirteen in February 1986, wouldn't be neglected or physically abused, but she'd bear witness to a lot of cruelty. Linda had a puppy named Pierre that she'd tote around wherever she went. The dog, which looked like a little rug, had an unusually long tail. One day, Linda ordered her male companion to chop it off. Loyd did as she'd requested, performing the in-home surgery. Afterward, Pierre wouldn't stop howling, and in the succeeding days the pooch's body swelled up and he refused to eat. Although the dog would get better, Karen found the episode profoundly unsettling. She didn't understand how people could inflict so much pain on a helpless animal.

Linda wasn't any kinder to Mildred Markham, calling the old woman stupid for drinking milk that had been purchased for the dog. It wasn't clear if Markham knew she was getting berated. Regardless, she absorbed her supposed granddaughter's insults in silence. At night, she and Loyd retired to a bedroom outfitted with nothing but a dirty mattress and a tattered blanket. One room over, Karen would watch Linda take off her shoulder-length blond wig before going to sleep each night. Underneath those fake tresses, she didn't have much hair at all.

The few times Jane came over to check on her younger sister, she was disturbed to see what Linda Lynch had done with the place. The high school sophomore called her mother to say that Markham and Loyd were living in filth, and to report that Linda had brought in her own living room furniture and dining room set. Queen Snell wasn't concerned. Her friend had told her that she'd found and killed a big snake on Queen's bed. That was a sign, Linda had explained, that Queen had been right to run away from her bad relationship.

THE QUEEN

While Jane didn't believe any of that voodoo nonsense, Karen wasn't sure what to think. The sixty-year-old Linda Lynch treated the thirteen-year-old girl as a confidant. Linda would spend hours driving Karen around the northern Panhandle in her red pickup, pointing out all the places she was planning to buy. She said they were going to leave Graceville very soon, and that they'd move into a brick house with a pool. She cruised by that brick house again and again, as if she was trying to will it into her possession.

The Snells didn't have much money. Karen heard Linda complain to the mailman and neighbors about the ragged condition of her stopgap home, and she disparaged Queen's green Ford LTD as an "old-ass car." This wasn't the life she felt she deserved. She'd have to go somewhere else, and con someone else, to ascend to her rightful station.

As soon as the 1986 school year was over, Jane and Karen got on a plane to join their mother in New York. When the whole family returned to Graceville in 1987, they came back to an empty house. Linda, they'd find out, had put everything the Snells owned into a storage facility, and she hadn't kept up with the rental fees. Queen couldn't afford to get their stuff out of hock. All of their belongings—the living room furniture, the girls' Barbie dolls, and one of her youngest daughter's trophies—were gone. So was Linda Lynch. Queen Snell and her daughters would never get the chance to ask her why she'd done what she'd done, and whether she'd gotten what she wanted.

Jane had come home to Florida well before her mom and her sisters—she'd hated New York, and her best friend's family had agreed to take her in. The first night she was back in town, staying temporarily with an old neighbor, she saw an ambulance stop in front of her mother's house. Jane watched as Mildred Markham was carried out on a stretcher. Two months later, Markham would be dead.

★ ★ ★

Linda Taylor had brainwashed Mildred Markham. That was the only explanation Markham's real granddaughter could come up with. Theresa

Davis wasn't sure where Taylor and her grandmother had met—one possibility was that they'd crossed paths when they'd been patients at the same Chicago hospital—and she wasn't sure what this Linda person had said or done to insinuate herself into Markham's life. All she knew for certain was that in the early 1980s, Markham had started telling her friends and relatives that Linda was her long-lost daughter.

Markham, who was seventeen years older than Taylor, was born in Louisiana around 1909 but had lived in Chicago for most of her life. In 1937, she'd married James Monroe Markham in a wedding officiated by the pastor of the Ebenezer Missionary Baptist Church, a South Side institution known as the birthplace of gospel music. James was a Pullman porter for the Illinois Central Railroad, one of the few decent-paying, high-status positions available to a black man in Chicago at that time, while Mildred worked out of their home as a seamstress and helped raise their granddaughter. A 1945 item in the *Defender*, which noted that Mildred and Theresa had "spent their vacation touring Florida and Alabama," said that "Mrs. Markham is well known for her work in charity throughout the community."

Theresa Davis's grandparents had been her primary caregivers, and they'd ensured that she'd grown up in a stable and loving household. After Markham became a widow in the spring of 1983, Davis wanted to make sure her grandmother was similarly safe and comfortable. But when she asked Markham to come live with her, the septuagenarian demurred. All she wanted to talk about was Linda.

James Markham had still been alive when his wife first started seeing Taylor. As soon as Markham's husband died, her newfound daughter began coming by a lot more often and telling the old woman she'd take care of all her needs. Markham thought that sounded great.

Davis discovered that her grandmother was missing on a Saturday morning in 1983, when she went to Markham's Chicago apartment and found the place empty. Markham's furniture, sewing machine, fur coats, and jewelry had been carted off. The money in her bank account was gone, too. Markham's neighbor told Davis she'd left willingly—that she'd actually been grinning as she walked out the door, telling anyone who'd listen that she was going with her daughter.

A month or two later, Davis got a letter from her grandmother. She said she was with Linda in Kankakee County, Illinois, and was ready to come home. When Davis and her husband traveled from Chicago down to Pembroke Township to search for Markham, the place where she'd been living was fenced in and locked up. Nobody seemed to know where she and Taylor had gone.

A few months after that, Davis would get a second letter, this one postmarked in Florida. Markham told her granddaughter that she was being mistreated—that Linda wouldn't let her stay in the main house. This time, Davis tried and failed to track down her grandmother from afar. She'd never see her again.

At around the time Markham wrote to her granddaughter from Florida, Taylor's son Johnnie Harbaugh and his wife, Carol, came to the Panhandle for a visit. On that trip, they met Markham for the first time. It didn't take them long to gather that she was being held against her will. They watched Taylor scream at the seventy-five-year-old and lock her in a room, and they heard Markham say she wasn't getting enough to eat. Markham begged the Harbaughs to take her back to Chicago. Thirty years later, Johnnie wouldn't have a clear memory of what happened next—maybe Markham had changed her mind and decided to stay in Florida, or perhaps he'd concluded that he didn't want to get involved. Carol would remember the chain of events more distinctly. Johnnie had backed off, she'd recall, after his mother had warned him, "You even think about it, and I'll blow your head off."

Taylor had good reason to want Mildred Markham to remain under her control. Unlike Queen Snell, Markham had substantial money and property. On October 29, 1985—five days after the *Miami Herald* reported that a plastic surgeon had burned Linda Ray Lynch's face and kept her a prisoner in a motel—Markham deeded 185 acres of land to Linda Lynch and Clifford L. Harbaugh. Clifford, Taylor's oldest son, would later deny having any knowledge of that deal. It's undeniable, though, that Markham was fleeced. Although the document spelled out that Markham would be paid $150,000 for that acreage—a parcel her husband James had bought in Lincoln County, Mississippi, with savings he'd accrued as a railroad man—there's no indication that any cash ever changed hands.

Four months after Taylor secured possession of Markham's land holdings, Taylor's faux father married her faux mother. The couple's Florida marriage record identified the groom as Willtrue Loyd and the bride—Mildred Markham—as Constance C. B. Wakefield Rayner. The shaky signature on that document—"Constance Wakefield"—appeared to have been written by the same hand that had scrawled Markham's name on that warranty deed in October 1985.

Although Loyd and Markham slept together on a dirty mattress, Karen Snell didn't think the newlyweds were romantically involved. The thirteen-year-old did, however, see Loyd strike his wife. The Graceville Police Department investigated another domestic dispute at the Snells' house on May 16, 1986, this one involving Linda Springer and Mildred Loyd. There's no record of how that dispute was adjudicated. There's also no reliable third-party account of the incident that put Mildred Markham into a coma.

* * *

When Markham was admitted to Flowers Hospital in Dothan on August 10, 1986—more than likely the day Jane Snell saw her getting carried away on a stretcher—her eyes were closed and she couldn't speak. Willtrue Loyd told the attending physician that his wife, who he said was named Constance, had fallen a week earlier and hit her head. She'd suffered from increasingly severe headaches after that fall, Loyd said, and had lost consciousness while sitting in a chair. Bruce Woodham, a neurosurgeon, diagnosed Markham with a subdural hematoma in the right frontal and temporal regions of her brain as well as with herniation syndrome—a displacement of the brain caused by pressure in the skull. "I believe that she has an imminent chance of dying," the doctor wrote after conducting his initial examination. "I have discussed this situation with the husband. He understands the bleak outlook that we have here."

Woodham operated immediately, sawing open Markham's skull to remove the clotted blood and to relieve the pressure on her brain. Although Markham survived the surgery, her condition did not improve. Forty-four days later, the surgeon wrote that she had "become a chronic akinetic mute." Markham was left in a vegetative state, able to suck and chew but totally unresponsive to sound and light. On September 24, she was released from the hospital and brought back to Queen Snell's house in Graceville. Markham had a feeding tube and a catheter, and her discharge instructions called for her body to be turned every two hours. A county home health certification form indicated that her husband was capable of "providing adequate care."

Mildred Markham died less than two weeks later. The Graceville police reported that Willtrue Loyd found her in her bed at 5:57 a.m. on October 5, 1986, four or five hours after she'd stopped breathing. Markham's death certificate, which identified her as Mildred Constance Raner Loyd, didn't include a Social Security number. It was also peppered with false information. The document stated that Markham was a citizen of Patricia Parks's home country of Trinidad. It also said she was the daughter of Edith Wakefield, the woman who, during 1964's Lawrence Wakefield heirship case, Linda Taylor had asserted was her own mother. The medical examiner from Florida's Fourteenth Judicial Circuit, finding nothing untoward, gave his permission to have Markham's body cremated. There would be no autopsy.[*]

Markham, like Sherman Ray, had two life insurance policies. Taylor was the beneficiary of both. The medical examiner's records suggest that Gulf Life Insurance Company paid Taylor's claim without much fuss. Union Fidelity Life Insurance Company, however, asked a lot of questions.

The Union Fidelity plan Mildred Markham had signed up for was touted by seventy-something celebrity pitchman Danny Thomas as "one

---

[*] The medical examiner, Dr. William Sybers, would plead guilty to manslaughter in 2003 after standing accused of killing his wife by injecting her with the poison succinylcholine. Sybers, who died in 2014, continued to profess his innocence even after taking that plea deal. "If I had truly killed my wife," he told the *New York Times*, "I would have ordered a cremation."

of the best life insurance plans available today." It wasn't. In 1987, the magazine *Money* warned its readers that mail-order term life insurance was typically a very bad deal. Such policies, which were advertised relentlessly on daytime television, paid out a piddling sum upon the death of an older customer—$3,000, for instance, for the non-accidental death of a seventy-five-year-old woman. On the plus side, Union Fidelity plans were cheap, costing just $24.45 per month for the maximum amount of coverage. The company also vowed that no physical examinations or health questions were required, and that no one between the ages of forty and seventy-four could be turned down "for any reason whatsoever."

Mildred Markham's enrollment form was dated July 28, 1986, just less than a week before she'd supposedly fallen and hit her head. Markham, who'd bought the maximum five units of coverage, should've been ineligible for the plan given that she was seventy-seven years old. Her age, though, was listed as fifty-nine on the date the policy was issued. The two signatures on the form—Mildred Rayner, the policyholder, and her daughter Linda Lynch, the beneficiary—looked remarkably similar, suggesting that one individual had handled all the paperwork.

No matter what was written on that form, Union Fidelity wouldn't have to pay up if Markham had died of natural causes, as the policy covered only accidental deaths during the first two years. But after some back-and-forth with Markham's neurosurgeon, the medical examiner's office decided her death had indeed been accidental—a consequence of the fall she'd suffered two months earlier. Union Fidelity wasn't convinced. In June 1987, with the claim still unpaid, Sandy Paderewski filed a civil complaint on behalf of his client Linda Ray Lynch. The case would eventually go to arbitration, and the two sides would reach a settlement in the latter part of 1988. Although the terms of that agreement were confidential and thus can't be verified, the lawyer who represented Union Fidelity would remember losing the case. The company's newspaper ads promised a payout of $41,500 when a fifty-nine-year-old woman died accidentally. Linda Taylor likely got close to that amount.

Perhaps it was a coincidence that Mildred Markham went into a coma immediately after the con artist who was holding her captive purchased a life insurance policy in her name. It's also possible that Markham fell and hit her head, and that Taylor then sent away for mail-order life insurance, fudging the date on the enrollment form to make it seem as though she'd applied before Markham's brain injury. Or maybe Taylor, with or without an accomplice, killed Markham for her money.

When Theresa Davis learned that her grandmother was dead, she immediately suspected that Taylor was responsible, and she was sure it hadn't been an accident. Bruce Woodham, the neurosurgeon, would later say he couldn't be certain that Mildred Markham's injuries were the product of an accidental fall as opposed to, say, a push down a flight of stairs or a strike from a blunt instrument. But without an autopsy, it was impossible to tell what had caused Markham's brain to bleed, and since her corpse was quickly cremated, no such determination would ever be made. Mildred Markham's death, like the deaths of Patricia Parks and Sherman Ray, would remain unexplained and unprosecuted. And Mildred Markham's family, like the families of Patricia Parks and Sherman Ray, would have no doubt that Linda Taylor was a killer.

Taylor didn't stop preying on Markham after the old woman took her last breath. Less than a month after her phony mother was cremated, Taylor started collecting government checks in Mildred Markham's name. Between 1986 and 1993, she'd nab more than $60,000 in ill-gotten benefits. This Taylor scam wouldn't come to an end until she was sixty-seven years old, when federal agents would get a tip on a toll-free hotline.

CHAPTER 18
Deficits of Memory

Mark Squeteri had never been on a stakeout before. The twenty-eight-year-old, a special agent for the United States Railroad Retirement Board, mostly investigated benefit fraud—making sure, for instance, that people collecting unemployment from the federal agency didn't have hidden stashes of undeclared income. It was a stultifying gig, one that required the young bureaucrat to sit behind a desk making phone calls and writing reports. For Squeteri, who worked out of the RRB's main office in Chicago, the opportunity to spend time on a seedy commercial strip in Tampa was something to be cherished.

Squeteri's search had kicked off in October 1993, when the RRB got a tip on its fraud hotline that a woman who went by Linda Springer had been stealing pension checks made out to Mildred Markham. In the months after getting that call, Squeteri had gone to Florida multiple times. His detective work eventually led him to a spot on North Nebraska Avenue just east of I-275, a stretch of road dominated by used car lots and road-side inns. Squeteri set up outside the Sulphur Springs post office, a squat white building that had once been an A&P grocery store. He was on the lookout for a woman whose rap sheet had entries dating back almost fifty years, and who'd been arrested in at least six different states.

The special agent knew that Linda Springer was a thief, and he suspected she might be a murderer. If he didn't catch her, it was unlikely anyone ever would.

* * *

Mildred Markham's husband had commenced his career as a Pullman porter in the mid-1930s, right around when the newly constituted Railroad Retirement Board began sending money to eligible retirees. James Markham, who was born in 1896, had started getting a monthly pension after retiring at seventy, and Mildred had become eligible for survivors' benefits upon his death in 1983. The RRB should've cut off those benefits when she died in 1986. Instead, her checks had been redirected to Linda Springer. As of the fall of 1993, she'd received $62,315.44 in unwarranted payments.

When Squeteri fielded that hotline call, he didn't just get a heads-up that someone was stealing government funds. The agency's confidential informant also guided Squeteri and his boss, Terrence Hake, toward the conclusion that Linda Springer was Linda Taylor, the notorious Chicago welfare queen.

In the early 1980s, Hake had been the key figure in the FBI's Operation Greylord, going undercover in the guise of a corrupt lawyer to catch Cook County attorneys and judges soliciting and collecting bribes. A decade later, having moved on to a mellower gig at the RRB, Hake asked his contacts at the FBI to pass along Taylor's file. Mark Squeteri had never seen anything like it. He pored over pages full of aliases, plus reports about multiple kidnappings and a possible homicide—the 1975 death of Patricia Parks, which the FBI had known about but had declined to pursue.

As soon as Squeteri saw that file, he understood he'd stumbled onto a big case. When he started to dig into Taylor's life in Florida, he got the sense he might be embarking on a life-changing investigation.

Everything about Mildred Markham's death certificate looked dubious. While her Cook County marriage license indicated that she'd been born around 1909 and that her maiden name was Hampton, Markham's Florida death record asserted that she was nearly twenty years younger and that her parents' surnames were Raner and Wakefield. Most notably, the Florida document listed Markham's Social Security number as "None"—an omission that ensured her death wouldn't be reported to the federal government. So long as the Railroad Retirement Board believed that Mildred Markham was still alive, it would keep on mailing her checks.

On October 1, 1993, the RRB sent $820.37 to Markham care of Linda L. Springer, P.O. Box 8334, Tampa, Florida. Later that month, that same U.S. Treasury check was transferred to a doctor's office as payment for cosmetic surgery. The back of the check—the eighty-fourth and final one Taylor would receive from the agency—was signed by both Linda Springer and Mildred Markham, the latter of whom had been dead for seven years.

Squeteri tracked down the plastic surgeon's administrative assistant, who said the patient who'd proffered that check matched a photograph of Linda Taylor. He also interviewed Taylor's son Paul, Markham's neurosurgeon, the chief of the Graceville Police Department, and four other potential witnesses. The special agent left those conversations convinced that Mildred Markham's death hadn't been an accident.

Squeteri's personal theory was that Taylor had killed Markham to get her pension money, and that she'd done it by shoving the old woman down some stairs. In the early stages of their inquiry, Squeteri and his boss, Terrence Hake, ran that idea by a figure from Taylor's past. Jim Piper, who'd prosecuted Taylor for welfare fraud in the 1970s, told them he believed she was definitely capable of killing someone.

Although Squeteri had no concrete evidence that Linda Taylor had murdered Mildred Markham, he did have solid proof that she'd stolen from the Railroad Retirement Board. On October 28, 1993, he secured a federal warrant calling for Taylor's arrest on check fraud charges.

To arrest Taylor, Squeteri would have to find her. Most of the people he talked to in Florida said he was doomed to failure—that the woman he was looking for had a tendency to vanish. By February 1994, Squeteri had decided his only move was to wait her out. He'd go to the spot in Tampa where she picked up her mail, and he'd bide his time until he caught sight of his quarry.

Squeteri lingered on North Nebraska Avenue for days, peering out the window of his car in search of a woman who resembled Taylor's nearly two-decades-old Chicago mug shots. On February 23, he spotted a suspect behind the wheel of a red 1992 Mercury Cougar. When she parked and went inside the post office, Squeteri ran the plates on the Mercury. He got a hit. He'd found Linda Taylor.

When Taylor came back out, Squeteri told her she was under arrest. He spelled out everything he'd learned about her criminal history—her aliases and arrests and the offense that had made her infamous.

"Linda, why'd you do this again?" the special agent asked.

Squeteri thought she looked surprised, as though she couldn't believe he'd uncovered her secret past. It was also possible he was flattering himself. She told Squeteri she hadn't done anything, and that he must've gotten her confused with someone else—she wasn't Linda Taylor or Linda Springer or the welfare queen.

* * *

In the fourteen years since she'd emerged from an Illinois prison, Taylor had perpetrated all sorts of criminal acts and had faced almost no consequences. Now she was charged with six felony counts of illegally cashing U.S. Treasury checks, a crime that carried a maximum sentence of ten years.

Thanks to Mark Squeteri, the federal prosecutors tasked with trying Taylor's case had some idea of her background. The indictment they filed in March 1994 in the U.S. District Court for the Middle District of Florida identified the defendant as Linda Taylor, Linda Springer, Linda Bennett, Linda Lynch, Linda Ray Lunch, Constance Wakefield, Constance W. Womack, Constance Green, Martha Lee Davis, and Mildred Markman. But Squeteri didn't see that indictment as the end of his investigation. The special agent was certain he was just getting started.

In the week after he arrested Taylor, Squeteri interviewed Queen, Jane, and Karen Snell, who told him what they knew about the woman who'd squatted in their house and disposed of all their possessions. He also talked to the funeral director who'd arranged Mildred Markham's cremation and the owner of the crematorium that had incinerated

Markham's body. The U.S. attorney's office, in the meantime, acquired Markham's medical records, as well as correspondence from Union Fidelity Life Insurance Company, the firm that had resisted paying the accidental death claim filed by Markham's ersatz daughter, Linda Lynch. The main prosecutor attached to the case told Squeteri that they'd soon have enough to charge Linda Taylor with murder.

Taylor had been released on $25,000 bond the day after she'd been arrested. In a financial affidavit, she identified herself as an unemployed widow. Although she owned 185 acres of Mildred Markham's land in Mississippi, Taylor attested that she had no real estate holdings, and said the only income she'd received in the previous twelve months was $300 to $400 from her children. Another form listed her residence as 7007 North Nebraska Avenue. That was the address of the Haven Motel, a low-rent lodge three blocks north of the post office where Squeteri had spotted Taylor driving a red Mercury Cougar. At the time of her arrest, Taylor lived alone. Her companion, Willtrue Loyd, had died of natural causes a year and a half earlier, at the age of seventy-two.

At her arraignment on March 31, Taylor pleaded not guilty to six counts of fraud. Three weeks later, her public defender, Craig Alldredge, was granted a continuance so she could receive treatment for a heart condition. But his client's heart troubles weren't Alldredge's biggest concern.

In 1978, three of Taylor's lawyers in Chicago had said she "was incapable of knowing whether or not she was telling the truth." That same year, another of her attorneys had noted that two psychiatrists had previously said she was "psychotic and unable to understand the nature of the proceedings of which she was a defendant."

Alldredge came to a similar conclusion in 1994, telling a judge that Taylor wasn't able to assist in her own defense. Every time he tried to discuss the case with her, he wrote, "she was vague, tangential, and related facts which were extremely improbable, if not impossible." When he "attempted to investigate these facts," Alldredge said, "it became clear that in many instances that which she related did not exist."

* * *

It wasn't up to Craig Alldredge to determine whether Taylor was competent to stand trial. In 1994 and 1995, a succession of mental health professionals would conduct their own assessments on behalf of the defense attorney and the district court. The experts who examined Taylor were operating at a severe information disadvantage, relying on an inveterate fabulist to tell them who she was and what she'd done.

"It is difficult to say what type of problems she may have," psychologist Michael Gamache wrote after putting the sixty-eight-year-old Taylor through a battery of tests. "Her symptoms are truly bizarre and unusual." Those bizarre and unusual symptoms manifested themselves in what Gamache termed a "peculiar, disorganized, and inconsistent history." Taylor first claimed to have been born in Trinidad, then Chicago. Gamache noted that she was obsessed with someone named Lawrence Wakefield, a man she said was her biological father. "She described his death in considerable detail, and remarked in particular on police officers and federal agents pulling bags of money out of his house," he wrote. Taylor told Gamache she'd been so distraught after Wakefield's death in 1964 that she'd attempted suicide.

Taylor laid out a long litany of alleged maladies. She'd been hit by a police car at the age of five "and suffered a fractured rib cage and legs," Gamache recorded. More recently, she "had been the subject of both abdominal and brain surgery." Although Taylor told the psychologist she'd never been treated for mental health issues, Gamache thought something was amiss. She failed to understand common proverbs, "struggled to recognize irregularities in absurd statements," and reported perceiving auditory hallucinations. "I heard a voice last night, they told me to live on and be happy," she said. "I was just lying in bed reading the Bible...it was a woman's voice...like maybe the Virgin Mary."

When Gamache asked Taylor about the criminal charges she was facing, she rambled "about death certificates, her mother traveling in Uganda, and multiple surgeries." She also said her case centered on clearing her name, "literally meaning clearing up some misunderstanding about aliases." She responded to a question about the possibility of spending the rest of her life in prison by saying, "Life is uncertain, but death is for sure."

Gamache was convinced that Taylor didn't belong in a courtroom. At the same time, he professed that he couldn't make a firm diagnosis. His best guess, he wrote, was that she had some kind of brain disease "or senile dementia complicated by an underlying psychopathology or mental illness, probably a psychotic disorder or delusional disorder."

Eight days later, Taylor submitted to another examination, this one conducted by a court-appointed psychiatrist. Dr. Donald Taylor described his subject as agitated, digressive, and vague. Under his questioning, she explained that she'd been abandoned by her mother and she again appeared preoccupied by the death of her purported father, saying she'd won a court battle over the rights to Lawrence Wakefield's fortune and "that the estate was worth seven million dollars but that the money is being held by the Federal government in a bank in Chicago." In a section marked "Educational History," the psychiatrist wrote that Taylor said she'd been raped multiple times by a teacher when she was ten years old, and that she'd been afraid to go to school after those sexual assaults. She also reported being mistreated because of her mixed-race heritage—that "she was too black to be accepted at white schools and vice versa."

Donald Taylor believed that his subject was experiencing "deficits of memory, calculations, and abstract thought." She could name Bill Clinton but couldn't remember Ronald Reagan or any other president, and she could spell *world* forward but not in reverse. "She indicated she has had both male and female voices talking to her several times a week for two years," he wrote. "She also occasionally sees the vision of a woman in her home."

At the end of his report, the psychiatrist said that Linda Taylor might be suffering hallucinations due to a head injury or brain tumor. He also suggested that she might have a factitious disorder—that she could be exaggerating her symptoms, or perhaps even causing her health problems intentionally. Either way, Donald Taylor said, she was likely incapable of consulting with her attorney. And so, on June 1, 1994, in the U.S. District Court for the Middle District of Florida, a judge ordered that Linda Taylor be committed for psychiatric treatment. After four months, she'd be reevaluated to determine if her trial could proceed.

* * *

On her first day at the Federal Medical Center in Lexington, Kentucky, Taylor told a nurse she enjoyed sewing and crafts, and that she'd like a visit from the chaplain. She also checked boxes denoting that she'd been afflicted with twenty-six different medical conditions, among them rheumatic fever, broken bones, recurrent back pain, foot trouble, neuritis, depression or excessive worry, amnesia, and nervous trouble. A staff member wrote that the new prisoner suffered from the delusion that "white women killed her father."

The federal prison at Lexington, which had been founded in the 1930s as a "narcotic farm" for recovering addicts, held roughly two thousand women, more than half of whom had been locked up on federal drug charges. Taylor, who was housed in Lexington's mental health wing, didn't do much socializing, preferring to spend her time knitting and watching television. Nurses described her as pleasant and cooperative, although she did complain about the diet she was given to help control her diabetes. Her charts indicated she'd gotten agitated with another inmate only once, when her roommate moved out and made off with a set of blinds.

Within twenty-four hours of her commitment, Taylor consented to taking major tranquilizers ("I WONT. MEDIC. FOR MY NEARVES," she wrote on one form) and antidepressant medication ("I NEED SOME FOR DERASON"). On August 31, a week after she'd arrived in Kentucky, her daily Prozac dosage was doubled to forty milligrams.

The next day, prison psychologist Katherine Freiman tried giving Taylor an exam designed to diagnose, among other things, depression, hysteria, psychopathy, paranoia, and schizophrenia. The Minnesota Multiphasic Personality Inventory comprised 567 true-or-false statements, including

"Evil spirits possess me at times," "I have never been in trouble because of my sex behavior," and "I think a great many people exaggerate their misfortunes in order to gain the sympathy and help of others." Taylor refused to play along, saying she didn't have her glasses.

During her next session with Freiman, Taylor became "frustrated and angry." She passed on taking one test because she said she was hungry, then decided she didn't want to eat. She cut a different exam short because she claimed she had a headache. She was unable or unwilling to do simple arithmetic, couldn't repeat the phrase "no ifs, ands, or buts," and did not "appear able to write a sentence." Her performance on a card-sorting task, the psychologist wrote, "suggested a passive-aggressive stance as she was able to state the difference between a correct and an incorrect response, but continued to sort the cards incorrectly."

Taylor was more willing to share her version of her life story. She told Freiman and other hospital staff that she'd grown up with white foster parents in Arkansas and Missouri. These white people had kidnapped her and her sister, Mary, and they'd called her a nigger, beaten her with an electrical cord, and forced her into prostitution.

Early in her hospitalization, Taylor had told the medical center's chief psychiatrist that she was "searching for my real mother and sister. I found only impersonators!" Later, she'd insist that Mildred Markham was her real mother. Markham, she said, had come into her life after Lawrence Wakefield's death—she'd been one of many women who'd tried to establish their maternity so they could get a chunk of Taylor's sizable inheritance. Markham had been the only one of these contenders who "had blood similar enough to her own to be her mother." Taylor said that Markham was now eighty-nine years old and doing missionary work in South Africa. She explained that she'd "been cashing her mother's checks in order to send her a package of items she needed on her mission."

The staff at the Federal Medical Center knew of one source who could potentially corroborate Taylor's stories. On September 25, Sandra Smith surprised her mother by making the 360-mile trip from Chicago to Lexington. Three days later, she told a social work intern that Taylor "needs some type of help."

Taylor had told the staff at Lexington that her daughter was a pediatrician. Smith, who'd taken her husband's last name upon getting remarried, was actually a cosmetologist. The forty-three-year-old Chicagoan said, per a memo jotted down by a social work intern, that it "bothers her that her mother truly believes she is a doctor." Smith, who thought Taylor was telling the truth about being Lawrence Wakefield's daughter, explained that her mother had been "mentally disturbed" ever since the policy king's death. "It would be wrong to say she is a habitual liar," Smith said. "I believe that the things she says, she truly believes in her mind that these things have occurred." Smith didn't think her mother should be in prison. She claimed she'd tried to get Taylor "committed to an institution" but, according to the social work intern, Smith alleged that her "brothers wouldn't go for it."

Lexington psychologist Katherine Freiman could only speculate about the precise nature of her patient's mental disturbance. It was possible, she wrote, that Taylor's "intense grief over the death of her father" could've made her delusional. "At times she appeared to be deliberately misrepresenting herself or willfully withholding information, and at other times, she appeared to be genuinely confused about events and their timing," Freiman continued. If Taylor was indeed suffering a cognitive decline, her impairment was "not extreme," as she had no trouble following the prison's rules. Taylor's "primary problem," the psychologist said, "appears to be delusional thinking compounded by borderline intellectual functioning, an impoverished early learning environment, and personality variables."

Freiman diagnosed Taylor with "personality disorder not otherwise specified"—an admission that she didn't have enough information to reach a firm conclusion. The psychologist added that Taylor exhibited traits of antisocial personality disorder, a condition characterized by a disregard for the consequences of one's actions and a total lack of remorse.

For all her uncertainty about Linda Taylor's affliction, Freiman had no doubt that her patient was competent to stand trial. Taylor knew the charges against her, understood the concept of a plea bargain, and remembered her attorney's name. She was thus able to assist in her own defense despite her "psychological and cognitive difficulties."

Just before her evaluation period was set to expire, Taylor underwent surgery to have a basal cell carcinoma excised from her forehead. After a few weeks of recovery, she was transported back to Florida, where she'd spend the next fifty-two days in the Pinellas County jail. A booking photograph taken on November 8, 1994, showed her scowling at the camera. She was wearing a powder blue top and had her hair in pigtails. Her forehead looked perfectly healed.

* * *

Despite Freiman's report, Taylor's lawyer, Craig Alldredge, wouldn't concede his client's mental competency. At a hearing on December 14, 1994, three defense witnesses—a clinical psychiatrist, a registered nurse, and Michael Gamache, the psychologist who'd examined Taylor seven months earlier—attested that "the defendant's condition has deteriorated within the last three weeks." In a ruling issued the following day, a judge wrote that "the defendant may be suffering from...brain damage, and an examination for that condition seems appropriate." Taylor was again declared incompetent and sent away for four more months of treatment.

Taylor would split that time between the Federal Medical Centers in Lexington and Fort Worth, Texas. In Kentucky, she said she'd seen visions of "green snakes." In Texas, she described hallucinations of a "dog having puppies." Personnel in both facilities said she was uninterested in social interaction and her own personal hygiene. "Attempted to stress need for bathing to patient but to no avail. Back to bed where she remained all day," a nurse wrote on January 29, 1995. "Sleeping entire shift except to eat and pill line, have to awaken for both," a staffer reported three weeks later.

Again, Taylor obstructed most attempts at psychological testing, as she "was uncooperative and complained of needing corrective lenses." Sandra Lang and Robert Gregg, a pair of psychologists in Fort Worth, noted just one specific result, reporting that Taylor "obtained a Full Scale IQ of 75" on the Wechsler Adult Intelligence Scale-Revised, a score near the cutoff point for intellectual disability. But like their counterpart in Lexington, Lang and Gregg argued that Taylor had the mental capacity to go before a judge. "When asked about her desires for the outcome of her case," the psychologists wrote, Taylor "adamantly stated [that] the case against her is 'weak as water.'"

* * *

Taylor was in good spirits when she left the Federal Medical Center in Fort Worth in April 1995. A nurse reported that her affect was "bright" and that she hadn't complained of any physical discomfort. The U.S. Marshal charged with transporting her acknowledged receipt of both the prisoner and her personal funds: $13.13.

Taylor's attorney didn't contest the findings in her latest prison medical report. Rather, Craig Alldredge made the case that his client had been mentally ill when she'd stolen Mildred Markham's pension checks, and therefore hadn't been responsible for her actions. Taylor's plea of not guilty by reason of insanity occasioned two more mental health assessments, one each by the defense and the prosecution. Both experts went to check on Taylor at Tampa's Hillsborough County jail. Both were alarmed by what they saw.

The government's examiner, a psychiatrist named Arturo Gonzalez, described Taylor as disheveled and disoriented. She claimed to have visions of a man who may or may not have been her father, and she told the psychiatrist she was currently on trial for having killed her mother in 1934. "The report from the last federal facility indicates that she was competent to proceed," Gonzalez wrote, "and I certainly don't know how they arrived at that conclusion if they were looking at the same individual that we evaluated today." He believed that Taylor had dementia, and that there was no way she'd ever be able to defend herself in court.

The defense expert, Michael Gamache, agreed that Taylor was delusional and unstable. Gamache, who was assessing Taylor for a third time, wrote that she was "in the worst condition that I have seen." Staffers at the jail told him "that they have had considerable difficulty in getting her to keep her clothes on. She disrobes for no apparent reason and then appears to be grossly confused." Taylor had also been picking at her body incessantly, "which has apparently led to a very serious wound in the center of her forehead at the scalp line."

Gamache had long suspected that Taylor was suffering from a brain disease, and he'd suggested months earlier that she get a full neurological workup. That had never happened. Instead, she'd been passed from doctor to doctor, with no one getting a firm grasp on what, if anything, was ailing her. Gamache reported that he'd checked in with Taylor's daughter, Sandra Smith, who'd told him that her mother had "been experiencing a deteriorating mental state for at least the last ten years." If that was the case, Gamache decreed, Taylor "was not truly capable of appreciating the wrongfulness of her actions or the probable consequences."

With that, the federal courts were done with Linda Taylor. On July 5, 1995, Judge H. Dale Cook ruled that the "defendant remains mentally incompetent to proceed and that there is no likelihood that she will be returned to mental competency in the foreseeable future." He ordered Taylor released from federal custody and involuntarily committed to a mental health facility under the care of the State of Florida. Eight months later, in March 1996, the federal government would dismiss its indictment against Taylor. She was seventy years old. She'd never be in trouble with the law again.

* * *

Mark Squeteri was sure it was all a con. Linda Taylor hadn't been confused when she'd stolen Mildred Markham's pension checks, and she hadn't been out of it when he'd peppered her with questions outside that post office in Tampa. Squeteri thought she was just a liar, and that she'd lied to all those doctors just as she'd lied to everyone else.

In the first few months after he arrested Taylor, the special agent from the Railroad Retirement Board had thought he was going to help convict her of murder. But when Taylor was first declared incompetent, Squeteri got assigned to other investigations. Over the next year, the case he thought might make his career would crumble into nothing.

Throughout her life, Taylor preyed on people and systems that were ill-equipped to handle her deceptions. It's possible that, in the mid-1990s, she got out of federal prison by pretending she was losing her mind. Her confusion and hallucinations also could've been the product of dementia. Squeteri was no mental health expert, but he didn't trust the psychiatrists and psychologists who'd concluded that Taylor wasn't accountable for what she'd done. And so the special agent decided he needed to pay her one more visit.

If Taylor had conned the U.S. government, it didn't look as though that scheme had redounded to her benefit. The judge in her criminal case had initially sent her to a crisis center for those deemed a threat to themselves or others. Patients' shoelaces, combs, toothbrushes, and pens were confiscated upon admission, lest they be used to inflict harm. When Squeteri located Taylor, she was in a locked facility, a place where she couldn't come and go as she pleased. Although the investigator wasn't able to see Taylor himself, he did find the nurse responsible for her care. "Do you really think this lady is mentally ill," he asked, "or do you think she's faking it?"

The nurse told him there was no question that Taylor was genuinely sick. Squeteri didn't believe it, but there was nothing he could do. She was somebody else's problem now.

* * *

By the time Mark Squeteri went to check on Linda Taylor, it had been a decade since she'd been referenced by name in the *Chicago Tribune* and five years since she'd been mentioned in any major newspaper. To some degree, Taylor disappeared from public view because her story had run its course: She'd been arrested, tried, and locked up, and Ronald Reagan's claims about her had been litigated, relitigated, and re-relitigated. But

Reagan himself also did his part to turn the spotlight away from the woman in Chicago with the hundred different names.

In the early days of his White House tenure, Reagan cited Taylor as the living embodiment of the supposed epidemic of welfare fraud. When he slashed the budgets for Aid to Families with Dependent Children and the food stamp program, the president's critics said he was consigning millions of Americans to poverty. In Reagan's telling, though, all he'd done was cut off a whole bunch of undeserving Linda Taylors. After he accomplished that mission, Reagan had little political use for Taylor's story, and he stopped telling it in both public and private. During his second term, he focused on a new line of attack, one that characterized welfare recipients as shiftless rather than devious.

At a meeting with congressional leaders in January 1986, Reagan explained that official unemployment statistics weren't accurate because some people "don't want to work." By way of example, he described a "fellow on welfare" who hung up the phone when presented with a job offer. This tale enraged Democratic speaker of the house Tip O'Neill. "I thought you would have grown in five years," O'Neill told Reagan, saying that this new, unsourced anecdote was just as absurd as "your story about the Chicago welfare queen."

A few days after that meeting, Reagan attacked "the welfare culture" in his State of the Union address, blaming public aid programs for "the breakdown of the family," as well as "child abandonment, horrible crimes, and deteriorating schools." Reagan had talked about the dangers of welfare dependency since he was the governor of California. Charles Murray's 1984 book, *Losing Ground*—which contended that government poverty-reduction efforts actually deepened poverty, particularly among black Americans, by discouraging job seeking and eroding personal responsibility—gave those old talking points a new intellectual sheen.

Murray saw himself as a teller of uncomfortable truths. In the proposal for *Losing Ground*, the conservative social scientist wrote that "a huge number of well-meaning whites fear that they are closet racists, and this book tells them they are not. It's going to make them feel better about things they already think but do not know how to say."* The book's final chapter suggested eliminating the safety net of AFDC, food stamps, and Medicaid for working-age people, a move Murray believed would inspire—or, failing that, force—the needy to get their own houses in order. "When reforms finally do occur," he wrote, "they will happen not because stingy people have won, but because generous people have stopped kidding themselves."

Murray was right that the American welfare system was in many ways counterproductive. Any outside income AFDC recipients received got subtracted from their monthly checks, a rule that discouraged on-the-books work. His contention that welfare was a major driver of illegitimacy, though, was refuted by most credible economists and social scientists. Murray also failed to foreground the fact that 60 percent of AFDC families were nonblack, and he glossed over the fact that the program's already meager benefit levels had been continually decimated by inflation.

For all its faults, *Losing Ground* succeeded in reframing the public aid debate. The problem that needed solving, Murray and Reagan argued, wasn't poverty—it was welfare. In 1981, Reagan had said his cuts to social services wouldn't harm the truly needy. By 1986, when the president's tax cuts were helping the rich get a whole lot richer, Reagan was suggesting that what the needy really needed was self-determination. Every man, woman, and child on welfare, he said in the State of the Union, deserved "real and lasting emancipation, because the success of welfare should be judged by how many of its recipients become independent of welfare."

At the tail end of 1986, Reagan's welfare task force proposed that the federal government declare its own independence from the public aid business by ceding decision-making to the states. The Democratic Congress wasn't having it, however, and the reform bill Reagan eventually signed—the bipartisan Family Support Act of 1988—did little to change

---

* A decade after *Losing Ground* came out, Murray (with coauthor Richard J. Herrnstein) would publish *The Bell Curve*, which postulated a genetic link between race and intelligence and argued that "America's fertility policy...subsidizes births among poor women, who are also disproportionately at the low end of the intelligence distribution."

the status quo. It would take a Democratic president to finish what Reagan started.

* * *

Three weeks into his first presidential campaign, Bill Clinton announced his mission to forge "a new covenant, a solemn agreement between the people and their government." Whereas the Reagan and George H. W. Bush administrations "exalted private gain over public obligations," Clinton vowed to ensure that "people who work shouldn't be poor." The flip side of that imperative, he said in October 1991, was that the poor needed to get to work. To that end, the Arkansas governor promised that his administration was "going to put an end to welfare as we know it."

Clinton was something of a welfare wonk, having helped put together the Family Support Act as the chair of the National Governors Association. Even so, his pledge to kill off welfare was less an actual policy proposal than a signal that he was a different kind of Democrat, one who didn't hew to liberal orthodoxy. With AFDC caseloads expanding, Clinton's message felt increasingly urgent. He wasn't the only political candidate delivering it.

In Louisiana, where Aid to Families with Dependent Children took up just 2 percent of the state's annual budget, David Duke pronounced that cheats, chiselers, and parasites were pillaging the treasury. The white supremacist–cum–Republican state legislator suggested that women on welfare be paid to get birth control implants, and he clucked his tongue at an unidentified New Orleans mother with eight children whose "welfare family could cost taxpayers over a million dollars." Duke used that not-very-coded rhetoric to secure a second-place finish in the 1991 Louisiana governor's race, winning a majority of the state's Republicans and 55 percent of the white vote. "Perhaps the messenger was rejected in this state of Louisiana, but the message wasn't," he said upon conceding defeat. "The people believe in what I believe."

Unlike Duke and Reagan, who appealed to anti-welfare prejudices by telling extravagant stories about immoral women, Clinton preached empathy. He explained that mothers felt trapped by welfare, unable to work outside the home because they couldn't afford child care or risk losing Medicaid coverage. The nuance Clinton spoke with on the campaign trail didn't matter at the ballot box. "Put an end to welfare as we know it" was the perfect pander to white, welfare-hating voters, a slogan that a Clinton-affiliated pollster described as "pure heroin." Clinton's adviser Bruce Reed called the catchphrase a "guiding star."

The new president didn't follow that guiding star after beating Bush and Ross Perot in 1992, choosing instead to make health care his top priority. When the White House did finally focus on welfare two years later, polling data revealed the widespread belief that the poor had it way too easy. One survey found that "welfare is considered odious by every demographic subgroup" and showed that a clear majority of respondents thought all recipients ought to work for their checks, that no one should get benefits for more than two years, and that mothers didn't deserve more financial support if they had additional children while already on the rolls.

In his 1994 State of the Union address, Clinton told the American people what they wanted to hear. "We'll say to teenagers, 'If you have a child out of wedlock, we will no longer give you a check to set up a separate household,'" the president declared, failing to acknowledge that unwed teen mothers represented just 2 percent of parents on AFDC. Clinton also said the government would provide welfare recipients with "the support, the job training, the child care you need for up to two years." After that cutoff date, enrollees were to be given subsidized public sector jobs if they couldn't find work with private employers.

Clinton argued that this approach would be better for both the government and the poor. He made that case by showcasing an anti–Linda Taylor, a woman who'd demonstrated her virtue by leaving the welfare system behind rather than bleeding it dry. Clinton said that unnamed public aid recipient had once been asked, "What's the best thing about being off welfare and in a job?" Her reply: "When my boy goes to school and they say, 'What does your mother do for a living?,' he can give an answer." The lesson of this anecdote, the president said, was that "these people want a better system, and we ought to give it to them."

* * *

Clinton's welfare plan never came up for a vote. Providing welfare recipients with subsidized jobs would've cost a tremendous amount of money, and no one had an appetite for ending welfare by raising federal spending. In November 1994, Republicans gained majorities in both houses of Congress, and the president lost control of his domestic agenda. Speaker of the House Newt Gingrich and the GOP had a different kind of covenant in mind, one in which the government did away with public aid and the needy took care of themselves.

Gingrich, like Charles Murray, argued that dismantling the welfare system would be an act of mercy. "By creating a culture of poverty, we have destroyed the very people we are claiming to help," he said. Gingrich blamed welfare for every conceivable social ill. On the stump, he'd declare that "you can't maintain civilization with 12-year-olds having babies and 15-year-olds killing each other and 17-year-olds dying of AIDS." Gingrich knew exactly how his words would be received. When the *New York Times'* poverty reporter Jason DeParle suggested to the congressman that "12-year-olds having babies" was a modern spin on Reagan's welfare queen, Gingrich "responded with the smile of a man well-pleased with his cleverness." He told DeParle, "Congratulations! You cracked the code!"*

Nearly six hundred witnesses testified in a slew of congressional hearings on welfare in 1995 and 1996. Just seventeen identified themselves as current or past welfare beneficiaries. Among them was Democratic representative Lynn Woolsey, the self-described first former welfare mother to serve in Congress, who credited public assistance with keeping her family afloat after her husband left her and their three children.

---

* DeParle, for his part, later reported getting a letter from a *Times* reader that called welfare recipients "low-life scum" and "human garbage." Another said, "I as a middle class white person is paying for their children because the bloods can't keep it in their pants."

Woolsey's message mostly went unheeded, even by some on the Left who insisted they weren't trafficking in stereotypes. "This issue is not, as is often portrayed, a caricature about Cadillac welfare queens...living in some big city, collecting a multitude of checks with which to buy a Cadillac and color television, and living the life of leisure," said Senator Byron Dorgan, a North Dakota Democrat. After disavowing Linda Taylor's nickname, Dorgan noted that greed and laziness were indeed endemic among the nation's poor—that "there are able-bodied people who make welfare a way of life and should go to work." Regardless of whether he used the term *welfare queen*, Dorgan had captured the essence of what it stood for.

As he campaigned for reelection, Clinton had yet to fulfill his promise to put the welfare system out of its misery, having vetoed a pair of Republican-backed proposals he'd deemed too extreme. If he didn't agree to something, his advisers feared, he'd risk losing out on a second term.

In the summer of 1996, Congress presented Clinton with the Personal Responsibility and Work Opportunity Reconciliation Act, a bill that proposed transforming the safety net in ways that, a little more than a decade earlier, only Charles Murray had dared to imagine. Aid to Families with Dependent Children would be replaced by a program called Temporary Assistance for Needy Families. As that name implied, payments made under the system would be time-limited, with most beneficiaries getting cut off after a maximum of five years. TANF would be paid for with the help of federal matching funds, delivered in the form of block grants to the states. Those grants wouldn't be indexed to inflation, meaning the pot of money would get smaller every year. When those funds ran out, it wouldn't matter how destitute you were—the government wouldn't provide you with any cash to live on.

The legislation passed 256 to 170 in the House and seventy-four to twenty-four in the Senate, with support from Democrats including Joe Biden and John Kerry. A few weeks after that vote, the *New Republic* ran a photo on its cover of a black woman holding an infant while smoking a cigarette. That image, which ran under the headline "Day of Reckoning," teased an editorial titled "Sign It." Against the advice of the liberals on his staff, Clinton did. "Today we are ending welfare as we know it," the president said in a ceremony at the White House Rose Garden on August 22, 1996. In November, he'd beat his Republican opponent Bob Dole in a landslide.

In his speech in the Rose Garden, Clinton explained that he'd pursued reform out of a desire "to overcome the flaws of the welfare system for the people who are trapped on it." He was introduced that afternoon by a woman he said had broken free from that trap.

"I am here today to talk about how much getting off assistance and getting a job meant to me and my children," said Lillie Harden, the anti–Linda Taylor whom Clinton had singled out for praise at the 1994 State of the Union. The Arkansas native told the assembled crowd that she'd spent two years on welfare in the early 1980s, taking home $282 per month. After enrolling in a job training program created by then-governor Clinton, she'd found work as a cook. Harden described Clinton as "the man who started my success" and ensured "my children's future." When the president took the stage, he thanked her "for the power of your example." In his autobiography, Clinton would call Harden's story "the best argument I've ever heard for welfare reform."

That argument wasn't as straightforward as it appeared. Two months after the Rose Garden ceremony, the *Arkansas Democrat-Gazette* published a front-page article revealing that Harden had gotten AFDC and food stamps off and on after graduating from her job training program. The newspaper also reported that Harden had at times failed to tell the local housing authority about her income, likely because an honest accounting would've imperiled her rent subsidy.

There was enough fodder in that article for a hard-liner to label Lillie Harden a welfare cheat. Her story, when told in full, could've also been used to highlight the importance of the safety net, which allowed Harden to pay her bills when she was in between jobs. But that Arkansas newspaper item wasn't picked up by the national media. While Reagan's critics on the Left had been highly motivated to prove he was lying about the woman in Chicago, nobody called Clinton out on the imperfections in his perfect welfare-to-work story. Welfare was complicated. Americans were in the mood for simple answers, even if those answers didn't happen to be true.

* * *

Johnnie Harbaugh wasn't sure how his mother had landed in an institution in Tampa. At some point in the mid-1990s, his sister, Sandra, called him to say that Taylor had been sent to a state mental health facility. Although Johnnie was willing to interrupt his Florida vacation to look in on her, he knew better than anyone that Taylor wasn't to be trusted. One time, when she'd been staying with Johnnie in Chicago, she'd swiped checks from her own grandson, lifting them right out of the kid's drawer. After that, Johnnie and his wife, Carol, had taken to padlocking their interior doors whenever she was around. She'd stolen from her oldest son Clifford's family, too, writing a check on their account for $700. She also had a habit of lying to Clifford about her health, telling him she was near death to elicit sympathy and money.

But as soon as Johnnie saw Taylor in Tampa, he knew this wasn't a con. She was wearing shoes that were way too big for her, and she had bald patches all over the top of her skull. She sounded as bad as she looked—ranting and raving, making up crazy things. She couldn't even remember her own son. She clearly needed help. Johnnie just wasn't sure he could be the one to give it to her.

Taylor had been a horrible parent. She'd hit Johnnie and abandoned him, and she'd made him lose faith in himself and other people. Growing up, he'd tried to be as cold as she was, getting in trouble with the law enough times that his rap sheet ran to multiple pages. By 1995, though, it had been more than twenty years since Johnnie had been arrested. The forty-five-year-old drove a big rig, and he'd watch the landscape roll past on long cross-country trips, just as he'd done as his mother's passenger in the 1950s. She'd made him who he was, and he hated and loved her for it.

In that Tampa institution, Taylor did eventually recognize her son's face. Once she figured out who he was, she begged Johnnie to take her to Chicago. None of her other children had claimed her. If Johnnie didn't accept responsibility for his mother, she'd be sent to a Salvation Army shelter for homeless women. Faced with that choice, he did what she would've done: He got in his car and drove away.

A couple of hours later, Johnnie pulled over to the side of the road. Years earlier, when he'd been a guest at Taylor's place in the Florida Panhandle, he'd had the chance to save Mildred Markham. Taylor's elderly captive had pleaded with him to rescue her, and he'd done nothing. Now he couldn't stop thinking about his mother, disoriented and locked away, with shoes that didn't fit and no one to look after her. Johnnie turned to his wife and asked what she would've done if Taylor were her mother; Carol said she wouldn't have left the institution without her. And so he turned the car around.

* * *

At Johnnie and Carol's apartment in Chicago, Taylor and her caretakers fell into a routine. Each morning, her daughter-in-law would wake Taylor up to give her an insulin injection. She would then go back to bed, where she'd stay all day. On Tuesdays, Sandra would come over to give her mother a bath and shampoo what remained of her hair.

After a few months, Sandra brought Taylor to live with her in Hazel Crest, a formerly all-white suburb south of Chicago that by 1990 had become predominantly black. As Taylor's dementia got worse, she began sneaking out of her daughter's house at night, wandering the streets with no clothes on. Taylor didn't know where she was, but she had an idea where she was going. When someone would find her a few doors down from Sandra's place, she'd explain that she'd been on her way to Hawaii.

Eventually, minding Taylor became too much for Sandra to handle, and she put her mother in a nursing home. Taylor convalesced there in near-total anonymity, her presence in Illinois unknown to the police officers who'd chased after her, the politicians who'd villainized her, and the supposed friends whose lives she'd destroyed.

THE QUEEN

Johnnie Harbaugh didn't visit his mother on any regular schedule, but on Thursday, April 18, 2002, he felt compelled to see her. Taylor's health had declined still further, and she'd been admitted to Ingalls Hospital in Harvey—the same suburban enclave where, twenty-five years earlier, the State of Illinois had opened a special court to handle the flood of welfare fraud prosecutions that had followed Taylor's high-profile conviction. On the night of Johnnie's visit, the seventy-six-year-old Taylor was in a huge amount of pain. She told her son she had a spider in her chest, and he watched her beat herself in the sternum, again and again. Johnnie couldn't bear to be there for more than twenty minutes. On his way out of the building, he just missed seeing his sister, Sandra. Neither of them was in the room when their mother died.

* * *

Linda Taylor was pronounced dead at 7:11 p.m. The cause was acute myocardial infarction—a heart attack.

Taylor's death certificate, which the funeral director filled out with Sandra's help, identified her as Constance Loyd. She'd conjured that first name halfway through her life, bestowing it on herself, her daughter, and her pseudo-mother, Mildred Markham. She'd taken the last name from the man who'd killed one of her husbands, a confederate she'd lived with for a decade afterward. Her age was given as sixty-seven, a nine-year understatement. Her father was listed as Lawrence Wakefield, the man she'd seen as her protector and ticket to prosperity, and whose fortune had just eluded her grasp. Her mother was marked down as Edith Elizabeth Jarvis, the woman who'd given birth to Wakefield in 1904. Taylor's race was recorded as white.

It's unclear whether these biographical details represented the truth as Taylor's daughter understood it or if Sandra had chosen a set of facts she thought her mother would've chosen for herself. Linda Taylor, or Constance Loyd, was born Martha Louise White in 1926, on a cold and rainy day in Golddust, Tennessee. Her father was a black man she likely never met. Her mother, Lydia, was the white great-granddaughter of a

Confederate soldier. Taylor had been taught as a child that her parentage defined who she was and limited who she could be. She'd lived her life in defiance of that proposition, constructing whatever past and present best suited her needs. Taylor wielded personas as weapons, using her shifting identities to acquire what she felt she deserved.

Taylor's white relatives had come out of Cullman County, Alabama, a notoriously racist locale where black people weren't safe after sundown. Her wake was held at a funeral home in Oak Lawn, Illinois, a Chicago suburb that systematically excluded blacks up through the 1990s. Johnnie spent an hour in the presence of his mother's body, which was displayed in a simple pine box. When the viewing was over, her corpse was cremated.

The Monday after Taylor died, she was given a Catholic funeral Mass at St. Ethelreda, a majority-black parish on the Southwest Side. Taylor had bonded with Patricia Parks over their shared Catholicism, and she'd professed to be Catholic during her stint at the Federal Medical Center in Lexington. But if she'd had a sincere relationship with a higher power, Johnnie hadn't known about it.

The Mass was arranged by Sandra's sons, Hosa and Duke, who as kids had been left in Taylor's negligent care. Clifford, who'd left home as a fourteen-year-old in the 1950s, flew in for the service. So did Paul, the son Taylor had cast aside in the 1960s, leaving him to spend his formative years in a state-run home in Illinois.

Paul had tried to forget about his mother, but family had never stopped mattering to him. Like Johnnie, he'd met up with Taylor again as an adult, and he and his mother had both ended up in Florida, at times living within miles of each other. When Taylor's memorial was over, it was Paul who took the small box containing her ashes. Nobody else had wanted them.

Acknowledgments

Writing a book can be isolating, especially the part when you have to write the book. But thinking back on the years I've spent puzzling through Linda Taylor's life, I'm overwhelmed with gratitude for the absurd number of people who've helped me. It all started in 2012, with an instant-messenger exchange with my first journalistic mentor, Tom Scocca. During that conversation, Tom sent me a link to an old magazine article about Taylor and encouraged me to figure out who she was and how she'd become a symbol for greed and sloth—questions I wouldn't have known how to approach without the skills Tom had taught me at the *Washington City Paper*.

I've spent the past fifteen years at *Slate* as part of the brainiest, sprightliest crew in all of media. My second journalistic mentor, David Plotz, gave me and so many of my colleagues the time and space to do ambitious work. He guided me and urged me on as I put together the article, published in 2013, that I've expanded into this book. This project never would've existed without his wisdom and support. Will Dobson, who edited that piece, listened to me ramble about warranty deeds and spent weeks of his life—OK, months—helping me fashion a coherent narrative. I feel preposterously lucky to have landed in the same place as Julia Turner, the sharpest and zazziest friend and colleague of them all. She made it possible for me to see this through to the end.

I owe an enormous amount to dozens upon dozens of *Slate*sters, past and present, folks who contributed to my original essay and have buoyed

Acknowledgments

me with advice and good cheer. Thank you to Lowen Liu, Allison Benedikt, Laura Bennett, Gabriel Roth, Jacob Weisberg, Dan Check, Chad Lorenz, Leon Neyfakh, Ava Lubell, Laura Miller, June Thomas, Chris Suellentrop, Jack Shafer, Jessica Winter, John Dickerson, Emily Yoffe, Jill Pellettieri, Vivian Selbo, Lisa Larson-Walker, Holly Allen, Bill Smee, Andy Bowers, Chris Kirk, Ben Blatt, and my podcast partners Stefan Fatsis, Mike Pesca, and the unforgettable Zelmo Beaty.

My agent, Alia Hanna Habib of the Gernert Company, believed in me and this story from the outset. Her steady hand and peerless editorial judgment got me across the finish line. Alia's former colleagues David McCormick and Leslie Falk of McCormick Literary have also been unfailingly helpful, as has my film agent Joe Veltre at Gersh.

Enlisting Leonard Roberge to help me figure out how this whole book-writing thing works was one of the wisest choices I've ever made. Not having appraised other freelance book editors, I can still say with confidence that Leonard is the greatest freelance book editor on the planet—diligent and perceptive, with no tolerance for lazy thinking. Bringing on Anna Kordunsky to fact-check the manuscript was another fabulous decision. Anna spiffed up my prose and saved me from innumerable missteps. Any mistakes that remain are mine alone.

My editor, Vanessa Mobley at Little, Brown, saw the potential in this book, and she put everything she had into ensuring that its potential was realized. Vanessa is brilliant, patient, and humane. She talked me through the knottiest of problems and gave me the strength I needed to get this project done. And huzzahs and thank yous to the whole peerless team at Little, Brown: publisher Reagan Arthur, production editor Michael Noon, copyeditor Nell Beram, publicist Alyssa Persons, marketing director Pamela Brown, and editorial assistants Joseph Lee and Sareena Kamath.

I'm beholden to everyone who worked with me to unearth and sift through the materials that helped bring Linda Taylor's story to life. Among those kind souls are Alice Crites, Rebecca Journey, John Kruzel, Ciara McCarthy, Mariana Zepeda, Peter Morris, Cyndy Richardson, Lara Hale, Evin Demirel, Pam Williams, Becca Bender, Ian Philbrick, Steven

Acknowledgments

Wright, and Jacob Rosinplotz. Special thanks to Michael Ravnitzky for his FOIA wizardry; the indefatigable Kim Stankiewicz of Chicago Ancestry, who tracked down a huge number of legal records; and Adam Hirsch, Sam Sedaei, and Thomas Miller, who shook loose the long-buried files from the Lawrence Wakefield probate case.

Thank you also to the archivists and librarians who helped guide my research, among them John Reinhardt and the staff at the Illinois State Archives, Deb Bier at the Peoria Public Library, and Arlene Balkansky at the Library of Congress. Betty Taylor of Alabama's Marshall County archives and Whit Majors from Florida's District Fourteen Medical Examiner's Office found documents I wasn't sure existed. The scholars Martin Gilens, Julilly Kohler-Hausmann, Robert Lombardo, and Jim Ralph inspired me with their writing and their magnanimity, as did authors Dave Baron, Lou Cannon, and Ethan Michaeli.

I couldn't have written about Taylor without the help of scores of people whose lives intersected with hers. Among them were Grady Mooney, who showed me around the remnants of Golddust, Tennessee; Ruth Cobb, Jill Vernon, and Bob Vogler, who shared materials on the Illinois Soldiers' and Sailors' Children's School; and Jack Sherwin, Ron Cooper, Jim Piper, Bridget Hutchen, Skip Gant, David Thompson, Craig Alldredge, Sandy Paderewski, Norris Bishton, Leon Wexler, Charlotte Nesbitt-Langford, and Linda Giesen, who walked me through reams of court and prison records.

I'm indebted to Taylor's relatives, George Bliss's colleagues and children—especially Bliss's oldest son, Bill—and the Parks, Moore, Ray, Snell, and Markham families. It's humbling to know that so many people entrusted me with their stories. I hope that I did them justice.

Rich So, Ben Healy, Laurel Wamsley, Stephanie Foerster, and Pat Stack made my frequent trips to Chicago a lot less lonely. Steve Feinstone and Frank Foer very generously offered me places to write. Bryan Curtis, John Swansburg, Melonyce McAfee, and Dan Engber did me the amazing kindness of reading my work in progress and suggesting all manner of improvements. My dear friend Jordan Hirsch read the book, schlepped to the Louisiana Supreme Court on my behalf, and spent hours with me on

Acknowledgments

the phone talking through themes and character arcs and plot developments. Big books have big problems—thanks to James Carmichael, John Mangin, Chris Park, Reihan Salam, and Jesse Shapiro for helping me solve them, and for keeping me motivated and entertained. And thank you to Hanna Rosin, Brendan Koerner, Patrick Keefe, Luke O'Brien, Alan Siegel, Dave McKenna, Jordan Ellenberg, Wendy Jacobson, Gabe Mendlow, Dr. Ted Bloch III, Dr. Frank Wilklow, John Bronsteen, Abby Dos Santos, Ryan Boehm, Kevin Maney, David Sarma, Jackie Delamatre, Adam Nielsen, Ellie Davis, Steven Ehrenberg, Heather McDonald, Adam Graham-Silverman, Tony Valadez, and Christopher Seidman for their advice and encouragement.

Lauren Levin is the smartest and most compassionate person I know. Our conversations help me see connections I wouldn't otherwise see, and my life wouldn't be as rich or as fun without my big sister. Having Alan and Marilyn Levin as my parents is the best thing that ever happened to me. They made me who I am and got me to where I am. I'm grateful for the love and support of my grandparents Irv and Lil Levin and Irwin and Fay Miller, my Uncle Sidney Levin, and all my aunts, uncles, and cousins in Louisiana, Texas, and beyond. Thank you to Michael Seidman and Lynda Couvillion for being my family away from home. And to Jess: Your belief in me helped me believe in myself. Thank you. I love you. It's done!

Timeline of Linda Taylor's Life

1926: Linda Taylor is born Martha Louise White in Golddust, Tennessee. Later in the year, her mother Lydia marries Joseph Jackson Miller in Mississippi County, Arkansas.

1940: Taylor is identified in the census as Martha Miller, a white 13-year-old living in Burdette Township, Mississippi County, Arkansas. She also gives birth to a son, Clifford.

1944: Under the name Martha Gordon, Taylor is arrested in Port Orchard, Washington, for vagrancy, and under the name Martha Davis, she's arrested in Seattle for disorderly conduct.

1945: Taylor has a chance encounter with her uncle Hubert Mooney in Oakland, California, and they spend a night out on the town with friends. A week later, Taylor is arrested for malicious mischief under the name Connie Reed and asks Mooney to bail her out of jail.

1946: Under the name Betty Smith, Taylor is arrested in Oakland on the suspicion she's engaging in prostitution and infected with a venereal disease.

1948: Under the name Connie Harbaugh, Taylor is arrested in Oakland for contributing to the delinquency of a minor. She marries navy enlisted man Paul Harbaugh and gives birth to a second son, who's also named Paul.

1950: Taylor gives birth to a third son, Johnnie, in Arkansas.

1951: Taylor gives birth to a daughter, Sandra, in Arkansas.

1952: Taylor gets divorced from Paul Harbaugh in Tennessee and marries Troy Elliott in Arkansas.

1956: Taylor gives birth to a fourth son, Robin, in Arkansas.

1959: Taylor helps Avalon and Annie Mae Moore's family escape the deprivations of sharecropping in Arkansas. They move together to Peoria, Illinois, where Taylor files a lawsuit alleging her children Paul and Sandra were injured in a school explosion there. The lawsuit is dismissed a little more than seven years later.

1963: After relocating from Peoria to Chicago, Taylor is arrested under the name Beverly Singleton for assaulting a twelve-year-old girl.

1964: Under the name Constance Wakefield, Taylor presents herself as the daughter of Lawrence Wakefield, a wealthy and recently deceased Chicago policy king. Thanks in part to testimony from Taylor's mother and her Uncle Hubert, a probate court judge rules she's not Wakefield's heir and sentences her to six months in jail for contempt, though she'll never serve that time.

1967: Taylor is arrested in Chicago for endangering the life of a child, unlawful use of a weapon, and kidnapping. She won't be prosecuted for any of these alleged crimes.

1969: Taylor marries Willie Walker in Chicago. She also succeeds in getting the Veterans Administration to classify her daughter Sandra as a "helpless child" owing to the girl's supposed injuries from the Peoria school explosion.

1971: Willie Walker files for divorce from Taylor.

1972: Under the name Connie Jarvis, Taylor gives Chicago Police Department detective Jack Sherwin a false burglary report. Taylor is also arrested for welfare fraud by the Michigan State Police under the name Connie Green. She skips bail in Michigan and never serves time for the offense.

1973: Taylor marries Aaron Bennett in Chicago and files for divorce a few months later.

1974: In August, Taylor marries Lamar Jones in Chicago. That same month, Sherwin finds multiple public aid identification cards in Taylor's Chicago apartment after she calls in another phony burglary. The detective arrests Taylor on behalf of the State of Michigan, where she has an outstanding felony warrant. In September, the *Chicago Tribune*'s George Bliss writes his first story about Taylor. Later that month, Taylor fails to appear at a Chicago court hearing. She's found shortly thereafter in Tucson, Arizona; the *Tribune*, in reporting her jailing in Arizona, refers to Taylor as the "welfare queen" for the first time. Taylor is brought back to Chicago, and in November she's indicted for theft, perjury, and bigamy. Toward the end of the year, Taylor moves in with Patricia Parks.

1975: While under Taylor's care, Parks dies of a barbiturate overdose. Taylor, whom Parks had made the trustee of her estate, is investigated for Parks's killing but isn't arrested or charged with a crime.

1976: In January, Republican presidential candidate Ronald Reagan begins referring to a woman in Chicago—Taylor—who "used 80 names, 30 addresses, 15 telephone numbers" to scam the public aid system. Also in January, Taylor, using the name Linda C.B. Wakefield, marries Sherman Ray in Chicago. In February, she's arrested in Chicago and charged with burglary after stealing a television, fur coat, and household goods from her ex-roommate. Later in the year, Taylor kidnaps Ray's niece, Diana; she isn't arrested or charged with a crime.

1977: Two and a half years after Taylor's arrest by Jack Sherwin, her welfare fraud trial finally begins. A Chicago jury finds her guilty of theft and perjury, and she's sentenced to three to seven years in state prison.

1978: Taylor begins serving her sentence in Dwight Correctional Center. She's also sentenced to a concurrent five-and-a-half-year prison term after pleading guilty to the burglary charges from 1976.

1980: Illinois' state parole board releases Taylor from prison after she's been incarcerated for a little more than two years. Reagan, who makes campaign fodder of the "woman in Chicago [who] received welfare benefit[s] under 127 different names," beats Democratic incumbent Jimmy Carter to win the presidency.

1983: Taylor's husband Sherman Ray is shot and killed in Momence, Illinois, by Willtrue Loyd—a man Taylor falsely claimed was her father. After Ray's killing, Taylor, Loyd, and Mildred Markham—a woman Taylor falsely claimed was her mother—move together to Florida.

1984: Reagan wins re-election.

1985: Under the name Linda Ray Linch, Taylor is arrested in Holmes County, Florida, for stealing four bulls. Taylor, as Linda Ray Lynch, also alleges that she's been mutilated by an unlicensed plastic surgeon. Markham deeds 185 acres of land in Mississippi to Taylor and Taylor's son Clifford. Taylor meets Queen Snell and Snell's three daughters.

1986: Taylor moves into the Snells' home in Graceville, Florida. Markham dies in Florida after suffering a head injury; her death is ultimately ruled accidental. Taylor begins receiving Markham's pension checks from the U.S. Railroad Retirement Board.

1987: Under the name Linda C. Lynch, Taylor is arrested in Jasper, Florida, for stealing a refrigerator.

1988: Taylor receives separate life insurance settlements stemming from the deaths of Ray and Markham.

1994: Under the name Linda Springer, Taylor is arrested in Tampa, Florida, and charged with illegally cashing Markham's federal pension checks. She's sent to a federal mental health facility and found incompetent to stand trial two separate times.

1995: Taylor is found incompetent to stand trial a third time. She's released from federal custody and committed to a state facility in Tampa.

1996: Federal prosecutors drop their indictment against Taylor. Around 1996, Taylor's son Johnnie picks her up from the state facility in Tampa and brings her with him to Illinois. Taylor lives with Johnnie for a short period, then moves in with her daughter, Sandra.

2002: Taylor dies in Chicago at the age of 76 under the name Constance Loyd.

Bibliography

A NOTE ON SOURCES

The Queen tells the story of Linda Taylor's life from beginning to end. Taylor was in the public eye for only a very brief period: the handful of years in the mid-1970s when she became known as the "welfare queen." In writing about her rise to infamy, I relied on contemporaneous reporting from the *Chicago Tribune*, the *Chicago Defender*, the *Chicago Sun-Times*, the *Chicago Daily News*, wire services, and national news outlets as well as television footage from CBS, NBC, and ABC. The task of hunting down primary sources was complicated by Taylor's deployment of dozens upon dozens of aliases. Ultimately, I was able to dig up police reports and court files from multiple jurisdictions, and I obtained FBI files and investigation records via the Freedom of Information Act. Among the interviews I conducted about Taylor's entanglements with the Chicago police and the Cook County courts, I had particularly fruitful conversations with detective Jack Sherwin, who died in 2018, and defense attorney Isaiah "Skip" Gant.

Records on the Illinois Legislative Advisory Committee on Public Aid came via the Illinois State Archives. Audio recordings of Ronald Reagan's campaign speeches and radio addresses were acquired from the Hoover Institution. Rick Perlstein's *The Invisible Bridge* was a tremendous resource on Reagan's rise as a political figure, while Martin Gilens's *Why Americans Hate Welfare* and the work of historian Julilly Kohler-Hausmann supplied crucial context on the history of public aid in the United States. George Bliss's son Bill provided photographs and documents from the Bliss family archives, and the reporter's colleagues—among them Bernard Judge, Bill Mullen, Chuck Neubauer, and Bill Recktenwald—offered sharp insights on his journalistic career. Patricia Parks's family was exceedingly generous in sharing their memories of her life and death.

The material on Taylor's life prior to the 1970s was based mostly on original reporting, with an emphasis on interviews, court files, and records attained through FOIA requests. The documents from the 1964 case in which Taylor attempted to win Lawrence Wakefield's fortune—a trove that had been sealed for more than fifty years—were indispensable both in recreating that proceeding and in providing avenues of research into Taylor's childhood in Tennessee and Arkansas in the 1920s and 1930s and her life in Washington State and California in the 1940s. Lawyer Norris Bishton was a key source for the events before, during, and after the Wakefield case. Taylor's cousins Joan Shefferd, Betty Hudson, and Sarah Mooney Hankey shared photographs and stories that shed light on her early years. Her son Johnnie Harbaugh illuminated Taylor's fraught relationships with her children. Taylor's marriage to Paul Harbaugh was elucidated by court and military records, Veterans Administration documents procured via FOIA, and interviews with Paul's widow, Jean Harbaugh. The narrative of Taylor's relationship with the Moore family came from conversations with Avalon and Annie Mae Moore's daughters Bobbie Moore Lanier, MaLoyce Bell, and Justine Oliver. Interviews and FBI and police records allowed me to describe Taylor's history of both alleged and documented kidnappings.

After Taylor went to prison in 1978, she essentially dropped out of sight. I was able to track her movements in Florida and Illinois with the help of court records, documents from federal agencies, and interviews with those who crossed her path in the 1980s and 1990s. Information on her stint in Dwight Correctional Center came from the Illinois Prisoner Review Board. My account of Sherman Ray's killing relied on VA, court, police, and coroner's records, plus interviews with Ray's sister Patricia Dennis and niece Diana Hibbler. I reconstructed Mildred Markham's

Bibliography

death with the assistance of Markham's granddaughter Theresa Davis and court and coroner's records. Jane Snell-Simpson and Karen Walker helped me tell the story of Taylor's entanglement with the Snell family in the mid-1980s. My reporting on Taylor's arrest by federal authorities in Florida and the details of her psychological evaluations was sourced from court records, documents obtained via FOIA from the Department of Justice and the Federal Bureau of Prisons, and interviews with Railroad Retirement Bureau special agent Mark Squeteri. Jason DeParle's reporting in the *New York Times* and his book *American Dream* were incredibly useful for understanding the political and policy goals of the Clinton-era welfare reform push. Taylor's son Johnnie also shared invaluable recollections of his mother's final years.

ARCHIVAL AND UNPUBLISHED SOURCES

BOP — Federal Bureau of Prisons
CCCC — Circuit Court of Cook County
CCCO — Cook County Clerk's Office
CPD — Chicago Police Department
EOUSA — Executive Office for United States Attorneys, U.S. Department of Justice
FBI — Federal Bureau of Investigation
FOIA — Information obtained under the Freedom of Information Act
IDC — Illinois Department of Corrections
IDPA — Illinois Department of Public Aid
ILGA — Illinois General Assembly
IPRB — Illinois Prisoner Review Board
ISA — Illinois State Archives
KCSP — Kankakee County Sheriff's Police
LAC — Legislative Advisory Committee on Public Aid
MSP — Michigan State Police
NCJRS — National Criminal Justice Reference Service
RRB — Railroad Retirement Board
VA — Department of Veterans Affairs

SELECTED BIBLIOGRAPHY

Alexander, Donald Crichton. *The Arkansas Plantation, 1920–1942*. New Haven: Yale University Press, 1943.

Bibliography

Angelou, Maya. *The Collected Autobiographies of Maya Angelou*. New York: Modern Library, 2004.

Appleyard, R.W. *Photographic Memories: South Haven, Michigan*. Historical Association of South Haven, 1996.

Bagwell, Beth. *Oakland: The Story of a City*. Novato, CA: Presidio Press, 1982.

Baron, Dave. *Pembroke: A Rural, Black Community on the Illinois Dunes*. Carbondale: Southern Illinois University Press, 2016.

Barton, Glen T. and J. G. McNeely. "Recent Changes in the Status of Laborers and Tenants on Arkansas Plantations." *The Journal of Land & Public Utility Economics* 15, no. 2 (May 1939).

Blalock, H. W. "Plantation Operations of Landlords and Tenants in Arkansas." University of Arkansas, College of Agriculture, Agricultural Experiment Station, *Bulletin No. 339* (May 1937).

"Blytheville in Arkansas." Pamphlet. Blytheville Chamber of Commerce, c. 1936.

Bolitzer, Alfred A. et al., eds. *A Time for Choosing: The Speeches of Ronald Reagan, 1961-1982*. Chicago: Regnery, 1982.

The Call of the Alluvial Empire. Booklet. Memphis, TN: Southern Alluvial Land Association, 1917.

Cannon, Lou. *Governor Reagan: His Rise to Power*. New York: Public Affairs, 2009.

Cannon, Lou. *President Reagan: The Role of a Lifetime*. New York: Public Affairs, 2000.

Carleson, Robert B. *Government Is the Problem: Memoirs of Ronald Reagan's Welfare Reformer*. Susan A. Carleson and Hans Zeiger, eds. Alexandria, VA: American Civil Rights Union, 2010.

Carmer, Carl. *Stars Fell on Alabama*. Tuscaloosa: University of Alabama Press, 1990.

Chicago Riot Study Committee. *Report to the Hon. Richard J. Daley*. Chicago, 1968.

Chipman, Irene Yochum. *Gold Dust Tennessee*. N.p., n.d., Lauderdale County Library.

Cleckley, Hervey M. *The Mask of Sanity: An Attempt to Clarify Some Issues About the So-Called Psychopathic Personality*. Emily S. Cleckley, pub. St. Louis: Mosby, 1988.

Clinton, Bill. *My Life*. New York: Alfred A. Knopf, 2004.

Cobb, Ruth A. *A Place We Called Home: A History of Illinois Soldiers' Orphans' Home 1864–1931, Illinois Soldiers' and Sailors' Children's School 1931–1979*. Normal, IL: Illinois Soldiers' and Sailors' Children's School Historical Preservation Society, 2007.

Committee to Study the ADC Program in Cook County. *Facts, Fallacies and Future: A Study of the Aid to Dependent Children Program of Cook County, Illinois*. Chicago: Greenleigh Associates, 1960.

Cooley, Robert with Hillel Levin. *When Corruption Was King: How I Helped the Mob Rule Chicago, Then Brought the Outfit Down*. New York: Carroll and Graf, 2004.

Cox, Anna-Lisa. *A Stronger Kinship: One Town's Extraordinary Story of Hope and Faith*. New York: Little, Brown and Company, 2006.

Dallek, Matthew. *The Right Moment: Ronald Reagan's First Victory and the Decisive Turning Point in American Politics*. New York: Oxford UP, 2000.

Bibliography

DeParle, Jason. *American Dream: Three Women, Ten Kids, and a Nation's Drive to End Welfare*. New York: Penguin, 2005.

Dew, Lee A. "The J.L.C. and E.R.R. and the Opening of the 'Sunk Lands' of Northeast Arkansas." *Arkansas Historical Quarterly* 27, no. 1 (Spring 1968).

Dowdy, G. Wayne. *Crusades for Freedom: Memphis and the Political Transformation of the American South*. Jackson: University Press of Mississippi, 2010.

Ducoff, Louis J. *Wages of Agricultural Labor in the United States*. USDA Technical Bulletin no. 895 (July 1945).

Dugger, Ronnie. *On Reagan: The Man & His Presidency*. New York: McGraw-Hill, 1983.

DuRocher, Kristina. *Raising Racists: The Socialization of White Children in the Jim Crow South*. Lexington: University Press of Kentucky, 2011.

Dygert, James H. *The Investigative Journalist: Folk Heroes of a New Era*. Englewood Cliffs, N.J.: Prentice-Hall, 1976.

Edrington, Mabel Flannigan. *History of Mississippi County, Arkansas*. Ocala, FL: The Ocala Star–Banner, 1962.

Edsall, Thomas Byrne and Mary D. Edsall. *Chain Reaction: The Impact of Race, Rights, and Taxes on American Politics*. New York: Norton, 1992.

Fite, Gilbert C. *Cotton Fields No More: Southern Agriculture 1865–1980*. Lexington: University Press of Kentucky, 1984.

Fremon, David K. *Chicago Politics, Ward by Ward*. Bloomington, IN: Indiana University Press, 1988.

Fronczak, Paul Joseph with Alex Tresniowski. *The Foundling: The True Story of a Kidnapping, a Family Secret, and My Search for the Real Me*. New York: Howard Books, 2017.

Gaines, William. "Lost art of infiltration." *Journalism* 8, no. 5 (October 2007).

Gardiner, John A. and Theodore R. Lyman. "Responses to Fraud and Abuse in AFDC and Medicaid Programs," report prepared for the National Institute of Justice, U.S. Department of Justice, January 1983.

Generous, William Thomas. *Sweet Pea at War: A History of USS Portland*. Lexington: University Press of Kentucky, 2005.

Gilens, Martin. *Why Americans Hate Welfare: Race, Media, and the Politics of Antipoverty Policy*. Chicago: University of Chicago Press, 1999.

Grimshaw, William J. *Bitter Fruit: Black Politics and the Chicago Machine, 1931–1991*. Chicago: University of Chicago Press, 1992.

Hake, Terrence with Wayne Klatt. *Operation Greylord: The True Story of an Untrained Undercover Agent and America's Biggest Corruption Bust*. Kindle edition. Ankerwycke/ the American Bar Association, 2015.

Hare, Robert D. *Without Conscience: The Disturbing World of the Psychopaths Among Us*. New York: Guilford Press, 1999.

Harrington, Michael. *The Other America: Poverty in the United States*. New York: Macmillan Publishing Company, 1962.

Bibliography

Hegarty, Marilyn E. *Victory Girls, Khaki-Wackies, and Patriotutes: The Regulation of Female Sexuality during World War II*. New York: New York University Press, 2008.

Heinicke, Craig. "Southern Tenancy, Machines, and Production Scale on the Eve of the Cotton Picker's Arrival." *Social Science History* 23, no. 3 (Fall 1999).

Heise, Kenan. *They Speak for Themselves: Interviews with the Destitute in Chicago*. Chicago: Young Christian Worker, 1965.

Herrnstein, Richard J. and Charles Murray. *The Bell Curve: Intelligence and Class Structure in American Life*. New York: Free Press, 1996.

Hirsch, Arnold. *Making the Second Ghetto: Race & Housing in Chicago 1940–1960*. Cambridge: Cambridge University Press, 1983.

Hobbs, Allyson. *A Chosen Exile: A History of Racial Passing in American Life*. Cambridge, MA: Harvard University Press, 2014.

Holley, Donald. "Leaving the Land of Opportunity: Arkansas and the Great Migration." *Arkansas Historical Quarterly* 64, no. 3 (2005).

House Committee on Ways and Means, *1996 Green Book: Background Material and Data on Programs Within the Jurisdiction of the Committee on Ways and Means*. WMCP 104-14. Washington, DC: U.S. Government Printing Office.

Hutchinson, William Thomas. *Lowden of Illinois: The Life of Frank O. Lowden*. University of Chicago Press, 1957.

Johnson, Marilynn S. *The Second Gold Rush: Oakland and the East Bay in World War II*. Berkeley: University of California Press, 1994.

Jones, Bouillon, Thiry, and Sylliaasen, Architects. "Orchard Heights, Washington: Housing Project Developed Under FPHA, Region 7." *Pencil Points: Progressive Architecture*, January 1945.

Kaelber, Lutz. "Eugenics/Sexual Sterilizations in North Carolina," University of Vermont, October 2014, www.uvm.edu/~lkaelber/eugenics/NC/NC.html.

Kirby, Jack Temple. "The Transformation of Southern Plantations c. 1920–1960." *Agricultural History* 57, no. 3 (July 1983).

Klatt, Wayne. *Chicago Journalism: A History*. Jefferson, NC: McFarland, 2009.

Kohler-Hausmann, Julilly. *Getting Tough: Welfare and Imprisonment in 1970s America*. Princeton, NJ: Princeton University Press, 2017.

Kohler-Hausmann, Julilly. "'The Crime of Survival': Fraud Prosecutions, Community Surveillance and the Original 'Welfare Queen.'" *Journal of Social History* 41, no. 2 (2007).

Laws of the Various States Relating to Vagrancy. Michigan State Library Legislative Reference Department. Lansing, MI: State Printer, 1916.

Levine, Marc V. and Sandra J. Callaghan. *The Economic State of Milwaukee: The City and the Region*. Milwaukee: Center for Economic Development, 1998.

Lindberg, Richard C. *To Serve and Collect: Chicago Politics and Police Corruption from the Lager Beer Riot to the Summerdale Scandal, 1955–1960*. Carbondale: Southern Illinois University Press, 1998.

Bibliography

Lombardo, Robert M. *Organized Crime in Chicago: Beyond the Mafia*. Chicago: University of Illinois Press, 2013.

MacLeod, Laurie, Darrel Montero, and Alan Speer. "America's Changing Attitudes Toward Welfare and Welfare Recipients, 1938-1995." *Journal of Sociology and Social Welfare* 26, no.2 (June 1999).

Merriner, James L. *Grafters and Goo Goos: Corruption and Reform in Chicago, 1833–2003*. Carbondale: Southern Illinois University Press, 2004.

Michaeli, Ethan. *The Defender: How the Legendary Black Newspaper Changed America*. Boston: Houghton Mifflin Harcourt, 2016.

"Mississippi County, Arkansas: It's the Soil!" Pamphlet. Blytheville Chamber of Commerce, c. 1936.

Morris, Billie. *Lauderdale County*. Images of America Series. Charleston, SC: Arcadia Publishing, 2012.

Murch, Donna Jean. *Living for the City: Migration, Education, and the Rise of the Black Panther Party in Oakland, California*. Chapel Hill, NC: University of North Carolina Press, 2010.

Murray, Charles. *Losing Ground: American Social Policy, 1950-1980*. Kindle edition. BasicBooks, 2015.

Murray, Pauli, ed. *States' Laws on Race and Color*. Cincinnati: Woman's Division of Christian Service, 1951.

Pascoe, Peggy. *What Comes Naturally: Miscegenation Law and the Making of Race in America*. New York: Oxford University Press, 2009.

Perlstein, Rick. *The Invisible Bridge: The Fall of Nixon and the Rise of Reagan*. New York: Simon & Schuster, 2014.

"Productivity of Farm Labor, 1909 to 1938." U.S. Department of Labor, *Monthly Labor Review* 49 (July–December 1939).

"Profiles—Black Advocates in the Forefront of Trial Litigation." *National Black Law Journal* 3 no. 1 (1973): 75–79.

Pryor, Richard with Todd Gold. *Pryor Convictions and Other Life Sentences*. New York: Pantheon Books, 1995.

Reagan, Ronald. *Reagan, in His Own Hand*. Kiron K. Skinner, Annelise Anderson, and Martin Anderson, eds. New York: Free Press, 2001.

Reese, Ellen. *Backlash Against Welfare Mothers: Past and Present*. Berkeley: University of California Press, 2005.

Richter, Jeremy W. "Alabama's Anti-Miscegenation Statutes." *Alabama Review* 68, No. 4 (October 2015).

Rolph, Stephanie R. "Courting Conservatism: White Resistance and the Ideology of Race in the 1960s," in Laura Jane Gifford and Daniel K. Williams, eds., *The Right Side of the Sixties*. New York: Palgrave Macmillan, 2012.

Royko, Mike. *Boss: Richard J. Daley of Chicago*. New York: Signet, 1971.

Bibliography

Self, Robert O. *American Babylon: Race and the Struggle for Postwar Oakland*. Princeton: Princeton University Press, 2003.

Shirley, Craig. *Reagan's Revolution: The Untold Story of the Campaign That Started It All*. Nashville: Thomas Nelson, 2010.

Smith-Pryor, Elizabeth M. *Property Rites: The Rhinelander Trial, Passing, and the Protection of Whiteness*. Chapel Hill: The University of North Carolina Press, 2009.

Snowden, Deanna. *Mississippi County, Arkansas: Appreciating the Past, Anticipating the Future*. Little Rock, AR: August House, 1986.

Solinger, Rickie. *Wake Up Little Susie: Single Pregnancy and Race Before Roe v. Wade*. New York: Routledge, 1992.

Sparks, Holloway. "Queens, Teens, and Model Mothers: Race, Gender, and the Discourse of Welfare Reform," in Sanford F. Schram, Joe Soss, and Richard C. Fording, eds., *Race and the Politics of Welfare Reform*. Ann Arbor: University of Michigan Press, 2003.

Stephens, Oren. "Revolt on the Delta: What happened to the sharecroppers' union." *Harper's*, November 1941.

Svahn, John A. (Jack). *"There Must Be a Pony in Here Somewhere." Twenty Years with Ronald Reagan: A Memoir*. Minneapolis: Langdon Street Press, 2011.

Thompson, Nathan. *Kings: The True Story of Chicago's Policy Kings and Numbers Racketeers*. Chicago: Bronzeville Press, 2006.

Travis, Dempsey J. *Racism: 'Round 'n 'Round It Goes*. Chicago: Urban Research Press, 1998.

Up from Dependency: A New National Public Assistance Strategy. Report to the President by the Domestic Policy Council Low Income Opportunity Working Group. Washington, DC: U.S. Government Printing Office, December 1986.

U.S. Department of Health and Human Services (HHS). *Aid to Families with Dependent Children: The Baseline*. Washington, DC: Office of Human Services Policy, June 1998.

U.S. General Accounting Office (GAO). *Bureau of Prisons Health Care: Inmates' Access to Health Care Is Limited by Lack of Clinical Staff*. Report to the Chairman, Subcommittee on Intellectual Property and Judicial Administration, Committee on the Judiciary, House of Representatives, February 1994.

U.S. Senate, "Fraud, Abuse, Waste, and Mismanagement of Programs by the Department of Health, Education, and Welfare," *Hearings before the Permanent Subcommittee on Investigations of the Committee on Governmental Affairs*, 95th Congress, 2nd session, July 20, 1978. Online at https://www.ncjrs.gov/pdffiles1/Digitization/51993NCJRS.pdf.

U.S. Senate, *Hearings on H.R. 12276 before the Subcommittee of the Committee on Appropriations*, District of Columbia Appropriations for 1963, 87th Congress, 2nd Session, 1962.

U.S. Senate, *Hearings before the Subcommittee to Investigate Juvenile Delinquency,*

Bibliography

Committee on the Judiciary, 96th Congress, 5th session, Chicago, IL—May 27, 1977; and Washington, DC—June 16, 1977.

Volanto, Keith J. "The AAA Cotton Plow-Up Campaign in Arkansas." *Arkansas Historical Quarterly* 59, no. 4 (Winter 2000).

Walker, Daniel, et al. *Rights in Conflict: The violent confrontation of demonstrators and police in the parks and streets of Chicago during the week of the Democratic National Convention of 1968*. Chicago: Bantam Books, 1968.

Weisberg, Jacob. *Ronald Reagan*. The American Presidents Series: The 40th President, 1981–1989. New York: Henry Holt, 2016.

Wendt, Lloyd. *Chicago Tribune: The Rise of a Great American Newspaper*. Chicago: Rand McNally, 1979.

Whayne, Jeannie. *Delta Empire: Lee Wilson and the Transformation of Agriculture in the New South*. Baton Rouge: Louisiana State University Press, 2011.

Whayne, Jeannie. "The Power of the Plantation Model: The Sunk Lands Controversy." *Forest & Conservation History* 37, no. 2 (April 1993).

White, Walter Francis. *A Man Called White: The Autobiography of Walter White*. Athens, GA: University of Georgia Press, 1995.

"Widner-Magers Farm Historic District," National Register of Historic Places registration form, U.S. Department of the Interior, January 29, 2007.

Wiedrich. Bob. *Windy City Watchdog: A Chicago Reporter's War on Organized Crime*. Xlibris, 2009.

Williams, Lucy A. "Decades of Distortion: The Right's 30-year Assault on Welfare." Political Research Associates, December 1997.

Wilkerson, Isabel. *The Warmth of Other Suns: The Epic Story of America's Great Migration*. New York: Vintage Books, 2010.

Wilson, William Julius. *The Truly Disadvantaged: The Inner City, the Underclass, and Public Policy*. Chicago: University of Chicago Press, 1990.

Witcover, Jules. *Marathon: The Pursuit of the Presidency, 1972-1976*. New York: Viking Press, 1977.

Woodruff, Nan E. "The Failure of Relief During the Arkansas Drought of 1930–1931," Arkansas Historical Quarterly 39, no. 4 (1980)

X, Malcolm with Alex Haley. *The Autobiography of Malcolm X*. New York: Random House, 1992.

COURTS

CCCC, *People of the State of Illinois v. Linda Taylor AKA Connie Walker AKA Linda Bennett AKA Sandra Brownlee AKA Linda Jones AKA Connie Jarvis*, case no. 75-6049.

CCCC, *People of the State of Illinois v. Linda Taylor*, case no. 76-1170 [*Linda Taylor burglary case*].

Bibliography

CCCC, *People of the State of Illinois v. Sandra Brownlee*, case no. 75–6048.

CCCVB, *The People of the State of Michigan v. Connie Green*, preliminary examination, February 25, 1972, file no. 1691.

CCCC, Probate Division. *In the Matter of the Estate of Lawrence Wakefield, Deceased*, file no. 64-P-1834, docket no. 664 [*Wakefield estate*].

CCCC, Probate Division. *In the Matter of the Estate of Patricia Parks AKA Patricia M. Parks, Deceased*, file no. 75-P-5014, docket no. 807 [*Estate of Patricia Parks*].

CCCC, Chancery Division. *Willie E. Butler, and Rose Butler, his wife v. Sherman F. Ray, and Linda C. Ray, his wife; Willtrue Loyd AKA William Willtrue Loyd and unknown others*, case no. 78-5514.

CCCC, Chancery Division. *National Homes Acceptance Corporation v. Sherman F. Ray, et al.*, case no. 77-8131

CCCC, Chancery – Divorce Division. *Patricia Marva Parks v. John E. Parks, John G. Parks and Emma Parks*, case no. 73-D-21775.

Circuit Court of Peoria County (IL). *Paul Harbaugh and Sandra Harbaugh, Minors, by Their Mother and Next Friend, Connie Harbaugh v. Peoria Board of Education and Central Illinois Light Company*, case no. 54495, 1960–1967.

12th Judicial Circuit Court of Florida in and for Sarasota County. *Linda C. Ray v. Veterans Life Insurance Company*, case no. 85-4046.

United States District Court for the Middle District of Florida, Tampa Division. *United States of America v. Linda Springer*, case no. 94-59-CR-T-21 (B).

ARCHIVAL COLLECTIONS

American Presidency Project, University of California, Santa Barbara.

Chicago History Museum

Chicago Tribune Oral History Archive

HistoryMakers digital archive

Hoover Institution Archives

Illinois General Assembly digital archive

Illinois State Archives

Marshall County, Alabama Archives

National Archives/National Personnel Records Center

Ronald Reagan Oral History Project, Miller Center of Public Affairs, University of Virginia

Seattle Municipal Archives

U.S. Navy/National Archives Catalog

Washington State Archives, Puget Sound

Notes

CHAPTER 1

Author interviews with Jack Sherwin, Susan Sherwin, Jerry Kush,
Jim Mott, Lamar Jones.

1   **a $1,000 haul:** "Fifth Jewel store robbed here in a week," *Chicago Tribune*, February 6, 1974.
1   **A month earlier:** "Woman shot; dies in arms of priest," *Chicago Tribune*, July 17, 1974.
1   **970 murders:** CPD, annual statistical summary.
2   **There were nearly:** CPD, annual statistical summaries.
2   **Four days earlier:** Supplemental answer and offer of proof to defendant's pretrial motion, *People of the State of Illinois v. Linda Taylor AKA Connie Walker AKA Linda Bennett AKA Sandra Brownlee AKA Linda Jones AKA Connie Jarvis* (henceforth *Illinois v. Linda Taylor*), CCCC.
3   **Taylor appeared to be:** Mug shots, CPD/FOIA.
3   **A large green refrigerator:** A list of allegedly stolen items appears in Sherwin's communication with the Michigan State Police, complaint report, August 25, 1974, MSP/FOIA.
3   **a window in her kitchen:** "Queen of welfare cheats—who is she?," *Dow Jones –Ottaway News/Pocono Record* (Stroudsburg, PA), February 13, 1975.
4   **"every person having":** Standard form, Chicago restrictive covenant, 1927.
4   **Mahalia Jackson moved:** "2 Homes Fired; Guard Chatham," *Chicago Defender* (Chicago, IL), April 26, 1956.
5   **But between 1967 and 1977:** Levine and Callaghan, *The Economic State of Milwaukee*, Chapter 5.

Notes

5   **White flight:** "Work," *Encyclopedia of Chicago* online.

6   **"pent-up aggressions":** Chicago Riot Study Committee, *Report to the Hon. Richard J. Daley,* p. 72.

6   **"unrestrained and indiscriminate police violence":** Walker, et al., *Rights in Conflict,* p. vii.

7   **The dental clinic at Great Lakes:** "Dentistry is Becoming a New Health Science," AP/*News Journal* (Mansfield, OH), June 25, 1967.

7   **prime recruiting ground...violent confrontations:** "New Gang Wars Disrupt City," *Chicago Defender,* September 16, 1968.

8   **On Saturday, August 17:** Lamar Jones testimony, November 12, 1974, *Illinois v. Linda Taylor.*

8   **four different names:** Interview with a postman at the USPS South Chicago station, October 1974, FBI/VA/FOIA.

9   **given her age as twenty-seven:** Marriage license, August 17, 1974, FBI/FOIA.

CHAPTER 2

Author interviews with Jack Sherwin, Ruth Hedlund, William Buhl,
Charles Bailey, Robert Rank, Erma Williams, Charles Reavy, Bob
Dell, Major Schutt.

11   **In March 1972:** Sherwin testimony, February 24, 1977, *Illinois v. Linda Taylor.*

11   **lost more than $8,000 worth:** Supplemental answer and offer of proof to defendant's pretrial motion, January 13, 1976, *Illinois v. Linda Taylor.*

11   **He'd also gone:** Complaint report, April 2, 1972, MSP/FOIA.

11   **He'd asked the troopers:** Ibid.

12   **the state troopers had sent him:** Complaint report, March 19, 1972, MSP/FOIA.

12   **Ed Hedlund advertised on the front cover:** South Haven, Michigan: city directory, special residential edition, 1972.

12   **In the early twentieth century:** Appleyard, *Photographic Memories: South Haven.*

12   **at first Hedlund:** "South Haven turns upscale," *Ludington Daily News* (Ludington, MI), September 24, 1987.

13   **She also showed off:** "Medical 'practice' just that for Welfare Queen," *Chicago Tribune,* July 14, 1975.

13   **blacks had won elected office:** Cox, *A Stronger Kinship,* Chapter 2.

13   **Between 1940 and 1970:** U.S. census data for Van Buren County, Michigan.

13   **She put down $400:** Interview with Ed Hedlund, additional complaint report, February 13, 1972, MSP/FOIA.

13   **Bailey had met Taylor in Chicago:** Interview with Bailey, additional complaint report, February 13, 1972, MSP/FOIA.

Notes

13   **daughter of a spiritual adviser:** April 16, 1970.

14   **She charged $100 per session:** "Medical 'practice' just that for Welfare Queen."

14   **Taylor called the teenager:** Bailey testimony, *People of the State of Michigan v. Connie Green,* preliminary examination, February 25, 1972, circuit court for the county of Van Buren.

15   **Dr. Shfolia ... Dr. Whoyon:** Interview with Bailey, additional complaint report, February 13, 1972, MSP/FOIA.

16   **Around Christmastime:** Ibid.

17   **The nanny, Virginia Griffin:** Griffin testimony, *Michigan v. Connie Green,* preliminary examination.

17   **"little black baby":** Jessie Dinkins testimony, *Michigan v. Connie Green,* preliminary examination.

18   **"was a disgrace":** Ibid.

18   **$236 every two weeks:** Payment of $472 per month in biweekly increments per Erma Williams testimony, *Michigan v. Connie Green,* preliminary examination.

18   **An authorization form listed:** "Welfare fraud—an easy game: 5 fictitious children go undetected for 3 months," *Detroit News,* February 10, 1975.

18   **so many small children:** Williams testimony, *Michigan v. Connie Green,* preliminary examination.

18   **just five months apart:** "Welfare fraud—an easy game," *Detroit News,* February 10, 1975.

19   **buy sixty-seven acres of land:** Progress report, November 1974, LAC/ISA.

19   **Hale called the police:** Complaint report, February 12, 1972, MSP/FOIA.

19   **The state troopers knocked:** Ibid.

19   **Inside the glove box:** Additional complaint report, February 12, 1972, MSP/FOIA.

19   **he found Charles Bailey:** Interview with Bailey, complaint report, MSP/FOIA.

20   **Griffin would later confess:** Interview with Griffin, additional complaint report, February 21, 1972, MSP/FOIA.

20   **"spilled the beans":** Interview with Bailey, additional complaint report, February 18, 1972, MSP/FOIA.

20   **On February 19, 1972:** Additional complaint report, February 19, 1972, MSP/FOIA.

20   **Taylor was a flight risk:** *Michigan v. Connie Green,* preliminary examination.

21   **"going to Florida":** Interview with Griffin, additional complaint report, February 21, 1972, MSP/FOIA.

22   **sent Sherwin a fingerprint card:** Sherwin testimony, February 24, 1977, *Illinois v. Linda Taylor.*

Notes

22   **less than 10 percent of the time:** CPD, annual statistical summary.

23   **in February 1967:** Criminal history, CPD/FOIA.

CHAPTER 3

Author interviews with Jack Sherwin, Jerry Kush, Etta Tomczyk,
Walter McWilliams, Bill Bliss, Larry Bliss, J. Terrence Brunner,
William Crawford, Jerry Crimmins, William Gaines, Bernard
Judge, Charles Mount, Bill Mullen, Chuck Neubauer, Bill Reckten-
wald, James Strong, Pam Zekman, George Groble.

25   **Sherwin walked into the front room:** Sherwin testimony, February 24, 1977, *Illinois v. Linda Taylor*.

25   **short-sleeved brocade dress:** Mug shot, August 25, 1974, CPD/FOIA.

25   **slammed the cardboard suitcase shut:** Sherwin and James McEnroe testimonies, February 24, 1977, *Illinois v. Linda Taylor*.

26   **driver's license that said Linda Bennett:** Michael Golden testimony, February 24, 1977, *Illinois v. Linda Taylor*.

26   **six police department inventory forms:** Inventory forms, August 25, 1975, CPD/FOIA.

26   **"I know you by the name":** Sherwin court testimony quoted in "Multiple identification cards led to 'Welfare Queen' arrest," AP/*Reno Evening Gazette*, March 8, 1977.

26   **He typed the name:** Arrest report, August 25, 1974, CPD/FOIA.

28   **fifty-four aliases:** Chicago office memo, November 26, 1974, FBI/FOIA.

28   **the pointed chin:** Martha Gordon mug shot and booking card, October 24, 1944, Kitsap County Sheriff's Office/Washington State Archives, Puget Sound.

28   **incapacitated by heart disease:** Eligibility questionnaire, Illinois Department of Public Aid, FBI/FOIA.

28   **sent her $416.70 each month:** Check images, FBI/FOIA.

28   **By the following January:** Certification of the comptroller of the State of Illinois, *Illinois v. Linda Taylor*.

28   **"Flordia":** Application for assistance, October 23, 1973, FBI/FOIA.

28   **a check for $306:** Memra Taylor testimony, March 8, 1977, *Illinois v. Linda Taylor*.

28   **A day after that:** Image of check issued November 1, 1973, FBI/FOIA.

28   **Three days after Sherwin:** Certification of the comptroller, *Illinois v. Linda Taylor*.

29   **She scrawled the words:** Application for assistance, Illinois Department of Public Aid, April 29, 1974, FBI/FOIA.

Notes

29   **This time, her request:** Etta Tomczyk testimony, grand jury indictment, February 6, 1975; and summary of Tomczyk's testimony by assistant state's attorney James Sternik, March 17, 1977, *Illinois v. Linda Taylor*.

29   **Maybe they'd have better:** George Bliss, "Her welfare, other frauds safe under wraps of U.S., Illinois bureaucracy," *Chicago Tribune/Tri-City Herald* (Kennewick, WA), October 10, 1974.

31   **"doctor collected $50":** "Four accused of falsified charges for services," August 26, 1974.

31   **Bliss blew out:** "$2.14 million in welfare paid to 20 doctors," August 27, 1974.

31   **"A nurse at Bethany Brethren":** "Reports used in fraud probe," August 28, 1974.

31   **eleven articles on page one:** *Chicago Tribune* digital archive/newspapers.com.

31   **more than one hundred people:** Dygert, *The Investigative Journalist*, p. 130.

32   **"should not have been allowed":** Harry Kariher quoted in "So What If He's a Little Messy?," *Phoenix New Times*, February 20–26, 1985.

32   **He hung out with them:** George Bliss, interview by Judy Pasternak of Northwestern University's Medill School of Journalism, February 26, 1976, Chicago History Museum.

32   **He'd flash a badge:** Ibid.

33   **abuses at Cook County's juvenile home:** "Orders juvenile home quiz: Judge probes girls' stories of indignities," September 12, 1950; "Juvenile home evidence given to prosecutor," September 13, 1950; "New juvenile home evidence given in quiz," September 16, 1950.

33   **On June 20, 1959:** "Obituary: Mrs. George Bliss," *Chicago Tribune*, June 21, 1959.

33   **forging their time sheets:** "Scandal hits sanitary unit," *Chicago Tribune*, May 17, 1961.

33   **He would build:** "BGA's George Bliss Rejoining Tribune," AP, October 15, 1971.

33   **188 phony jobs...$1 million:** "Pulitzer Prize Won By Bliss of the *Tribune*," May 8, 1962.

33   **more than eight hundred thousand readers:** "Dave Felts Column," *Southern Illinoisan* (Carbondale, IL), January 22, 1959; "Times Sets New Sales, Ad, Circulation Records," *Los Angeles Times*, February 2, 1964.

33   **1.2 million on Sundays:** advertisement in *Chicago Tribune*, February 11, 1963.

34   **Chicago newspaper columnist:** "OK, uncle, Mike's jingling the bell," *Chicago Tribune*, December 6, 1991.

34   **Bliss wanted to dig up:** Bliss, interview by Pasternak, 1976.

34   **found $750,000 in cash:** "Demands Probe of Closet Story," *Chicago Tribune*, January 12, 1971.

34   **heart attack victim:** "Heart Victim Is Left in Flat; Had Only $2," June 9, 1970.

Notes

35 **"gun battle":** "Exclusive: Hanrahan, Police Tell Panther Story," December 11, 1969.

35 **"not a single black vote":** "Miscarriage of justice," October 28, 1972.

35 **Clayton Kirkpatrick:** Bernie Judge, *Tribune* oral history interview: Klatt, *Chicago Journalism: A History*, p. 238.

36 **won journalism's top prize:** "Chicago vote fraud disclosures earn top local reporting award," *Chicago Tribune*, May 8, 1973.

36 **In 1974, [Bliss's] byline:** *Chicago Tribune* digital archive/ProQuest.

36 **"word has spread among":** "State blames county for welfare cheats," *Chicago Tribune*, August 6, 1974.

38 **Linda Taylor received:** "Cops find deceit—but no one cares," September 29, 1974.

39 **"Miss Taylor may be involved":** "Panel probes welfare cheating charges," *Chicago Tribune*, September 30, 1974.

39 **"at least 16":** "Probe Welfare Fraud Ring: Link County Workers to $160,000 Loss," July 15, 1971.

39 **more than eleven hundred newspapers:** "Says UPI President Beaton: Subscribers' advice will help the future," UPI/*Daily Journal* (Franklin, IN), April 18, 1974.

40 **"well-organized scheme":** "Welfare Checks Help Cheater's Lifestyle," UPI/*Sarasota Herald–Tribune*, October 2, 1974.

40 **In many newspapers:** "Welfare bonanza keeps woman in big cars—cops," UPI/*Morning Herald* (Hagerstown, MD), October 1, 1974.

40 **"Welfare queen arrested":** *Democrat and Chronicle*, October 1, 1974.

40 **"Madame X":** "Woman in Mink with $60,000 Lived on Relief in a Hotel, Inquiry by State Discloses," October 30, 1947.

40 **"theme of the undeserving poor":** *New Yorker*, November 22, 1947.

41 **"unscrupulous parasites":** "Relief and its abuses," June 6, 1933.

41 **By November:** "Special Court set up to try relief families," November 3, 1933.

41 **That same month:** "Jails mother 30 days for relief fraud," *Chicago Tribune*, November 11, 1933.

41 **"women relief cheaters":** "Women relief cheaters: How they operate," January 22, 1951.

41 **"feed steaks" ... "$61,500 relief jackpot":** "Children Without Fathers: The Shocking Truth About the Aid to Dependent Children Welfare Program," *Reader's Digest*, November 1961.

41 **"1958 air-conditioned Cadillac":** "Welfare: has it become a scandal?," *Look*, November 7, 1961.

41 **called out:** "California Cleans Up Its Welfare Mess," *Reader's Digest*/*Abilene Reporter–News* (Abilene, TX), October 28, 1973.

42 **Cash declined:** "Johnny Cash Won't Sing Nixon Request," UPI/*Bridgeport Telegram* (Bridgeport, CT), March 31, 1970.

42 **an estimated 24.3 million people:** U.S. Census Bureau, "Characteristics of the Population Below the Poverty Level: 1974," *Current Population Reports: Consumer Income,* January 1976.

42 **roughly fourteen million Americans:** "Supplemental Nutrition Assistance Program (SNAP): A Short History," U.S. Department of Agriculture, www.fns.usda.gov/snap/short-history-snap.

42 **7.8 million children:** Table 2.1 in U.S. HHS, *Aid to Families with Dependent Children: The Baseline,* June 1998, p. 15.

42 **"Department of Agriculture is receiving":** Harvey column, May 10, 1973.

42 **"welfare mothers are being urged":** "High food prices more than a nuisance to the poor; even neckbones too expensive," *Chicago Tribune,* July 29, 1973.

42 **headline on the front page:** *Lubbock Avalanche-Journal* (Lubbock, TX), October 1, 1974.

42 **The median household income:** Table A in U.S. Census Bureau, "Household Money Income in 1974 and Selected Social and Economic Characteristics of Households," *Current Population Reports: Consumer Income* 60, no. 100, August 1975.

43 **sticker price of a 1974 Cadillac Eldorado convertible:** NADA guides online.

43 **On September 30, 1974:** Criminal history, CPD/FOIA.

44 **Don Moore wrote a letter:** Moore to Rochford, October 7, 1974, ISA.

CHAPTER 4

Author interviews with Lamar Jones, Jack Sherwin, Joel Edelman,
Ward Hamlin Jr., Peter Hannaford, Neal Caauwe, Johnnie
Harbaugh, Bridget Hutchen, Bernard Carey, Kenneth Gillis, Jeffrey
Simon.

46 **the U.S. Department of Agriculture began:** Interview with a USDA special agent, November 1974, FBI/FOIA.

46 **the twelve-person, bipartisan group:** History of LAC, handout, ISA.

46 **26 cents per person per meal:** "Demand More Aid for Poor Here," *Chicago Defender,* March 3, 1969; "The Why's and What's of Welfare," *Chicago Tribune,* August 11, 1969.

47 **"hardly enough":** Senator Fred J. Smith to LAC, quoted in "Sen. Smith Opens War On Swank For Disregarding Needs Of Poor," *Chicago Defender,* April 19, 1969.

47 **some committee members:** "State Hunts Missing Fathers," AP/*Freeport Journal–Standard* (Freeport, IL), April 29, 1964.

Notes

47   **the total abolition of public aid:** Representative Rae C. Heiple II quoted in "Lawmaker Asks Stop to Poor Relief," UPI/*Daily Herald*, March 14, 1963.

47   **remained in the ADC program:** DeParle, *American Dream*, Chapter 5.

47   **"Suitable home" and "man in the house" provisions:** Kohler-Hausmann, "The Crime of Survival," p. 332.

47   **The practice didn't end:** Kaelber, "Eugenics/Sexual Sterilizations in North Carolina."

47   **could be jailed:** "Illinois Gets a Warning on Children's Aid," *Chicago Tribune*, May 3, 1962.

47   **"hostility to this most disadvantaged segment":** Committee to Study the ADC, *Facts, Fallacies and Future*, p. 4.

47   **"There is a good probability":** Ibid., p. 6.

48   **reported, thirty-nine states:** "Picture Of Typical Welfare Recipient False?," AP/*Wilmington News-Journal* (Wilmington, OH), January 11, 1972.

48   **In 1968, the Supreme Court…two years later, the justices:** *King v. Smith*, 1968; *Goldberg v. Kelly*, 1970.

48   **In 1959, 22.4 percent:** Table A-1 in U.S. Census Bureau, "Poverty in the United States: 2000," *Current Population Reports: Consumer Income*, September 2001.

48   **Between 1963 and 1973:** Caseload data, AFDC, Office of Family Assistance of the Administration for Children and Families.

49   **rising to $1.5 billion:** Department of Public Aid, financial report, ISA.

49   **"is really the reform":** Richard Cloward (Columbia University) quoted in "The Welfare Crisis—A Human Crisis," February 7, 1971.

49   **"fiscal chaos, and perhaps bankruptcy":** "Dems Hit Welfare Slash Plan; Republicans Call It Necessary," *Chicago Tribune*, October 7, 1971.

49   **In 1972, he called:** "Money main school problem, Moore tells Dist. 145," *Suburbanite Economist*, October 15, 1972.

49   **"both black and white people":** "Senate Bill Would Block Bus Use for Integration," UPI/*Galesburg Register-Mail* (Galesburg, IL), April 13, 1973.

49   **186 black constituents and 15,697 white ones:** Data for Midlothian in "General Population Characteristics: Illinois," *1970 Census of Population*, U.S. Census Bureau, p. 13.

49   **"that some of these people":** July 1974, LAC/ISA.

49   **"cancer eating at":** "Reagan Asks Sweeping Changes in Welfare, Medi-Cal Programs," *Los Angeles Times*, January 13, 1971.

50   **"Reagan Revolution":** "Reagan the Revolutionary," *Washington Star* Syndicate/*Emporia Gazette* (Emporia, KS), September 4, 1971.

50   **study what Reagan had done:** Don Moore to LAC, ISA.

50   **threatened to sue:** "Lawsuits peril new welfare plan," *Chicago Tribune*, August 20, 1973.

50   **override the governor's veto:** "Override welfare veto," *Chicago Tribune*, November 9, 1974.

50   **On June 21, 1974:** "High-salary workers collecting public aid."

50   **"that cheating amounts":** "Slash in funds could cripple fight against welfare cheats: Scott," *Chicago Tribune*, June 22, 1974.

51   **Edelman officially signed on:** Edelman to Moore, September 5, 1974, LAC/ISA.

51   **On their first day:** Edelman to Ronald Zumbrun regarding Dave Todd, September 1974, LAC/ISA.

52   **Taylor's new home:** Classified ad, *Tucson Daily Citizen*, September 30, 1974.

52   **1974 Chevrolet Impala station wagon:** Prosecutor's statement, March 17, 1977, *Illinois v. Linda Taylor.*

52   **She carried Illinois driver's licenses:** List of documents seized in Arizona, FBI/FOIA.

52   **One identified her as:** "Flimflam: Welfare schemer's frauds may top $1 million," *Detroit News*, February 9, 1975.

52   **Joe Fick:** Supplementary complaint report, MSP/FOIA.

52   **A photo published:** "Suspect held here in Chicago fraud," October 11, 1974.

53   **The cops impounded:** List of documents seized in Arizona, FBI/FOIA.

53   **"avalanches of abundance":** Text of the ad can be seen in "Is it true? This Amazing PSYCHIC PERCEPTOR brings you Wealth, Love and Power Beyond Belief!," *Florence Times—Tri-Cities Daily* (Florence, AL), August 1, 1976.

53   **Taylor's daughter, Sandra:** "Fraud suspect going to Chicago," *Tucson Daily Citizen*, October 12, 1974.

53   **placed her under arrest for grand theft:** Arrest report, October 12, 1974, CPD/FOIA.

54   **In his October 12 piece:** "'Welfare queen' jailed in Tucson," *Chicago Tribune*.

54   **"I'm already a drone bee":** "'Get Serious, Baby! I'm Not Slaving So Kids Can Make The Scene!,'" November 4, 1967.

54   **"Mary Black":** "Rehabilitation Could Help in Some Welfare Cases," July 25, 1969.

55   **"woman who's been dubbed":** "To Illinois Welfare Queen Everyone Is Stupid," Gannett/*El Paso Times*, December 4, 1974.

55   **"turns from black to Latin":** "Welfare scandal could be nation's biggest: probers," UPI/*Daily Herald*, November 27, 1974.

55   **Peter Hannaford filed that clip away:** Peter Hannaford papers, Hoover Institution archives, box twelve, folder twelve.

56   **On October 24, 1974:** LAC progress report, November 1974, LAC/ISA.

56   **Paris, France:** Using the name Sandra Harbaugh, Brownlee also listed her place of birth as Paris, France, on her 1972 marriage application. Record via FBI/FOIA.

Notes

56   **she'd cashed welfare checks:** Interview with Brownlee, October 29, 1974, FBI/FOIA.

56   **"She is not sure of her origin":** Interview with Brownlee, December 17, 1974, FBI/FOIA.

57   **Johnnie Harbaugh had been arrested:** John A. Wakefield criminal history, CPD/FOIA.

58   **On October 24:** LAC progress report, November 1974, LAC/ISA.

58   **In 1975, the Tribune reported:** "Police surrender secret files on four," April 10, 1975.

58   **"Two members of the legislative committee":** George Bliss and Charles Mount, "State employes helped 'Welfare Queen'—legislator," *Chicago Tribune,* October 26, 1974.

59   **$4.3 million...largest cash heist:** "Two vault suspects seized in W. Indies," *Chicago Tribune,* October 31, 1974.

59   **had been tied up with the vault break-in:** LAC progress report, November 1974, LAC/ISA.

59   **Bliss had called the legislative committee:** Ibid.

60   **Kenneth Gillis encouraged:** LAC progress report, November 1974, LAC/ISA.

60   **Aaron Bennett was decidedly uncrushed:** "Flimflam: welfare schemer's frauds may top $1 million."

60   **Sherwin testified about:** November 1974, *Illinois v. Linda Taylor.*

61   **"may be only a fraction":** "Jury indicts 'Welfare Queen,'" November 14, 1974.

61   **The legislative committee's after-action report:** LAC progress report, November 1974, LAC/ISA.

CHAPTER 5

Author interviews with John Parks, John Paul Parks, Patricia
Bridgetta Parks, Kenneth Gillis, James Piper, Bridget Hutchen.

63   **"Linda Mallexo":** "Welfare Queen's role—Was it voodoo spell?," *Chicago Tribune,* June 29, 1975.

63   **Parks would be dead:** Ibid.

64   **"My friend, Linda":** Last will and testament of Patricia Parks, December 11, 1974, CCCC Probate Division.

64   **She "is without a doubt":** "More agencies join 'welfare queen' quiz," *Chicago Tribune,* December 1, 1974.

64   **"like some science fiction story":** "Welfare and Pension Swindle Laid to Woman of Many Aliases," *New York Times,* December 15, 1974.

Notes

65   **"most of the investigators' stories":** "'Welfare queen' denies fraud rap," UPI/*Baltimore Afro-American*, December 10, 1974.

65   **in a private letter:** Edelman to *Chicago Tribune* editor Clayton Kirkpatrick, February 17, 1976, LAC/ISA.

65   **He repeatedly asked:** Trainor to Moore, February 5, 1975, LAC/ISA.

65   **In January 1975:** Trainor to Moore, January 9, 1975, LAC/ISA.

65   **"still receiving inquiries":** Caauwe and Pennix to Moore, January 1975, LAC/ISA.

66   **declared in a memo:** Chicago office memo, January 21, 1975, FBI/FOIA.

66   **On November 12 and 13, 1974:** Chicago office memo, December 19, 1974, FBI/FOIA.

66   **On a handwriting assessment form:** FBI/FOIA.

67   **disguised her true handwriting:** Chicago office memo, December 19, 1974, FBI/FOIA.

68   **"tired of my sick butt":** Testimony of Patricia Parks, April 29, 1974, *Patricia Parks v. John Parks*, CCCC.

68   **"physically ill and in a weakened condition":** Petition, February 5, 1975, *Patricia Parks v. John Parks*.

69   **Five months earlier:** Last will and testament of Patricia Parks, December 11, 1974, CCCC Probate Division.

69   **Now she updated that will:** Codicil to Parks's last will and testament, May 29, 1975, CCCC Probate Division.

69   **"for the consideration of one dollars":** Quitclaim deed, April 30, 1975, Cook County Recorder of Deeds.

69   **Relationship: "friend":** Coroner's certificate of death, Patricia Parks, June 15, 1975, CCCO.

70   **ex-husband would get custody:** Order, July 21, 1975, *Patricia Parks v. John Parks*.

71   **"lingerie and various personal items":** Petition, February 5, 1975, *Patricia Parks v. John Parks*.

71   **Patricia's attorney also said:** Claim against the estate, March 12, 1976, *In the Matter of the Estate of Patricia Parks AKA Patricia M. Parks, Deceased*, CCCC Probate Division.

71   **had changed the locks:** "'Squatter' claims her house: 'Welfare Queen' is locked out," June 22, 1975.

71   **sporty striped twinset:** Photo in *Chicago Tribune*, June 23, 1975.

71   **headed out to South Phillips Avenue:** "Welfare Queen brings help, but still can't get house," *Chicago Tribune*, June 23, 1975.

72   **"learned that Mrs. Parks reportedly":** "Probe death of Welfare Queen's friend," June 26, 1975.

Notes

72 **"an excessive amount of medical drugs":** "Welfare Queen's role—Was it voodoo spell?"

72 **"housekeeper, nurse, and companion":** "Probe Patricia Parks death," June 28, 1975.

73 **"a paid housekeeper for Mrs. Parks":** "Welfare Queen's role—Was it voodoo spell?"

73 **was her sister:** "'Welfare Queen' raps cops," February 5, 1975.

73 **"get out of the city":** "Run Them Out of Town," July 16, 1966.

73 **The *Defender*'s reply:** "An Editorial: Let's Face Facts," July 18, 1966, cited in Michaeli, *The Defender*, p. 418.

73 **daily circulation of twenty-five thousand…751,000:** "Chicago Defender now a newspaper historical site," UPI/*Daily Dispatch* (Moline, IL), May 6, 1975; "Once stodgy Chicago Tribune takes on new (out)look," Lindsay-Schaub/*Southern Illinoisan* (Carbondale, IL), November 14, 1976.

74 **"evidently was the subject of voodoo sessions":** "Welfare Queen's role—Was it voodoo spell?"

74 **"I don't believe in that mess!":** "'Welfare queen': Denies voodoo in death," June 30, 1975.

76 **Patricia Parks, negro female:** Cook County state's attorney's office to FBI, July 9, 1975, FBI/FOIA.

77 **Between 1968 and 1975:** Investigation report, November 1974, FBI/FOIA.

77 **"has a mental age of 10":** Ibid.

77 **George Bliss had been assigned:** "The reporter who taught how to give," *Chicago Tribune*, September 13, 1978.

77 **The FBI learned:** Interview with a teacher at Our Lady of the Angels School, March 1975, FBI/FOIA.

77 **She'd also gotten married in 1972:** Chicago office memo, July 26, 1976, FBI/FOIA.

77 **received a curt reply:** FBI to SAC, Chicago, July 18, 1975, FBI/FOIA.

CHAPTER 6

Author interviews with Jim Lake, John Sears, Peter Hannaford, Bill Mullen, Lou Cannon, Isaiah "Skip" Gant, Jim Piper, Steven Lubet, Sam Adam, Sr., Thomas Geraghty, Arnette Hubbard.

79 **In a radio commentary:** *Reagan in His Own Hand*, pp. 255–256.

79 **"preaching the gospel of free enterprise":** *CBS Evening News with Walter Cronkite,* January 6, 1975.

80 **"The astonishing thing is":** "Reagan's Theatrical Politics," November 19, 1975.

80 **"citizens' press conferences":** Perlstein, *The Invisible Bridge*, pp. 595–596.

Notes

80   **"throw old people in the snow":** Bo Callaway quoted in ibid., p. 596; and "Reagan Ford's big asset in NH," *Boston Globe,* January 10, 1976.

80   **"I guess I made a mistake":** Ibid., p. 596.

80   **federal taxes on alcohol:** "Reagan Soft-Pedals Revenue By Tax In Taxless NH," AP/*Biddeford-Saco Journal* (Biddeford, ME), January 16, 1976.

80   **"move elsewhere":** "Reagan Says Plan Could Harm Needy," *New York Times,* January 17, 1976.

81   **"No one knows":** "Reagan Soft-Pedals Revenue By Tax In Taxless NH."

81   **He also bunked there in April 1967:** Robert Lipsyte, "Clay Puts His Affairs in Order As Day of Decision Approaches," *New York Times,* April 27, 1967.

81   **an updated, fifty-four-count indictment:** *Illinois v. Linda Taylor.*

82   **Taylor testified:** *Estate of Patricia Parks.*

83   **"two men came in carrying guns":** "Miss Taylor Reports Robbery," *Chicago Tribune,* October 24, 1975.

83   **"blow his brains out":** "'Welfare queen' robbed," October 25, 1975.

83   **tried and failed to lay claim to the estate:** "Policy chief's estate case an 11-year game," February 20, 1975.

84   **1964 kidnapping:** "Probe aid queen tie to kidnapping," *Chicago Tribune,* March 21, 1975.

84   **she may have purchased children:** "Hint aid queen, baby-buying tie," *Chicago Tribune,* March 24, 1975.

84   **faking his own death:** "Ex-husband bilked her, 'welfare queen' charges," May 12, 1975.

84   **The AP reported:** "'Welfare Queen' reindicted on 54 counts of fraud," AP/*Dixon Evening Telegraph* (Dixon, IL), September 18, 1975.

84   **"was accused of covering up":** "Walker hid aid fraud: legislator," *Chicago Tribune,* January 10, 1975.

84   **yet another Pulitzer Prize:** "The hard work behind the Pulitzer," *Chicago Tribune,* May 4, 1976.

85   **At a $5-a-plate luncheon:** "Reagan Visits Cities In NC," AP/*Rocky Mountain Telegram,* January 27, 1976.

85   **to repay $1,511:** Audio recording, Hoover Institution archives.

86   **"might be a dangerous subject":** Dallek, *The Right Moment,* pp. 197–198.

87   **the term's vagueness:** Gilens, *Why Americans Hate Welfare,* p. 13; "The Outsize Hold of the Word 'Welfare' on the Public Imagination," *New York Times,* August 6, 2018.

87   **"I don't like to see my taxes":** "Goldwater, Rocky Clash on Welfare," *Des Moines Register,* July 20, 1961.

87   **"the welfare system, as we know it":** "Welfare Cheating: Address of Hon. Russell B. Long, Chairman, Committee on Finance and Supporting Materials," *Congressional Record,* September 30, 1972.

Notes

87   **a group of women in Prince George's County:** "Welfare Cheating Ring Uncovered," December 12, 1971.

87   **Department of Health, Education, and Welfare reported:** U.S. Senate, "Fraud, Abuse, Waste, and Mismanagement."

88   **A 1973 HEW survey:** "Payment Errors Found," *Washington Post*, December 21, 1973.

88   **"honest mistakes":** Ibid.

88   **the basic grant:** "State Legislator Proposes Welfare Payment Increase," AP/*Freeport Journal-Standard* (Freeport, IL), June 7, 1974.

88   **just more than $3,800:** "Public aid budget keeps going up and up...," Lindsay-Schaub/*Southern Illinoisan* (Carbondale, IL), March 11, 1975.

88   **A June 1976 survey:** "Majority ambivalent on welfare," *Chicago Tribune*, June 10, 1976.

88   **"the American way of life":** "The year was...1976," *Public Perspective*, May/June 2000.

89   **just more than 40 percent:** Gilens, *Why Americans Hate Welfare*, p. 106.

89   **In 1964, just 27 percent:** Ibid., p. 120.

89   **"more constructive or productive citizens":** Joseph Mitchell at the Citizens' Council Forum, quoted in Rolph, "Courting Conservatism."

90   **"I would do everything":** "Reagan would end busing," *Portsmouth Herald* (Portsmouth, NH), January 29, 1976.

90   **"that we had a racial problem":** Perlstein, *The Invisible Bridge*, p. 554.

90   **"the dumbest thing":** "'Closest Friend' Was Reagan Teammate," *Washington Post*, January 16, 1986.

90   **"strapping young buck":** "Reagan is Picking His Florida Spots," February 5, 1976.

91   **"give back to the people":** "A Reporter in Washington, DC," *New Yorker*, May 24, 1976.

91   **the Cook County judge decreed:** "Judge rules Linda can be called names—just 4," *Chicago Tribune*, January 27, 1976.

92   **asserting that five different judges:** Petitions for substitution of judge, December 13, 1974, *Illinois v. Linda Taylor*.

92   **"the Defendant does not know":** Motion to dismiss each count of each indictment, February 18, 1975, *Illinois v. Linda Taylor*.

92   **"so staggering in its wastefulness":** People's answer to defendant's pretrial motion, December 18, 1975, *Illinois v. Linda Taylor*.

92   **"bore the rhythm and intensity":** "The Alfano Murder Trial: Analyzing the System," January 24, 1971.

92   **a habit of swiping sugar:** "The Defiant One," *Chicago*, July 1999, p. 50.

93   **When Pincham was in high school:** Travis, *Racism*, pp. 82–83.

Notes

93 **stepped away from his firm briefly:** Pincham, interviewed by Adele Hodge, August 13, 2002, the HistoryMakers digital archive.

93 **"ye have done it unto me":** "The Alfano Murder Trial: Analyzing the System," *Chicago Tribune,* January 24, 1971.

93 **Jackson demanded:** "Rev. Jackson Calls for Hanrahan's Resignation, Replacement by Black," *Chicago Tribune,* August 27, 1971.

94 **His firm rented space:** "Black Businessmen Produce Jobs," *Chicago Defender,* October 14, 1968.

94 **"When you cut through everything":** "Judge rules Linda can be called names—just 4," January 27, 1976.

95 **"not the rich nor the famous":** "Profiles—Black Advocates in the Forefront of Trial Litigation."

95 **published a front-page report:** "Reagan Stories Don't Check Out."

96 **"an excellent example of reportorial journalism":** Melvin Mencher quoted in "Truth on the campaign trail," *Washington Star,* March 1, 1976.

96 **"In recent weeks, you've been":** ABC News, raw footage.

97 **the *New York Times* reprinted:** February 15, 1976.

98 **"latest con job":** "The Biggest Welfare Cheat of All," February 18, 1976.

98 **"stories are peopled":** "Reagan's Half-Truths," June 12, 1976.

98 **on the order of $40,000:** James Trainor to Don Moore, January 1975, ISA.

98 **"may have understated the facts":** "*Star* Lays Egg With Reagan Story," February 14, 1976.

CHAPTER 7

Author interviews with Jack Sherwin, Jim Piper, Johnnie Harbaugh,
Chuck Neubauer, James Strong, Bill Bliss, Bill Recktenwald, J.
Terrence Brunner, Bill Mullen, Ron Cooper.

101 **When Linda Taylor walked out:** NBC News, raw footage.

101 **on February 25, 1976:** George Bliss, "'Welfare Queen' charged with stealing furnishings," *Chicago Tribune,* February 26, 1976.

101 **a "fishing expedition":** Defendant's petition to suppress evidence, May 15, 1975, *Illinois v. Linda Taylor.*

102 **The day before:** Arrest report, continuation of narrative, February 24, 1976, *People of the State of Illinois v. Linda Taylor* (henceforth *Linda Taylor* burglary case), CCCC.

103 **he decided to wait:** Arrest report, continuation of narrative, February 27, 1976, *Linda Taylor* burglary case.

103 **assembled at 7450 South Normal:** "'Welfare Queen' charged with stealing furnishings."

Notes

103   **didn't appear to have anywhere to sleep:** Arrest report, continuation of narrative, February 27, 1976, *Linda Taylor* burglary case.

103   **"No matter how much money":** Sherwin account in arrest report, continuation of narrative, March 5, 1976, *Linda Taylor* burglary case.

104   **There was a bullet:** George Bliss and Lee Strobel, " 'Welfare Queen's' bond to remain at $50,000," *Chicago Tribune*, February 27, 1976.

104   **cadre of welfare cheaters:** "Panel probes welfare cheating charges," *Chicago Tribune*, September 30, 1974.

104   **"sought to publicize":** "Legislative Advisory Committee On Public Aid," *South Suburban Journal* (Harvey, IL), September 18, 1975.

104   **instructed the city's cops:** Superintendent James M. Rochford, notice on how to refer suspected fraud cases, January 14, 1975, ISA; George Bliss, "War on aid cheats saves $500,000 in 9 months," *Chicago Tribune*, September 22, 1975.

104   **from $100,000 to $188,000:** "Legislative Advisory Committee on Public Assistance, Budget for FY 1975," ISA; "Legislative Advisory Committee On Public Aid."

104   **saved taxpayers more than $1 million:** "Welfare: Finding Society's Cheaters," *Star-Tribune* (Harvey, IL), April 4, 1976.

104   **"the greater crimes are being committed":** Moore speech transcript, ISA.

105   **Moore's proposal to set up:** Moore on Senate Bill 1312, 79th Illinois General Assembly, May 20, 1975, session transcript, ILGA online archive.

105   **succeed in lobbying:** "Legislative Advisory Committee On Public Aid."

105   **"finder's fee" of up to $2,500:** "Senate Bill 1942 (Berning)," IDPA interoffice memos, May and June 1976, ISA; "Welfare cheat 'bounty bill' faces oblivion," *Chicago Daily News*, June 17, 1976.

105   **"too many people on welfare":** "Results of public opinion survey 'Viewpoint': December 1975–January 1976," state senator Thomas H. Miller to Don Moore, February 10, 1976, ISA.

105   **These volunteer guardians:** IDPA director's administrative files, 1962 to June 1989, ISA.

106   **launching a 24-hour, toll-free welfare fraud hotline:** IDPA news release, May 22, 1975, ISA.

106   **At 9:07 a.m. on August 14, 1975:** IDPA director's administrative files, 1975, ISA.

107   **more than five thousand tips:** Charles Conner to Robert Wessel, June 23, 1976, IDPA/ISA.

107   **Two-thirds of those callers:** "Tipsters on hotline aid war on welfare cheaters," *Chicago Tribune*, May 20, 1976.

107   **$25,135 a year to maintain:** "The Hot Line," fact sheet, IDPA director's administrative files, 1976, ISA.

Notes

107   **"been too successful"**: James Bailey quoted in "Tipsters on hotline aid war on welfare cheaters."

107   **"Big Brother's helper"**: "Public Aid's wrong number," October 28, 1975.

107   **"dangerous and un-American"**: October 28, 1975, IDPA/ISA.

108   **The "CHIGO PD" placard**: Mug shot, February 26, 1976, CPD/FOIA.

108   **A month before, she'd married:** Marriage license, January 22, 1976, VA/FOIA.

109   **Arthur Krueger:** Written statement, February 25, 1976, *Linda Taylor* burglary case.

109   **"split certain expenses"**: Brame statement in burglary police report, February 26, 1976, *Linda Taylor* burglary case.

109   **"feared that she would have trouble"**: Officer Raymond Howe, supplementary report, February 26, 1976, *Linda Taylor* burglary case.

109   **Brame's neighbors had seen:** Arrest report, continuation of narrative, February 26, 1976, *Linda Taylor* burglary case.

109   **at 1:30 a.m. on February 26:** Ibid.

110   **"deposition of Patricia M. Parks"**: Property inventory forms, February 27, 1976, *Linda Taylor* burglary case.

110   **"exorbitant, prohibitive, punitive"**: Defendant's bail reduction motion, April 12, 1976, *Linda Taylor* burglary case.

111   **"to have some respect for the court"**: "Dander up, bond down, for 'Queen,'" April 15, 1976, *Chicago Tribune.*

111   **"a champion of deception and deceit"**: Ibid.

111   **reducing his client's bail to $7,500:** Bail bond slip and cash deposit form, April 15, 1976, *Linda Taylor* burglary case.

111   **left the court no forwarding address:** Motion to revoke bond, June 7, 1976, *Linda Taylor* burglary case.

111   **the campaign's chartered plane:** Peter Hannaford interview, Ronald Reagan Oral History Project.

111   **Nancy Reagan urged:** Perlstein, *The Invisible Bridge,* p. 637.

112   **"collapse of the American will"**: Witcover, *Marathon,* p. 402.

112   **"We bought it"**: *The Panama Deception,* dir. Barbara Trent, 1992.

112   **"gross factual errors"**: Perlstein, *The Invisible Bridge,* p. 633.

112   **"The Panama Canal issue"**: Witcover, *Marathon,* p. 402.

112   **"Miss Sally Jones sitting at home"**: "Arithmetic plaguing Reagan in Ford fight," *New York Times,* March 25, 1976.

112   **Reagan reportedly demanded:** Witcover, *Marathon,* p. 411.

113   **"As much as I hate to admit it"**: Ibid., p. 419.

113   **"Welfare is destroying human beings"**: "Audio Recently Found of Ronald Reagan's Visit to Chattanooga in 1976," the *Chattanoogan* online, September 1, 2014.

Notes

113   **"What do you propose to do":** ABC News, raw footage.

113   **by wooing delegates:** Witcover, *Marathon*, pp. 440–441.

114   **"we've nominated the wrong man":** Shirley, *Reagan's Revolution*, p. xxiii.

114   **by drinking champagne:** "Reagan resumes career as radio commentator," AP/*South Mississippi Sun*, September 2, 1976.

114   **on airplanes and car rides:** *Reagan in His Own Hand*, p. xvi.

115   **"the 'welfare queen,' as she's now called":** Hoover Institution archives.

116   **"the abuses in the program":** "Interview with Managing Editors on Domestic Issues," December 3, 1981, American Presidency Project.

116   **"The new *Human Events* readership study":** advertisement, p. 17.

117   **a piece on police brutality:** "Police brutality in Chicago: Bad apples on the beat," February 9, 1974.

118   **it landed on the front page:** George Bliss and Chuck Neubauer, "Tax breaks for Daley pals told," *Chicago Tribune*, September 14, 1976.

118   **On the morning of July 8, 1976:** Arrest report, CPD/FOIA.

118   **grew by 151 percent:** U.S. Census Bureau data, cited in "Study finds 1 in 5 Chicagoans is poor; up 24% since 1970," *Chicago Tribune*, January 9, 1983.

118   **Sherman Ray's unemployment checks:** Chicago office memo, November 23, 1976, FBI/FOIA.

119   **April 1, then to May 6:** Memorandum of orders, *Illinois v. Linda Taylor*.

119   **twenty-two criminal judges:** "County justice system to be unveiled on local TV," *Chicago Defender*, December 20, 1975.

119   **350 pending cases:** "Continuances delay justice: 25 in County Jail wait years for trial," July 6, 1976.

119   **A mere thirty defense attorneys:** "Reformers move on court delays," *Chicago Tribune*, September 1, 1974.

119   **"Right after an incident":** "Criminal Courts Trials Mired in Endless Delays," May 19, 1971.

119   **"can't try every criminal case":** "Continuances try a judge's patience," November 22, 1976.

120   **"welfare abuse cannot be ignored":** "Walker announces task force to probe state welfare abuses," *Dixon Evening Telegraph* (Dixon, IL), September 10, 1974.

120   **even, hypothetically, $1 million:** "$1 million welfare fraud only misdemeanor— Rice," *Metro-East Journal* (East Saint Louis, IL), February 26, 1976.

120   **In November 1976, Piper:** Chicago office memo, November 17, 1976, FBI/FOIA.

120   **$3,250 . . . and $3,757.40:** Chicago office memo, July 26, 1976, FBI/FOIA.

121   **"Any federal prosecution would":** Ibid.

121   **"blew this matter way out of proportion":** Chicago office memo, January 26, 1977, FBI/FOIA.

Notes

121   **Illinois Supreme Court ruled:** *People of the State of Illinois v. Louise Brooks,* December 3, 1976.

121   **for up to twenty years:** "Chicago 'welfare queen' may get up to 20 years," *Journal and Courier* (Lafayette, IN), March 18, 1977.

121   **"on the docket too long":** "Scolds 'welfare queen's' lawyer," *Chicago Defender,* February 23, 1977.

CHAPTER 8

Author interviews with Isaiah "Skip" Gant, Jim Piper, Kenneth
Gillis, Jack Sherwin, Johnnie Harbaugh, David Grimes, Etta
Tomczyk, Bridget Hutchen, Robert Sklodowski, Bernard Judge.

123   **The air-conditioning didn't work:** "$92 million court repairs aimed at improving justice," *Chicago Tribune,* February 10, 1975.

124   **"trying a criminal case":** "Profiles—Black Advocates in the Forefront of Trial Litigation."

124   **When a gust of wind:** UPI Telephoto image in "More agencies join 'welfare queen' quiz," *Chicago Tribune,* December 1, 1974.

124   **A few months later, Taylor dressed:** CBS News, raw footage, c. February 1975.

124   **"brightly colored mod outfits":** "Welfare Queen Sentenced," AP/*Times and Democrat* (Orangeburg, SC), May 13, 1977.

125   **One year and ten continuances:** Memorandum of orders, *Illinois v. Linda Taylor.*

125   **her name was Linda Wakefield:** Taylor examination, February 24, 1977, *Illinois v. Linda Taylor.*

127   **"used eight of their ten":** Nathaniel Clay, "God and criminal justice," March 22, 1977.

127   **three of them black:** "'Welfare Queen's' trial goes on," March 8, 1977.

128   **"This woman is the fall guy":** "State 'welfare queen' a 'fall guy,' jury told," *Chicago Sun-Times,* March 5, 1977.

128   **Sherwin led off:** "Suspect had 4 bogus welfare ID cards, cop testifies," *Chicago Sun-Times,* March 8, 1977.

128   **"Is this your card?...not your card?":** Summary by Sternik in closing statement, March 17, 1977, *Illinois v. Linda Taylor.*

128   **"for a while...but not anymore":** "'Welfare Queen's' trial goes on."

129   **"During last year's race":** March 7, 1977, broadcast.

129   **a 230-word news brief:** "'Welfare queen' aliases cited by witness at trial."

129   **a front-pager on a Cook County court case:** "Father cleared of death plot on son," March 12, 1977.

Notes

131   **food vouchers…checks totaling $419.33:** Slimkowski and Memra Taylor trial testimonies, March 8 and 9, 1977, *Illinois v. Linda Taylor;* check images, FBI/FOIA.

131   **the intake worker got suspicious:** Etta Tomczyk testimony, grand jury indictment, February 6, 1975; and summary of Tomczyk's testimony by Sternik in closing statement, March 17, 1977, *Illinois v. Linda Taylor.*

132   **"suffered a setback":** "2 can't identify 'welfare queen,'" March 10, 1977.

132   **"key witness":** Chicago office memo, January 26, 1977, FBI/FOIA.

133   **on thirteen of the twenty-three checks:** Charles Mount, "'Welfare queen,' checks linked by writing expert," *Chicago Tribune,* March 12, 1977.

133   **"So the last shall come first":** Gant, closing statement, March 17, 1977, *Illinois v. Linda Taylor.*

134   **"You may feel that":** Ibid.; Clay, "God and criminal justice."

135   **"just a parasite":** Piper, closing statement, March 17, 1977, *Illinois v. Linda Taylor.*

135   **"sat stoically through":** "Welfare Queen guilty in fraud," AP/*San Bernardino County Sun,* March 18, 1977.

135   **"With her face pinched and drawn":** "Welfare Queen guilty," March 19, 1977.

135   **"You seriously offer that":** Court transcript, March 17, 1977, *Illinois v. Linda Taylor.*

136   **Operation Greylord…judges' chambers:** "BFI 'sting' hits lawyers, judges," *Chicago Tribune,* August 6, 1983; "Greylord's roots deep, intricate," *Chicago Tribune,* December 18, 1983.

136   **"I love people that take dough":** "Judge Liked 'People Who Take Dough,' Greylord File Shows," *Chicago Tribune,* April 27, 1985.

136   **Jones had insisted:** "Reveal death threats to Judge Mark Jones," *Chicago Defender,* October 29, 1975.

136   **"We, the jury, find the defendant":** Court transcript, March 17, 1977, *Illinois v. Linda Taylor.*

137   **"Mr. Piper had them put":** Ibid.

138   **The *Tribune* published:** Charles Mount, "'Welfare queen' found guilty in aid fraud case," March 18, 1977.

138   **"Miss Taylor showed no emotion":** "'Welfare Queen' convicted," March 18, 1977.

138   **"nervous and gloom-stricken":** Clay, "God and criminal justice."

138   **"Although it was obvious":** Ibid.

138   **When Taylor emerged:** CBS News, raw footage, March 17, 1977.

Notes

CHAPTER 9

Author interviews with Bill Bliss, Larry Bliss, William Crawford,
Jerry Crimmins, William Gaines, Bernard Judge, Bill Mullen,
Chuck Neubauer, Bill Recktenwald, James Strong, Jim Piper, Isaiah
"Skip" Gant, Phillip Wertz, Ward Hamlin Jr., Robert Sklodowski,
Jeffrey Simon, Bernard Carey.

141   **an enormous Bible:** "Welfare Queen Jailed," AP/*Mt. Vernon Register–News,*
March 26, 1977.

141   **"Since you came and searched my house":** "Welfare queen gives court
wrong address, goes to jail," *Chicago Tribune,* March 26, 1977.

141   **"she attended church meetings":** "Welfare Queen Jailed."

141   **"Judge, can I say something?":** Quoted in "Welfare queen gives court wrong
address, goes to jail."

142   **"She was so greedy she couldn't stop":** Court transcript, March 17, 1977,
Illinois v. Linda Taylor.

142   **"cold, calculated plan":** Quoted in "Illinois 'Welfare Queen' Sentenced," *Chicago Daily News/Waukesha Daily Freeman* (Waukesha, WI), May 13, 1977.

142   **"If there is anybody":** Ibid.

142   **Gant also cited:** Charles Mount, "Welfare queen gets 2-6 years in jail," *Chicago Tribune,* May 13, 1977.

142   **"Black schoolchildren in Chicago":** Quoted in "Illinois 'Welfare Queen' Sentenced."

142   **"telling me what to do":** "Welfare Queen Gets 2- to 6-Year Term," AP/*Decatur Herald,* May 13, 1977.

143   **For each of those counts:** Certified statement of conviction, *Illinois v. Linda Taylor.*

143   **"quietly replied 'No'":** "Welfare Queen gets 3 year jail term," May 14, 1977.

143   *Sun-Times* **added:** "'Welfare Queen' Linda Taylor gets two prison terms,"
May 13, 1977.

143   **"I'm concerned about":** "Mental Test for 'Queen' of Welfare," AP/*Mt.
Vernon Register–News,* April 1, 1977.

143   **"dishonesty, fraud":** Report and recommendation of the review board,
March 14, 1988, *In the Matter of William Starke,* Illinois Attorney Registration
and Disciplinary Commission.

144   **"If she was convicted":** "Convicted 'welfare queen' to undergo mental
exam," April 1, 1977.

144   **"was incapable of knowing":** Petition for behavioral clinic examination,
March 27, 1978, *Linda Taylor* burglary case.

144   **filed a notice of appeal:** May 12, 1977, *Illinois v. Linda Taylor.*

Notes

145   **"a bank telling a bank robber":** "$6 million aid quiz called flop," March 20, 1977.

145   **The four-part series:** "How ruses lure victims to child pornographers," *Chicago Tribune*, May 21, 1977.

145   **led to U.S. Senate hearings and the passage:** U.S. Senate, "Protection of Children Against Sexual Exploitation," *Hearings before the Subcommittee to Investigate Juvenile Delinquency*, Chicago, May 27, 1977; "Pleading the First," *Washington City Paper*, August 7, 1988.

145   **"We miss you around here":** Kirkpatrick to George Bliss, August 9, 1977, via Bliss family archive.

147   **"king of the family":** "Granddad of 57 Is Honored at Family Party," *Chicago Tribune*, December 18, 1966.

147   **around five thirty the next morning:** Case report, September 11, 1978, Cook County Medical Examiner's Office/FOIA.

147   **6:42 a.m. on September 11:** Pathological report and protocol, September 11, 1978, Cook County Medical Examiner's Office/FOIA.

147   **Bliss's friend John L. Sullivan:** Incident report, September 11, 1978, Oak Lawn Police Department/FOIA.

148   **the night of September 14, 1978:** Therese Bliss death certificate, CCCO.

148   **A toxicological analysis:** Toxicologist's report, September 13, 1978, Cook County Medical Examiner's Office/FOIA.

148   **It had been Bliss:** "The reporter who taught how to give," September 13, 1978.

148   **the paper's front-page obituary:** "Pulitzer Prize winner George Bliss dead," September 12, 1978.

149   **"hope that his death":** "George Bliss," September 12, 1978.

149   **"people like Bliss need":** "The lesson of Bliss' death," September 15, 1978.

149   **"really not enough":** Ward Hamlin Jr. quoted in "Welfare Queen's Sentence Draws Van Buren Echo," *Herald-Palladium* (Benton Harbor, MI), May 13, 1977.

150   **"on very similar charges":** Chicago office memo, May 27, 1977, FBI/FOIA.

150   **On June 20, 1977:** Conviction information, *People of the State of Illinois v. Sandra Brownlee*, CCCC.

150   **at least one newspaper:** "State welfare princess, mate get probation," AP/*Southern Illinoisan* (Carbondale, IL), June 21, 1977.

150   **to claw back $7,000:** "Welfare queen becomes case study," *Chicago Tribune*, October 29, 1977.

150   **Brownlee told her probation officer:** Restitution ledger, June 29, 1977, *Illinois v. Sandra Brownlee*.

150   **Piper affirmed:** "Illinois Welfare Queen out on bond, seeks aid," November 17, 1977.

150   **On November 18, 1977:** Memorandum of orders, November 18, 1977, *Linda*

Taylor burglary case; "'Welfare queen' jailed for missing court dates," *Chicago Tribune*, November 19, 1977.

151 **In January 1978:** Motion to withdraw as defendant's attorney, January 13, 1978, *Linda Taylor* burglary case.

151 **"had absolutely no cooperation":** John J. Wallace, motion to withdraw, February 24, 1978, *Linda Taylor* burglary case.

151 **That same month:** Memorandum of orders, February 3, 1978, *Illinois v. Linda Taylor*.

151 **"has been unable to substantiate":** Nicholas C. Avgerin, motion in the nature of discovery, March 27, 1978, *Linda Taylor* burglary case.

151 **petition was denied:** "'Welfare queen' given 5 1/2 years for burglary," *Chicago Tribune*, March 28, 1978.

151 **she pleaded guilty:** Change of plea, report of court proceedings, *Linda Taylor* burglary case.

151 **Sklodowski sentenced Taylor:** "'Welfare queen' given 5 1/2 years for burglary."

152 **amnesty to rule breakers:** "29 Agree To Return Welfare," *St. Louis Post-Dispatch*, January 11, 1976.

152 **"I think the welfare queen":** "Welfare cheats find 'easy street' has a dead end," March 26, 1978.

152 **"We don't prosecute the mother of 10":** "Welfare crooks employ new tactics," November 25, 1978.

152 **"The thing that made":** "Welfare fraud investigated," UPI/*Republican and Herald* (Pottsville, PA), November 22, 1978.

153 **"Chicago's second welfare queen":** "Probers think they have welfare queen successor," *Chicago Tribune*, January 21, 1977.

153 **"She had to write a report":** Quoted in "Criminal justice student indicted for welfare fraud," AP/*Decatur Herald*, April 29, 1978.

153 **"Atrocious things are going on":** "She's Known As Chicago's 'Welfare Queen,'" July 3, 1978.

153 **eight in-home client interviews per day:** "More Welfare Spending, Staff Needed," *Decatur Herald*, August 27, 1975.

154 **directly to currency exchanges:** Kohler-Hausmann, *Getting Tough*, p. 188.

154 **"The benefits were too low":** Ibid., p. 171.

154 **$317 per month:** "Public aid's housecleaning necessary to end abuses," Lindsay-Schaub/*Southern Illinoisan*, June 30, 1978.

154 **870 public assistance cases:** "Disposition of Public Assistance Cases Involving Questions of Fraud" (Report E-7), Department of Health, Education, and Welfare, 1970.

155 **2,638 cases:** Report E-7, Department of Health, Education, and Welfare, 1979.

Notes

155   **George Lindberg...said in 1977:** "Public Aid Fraud Not Overlooked," Lindsay-Schaub/*Decatur Herald*, April 10, 1977.

155   **a minimum of $50,000:** "Millions spent in detecting losses," Lindsay-Schaub/*Decatur Herald*, June 25, 1978.

155   **For every cheat you get:** "Needy, not the greedy should receive welfare," UPI/*Journal Gazette* (Mattoon, Illinois), November 22, 1978.

155   **A survey conducted in Illinois in 1978:** Samuel Skinner, remarks at Secretary's National Conference on Fraud, Abuse, and Error, December 1978, Department of Health, Education, and Welfare/NCJRS.

155   **close to $1 million...closer to $300,000:** "Too often, appearances deceiving in war against fraud," Lindsay-Schaub/*Decatur Herald*, June 29, 1978.

156   **partnered with George Bliss:** George Bliss and William Crawford Jr., "Inside $7 million Medicaid eye care fraud conspiracy," *Chicago Tribune*, June 13, 1976.

156   **twenty welfare fraud cases:** Notice, September 1977, LAC/ISA.

156   **"correct public aid fraud":** "Republicans fail to cut aid appropriation," *Pantagraph* (Bloomington, IL), April 30, 1976.

156   **"I am aware of the fact":** 79th Illinois General Assembly, April 29, 1976, session transcript, ILGA online archive.

157   **"'Welfare cheaters' has become":** "Leaders Meet on Poor," *Chicago Defender*, November 26, 1977.

157   **"I think they're trying":** "Democrats ask new aid fraud panel," *Chicago Tribune*, January 16, 1978.

157   **on February 16, 1978:** Warden Charlotte Sutliff to Sternik, February 28, 1978, *Illinois v. Linda Taylor*.

157   *New Republic* **would publish an essay:** "The President's Mind," April 7, 1982.

CHAPTER 10

Author interviews with Norris Bishton, Leon Wexler, Gerald
Mannix, Robert Lombardo, Arthur Engelland, Gus Redmond.

159   **decade-old refrigerator:** "Gambler Left Over $770,000, But Wouldn't Advance Maid $20," *Chicago Daily News*, February 22, 1964.

159   **the seventy-year-old woman:** Although many news reports indicated that she was sixty-six, Kennedy would later testify that she'd been born in December 1893. Testimony of Rose Kennedy, June 3, 1965, *In the Matter of the Estate of Lawrence Wakefield*, (henceforth *Wakefield* estate), CCCC Probate Division.

159   **travel by private ambulance:** "$500,000 Found in Home; Seize Policy Hoard After Owner Dies," *Chicago Tribune*, February 20, 1964.

159   **He also noticed:** Childs's account in "How Patrolman's Hunch Unveiled Riches," *Chicago Sun-Times*, February 23, 1964.

Notes

160   **At 3 p.m. on that second day:** Robert McDonald testimony, April 5, 1965, *People of the State of Illinois v. Rose Kennedy,* CCCC.

161   **almost fainted:** "$500,000 Found in Home: Seize Policy Hoard."

161   **Kennedy watched...in a small chair:** NEA Telephoto image in *Jacksonville Daily Journal* (Jacksonville, IL), February 23, 1964.

161   **The money filled thirty-two sacks:** "$500,000 Found in Home: Seize Policy Hoard."

162   **"the government would":** "Final Tally of Cache Is $763,223," *Chicago Sun-Times,* February 21, 1964.

162   **He'd died at 8:55 p.m.:** Lawrence Wakefield death certificate, CCCO.

162   **"I loved him and I am sorry":** June Kaufman testimony, April 5, 1965, *Wakefield* estate.

163   **eventually counted:** "The Fight Begins for Policy Hoard," *Chicago Daily News,* February 21, 1964.

163   **$763,223.30:** "Big Crowd at Policy Boss Rites," *Chicago Daily News,* February 25, 1964.

163   **"They just wanted to see":** "Money Man Popular in Death: Chapel Flooded With Calls About Policy Future," February 22, 1964.

163   **None of them brought flowers:** "'Friends' Jam Chapel to View Policy King," *Chicago Tribune,* February 24, 1964.

163   **"an unostentatious man":** "1,100 At Church for Last Rites of Policy Boss," *Chicago Tribune,* February 26, 1964.

165   **A day earlier:** "The Policy Plot Thickens Around $760,000 Trove," April 17, 1964.

166   **"known to a generation":** "Over $250,000 Cache Found by Raiders; Believed Policy Money," February 20, 1964.

166   **$50-million-a-year business:** "Betting on the Numbers—A $50 Million-a-Year Game," February 21, 1964.

166   **"less than half":** "The Players Get a Raw Deal," February 21, 1964.

167   **"all taken from poor Negroes":** X and Haley, *The Autobiography of Malcolm X,* p. 248.

167   **Wakefield had been arrested:** "Hundreds at Rites for 'Shabby' Chi Policy Man Who Left Over $700,000 in Home," ANP/*Pittsburgh Courier,* February 29, 1964.

166   **"risk[ed] their insurance policy":** "Who Will Get Policy Baron's Fortune?"

167   **"Big" Ed Jones:** "The Emperor Jones," *Time,* May 27, 1946.

167   **paid a $100,000 ransom:** "Ted Roe Bares Inside Story of Jones Kidnaping," *Chicago Tribune,* June 23, 1951.

167   **"behind an appearance":** "Count $763,000 in Policy Hoard," February 21, 1964.

167   **"Two men from the crime syndicate":** "Escapes Crime Syndicates; 'Shabby' Policy Man Leaves over $800,000," *Pittsburgh Courier,* February 29, 1964.

Notes

167   **"a penny in the house":** "Count $763,000 in Policy Hoard."

167   **$250,000 ... $7,500:** "Betting on the Numbers—a $50 Million-a-Year Game" and "$750,000! And Policy Hoard Count Goes On," *Chicago Daily News*, February 20, 1964.

168   **"an unattractive token operation":** "Who Will Get Policy Baron's Fortune?"

168   **Kennedy's version of events:** "Housekeeper of Wakefield Weeps, Freed," *Chicago Tribune*, March 25, 1964.

168   **In May, Constance Wakefield:** Petition, May 19, 1964, *Wakefield* estate.

168   **"suffered recurring illness":** Affidavit and motion for continuance, August 4, 1964, *Wakefield* estate.

168   **"she apparently had fainted":** "Alleged Policy King Heir Faints at Hearing," October 14, 1964.

169   **Hospital records:** Norris Bishton testimony on legal costs, December 9, 1964, *Wakefield* estate.

169   **In September, a probate judge:** Order, September 29, 1964, *Wakefield* estate.

169   **receipt for $54.90 ... stud fee of $25:** Deponent's exhibits, *Wakefield* estate.

169   **a brown leather billfold:** *Wakefield* estate.

170   **Jim and Virginia Collins:** Deponent's exhibit, *Wakefield* estate.

170   **The first will:** *Wakefield* estate.

170   **The second will:** Ibid.

171   **hiring the president:** Donald Doud to Norman J. Barry, detailed bill, January 11, 1965, *Wakefield* estate.

172   **Linda Taylor took the stand:** Court transcript, *Wakefield* estate.

172   **That certificate:** Constance Beverly Wakefield delayed record of birth, CCCO.

172   **The petitioner had asked:** Blowitz to Judge Kogut, November 9, 1964, *Wakefield* estate.

174   **Barry then took over:** Court transcript, November 9, 1964, *Wakefield* estate.

CHAPTER 11

Author interviews with Norris Bishton, Leon Wexler, Gerald
Mannix, Johnnie Harbaugh, John Owens, Shelby Tuitavuki, Joan
Shefferd, Betty Hudson, Sarah Mooney Hankey.

177   **"Are you acquainted with":** Hubert Mooney examination, November 9, 1964, *Wakefield* estate.

178   **"If we would feel":** Court transcript, November 9, 1964, *Wakefield* estate.

179   **"Just say her attorney":** "The Fight Begins for Policy Hoard."

179   **"I hope she has a good time":** "Police Raid Ruled Illegal: Blonde Woman Renews Claim on $761,385," April 4, 1964.

180   **series of pencil marks:** Doud to Barry, detailed bill.

180   **"the biggest morass":** Bishton testimony on legal costs, *Wakefield* estate.

180   **Eighty-seven long-distance phone calls:** Ibid.

181   **purchasing his star witness's testimony . . . "strictly a fishing expedition":** Court transcript, November 10, 1964, *Wakefield* estate.

181   **eleven black people:** Data for Cullman precinct, 1930 U.S. population census.

181   **zero people . . . had not changed:** Data for Summit precinct (1930) and Brooksville Division (1960), U.S. population census.

181   **"the only strictly white town":** "Only One Negro," *Tensas Gazette* (Saint Joseph, LA) and *Hinds County Gazette* (Raymond, MS), April 10, 1908.

181   **"not to have to stop at Cullman for any purpose":** "To Try 2 Boys With Murder Attempt In Morgan County, Ala.," *New Journal and Guide* (Norfolk, VA), February 1, 1936.

182   **"You ought to have":** "Ozie Powell and 'killer' sheriff," *Pittsburgh Courier,* February 1, 1936.

182   **After Mooney was excused:** Constance Wakefield examination by Mannix, November 10, 1964, *Wakefield* estate.

183   **On April 25, 1946:** Arrest and booking report, Oakland Police Department, *Wakefield* estate; "Seek contempt ruling in will of Wakefield," *Chicago Tribune,* November 11, 1964.

183   **Two years later:** Arrest and booking report, Oakland Police Department, March 18, 1948; Constance Wakefield examination by Mannix.

183   **When she was fingerprinted:** Constance Wakefield examination by Mannix.

183   **On the afternoon of November 10:** Sergeant Burton J. Buhrke examination, *Wakefield* estate.

184   **"Everything is fictitious":** Court transcript, November 10, 1964, *Wakefield* estate.

184   **Betty Day . . . swore she'd been present:** Day examination, November 9, 1964, *Wakefield* estate.

184   **he'd recently been arrested:** "Charge Doctor in Dope Sale to Juveniles," *Chicago Tribune,* January 5, 1963.

184   **In 1970, though, Sill was arrested again:** "Doctor Charged With Drug Abuse," AP/*Dispatch* (Moline, IL), August 12, 1970.

185   **"a little court deal":** Hubert Mooney examination, November 10, 1964, *Wakefield* estate.

185   **three days later, Lydia Blount:** Examination by Blowitz, November 12, 1964, *Wakefield* estate.

187   **I said, "[Martha] is up here":** Hubert Mooney examination, November 12, 1964, *Wakefield* estate.

187   **135 times:** Blount examination, November 13, 1964, *Wakefield* estate.

188   **rented a car:** Bishton testimony on legal costs, *Wakefield* estate.

Notes

189   **"smart little while":** Sarah Jane Mooney examination, November 13, 1964, *Wakefield* estate.

189   **"Yes, yes, I guess I was":** Ibid.

189   **a photograph taken in 1942:** State of Illinois exhibit, *Wakefield* estate.

189   **It had been twenty-two years:** Thelma Helms examination, November 12, 1964, *Wakefield* estate.

190   **"because of his age":** Court transcript, November 16, 1964, *Wakefield* estate.

190   **"to strike and dismiss":** Mannix to Kogut, court transcript, November 16, 1964.

190   **Rose Kennedy got:** "Woman to Get $431,385 of Policy Hoard," *Chicago Tribune,* September 16, 1965.

190   **ordered to pay roughly $23,000:** Order, December 10, 1964, *Wakefield* estate.

190   **On November 29, 1966:** Reversing and remanding order, Appellate Court of Illinois, First District, *Wakefield* estate.

191   **would fail to show up:** Order, March 7, 1967, *Wakefield* estate.

191   **ran a photo of the "phony heiress":** "Phony heiress of policy king gets 6 months."

192   **ice-skating rink:** "Neighbors' Zest Overflows—Into Ice Rink," *Chicago Tribune,* March 1, 1964.

192   **95 percent white . . . 99 percent black:** Data from 1960 for Lincoln Park and Grand Boulevard in *Encyclopedia of Chicago* online.

192   **Forty-Third and South Calumet:** Changes of address made by Connie Harbaugh compiled by the VA, provided in FBI Chicago office memo, June 25, 1975, FBI/FOIA.

193   **she'd started hearing voices:** Katherine Freiman forensic evaluation of Linda Springer, October 4, 1994, *United States of America v. Linda Springer* (henceforth *USA v. Springer*), Federal Bureau of Prisons/FOIA.

193   **"a Portuguese or something":** Examination, November 10, 1964, *Wakefield* estate.

193   **"she is supposed to be":** Examination, November 13, 1964, *Wakefield* estate.

CHAPTER 12

Author interviews with Joan Shefferd, Irene Greer Chambers, Betty Hudson, Sarah Mooney Hankey, Grady Mooney, Ed Stacy, Norris Bishton.

195   **a rainstorm on a frigid winter day:** Thelma Helms examination, November 12, 1964, *Wakefield* estate.

195   **Marvin White, wasn't around:** Sarah Jane Mooney examination, November 13, 1964, *Wakefield* estate.

Notes

196   **arrested twice for vagrancy:** Register of prisoners committed to county jail, Marshall County, Alabama archives.

196   **"any person who is":** *Laws of the Various States Relating to Vagrancy,* p. 9.

196   **a handwritten note:** Complainant exhibits, *Marvin White v. Lyde White,* circuit court of Marshall County, Marshall County, Alabama archives.

196   **Lydia was fourteen:** Birth date (April 12, 1908) per Lydia Blount obituary in *Searcy Daily Citizen,* August 9, 2003.

196   **filed for divorce:** Petition, October 14, 1927, *Marvin White v. Lyde White.*

196   **He later helped send Head to prison:** Marvin White testimony, court transcript, March 14, 1927, *Arthur Head v. State of Alabama,* Alabama Court of Appeals.

197   **Golddust...got its name:** Chipman, *Gold Dust Tennessee,* pp. iii–iv.

197   **Lydia arrived in Golddust:** Helms examination, November 12, 1964, *Wakefield* estate.

197   **when she was fifteen years old:** Although Sarah Jane testified in 1964 that she would soon be turning eighty-four, the Social Security Death Index lists her birth date as November 21, 1882. The 1900 U.S. population census also lists her birth year as 1882. Social Security Death Index for Sarah Mooney; and U.S. census worksheet for Baileyton, Cullman County, Alabama, 1900.

197   **owned some land in Blount County:** Boaz Mooney certificate of the Register of the Land Office, March 1858, U.S. General Land Office Records, Ancestry.com.

197   **lynched in 1861:** "Bullet-Riddled Hat Hints Old Tragedy," *Decatur Daily* (Decatur, AL), July 12, 1964.

197   **owner of eight slaves:** U.S. census worksheet for Franklin County, Tennessee, 1830.

198   **Her maternal grandfather:** Civil War prisoner-of-war record for Alfred Rutledge, Ancestry.com; entry on Confederate Mound memorial plaque via Find a Grave.

198   **"eighty acres of hell":** "Chicago's forgotten Civil War prison camp," WBEZ, March 11, 2015.

198   **Martha Louise Rutledge Brown:** Tombstone image via Find a Grave.

198   **She'd given birth to Mary Jane:** Sarah Jane Mooney examination, November 13, 1964, *Wakefield* estate.

198   **just one rainy weekday:** U.S. Daily Weather Maps, National Oceanic and Atmospheric Administration Central Library.

199   **"Marv White":** Examination, November 13, 1964, *Wakefield* estate.

199   **"any white person and any negro":** Richter, "Alabama's Anti-Miscegenation Statutes," p. 346.

199   **That law had been upheld:** *Pace v. Alabama,* January 1883.

200   **in Osceola, Arkansas:** "Negro Lynched for 'Attacking' Child He Only Startled," *St. Louis Argus,* June 8, 1926; DuRocher, *Raising Racists,* pp. 146–147.

Notes

200 **In October 1926:** Marriage license, State of Illinois exhibit, *Wakefield* estate.

200 **"Old Man Joe Miller":** Sarah Jane Mooney examination, November 13, 1964, *Wakefield* estate.

200 **a Ford truck:** Hubert Mooney examination, November 13, 1964, *Wakefield* estate.

200 **As of the 1930 U.S. census:** U.S. census worksheet for Hector Township, Arkansas, April 1930.

201 **wolves, bobcats, and bears:** "Hometown—Dell, Arkansas," *Village News* (Blytheville, AR), March 28, 1979.

201 **drainage ditches ... shored up levees:** Whayne, *Delta Empire,* p. 146.

201 **"greatest cotton producing county":** Blytheville Chamber of Commerce pamphlet, c. 1936.

201 **The front of the Stacy family's residence:** Photograph of Stacy Brothers residence west of Wilson Junction, c. 1935, Central Arkansas Library online.

202 **a ceaseless drought:** Whayne, *Delta Empire,* p. 163.

202 **"how hard it was":** Woodruff, "The Failure of Relief During the Arkansas Drought of 1930–1931," p. 311.

203 **"eating watermelons":** Hubert Mooney examination, November 9, 1964, *Wakefield* estate.

203 **"the star plantation of the South":** Hutchinson, *Lowden of Illinois,* p. 220.

203 **"not only delighted":** Ibid., pp. 710–711.

203 **According to the 1940 census:** U.S. census worksheet for Burdette Township, Arkansas, April 1940.

203 **$298 ... $1,001:** Ducoff, *Wages of Agricultural Labor,* p. 96.

204 **U.S. Census Bureau had distinguished:** "Personal description" in Instructions to Enumerators, 1920 U.S. census.

204 **"Be particularly careful":** "Special Instructions: Color, Sex, and Age" in Instructions to Enumerators, 1890 U.S. census.

204 **"very nature of things":** Smith-Pryor, *Property Rites,* p. 107.

204 **prohibited the act of "concubinage":** Murray, *States' Laws on Race and Color,* p. 39.

205 **"There are lots of them":** Hubert Mooney examination, November 10, 1964, *Wakefield* estate.

205 **"no school I went to":** Helms examination, November 12, 1964, *Wakefield* estate.

205 **"they wouldn't allow":** Blount examination, November 13, 1964, *Wakefield* estate.

206 **would later estimate:** White, *A Man Called White,* pp. 48–49.

207 **"Why, Mister, you're leaving":** White, "I Investigate Lynchings."

207 **would introduce into evidence:** Barry statement, November 13, 1964; and State of Illinois exhibit, *Wakefield* estate.

Notes

CHAPTER 13

Author interview with Jean Harbaugh.

209 **"the vilest the health department":** "Filth, Rent Gouging Laid To Landlord: 18-Count Complaint Arrests Owner of 'Vilest Apartments,'" *Oakland Tribune,* August 4, 1942.

209 **front-page spread:** "Tenants Join City Health Officials In Charges Against Landlord Here," August 5, 1942.

209 **"filth and rubbish":** "Landlord Faces $1200 in Fines," *Oakland Tribune,* August 27, 1946.

209 **On February 4:** "City Police Study Child Abandonment," *Oakland Tribune,* February 5, 1948.

209 **"received information":** Arrest and booking report, Oakland Police Department, State of Illinois exhibit, *Wakefield* estate.

210 **"any house of prostitution":** California Welfare and Institutions Code, sections 700 and 702.

210 **As many as 21 percent:** Holley, "Leaving the Land of Opportunity," pp. 250–252.

210 **Between 14 and 18 percent:** Ibid., p. 250.

210 **"rotten dead Negro":** Angelou, *Collected Autobiographies,* p. 153.

211 **"go to the same schools":** June 1949 issue quoted in Johnson, *The Second Gold Rush,* p. 54.

211 **stayed open twenty-four hours:** Johnson, *The Second Gold Rush,* p. 143.

211 **featured a young black woman:** Dorothea Lange collection, Oakland Museum of California, the city of Oakland.

211 **passed over black women:** Ibid., p. 48.

211 **Between 1940 and 1947:** Self, *American Babylon,* p. 68.

211 **rented out chairs:** Johnson, *The Second Gold Rush,* p. 85.

212 **"such a small part of the city":** Ibid., p. 51.

212 **As of 1950, 85 percent:** Murch, *Living for the City,* p. 26.

212 **shook all day long:** Angelou, *Collected Autobiographies,* p. 158.

212 **"dusty bars and smoke shops":** Ibid., p. 159.

212 **"colored dances" on Monday nights:** Johnson, *The Second Gold Rush,* p. 169.

212 **"the influx of what might":** Quoted in Bagwell, *Oakland: The Story of a City,* p. 240.

213 **responded to this influx:** Ibid., p. 169; Self, *American Babylon,* p. 57.

213 **enlisted in the navy:** "Seventeen Are Accepted For Navy Service," *Jackson Sun* (Jackson, TN), July 16, 1942.

213 **Two months after:** Report of changes, USS *Portland,* September 1942, U.S. Navy/National Archives Catalog; Generous, *Sweet Pea at War,* pp. 85–86.

Notes

213 **Mooney went AWOL…bad conduct discharge:** Reports of changes, USS *Portland,* February and March 1943.

213 **ads for white-only positions:** 10th Street Market ads, *Oakland Tribune,* June 27 and September 22, 1944.

213 **"never thought about":** Hubert Mooney examination, November 9, 1964, *Wakefield* estate.

214 **The night's revelry began:** Hubert Mooney examination, November 10, 1964, *Wakefield* estate.

214 **"intended to hold":** Arrest and booking report, August 4, 1945, Oakland Police Department, *Wakefield* estate.

215 **"The landlord came into my apartment":** Constance Wakefield examination, November 10, 1964, *Wakefield* estate.

215 **"because that's useless":** Hubert Mooney examination, November 10, 1964, *Wakefield* estate.

215 **In January 1943:** Docket sheet, Seattle Municipal Court/Seattle Municipal Archives.

215 **A year and a half later:** Booking card, October 24, 1944, Kitsap County Sheriff's Office/Washington State Archives, Puget Sound.

215 **Less than a month:** Docket sheet, Seattle Municipal Court.

215 **more than 250,000…165,000 cases:** "Appendix D: A Summary of Venereal Disease Statistics" in U.S. Army Medical Department, *Preventive Medicine in World War II.*

216 **"loose women":** "Loaded? Don't take chances with pick-ups," poster, c. 1943.

216 **published a two-part series:** "Seattle Wages Relentless War on Organized Vice," April 1, and "Crackdown on Vice Scatters Disease-Bearers," April 2, 1943.

216 **"chief source of infection":** "Monthly Venereal Disease Index of Seattle, Washington," August 1943, Seattle Municipal Archives.

216 **unsanitary, overcrowded facility:** "Kimsey Wants Action on Jail," *Seattle Times,* June 27, 1943.

216 **"unfortunate unmarried mothers":** Florence Crittenton Home described in *Seattle Juvenile Court Report for 1928,* King County Superior Court/Kingcounty.org.

217 **"nothing to remind the girls":** "New Treatment Center Praised," January 23, 1944.

217 **17 percent…"large proportion":** Hegarty, *Victory Girls, Khaki-Wackies, and Patriotutes,* p. 76.

217 **Orchard Heights, a temporary housing project:** Jones, Bouillon, Thiry, and Sylliaasen, Architects, "Orchard Heights, Washington."

217 **At 4 a.m. on April 25, 1946:** Arrest and booking report, Oakland Police Department, *Wakefield* estate.

Notes

218   **arrested 753 people:** Johnson, *The Second Gold Rush,* p. 159.

218   **"laundry":** Arrest for malicious mischief, August 4, 1945, Oakland Police Department, *Wakefield* estate.

218   **usherette:** Arrest on suspicion of venereal disease, April 25, 1945, Oakland Police Department, *Wakefield* estate.

219   **apartment manager:** Arrest for contributing to delinquency of minor, March 18, 1948, Oakland Police Department, *Wakefield* estate.

219   **temperature taker:** Michael Gamache forensic evaluation of Linda Springer, May 10, 1994, *USA v. Springer,* BOP/FOIA.

219   **"If I accepted this offer":** Quoted in Hobbs, *A Chosen Exile,* p. 259.

220   **Two weeks after that arrest:** Marriage license, March 31, 1948, Alameda County Clerk-Recorder's Office.

221   **"no license may be issued":** California Civil Code, section 69.

221   **declare the state's miscegenation ban unconstitutional:** *Perez v. Sharp,* October 1, 1948.

221   **Joseph Harbaugh Sr. had been killed:** "Grief Welds Mather Hearts into One," *Pittsburgh Press,* May 22, 1928.

221   **As a teenager, Paul had worked:** Paul Stull Harbaugh World War II registration card, Ancestry.com.

222   **Harbaugh spent six weeks:** Paul Stull Harbaugh military records, National Archives/National Personnel Records Center.

222   **ferried personnel and supplies:** "General A. E. Anderson (AP-111)," Naval History and Heritage Command online, July 10, 2015.

222   **two days before he sailed:** Cruise number 31, April 2 to June 1, 1948, www.ussgeneralanderson.com (accessed October 2017).

222   **His petition:** Petition for adoption, Alameda County Superior Court, VA/FOIA.

223   **"would be sorry":** Bill for divorce, May 18, 1951, *Paul Stull Harbaugh v. Connie Martha Louise White Harbaugh,* circuit court of Shelby County, Tennessee.

224   **In January 1952:** Decree of divorce, January 4, 1952, *Paul Harbaugh v. Connie Harbaugh.*

224   **California's strict divorce laws:** Hayes, "California Divorce Reform," p. 660.

226   **At one thirty on a Monday morning:** "Staying In New Home Despite Bombing, Negro Family Says," *Jackson Sun,* June 29, 1953; Dowdy, *Crusades for Freedom,* p. 35.

226   **"I guess they meant":** "Negroes To Stay In All-White Area," UP/*Pampa Daily News* (Pampa, TX), June 30, 1953.

Notes

CHAPTER 14

Author interviews with Bobbie Moore Lanier, MaLoyce Bell, Justine Oliver, Johnnie Harbaugh, Joan Shefferd, Betty Hudson, Shelby Tuitavuki, Jimmy Fulton, Clark Forrest Jr., Jim Ralph.

228 **"I think that has been verified":** Hubert Mooney examination, November 10, 1964, *Wakefield* estate.

228 **August 1952...marriage license:** State of Illinois exhibit, *Wakefield* estate.

229 **In court in 1964:** Lydia Blount and Hubert Mooney examinations, November 12 and 13, 1964, *Wakefield* estate.

229 **"white children or Negro children":** Blount examination, November 13, 1964, *Wakefield* estate.

230 **"the world belongs to the colored races":** "Filipino's 'Movement' Going Strong Until Officers Arrive," *Blytheville Courier News* (Blytheville, AR), August 22, 1934.

231 **at least eight times:** Court transcript, November 6, 1950, *State of Louisiana v. Golda Forrest McDonald,* Supreme Court of Louisiana.

231 **In 1950, she was convicted:** "Slayer Is Given 10 Years: Mrs. McDonald Of Holden Area Must Go To Prison," *Enterprise-Journal* (McComb, MS), March 7, 1950; *State of Louisiana v. Golda Forrest McDonald.*

239 **"houses of vice are padlocked":** "Now They're Proud of Peoria," *Reader's Digest* (condensed from *Redbook*), August 1955.

239 **"They called Peoria":** Pryor and Gold, *Pryor Convictions and Other Life Sentences,* p. 15.

239 **"Peoria wasn't any better":** John Gwynn quoted in "The View From Peoria: It's Not Playing Well," *Washington Post,* June 30, 1974.

239 **In 1962, six members:** "Negroes File Civil Rights Damage Suit," AP/*Journal Gazette* (Mattoon, IL), October 25, 1962.

239 **brimming with job prospects:** "Segregation and Desegregation," Richard Pryor's Peoria online.

239 **any blacks on the payroll:** "Change and the Community Conscience," *Inter-Business Issues,* February 2015.

239 **two full-time black workers:** "Gwynn Attacks Mayor Day Statement, Says There IS Racial Tension in Peoria," *Peoria Journal Star,* June 22, 1963.

239 **"nasty work":** Pryor and Gold, *Pryor Convictions and Other Life Sentences,* p. 53.

240 **At 11:30 a.m. on December 21, 1959:** "Leak in Gas Main Triggers School Blast; 2 Men Hurt," *Peoria Journal Star,* December 22, 1959.

241 **"mother said he had blood on his shirt":** "Webster School Blast Burns 2, Knocks 28 Kids, Teacher Down," *Peoria Journal Star,* December 21, 1959.

241 **The adults at Webster School:** "Leak in Gas Main Triggers School Blast; 2 Men Hurt"; "Webster School Blast Burns 2, Knocks 28 Kids, Teacher Down."

Notes

241   **"injured and became ill":** Complaint at law, *Paul and Sandra Harbaugh v. Peoria Board of Education,* circuit court of Peoria County.

CHAPTER 15

Author interviews with Johnnie Harbaugh, Jean Harbaugh, Ron
Huber, Bob Vogler, Ted Amlong, Larry Sorrell, Bobbie Moore
Lanier, MaLoyce Bell, Ron Cooper, Bernard Carey, Jimmy Fulton.

243   **"possibly due to school explosion":** Medical record, July 28, 1960, VA/FOIA.

243   **"nearly total loss of hearing":** Williams AFB to Walter Reed Hospital, January 26, 1961, VA/FOIA.

244   **"permanent impairment of eyesight":** Answer of plaintiff, March 2, 1964, *Harbaugh v. Peoria Board of Education.*

244   **letter from President John F. Kennedy:** Motion to produce documents, May 20, 1966, *Harbaugh v. Peoria Board of Education.*

244   **had been injured in the fiery episode, too:** Answers to interrogatories, December 1, 1965, *Harbaugh v. Peoria Board of Education.*

244   **eight medical professionals...Grant Sill:** Ibid. and answers to interrogatories, February 29, 1964, *Harbaugh v. Peoria Board of Education.*

244   **Four months later:** Order of dismissal, March 20, 1967, *Harbaugh v. Peoria Board of Education.*

244   **Two years after that:** Answers to interrogatories, April 18, 1966, *Harbaugh v. Peoria Board of Education.*

245   **"keep him and send him to school":** VA/FOIA.

245   **The Veterans Administration had gotten word:** Lancaster (adjudication officer) to VA Chicago regional office, June 5, 1961, VA/FOIA.

245   **blood pressure of 220 over zero:** August 1958 hospitalization noted in Paul Stull Harbaugh disability appeal, March 8, 1960, VA/FOIA.

246   **"refuse to support":** Insurance claim, November 10, 1958, VA/FOIA.

246   **$14.10 for each:** Summary of payments and addresses, Chicago office memo, June 25, 1975, FBI/FOIA.

246   **"shortly after her husband's death":** Interview on March 6, 1975, FBI/FOIA.

246   **2020 North Cleveland Avenue:** Summary of payments and address changes, FBI/FOIA.

246   **"had deserted":** Lancaster to VA Chicago regional office, June 5, 1961, VA/FOIA.

247   **placed under the custodianship:** Department of Public Welfare to VA Chicago regional office, April 26, 1961, VA/FOIA.

247   **praying "to the Good Lord":** VA/FOIA.

Notes

247 **"We are sorry, but":** Williams (adjudication officer) to C. Wakefield, April 14, 1965, VA/FOIA.

247 **opened its doors in 1869:** "ISSCS—Proof of State Concern," *Pantagraph*, October 20, 1954.

247 **close to three hundred children:** "Altered Climate Marks Home for 270 Children," *Pantagraph*, December 12, 1965; Cobb, *A Place We Called Home*.

247 **"emotionally disturbed":** "Children Older, Problems Different, Officials Say," June 1, 1958.

248 **invitational track meet in 1964:** "ISSCS 1st In Own Track Meets," *Pantagraph*, May 21, 1964.

248 **In September 1964, a supervisor:** Dewett to VA, September 9, 1964, VA/FOIA.

249 **"as indicated by our records":** Williams to Illinois Department of Children and Family Services, October 2, 1964, VA/FOIA.

249 **On April 17, 1964:** "The Policy Plot Thickens Around $760,000 Trove."

250 **"declined prosecution":** Memo, February 24, 1965, FBI/FOIA.

250 **"kidnapped by two white men":** "Dead Policy King's $763,000 Demanded By His 'Daughter.'"

250 **"first unoccupied service station":** Chicago bureau memo, August 19, 1965, FBI/FOIA.

250 **"staying with relatives":** Chicago bureau memo, September 22, 1965, FBI/FOIA.

250 **"In view of background":** Chicago bureau memo, August 19, 1965, FBI/FOIA.

250 **on February 23, 1966:** Chicago bureau memo, FBI/FOIA.

251 **"Sandra Stienberg...has been missing":** "Seen This Girl?," March 3, 1966.

252 **"charged with being a runaway":** Chicago bureau memo, April 25, 1966, FBI/FOIA.

252 **Railroad firms had shipped:** "Chicago Snow Is Shipped to Dixie: Hundreds of Freight Cars Used," *Chicago Tribune*, February 11, 1967.

252 **"caused snow-fighting crews":** "3d Storm Blowing in Zero: Wind Sweeps 8-Inch Snow Into Drifts," February 6, 1967.

253 **A few hours later:** Chicago bureau memo, February 9, 1967, FBI/FOIA.

253 **the girl's name was Lena:** George Bliss and William Griffin, "Hint aid queen, baby-buying tie," *Chicago Tribune*, March 24, 1975.

253 **Martin Luther King Jr.'s headquarters:** "Modern Struggles, Modern Design—Dr. King and the story of Liberty Baptist Church," *Repeat: Writings on Architecture in Chicago and the World*, January 17, 2011.

253 **The Chicago police...to the collar:** Arrest reports, August 26, 1965, and June 2, 1967, CPD/FOIA.

Notes

254   **When they tracked down:** Chicago bureau memo, February 9, 1967, FBI/FOIA.

254   **On February 7:** Arrest report and criminal history, CPD/FOIA.

254   **She was arrested again:** Arrest report, February 22, 1967, CPD/FOIA.

254   **On March 6:** Arrest report, CPD/FOIA.

255   **On the afternoon of April 27, 1964:** "'She Took the Baby from My Arms'— Mother Tells How Boy Was Stolen," *Chicago Daily News,* April 28, 1964.

256   **"given the baby to another nurse":** "Baby Stolen From Parent At Hospital," UPI/*Courier-Journal* (Louisville, KY), April 28, 1964.

256   **two hundred police officers:** "Police Seek Baby Snatcher in Chicago," UPI/*Daily Register* (Harrisburg, IL), April 28, 1964.

256   **thirty-eight thousand Chicagoans:** "Fronczak File Grows in FBI's Hunt for Baby; 7,500 Suspects Are Eliminated," *Chicago Tribune,* February 15, 1965.

256   **"Our whole life" ... "I believe that God":** *Chicago Tribune* Press Service, July 26, 1964; AP, October 27, 1964; and AP, April 27, 1965.

257   **"Miss Taylor appeared one day":** "Probe aid queen tie to kidnaping," *Chicago Tribune.*

257   **Taylor told the *Chicago Daily News*:** "Ex-husband bilked her, 'welfare queen' charges," May 12, 1975.

257   **he "never knew":** Summary of June 10, 1976, interview, FBI/FOIA.

258   **On May 13, 1977:** "Welfare Queen Gets Two to Six Years in Jail," *Chicago Tribune.*

258   **The bureau has declined:** FBI Records Management to author, February 2015.

258   **identified as a potential witness:** Bishton testimony on legal costs, December 9, 1964, *Wakefield* estate.

258   **"known Taylor to dress as a nurse":** Arthur Krueger written statement, February 25, 1976, *Linda Taylor* burglary case.

259   **"as a registered nurse":** Katherine Freiman forensic evaluation of Linda Springer, October 4, 1994, *USA v. Springer,* BOP/FOIA.

259   **when Sherwin filled out:** Arrest report, August 25, 1974, CPD/FOIA.

259   **ran a front-page interview:** "Exclusive! Dead Policy King's $763,000 Demanded by His 'Daughter'; Has Papers to Prove Her Claim," April 18, 1964.

259   **"There is no remote possibility":** Fronczak and Tresniowski, *The Foundling,* p. 87.

260   **"was capable of anything":** "Son Suspects 'Welfare Queen' May Have Stolen Baby Paul Fronczak," abcnews.com, March 14, 2014.

260   **"a little boy":** Examination, November 9, 1964, *Wakefield* estate.

261   **black market for child adoption in Chicago:** "Probers Told Baby Selling Hub in Chicago," *Chicago Tribune,* January 6, 1959.

262   **determine his real name:** Virginia Griffin interview, additional complaint report, February 21, 1972, MSP/FOIA.

262   **"The mother states":** "Special Neuropsychiatric Examination," Sandra Harbaugh disability evaluation report, VA/FOIA.

263   **granted a stipend:** Investigation report, undated, VA/FOIA.

263   **married Roosevelt Brownlee:** Marriage record, June 26, 1972, FBI/FOIA.

263   **"partially deaf":** Report of field examination, October 4, 1972, VA/FOIA.

263   **a letter demanding $3,520:** VA investigation summary, June 30, 1976, FBI/FOIA.

264   **"the acorn seldom falls far from the oak":** "New 'welfare queen' makes her mark," July 2, 1977.

264   **"never learned the basis":** Interview summary, December 17, 1974, FBI/FOIA.

265   **"greater than average intelligence":** Interview summary, December 20, 1976, VA/FOIA.

265   **had shown up out of the blue:** Interview summary, June 10, 1976, FBI/FOIA.

266   **"dirty, hungry-looking":** Quoted in "Woman Is Charged In Burglary," UPI/*St. Louis Post-Dispatch*, February 26, 1976.

266   **two counts of child neglect:** Arrest report continuation of narrative, February 26, 1976, *Linda Taylor* burglary case.

CHAPTER 16

Author interviews with Linda Giesen, Frank Deere, Charlotte
Nesbitt-Langford, Magnolia Brison, Johnnie Harbaugh, Lou
Cannon, Jim Lake.

267   **New inmates came:** "'You feel like hell. You want out.... Tell all the people out there that this isn't fun,'" *Chicago Tribune Magazine*, May 20, 1979.

267   **prisoner A-87028...intake form:** Prison record and April 5, 1978, photograph, IPRB/FOIA.

268   **"a nationally known welfare cheat":** Carey, official statement of facts, IPRB/FOIA.

268   **one journalist argued:** "Dwight prison a monument to early women's lib movement," *Daily Leader* (Pontiac, IL), October 6, 1976.

268   **The cottages had balky plumbing:** "A warden's view of prison life," *Chicago Tribune*, May 20, 1979.

268   **"Tell all the people out there":** "'You feel like hell.'"

268   **"All this place does":** "Women in prison: You learn 'how to really hate.'"

269   **three-hundred-plus convicts:** "A warden's view of prison life."

Notes

269   **he'd later say:** "Judge wants Columbo behind bars," *Daily Herald*, December 18, 1988.

269   **"suburban sylph":** "'Can't never tell' at Columbo trial," *Chicago Tribune*, June 12, 1977.

269   **front-page billing:** "Columbo gets 200 years," August 9, 1977.

269   **"minor violation on her prison record":** "Follow-up: Welfare fraud winding down," March 25, 1979.

269   **Taylor was deemed:** Prisoner information card, Linda Bennett, IPRB/FOIA.

269   **The prison's doctors...Nitrospan:** Ibid.; Administrative Review Board meeting summary, revocation of good conduct credits, November 15, 1979, IPRB/FOIA.

269   **$5 a day as seamstresses:** "Rehabilitation? Women's skills training falls short," *Chicago Tribune*, August 5, 1980.

270   **"routine shakedown":** Resident disciplinary report, October 3, 1979, IPRB/FOIA.

270   **"set up by correctional guards":** Administrative Review Board meeting summary.

270   **She also requested:** Resident disciplinary report, October 3, 1979, IPRB/FOIA.

270   **"will no doubt resume":** Ginex to Prisoner Review Board, December 11, 1979, IPRB/FOIA.

271   **"be self-employed with sewing":** Early release worksheet, Linda Bennett, IPRB/FOIA.

271   **"At age 50":** Parole officer report, April 27, 1981, IPRB/FOIA.

271   **"she will remain":** Prisoner Review Board, order for discharge, IPRB/FOIA.

271   **seventy-seven indictments:** "30 more indicted in aid fraud sweep," February 16, 1978.

272   **"crying in front of the judge":** "State calls courts 'soft' on aid fraud," February 19, 1978.

272   **the *Tribune* wrote:** "31 more indicted in welfare fraud probe; total now 342," May 1, 1979.

272   **in excess of $100,000:** "Follow-up: Welfare fraud winding down," *Chicago Sun-Times*, March 25, 1979.

272   **"the new welfare queen":** "Woman to be arraigned in $118,456 aid fraud," *Chicago Tribune*, May 1, 1978; "New 'Welfare Queen' charged in 505 counts," *Chicago Tribune*, April 29, 1978.

272   **reached a plea deal:** Change of plea, January 8, 1979, *People of the State of Illinois v. Arlene Otis*, CCCC.

272   **"Ice Cream Welfare Queen":** "'Ice Cream' aid fraud suspect held," August 26, 1978.

Notes

273   **"with illegally collecting":** "Woman charged in rip-off of $200,000 in welfare," *Chicago Tribune,* May 19, 1980.

273   **"has not received":** "Alone for Christmas—fear is companion," December 4, 1979.

273   **an in-depth feature:** "There are crimes and there are crimes," *Chicago Lawyer,* February 1980.

274   **"bilking the welfare system":** "Grand jury indicts 27 more in welfare fraud," *Chicago Tribune,* November 15, 1978.

274   **disbanded its internal police force:** Gardiner and Lyman, "Responses to Fraud and Abuse in AFDC and Medicaid Programs," p. 55.

275   **631 people . . . $7.3 million:** "41 indicted on theft charges in $700,000 welfare fraud," *Chicago Tribune,* September 30, 1980.

275   **just above ten thousand reports per year:** IDPA statistics in "Aid abuse line works amid Gestapo charges," *Chicago Tribune,* July 17, 1980.

275   **57 to 60 percent of survey respondents:** MacLeod, Montero, and Speer, "America's Changing Attitudes Toward Welfare," p. 181.

275   **"accused of pulling off":** "Welfare Queen Surrenders: Accused of $289,000 Swindle," June 14, 1978.

276   **"on a par with somebody":** "Welfare Queen Sent to Prison: Invented 70 Children for $239,587," December 28, 1978.

276   **"possible record swindle":** "$300,000 Welfare Fraud Case Uncovered," *Los Angeles Times,* December 19, 1980.

276   **"My other car is a Rolls":** "California's 'welfare queen' holds credit fraud title here," *Chicago Tribune,* February 23, 1981.

276   **thirteen names . . . forty-nine dependent children:** "Woman Gets 8-Year Term in $377,000 Welfare Fraud," *Los Angeles Times,* June 24, 1983.

276   **"I think every year or so":** "Welfare Queens Are Exceptions," December 25, 1980.

277   **"She does have a Rolls-Royce":** "Information Please: The Public Gets Involved in Crime Detection," *Los Angeles Times,* January 7, 1981.

277   **"the promised land":** *Minneapolis Star,* June 25, 1981.

277   **"tracking welfare recipients":** *Arizona Republic* (Phoenix, AZ), June 16, 1978.

277   **"everything from guns":** "Prosecution is called key in preventing welfare fraud," *Courier-Journal* (Louisville, KY), June 4, 1980.

277   **"No one in the United States":** Q and A at the White House, Ronald Reagan Presidential Library and Museum online.

278   **"It's easy. They just lie":** Roza Gossage quoted in "Welfare," Reagan radio address on December 22, 1976, in *Reagan in His Own Hand,* p. 391.

278   **"stumbling through the palm trees":** "Memo to Jimmy: A lot of folks want your job," Gannett/*Statesman Journal* (Salem, OR), November 21, 1977.

Notes

278   **"There's a woman in Chicago":** "Stars at right: Simon Hoggart on the Bush and Reagan campaign trail in Texas," *Guardian*, May 3, 1980.

278   *Los Angeles Times* **said:** "Statistics Analyzed: Record Doesn't Always Support Reagan's Claims," April 12, 1980.

278   *Time* **said...** *New York Times* **said:** "Challenges to Statements Putting Reagan on the Defensive," *New York Times*, April 13, 1980.

279   **"crisis of confidence":** "The Malaise Speech," July 15, 1979, American Presidency Project.

279   **"I find no national malaise":** "A Vision for America," November 3, 1980, American Presidency Project.

279   **"so economically trapped":** August 3, 1980, speech transcript at the *Neshoba Democrat* online; and audio, Closed Captioning Project, YouTube.

280   **"the rebirth of code words":** September 16, 1980, American Presidency Project.

280   **1981 interview:** "Exclusive: Lee Atwater's Infamous 1981 Interview on the Southern Strategy," *Nation*, November 13, 2012.

280   **40 percent:** Edsall and Edsall, *Chain Reaction*, p. 150.

280   **"not make any special effort":** Survey form, 1976 preelection study, Survey Research Center, University of Michigan.

280   **"too many people":** "Reagan urges minorities to 'look beyond labels,'" AP/*Journal News* (White Plains, NY), August 5, 1980.

280   **A month later:** "Carter Says Reagan Injects Racism," *Washington Post*, September 17, 1980.

280   **"a racist in any degree":** News conference, September 18, 1980, American Presidency Project.

281   **"bitter racist diatribes":** "Race Issue in Campaign: A Chain Reaction," September 27, 1980.

281   **"We want that federal government":** "Thurmond at rally: U.S. needs a change," *Jackson Clarion-Ledger*, November 3, 1980.

281   **"those with true need":** February 18, 1981, American Presidency Project.

282   **"subject to almost inevitable fraud":** News briefing, May 2, 1977, American Presidency Project.

282   **"his well-worn campaign anecdotes":** "Still Learning to be the Opposition," *Washington Post*, February 15, 1981.

282   **"his famous 'welfare queen'":** "Reagans may attend summer wedding of Prince Charles, Lady Diana," UPI/*Galveston Daily News* (Galveston, TX), March 1, 1981.

282   **"$120 billion deficit coming":** "GOP Leader Says Reagan Hurting Minority Appeal," AP/*Alabama Journal*, March 2, 1982.

282   **"unfortunate if the president was misinformed":** "Reagan unverified on fraud stories," *New York Times*, March 25, 1982.

Notes

283 **An estimated 408,000:** "Cutbacks to Hit 1 Welfare Family in 5," *Washington Post*, September 22, 1981.

283 **roughly one million people:** "Reagan Weighs Plans to Cut Food Stamps Fund Even More," *New York Times*, November 13, 1981.

283 **a long front-page story:** "Reagan's 1st Year: Winners and Losers," December 27, 1981.

284 **would give him about 60 percent:** "Trimming social programs; Reagan and the fairness issue," *Christian Science Monitor*, June 29, 1982.

284 **"people who are embarrassed":** "Going Hungry in America," *Boston Globe Magazine*, May 23, 1982.

284 **67 percent:** Gilens, *Why Americans Hate Welfare*, p. 126.

284 **Just seventeen of the ninety people:** Ibid.

284 **"horror stories about the people":** Remarks in Bloomington, Minnesota, February 8, 1982, American Presidency Project.

285 **"neighbor caring for neighbor":** Remarks in New York, January 14, 1982, American Presidency Project.

285 **"Is it news that some fella":** "Reagan Pushes New Federalism," *Daily Oklahoman*, March 17, 1982.

285 **"a lot of stories of people":** "Reagan criticizes 'horror stories'—but look at some of his," *Boston Globe*, February 15, 1982.

285 **"He has several responsibilities":** "Reagan Quoted As Assailing TV Coverage of the Recession," *New York Times*, March 18, 1982.

CHAPTER 17

Author interviews with Diana Hibbler, Patricia Dennis, Theresa Davis, Karen Walker, Jane Snell-Simpson, Neil Fahrow, Timothy Nugent, Sandy Paderewski, David Thompson, Reta Hunter, Barbara B. Hunter, Johnnie Harbaugh, Carol Harbaugh, Dave Baron, Kenneth Lynch, Bruce Woodham, Byron Keith Lassiter, Thomas Ray Reynolds, Bill Tom Gavin, Tom Pelham, Mary Paul.

288 **He'd joined the Marine Corps:** Beneficiary identification record, VA/FOIA.

288 **twenty-nine of the men...114 were wounded:** 3rd Battalion, 3rd Marines command chronology, June 1969, 33USMC.com.

288 **"nervousness":** Veteran's application for compensation or pension, November 1969, VA/FOIA.

288 **The document, dated January 20, 1976:** Marriage license, VA/FOIA.

289 **showed footage of Ray:** March 7, 1977.

289 **AP snapped a picture:** "'Welfare Queen' Convicted," May 13, 1977, AP Images online.

Notes

289   **"mental condition":** Veteran's application for compensation or pension, October 1977, VA/FOIA; VA deferred rating decision form, December 1977, VA/FOIA.

290   **was just twenty-five years old:** John S. Ray death certificate, CCCO.

290   **a prominent Chicago entrepreneur:** "Honor Lena Bryant in Sunday tribute," *Chicago Defender,* April 26, 1975.

290   **Miss Black USA pageant:** "Beauty college," *Chicago Defender,* July 24, 1974.

292   **"no industry, no policeman":** "The 'rural South' looms just beyond suburbia," *Chicago Tribune Magazine,* December 13, 1981.

293   **"own part of 'America' forever":** Moscickis Realty ad quoted in "Pembroke: Promise of good life unfulfilled," *Chicago Tribune,* August 28, 1974.

293   **"preprogrammed for poverty":** "Dirt Poor," *Chicago Tribune Magazine,* February 28, 1999.

293   **A veteran of World War II:** World War II army enlistment records, Ancestry.com.

293   **nurse's aide at the VA hospital:** Arrest report, January 31, 1978, CPD/FOIA.

293   **a check issued to Loyd:** Arthur Krueger written statement, February 25, 1976, *Linda Taylor* burglary case.

293   **three of them went in together:** Complaint to foreclose mortgage, November 28, 1977, *National Homes Acceptance Corporation v. Sherman F. Ray, et al.,* CCCC Chancery Division.

293   **two-story stucco house:** Real estate sales contract, March 20, 1978, *Willie E. Butler, et al. v. Sherman F. Ray, et al.,* CCCC Chancery Division.

293   **loan backed by the Veterans Administration:** Advice regarding indebtedness of obligors on guaranteed or insured loans, September 6, 1978, VA/FOIA.

293   **A foreclosure action:** Complaint to foreclose mortgage.

294   **In July 1977, he forged:** Case summary, *Home Indemnity Co. v. The First National Bank of Waukegan and Willtrue Loyd,* Seventh U.S. Circuit Court of Appeals, LexisNexis.

294   **"deceptive practice":** Arrest report and mug shot, January 31, 1978, CPD/FOIA.

294   **shoplifting:** Criminal history and mug shot, September 4, 1980, CPD/FOIA.

294   **Ray was hospitalized:** Answer and counterclaim, October 24, 1985, *Linda C. Ray v. Veterans Life Insurance Company,* Sarasota County Circuit Court.

294   **the VA brushed off:** Kozlowski (adjudication officer) to Ray, November 23, 1982, VA/FOIA.

294   **seven-foot snake:** General case report, August 25, 1983, Kankakee County Sheriff's Police/FOIA.

294   **"would go down to pick corn":** Willtrue Loyd statement, September 27, 1983, Sherman Ray death inquest, Kankakee County Coroner, KCSP/FOIA.

Notes

294   **Metal pellets:** Report of coroner's physician, Sherman Ray death inquest, August 30, 1983, KCSP/FOIA.

295   **"usually associated with stupor":** Full autopsy report, October 3, 1983, Sherman Ray death inquest, KCSP/FOIA.

295   **"did not see the incident":** Timothy Nugent testimony, September 27, 1983, Sherman Ray death inquest, KCSP/FOIA.

296   **two life insurance plans:** National Home Life Insurance Company: Lassiter (Northern Service Bureau) to Kankakee County Coroner, June 12, 1984, KCSP/FOIA; Veterans Life Insurance: Policy application, July 31, 1982, *Linda C. Ray v. Veterans Life Insurance Company,* Twelfth Judicial Circuit Court of Florida (Sarasota County).

296   **On August 28, she sent:** Application for United States flag for burial purposes, VA/FOIA.

296   **A month after her husband's funeral:** Mortgage deed, October 1, 1983, Holmes County, Florida/MyFloridaCounty.com.

296   **"friendly to strangers unless":** "Farmers' mood: The Democrats...if it matters," *South Florida Sun-Sentinel* (Fort Lauderdale, FL), October 25, 1982.

297   **allegedly stealing the owner's refrigerator:** Incident report, June 17, 1987, Hamilton County Sheriff's Office.

297   **commandeering four bulls:** Complaint, October 1, 1985, *State of Florida v. Linda Ray Linch,* Holmes County Circuit Court.

297   **similar-looking bulls:** No information, November 15, 1985, *Florida v. Linch.*

298   **$738 civil judgment:** Final judgement, July 14, 1989, *Leroy Hunter v. Linda Lynch,* Suwannee County Circuit Court/MyFloridaCounty.com.

298   **"virtual prisoner":** "Patient: Ex-Doctor Ruined My Face," October 24, 1985.

299   **lost his medical license:** Final order, May 12, 1984, *Department of Professional Regulation v. Bernard Gross, MD,* Board of Medical Examiners, Florida Department of Health/public records request.

299   **Gross was charged:** Case information, Miami–Dade County Criminal Justice Online System.

299   **dismiss the case in 1986:** Order granting motion to dismiss without prejudice, June 23, 1986, *Linda Ray v. Stefano Dimauro, MD, et al.,* Eleventh Judicial Circuit Court of Florida (Dade County)/Miami–Dade County Civil, Family, and Probate Courts Online System.

299   **"reasonable investigation":** Ibid.; Florida Statutes sections 766.57 and 768.495.

299   **a payout of $100,000:** Complaint, September 19, 1985, *Ray v. Veterans Life.*

299   **settlement in January 1988:** Docket sheet, *Ray v. Veterans Life,* U.S. District Court for the Middle District of Florida, Tampa Division.

300   **more than 96 percent white:** U.S. census data, 1980.

Notes

300 **86.4 percent of its votes:** "Florida Panhandle Still Wallace's, but Slippage Is Seen," *New York Times*, August 3, 1975.

300 **members of the Dupree family:** "Friends Say Threats Led to Change in Burial Plans for Black Woman," AP, July 23, 1991.

301 **working dairy farm:** "List of property covered," financing statement for debtors Ken Lynch and Linda Lynch, May 8, 1985, *Charlotte Gruber v. Ken H. Lynch and Linda R. Lynch*, Fourteenth Judicial Circuit Court of Florida (Holmes County).

303 **foreclosed on in October 1985:** Notice of lis pendens, October 23, 1985, *The Federal Land Bank of Columbia, SC v. Charlotte Gruber, Linda Ray Lynch, and Ken H. Lynch,* Fourteenth Judicial Circuit Court of Florida (Holmes County).

305 **around 1909:** U.S. census worksheet for Ward 16, city of Chicago, 1940.

305 **In 1937, she'd married:** Marriage license, July 29, 1937, CCCO.

305 **birthplace of gospel music:** Ebenezer Missionary Baptist Church archives: organizational history, Chicago Public Library online.

305 **"spent their vacation":** "Mississippi Visitors," August 11, 1945.

306 **Markham deeded 185 acres:** Warranty deed, individual to individual, Holmes County, Florida/MyFloridaCounty.com.

307 **The couple's Florida marriage record:** February 25, 1986, Jackson County Clerk/MyFloridaCounty.com.

307 **Graceville Police Department investigated:** Mark Squeteri affidavit, October 28, 1993, *USA v. Springer*, U.S. District Court for the Middle District of Florida, Tampa Division.

307 **When Markham was admitted:** Flowers Hospital history and physical for Constance Loyd and operative report for Constance Loyd, August 10, 1986, EOUSA/FOIA.

308 **"become a chronic akinetic mute":** Flowers Hospital discharge summary, September 23, 1986, EOUSA/FOIA.

308 **"providing adequate care":** Home health certification and plan of treatment, September 23, 1986, EOUSA/FOIA.

308 **The Graceville police reported:** Death report, District Fourteen Medical Examiner's Office.

308 **Markham's death certificate:** Jackson County Health Department/District Fourteen Medical Examiner's Office.

308 **The medical examiner:** Investigative report, October 5, 1986, District Fourteen Medical Examiner's Office.

308 **"If I had truly":** "Examiner's Murder Case Becomes a Tangled Tale," September 21, 2003.

308 **Gulf Life Insurance Company paid:** Gulf Life Insurance Company to William Sybers, November 4, 1986; Sybers's office to Gulf Life Insurance Company, November 18, 1986, District Fourteen Medical Examiner's Office.

Notes

309   **warned its readers:** "TV insurance has low cost, low benefits, experts say," *Money/South Florida Sun Sentinel* (Fort Lauderdale, FL), July 20, 1987.

309   **$3,000 . . . seventy-five-year-old woman:** Union Fidelity ad, *Detroit Free Press*, March 16, 1987.

309   **Mildred Markham's enrollment form:** Exhibit, *Linda Ray Lynch v. Union Fidelity Life Insurance Company*, Twelfth Judicial Circuit Court of Florida (Sarasota County).

309   **medical examiner's office decided:** Sybers to Union Fidelity life claims department, June 9, 1987, District Fourteen Medical Examiner's Office.

309   **In June 1987:** Complaint, July 27, 1987, *Lynch v. Union Fidelity*.

309   **would reach a settlement:** Docket sheet, *Lynch v. Union Fidelity*, U.S. District Court for the Middle District of Florida, Tampa Division.

310   **she'd nab more than $60,000:** Squeteri affidavit, October 28, 1993, *USA v. Springer*.

CHAPTER 18

Author interviews with Mark Squeteri, Terrence Hake, Craig
Alldredge, Johnnie Harbaugh, Carol Harbaugh, Theresa Davis,
Jane Snell-Simpson.

312   **his career as a Pullman porter:** Employee service and earnings totals for James Monroe Markham, RRB/FOIA.

312   **began sending money:** "Judge Gives Different Ruling," UP/*Times* (Munster, IN), July 1, 1936; RRB, "Railroad Retirement Handbook," p. 2.

312   **born in 1896:** James Monroe Markham World War I registration card, Ancestry.com.

312   **Hake had been the key figure:** "August 5, 1983: Operation Greylord investigation revealed," *Chicago Tribune*, November 6, 1997.

313   **RRB sent $820.37:** Exhibit attached to Squeteri affidavit, *USA v. Springer*.

313   **Squeteri tracked down:** Squeteri affidavit, *USA v. Springer*.

313   **He also interviewed:** Written materials reviewed as part of the evaluation,

313   **On October 28, 1993:** Warrant for arrest, *USA v. Springer*.

314   **red 1992 Mercury Cougar:** Subject report for Linda Springer, U.S. Marshals Service/FOIA.

314   **The indictment they filed:** March 25, 1994, *USA v. Springer*.

314   **Queen, Jane, and Karen Snell:** Written materials reviewed, Freiman forensic evaluation.

315   **released on $25,000 bond:** Individual custody/detention report, U.S. Marshals Service/FOIA; appearance bond, *USA v. Springer*.

315   **In a financial affidavit:** February 24, 1994, *USA v. Springer*.

Notes

315   **7007 North Nebraska Avenue:** Defendant information relative to a criminal action in U.S. District Court, EOUSA/FOIA.

315   **had died of natural causes:** Investigation report, August 10, 1992, District Four Medical Examiner's Office.

315   **Three weeks later:** Motion for continuance of trial, April 18, 1994; order, April 19, 1994, *USA v. Springer*.

315   **"was incapable of knowing":** Petition for behavioral clinic examination, March 27, 1978, *Linda Taylor* burglary case.

315   **"she was vague, tangential":** Motion to determine competency of defendant, May 13, 1994, *USA v. Springer*.

316   **"It is difficult to say":** Michael Gamache forensic evaluation of Linda Springer, May 10, 1994, *USA v. Springer*, BOP/FOIA.

317   **Dr. Donald Taylor described:** Evaluation, May 18, 1994, *USA v. Springer*, BOP/FOIA.

318   **on June 1, 1994:** Mental competency hearing and order, *USA v. Springer*.

318   **Taylor told a nurse:** Psychiatric nursing database admission form for Linda Springer, August 24, 1994, BOP/FOIA.

318   **twenty-six different medical conditions:** Medical history report for Linda Springer, August 24, 1994, BOP/FOIA.

318   **"narcotic farm":** "Narcotic Farm Praised," AP/*Cincinnati Enquirer*, February 9, 1943.

318   **roughly two thousand women:** "Appendix III: Lexington Medical Referral Center" in U.S. Government Accountability Office, *Bureau of Prisons Health Care*, February 1994, p. 31.

318   **Nurses described . . . set of blinds:** Nursing notes, September 23, 1994, BOP/FOIA.

318   **Within twenty-four hours:** Consent forms for use of neuroleptic and antidepressant medication, August 25, 1994, BOP/FOIA.

318   **doubled to forty milligrams:** Federal prison system medication routine, August 1994, BOP/FOIA.

318   **tried giving Taylor an exam:** Freiman forensic evaluation.

318   **567 true-or-false statements:** "Test revised that gauges personality," *Atlanta Constitution*, January 23, 1990.

319   **"frustrated and angry":** Freiman forensic evaluation.

319   **they'd called her:** Psychosocial assessment, doctor's progress notes, September 22, 1994, BOP/FOIA.

319   **"my real mother and sister":** John Eisenbach, doctor's progress notes, August 25, 1994, BOP/FOIA.

319   **"had blood similar enough":** Freiman forensic evaluation.

319   **On September 25, Sandra Smith:** Nursing notes, September 25, 1994, BOP/FOIA.

Notes

319   **"needs some type of help"**: Telephone conversation summary, doctor's progress notes, September 28, 1994, BOP/FOIA.

320   **"bothers her"**: Conversation summary, doctor's progress notes, October 5, 1994, BOP/FOIA.

320   **"mentally disturbed"**: [Quoted in] Freiman forensic evaluation.

321   **"personality disorder not otherwise specified"**: "Diagnostic impression" in ibid.

321   **Taylor underwent surgery**: Record of medical care and operation report, September 29, 1994, BOP/FOIA.

321   **fifty-two days in the Pinellas County jail**: Individual custody/detention report, USM/FOIA.

321   **A booking photograph**: Pinellas County Sheriff's Office.

321   **a hearing on December 14, 1994**: Clerk's minutes, *USA v. Springer*.

321   **"the defendant's condition has deteriorated"**: Order, December 15, 1994, *USA v. Springer*.

321   **"green snakes"**: Psychiatric nursing database admission, January 17, 1995, BOP/FOIA.

321   **"dog having puppies"**: Psychiatric nursing assessment form, February 7, 1995, BOP/FOIA.

321   **"Attempted to stress need"**: Nursing notes, January 29, 1995, BOP/FOIA.

321   **"Sleeping entire shift"**: Progress notes, February 18, 1995, BOP/FOIA.

321   **"was uncooperative and complained"**: Sandra Lang and Robert Gregg forensic evaluation of Linda Springer, April 13, 1995, *USA v. Springer*, BOP/FOIA.

322   **affect was "bright"**: Progress notes, April 13, 1995, BOP/FOIA.

322   **$13.13:** Release authorization form, April 13, 1995, BOP/FOIA.

322   **"The report from the last federal facility"**: Gonzalez to Judge Thomas Wilson, June 7, 1995, *USA v. Springer*.

323   **"in the worst condition"**: Gamache to Alldredge, June 13, 1995, *USA v. Springer*, BOP/FOIA.

323   **he'd suggested months earlier**: Gamache to Jeff Carbia (assistant federal public defender), December 16, 1994, *USA v. Springer*, BOP/FOIA.

323   **"experiencing a deteriorating mental state"**: Gamache to Alldredge.

323   **"defendant remains mentally incompetent"**: Order, *USA v. Springer*.

323   **Eight months later**: Motion for order for dismissal, March 6, 1996, *USA v. Springer*.

324   **confiscated upon admission**: "'This is, literally, the last stop for some of them,'" *Tampa Tribune*, December 11, 1988.

324   **a decade since...five years since**: "The family is No. 1 casualty of welfare warfare," *Chicago Tribune*, October 2, 1985; "The hidden faces of the hungry," *St. Petersburg Times*, March 14, 1990.

325   **"don't want to work"**: Cannon, *President Reagan*, p. 439.

Notes

325   **"I thought you would have grown in five years":** "Speaker Calls President Insensitive," *Washington Post*, January 29, 1986.

325   **"a huge number of well-meaning whites":** "Daring Research Or 'Social Science Pornography'?," *New York Times*, October 9, 1994.

326   **"When reforms finally do occur":** Murray, *Losing Ground*, p. 236.

326   **60 percent of AFDC families:** "Aid to Families with Dependent Children and Related Programs" in House Committee on Ways and Means, *1996 Green Book*, p. 474.

326   **welfare task force proposed:** *Up from Dependency: A New National Public Assistance Strategy*, December 1986.

326   **"America's fertility policy":** Murray, *The Bell Curve*, p. 548.

327   **"a new covenant":** "The New Covenant: Responsibility and Rebuilding the American Community," speech at Georgetown University, October 23, 1991.

327   **2 percent of the state's annual budget:** "David Duke's Addictive Politics," *Time*, October 1, 1990.

327   **get birth control implants:** "Duke Presses Louisiana Birth Control," *Washington Post*, May 29, 1991.

327   **"welfare family could cost taxpayers":** "David Duke's Addictive Politics."

327   **"Perhaps the messenger":** "The numbers from Louisiana add up chillingly," *Baltimore Sun*, November 18, 1991.

328   **He explained that mothers:** "Clinton's Standard Campaign Speech: A Call for Responsibility," *New York Times*, April 26, 1992.

328   **"pure heroin" ... "guiding star":** DeParle, *American Dream*, p. 4.

328   **"welfare is considered odious":** Health and Human Services Department data cited in Sparks, "Queens, Teens, and Model Mothers," p. 180.

328   **2 percent of parents on AFDC:** HHS data cited in Sparks, "Queens, Teens, and Model Mothers," p. 180.

328   **"What's the best thing":** State of the Union address, January 25, 1994, American Presidency Project.

329   **"By creating a culture of poverty":** Jason DeParle, "Rant, Listen, Exploit, Learn, Scare, Help, Manipulate, Lead," *New York Times*, January 28, 1996.

329   **"you can't maintain civilization":** Jason DeParle, "House GOP Proposes 'Tough Love' Welfare Requiring Recipients to Work," *New York Times*, November 11, 1993.

329   **"responded with the smile":** DeParle, *American Dream*, p. 131.

329   **Nearly six hundred witnesses ... Just seventeen:** Sparks, "Queens, Teens, and Model Mothers," p. 184.

329   **"low-life scum" ... "their pants":** DeParle, *American Dream*, p. 133.

330   **"This issue is not":** Legislative hearing, July 18, 1996, *Congressional Record*.

330   **Joe Biden and John Kerry:** "The Failure of Welfare Reform," *Slate*, June 1, 2016.

Notes

330   *New Republic* **ran a photo:** August 12, 1996, issue.

331   **"Today we are ending":** Remarks and Q and A, American Presidency Project.

331   **"I am here today":** "Welfare Reform Bill Signing," August 23, 1986, C-SPAN.

331   **"the best argument":** Clinton, *My Life*, p. 330.

334   **published a front-page article:** "Welfare escape not simple or final for woman who won Clinton's praise," October 27, 1996.

334   **7:11 p.m.:** Constance Loyd death certificate, CCCO, Lincoln County, Mississippi, Chancery Clerk online.

Index

Index

Index

Index

Index

Index

Index

Index

Index

Index

Index

Index

Index